NATIONAL GANGS RESOURCE HANDBOOK
An Encyclopedic Reference

Introduction to Gangs
Comprehensive Bibliography
Major Gangs' Constitutions
National Gangs Directory

George W. Knox, Ph.D., Director
National Gang Crime Research Center
Chicago State University

"...the single most important reference tool no serious research library can afford to be without..."
John Morgan, Ph.D., D.Sc., Director
The Rhodes-Fulbright International Library

For Reference

Not to be taken from this room

Wyndham Hall Press

NATIONAL GANGS RESOURCE HANDBOOK
An Encyclopedic Reference

by George W. Knox, Ph.D.

International Standard Book Number

ISBN 1-55605-256-1 (paperback)
ISBN 1-55605-257-X (hardback)

Copyright © 1994 by George W. Knox

Printed in the United States of America

Wyndham Hall Press
Bristol, IN 46507-9460

TABLE OF CONTENTS

CHAPTER ONE
   UNDERSTANDING GANGS 1

CHAPTER TWO
   PRIMARY BIBLIOGRAPHY ON GANGS 17

CHAPTER THREE
   SECONDARY BIBLIOGRAPHY ON GANGS 62

CHAPTER FOUR
   MAJOR GANGS' CONSTITUTIONS 77

CHAPTER FIVE
   NATIONAL GANGS DIRECTORY 161

APPENDIX A
   STREETGANG TERRORISM OMNIBUS
      PREVENTION ACT 235

ABOUT THE AUTHOR 241

CHAPTER ONE

UNDERSTANDING GANGS

INTRODUCTION

Some of our literature on gangs tends to describe "social gangs[a]" which are similar to unsupervised play groups. Social gangs, according to this author, are not really gangs at all. While they could become real gangs they are little more than the kind of precocious youths represented in movie characters like Spanky and Alfalfa in "The Little Rascals"[1]. We should be less worried about the mischief caused by play groups. They do not represent a national crime problem.

This book provides a study of the criminal gang. The most essential feature of the criminal gang is that its members routinely engage in law violation behavior. This is done individually, in small groups, and often in an organized continuing fashion. The nature of this involvement with crime will be seen to provide the basis for examining gangs from a social organizational perspective.

This is the kind of gang that is seen in both juvenile and adult correctional institutions. Correctional officers do not see "social gangs", those who never come to the attention of the criminal justice system.[b] They see, rather, the hardcore law-offending gangs[2]. It is mostly the criminal gang member we find in our jails.

Law enforcement faces little problem from small cliques of unsupervised kids. Thus, police do not face a very high threat from so-called social gangs. Law enforcement officers are, however, often shot and killed by members of structured criminal gangs. It is the criminal gang that is the focus of this book. Later it will be shown how these gangs are classified in terms of the level of organizational sophistication.

You, and the public, are not worried about being killed by a random shooting where the shooter was Spanky or Alfalfa. You are probably concerned more about the hardcore criminal gang. Some of these well known criminal gangs are examined in detail in this book. Some gangs are highly structured and have written constitutions, some examples of these internal gang writings are provided in the appendices of this

---

[a] A "social gang" is what the author calls in later portions of this book a level zero gang. It is, at best, a "pre-gang" group. It commits few serious crimes. It is equivalent to a streetcorner play group such as Spanky and Alfalfa, et al, in the popular TV series "The Little Rascals".

[b] We cannot oversimplify the definition of gang by taking the viewpoint that any organized group containing offenders must necessarily constitute a gang. Were that kind of ambiguous definition used in gang analysis, then correctional officials would have to conclude that any "pro-social" club or organization behind the walls of correctional institutions constitutes a "social gang". That is not the perspective advanced in this book. Even though some wardens may use this definition of gangs, particularly in reference to Muslims.

book. Some gangs are little more than small units of persons often no more complicated in their hierarchy than a burglary or armed robbery "ring".

Regarding the study of gangs there are many questions that must be answered if we are to truly attain a social scientific perspective. This book seeks to provide a social scientific view of gangs. That means being interdisciplinary.[3] That also means relying, where possible, on good criminological research about gangs.

The ambiguity of defining characteristics of and about "gangs" in the literature can often mean more confusion the more we read. But there are two empirical questions about gangs in America that command our attention. (1) When does a loosely formed street corner group become a gang? And (2) if gangs are involved in crime, then how much of crime in America is explained by gang involvement? These two questions, so essential to the social scientific study of gangs, are not fully answered in the prior literature. Much new data is provided in this book to shed light on these and other important issues.

SOME PRELIMINARY CONSIDERATIONS

Some may say that gangs can be socially engineered (i.e., artificially created) and even experimentally manipulated (e.g., gang social service intervention, gang deprogramming services, or capable of being manipulated by political parties). The bottom line here is: can anything be done about the gang crime problem? Some may say that it is possible to exert much impact on gangs, perhaps even destroy them (e.g., gang busting). Others may say that through social services we can work directly with gangs and gang members; and perhaps show them a better way of life. The most extreme form of this therapeutic intervention would be that we can "deprogram" gang members. Before addressing the significance of such an assumption about social engineering and gangs, it is necessary to review some of the issues concerning gangs generally. Still others may say that as a crime problem no one has ever come up with the magic bullet of rehabilitation or prevention. Therefore it may be impossible to turn around the gang crime problem if we were to listen to some viewpoints. The truth is probably somewhere in between the two extremes that we can do a lot or we cannot do anything about the gang crime problem.

In this chapter we will only examine some of the general characteristics of gangs. In later portions of this text, however, the definitional overlap and variation in what constitutes a gang will be examined in much greater detail. This will involve the analysis of the gang in terms of what we know about social group formations generally.

The approach of this book is therefore incremental. It will address the major issues and at appropriate points in the book provide elements of a more integrated view of gangs, including a gang typology. The final chapter will review in detail the competing definitions of gangs and suggest an integrated definition of gang levels of "threat severity" and membership stages.

Gangs apparently need not have a publicly known label or name for their group[4], although most American gangs do.[5] Indeed in the early stage of gang formation the name itself emerges as a function of identity and crystallization. Gangs often do not consider themselves "gangs", but rather as types of "organizations". Gangs like the Gangster Disciples in Chicago deserve their preference for being called an organization, because they have been able to stage protests with several thousand members marching in unison in front of City Hall.

A historical review of American gangs would suggest that they emerged along racial and ethnic lines. Bonn (1984: 333), discussing gangs in the context of organized crime, reported criminal gangs existing in America as early as 1760. In the urban context, Bonn described gangs as clearly having ethnic homogeneity in terms of their organization. "Irish gangs were the first to emerge.." followed by German, Jewish and Italian gangs (Bonn, 1984: 333-334). This factor will be examined in much greater detail later in the book.

To some extent gangs gain legitimacy through the tendency of American culture to romanticize, and often idolize, gang exploits[6]. Al Capone as a gang leader has been significantly represented in fiction, myth, and through the Hollywood movie industry. As a byproduct of this element of culture, Chicago as a city must still today labor under the image of a "rat...tat...tat...tat" town associated with hoods carrying Thompson submachine guns. The cognitive map of many Americans places Chicago as "gangster land", which is not exactly a tourist attraction![7] And how does America compete as a tourist attraction, as a "peaceful place" in a democratic milieu, when gangs dominate the public imagination both here and abroad? The image of gang killings communicates "when travelling to America, bring your bullet proof vest".

There is also an important ideological factor involved in both the study of gangs and policy responses to the gang problem. Hagan (1987: 231-232) characterized the study of gangs as a fetish of criminologists during the 1950s and 1960s. While the gang problem did not disappear, the attention to gang research apparently did in the 1970s according to some sources. Hagan cited the literature review by Bookin-Weiner and Horowitz (1983) to the effect that ideological polarization in the 1970s was associated with a shift in analytical interests. Here the emphasis on macroanalytic problems such as social structure, SES (social economic status), and the community as the unit of analysis are characterized as being perhaps liberal while the emphasis on individual traits as explanations of criminal activity hold more weight for a conservative ideological orientation. The legitimacy of this claim is open to discussion[8], but perhaps rests with the common hypothesis that in some regard academic research follows the budgetary process. That is, in academia, the tail of funding for research can wag the dog of knowledge development.

This ideological factor cannot be overemphasized and we must be alert to its influence at all stages in the knowledge production process. By ideology we mean those values and assumptions about the world which have implications for the control and allocation of limited resources. In the study of sociology, for example, one of the concepts that students quickly learn is "value free". That is, one should not bring one's own values into play in research; for otherwise we are advancing not social science, nor policy for the improvement of corrections and criminal justice, but rather we are advancing ideology. The problem however is that society cannot be easily placed in an aseptic vacuum free from normative influences. That is, how we view the world may often influence how we portray the origin, structure, function, composition and policy recommendations for problems such as gang crime.

There has always existed a linguistic problem in the study of gang crime. The term "gang banger" itself is perhaps more fitting for use by sensational journalism than by a social scientist. It is a label containing stigma and implications that should engender fear and loathing. Indeed our language has much to do with the problem. When discussing "gangs" in America, one of the first things a student of criminology will learn is that in reviewing the literature what some conceive of as "gangs" are little more than conspicuously obnoxious youths running head strong against societal norms, as well as, of course, highly organized and armed groups with syndicated functions and hierarchical roles who are prone to violence.

The loose and pejorative use of the label "gang" is a source of confusion. We shall have to clarify our language to be able to objectively assess the gang problem in America today. The most common variation involves labelling all gang members in a tradition of much enmity (e.g., gang banger). Another variation, espoused by those in combat with gangs, is that some authors have apparently experienced the "Stockholm syndrome", or an over-identification with the rhetoric of gang members; almost in a tradition of Chicago's Rev. John Fry (Fry, 1969, 1973), that all that is important is that we "offer them something" (e.g., give them a bone), and we should therefore provide services and programs to serve them.[9] Both views suffer from a lack of clarity of what levels of gang sophistication we are talking about and the degree of individual integration into the gang subculture.

Vagueness and imprecision can get us into a lot of trouble. Mostly, it backfires in terms of social policy and legislation. Kasimar (1971: 52) described how the zeal of Detroit prosecutors to fight crime created a "public enemy act", as well as New Jersey which passed a law making "it a felony, punishable by 20 years' imprisonment, to be a gangster", were found to be unconstitutional, in New Jersey's case because of vagueness and uncertainty.[10] It also confuses us in the arena of social service intervention: some gangs at some stages of membership integration are clearly more "reachable" than others, and not paying attention to the details of such distinctions can mean exacerbating the very problem being used as a platform for social service intervention. Generally, what the study of gangs implies in criminology is some difference from loner or individual crime, chiefly in terms of a difference in organizational terms. A single gunman acting alone in a robbery, simply put, differs from a crime resulting from a gang. The gang implies something that the lone criminal offender does not have: some sense of organizational capability. The gang also implies a continuing or persisting threat over time that can increase. It is this emphasis on organizational characteristics that is common to the study of gangs, but which is at the same time most underdeveloped in the sense of linking what we know about social organization generally to the more specific problem of the study of gangs.

The study of gang crime has always implied some element of organizational life, although this aspect of gang analysis has not always emerged in the literature to the extent that we may desire. Indeed, there is radical disagreement on this issue. But this book develops such an organizational viewpoint, because it is also one that allows for more effective law enforcement, greater choices in managing the problem in the field of corrections, and much more latitude in addressing the gang problem from all levels of prevention --- primary, secondary, and tertiary (e.g., aftercare services).

Clearly, gangs do exist and their members do commit crimes. It is, then, a proper area of study for the social sciences. And yet some may say that gang research and analysis has barely risen above the level of an esoteric craft. These same cynics condemn not only intellectuals but applied knowledge as well, to the effect we really do not know much about crime, when in fact we do know some things. This book simply seeks to fill the gap in limited choices available for someone who has the responsibility for educating and training on the topic of gangs. The book therefore addresses many issues and includes many sources of data.

WHEN IS A GROUP A GANG?

Does calling a group a gang make it a gang? It probably depends on who uses the language. The voice of a community resident differs in definitive power from the voice of a United States Attorney or a local prosecutor.[11] The difference is power.

Legally, there are few statutes addressing this issue, and specific laws addressing gangs have only recently come into being.[12] There is the federal RICO statute and its many mini-RICO versions at the state level of criminal law. These define organizations engaged in violation of the law and can be used for both criminal and civil prosecution. Again, however, language is no friend of social science here. For example, Illinois as does many other states, has a "mob action" criminal statute which covers crimes committed in a group including civil protest demonstrations. Literally thousands of persons have been arrested under this statute for protests associated with the "right to life" movement and in protesting abortion. Does arrest for mob action make one a "mobster"?

The answer is most probably, NO. That is, most of those arrested for protesting the operation of an abortion clinic would probably reveal a pro-social motivation of a higher social purpose and an intent to be arrested, not to avoid arrest, in their behavior as a matter of civil disobedience. Indeed, they may be very religious persons who know that mass media attention to their cause is most likely under conditions of the arrest of their members. But does that make them "mobsters"? No! It is a matter of intention to avoid arrest as well. Groups like those with internalized higher moral imperatives such as those who may engage in civil disobedience --- for example to protect the environment --- knowing they will be arrested for their behavior, and willfully continuing such behavior as a moral protest, cannot be considered "gangs" in any sense used in this book. The reasoning here rests with the fact that their intent is not to do harm through violence or to benefit economically through criminal code violation, and further that in such civil disobedience they do not seek to evade arrest.

Thus, many persons being arrested for protesting abortion in the traditional civil disobedience style of political and moral protest cannot be considered gang members. However, in recent years violent attacks have been undertaken against individual physicians. Also, the medical buildings themselves have been burglarized, vandalized, and attacked in a different style where the perpetrators definitely do seek to cause harm and do seek to evade arrest. Such persons operating as a group would come under the umbrella of gang analysis.

A new law did recently criminalize some abortion protest behavior, it is called the FACE Act: Freedom of Access to Clinic Entrances Act. It is a federal criminal misdemeanor where the first offense can result in six months in prison and a fine of up to $10,000 for blocking the access to healthcare services of patients trying to use an abortion clinic. The first federal charges against violators of this Act were made in June of 1994.[13] So what we have here is a change from the time the first edition of this book appeared: a new criminal code defining that behavior as a crime. So the fact is the benefit structure here is ideological in nature, just as in political crime and in terrorism, and while we can expect this "gang" behavior to profile differently, it must still be treated analytically as gang crime if the abortion protestors violate the FACE Act. The fact that most do not try to evade arrest do however make them a unique exception to what we mean by gang crime.

The same problem arises in considering gangs. And in this regard we choose at this point to forcibly eliminate the phrase "gangster" from any subsequent discussion, because it confuses more than it contributes to the scientific understanding of the problem. It carries a value connotation and a culturally prescribed image of evil. One fact that will emerge in the study of gangs is that not all of the 24 hour day spent by gang members is spent in a relentless search for evil as if it were the only goal gang members had. Gang members are not alien invaders from another planet, they are from and live in our communities.

The term "gang banger" is similarly not to be found in the ensuing discussion unless in the context of views from persons interviewed who do not represent a social scientific view of the world. It is a label of derision just like gangster and mobster. It connotes more in terms of values of derogation and the psychology of enmity (Keen, 1986) than it does in terms of scientific classification.

Anyone who grew up in the 1950s or who watches such re-runs may recall a "gang" that was portrayed every Saturday morning at cartoon time on television. It was the series about "The Little Rascals". Is that what we mean by a gang? It too is a misrepresentation, albeit one that gives a favorable image to "gang". But that is Hollywood, and the reader of this book must be willing to break free of those kind of stereotypes created by culture. Alfalfa and Spanky and their associates typified much of urban adolescents, but they hardly typified what is meant today by an American gang-affiliated youth.

Do gangs necessarily have to have illicit goals, functions, or engage in law violation collectively or as individuals? Or can a gang have pro-social purposes? The answer is historical. That is, historically the phrase gang has encompassed both sets of group affiliation. In doing so the study of gangs has suffered from more than a small amount of measurement error. There must be both a qualitative and quantitative difference between a voluntary association composed primarily of youths which simply seeks to have a good time as compared to one that has a high degree of criminality in its everyday life. In other words, if any clique or group of three or more youths together, unsupervised constitutes a gang, then all of America has at one time or another been gang affiliated.

How much deviance or crime must a group be responsible for before it is considered a gang? Are the Boy Scouts a gang if one of the ranking members is in fact secretly a cat burglar or a semi-professional car thief? No doubt about it, some legitimate social organizations and groups do routinely experience what is called a succession of goals. That is, these groups may be formed initially for a certain specific purpose, but may later in time change and come to take on a new and entirely different goal and purpose. So it is analytically possible for even a legitimate group to transform itself into a gang.

If the road to hell is paved with good intentions, then how do we account for the type of organizational climate change that took place when the Rev. Jim Jones began having his religious followers carry out the practice of drinking poisoned Kool-aid?[14] The tragedy that occurred in Jonestown, where hundreds of people died in 1978 bears much significance to the study of gangs in that it was collective behavior and it ultimately had what must be regarded as a criminal outcome --- mass suicide. How do gangs differ from cults? A cult engaged in crime, over time, is a gang. Many "skinhead" groups and white racist groups can be considered gangs, because they often engage in what are called bias crimes.[15] But it means having more than the "skinhead", it means the actual commission of such acts of racial/ethnic/sexual preference bigotry in a manner that tends to violate another persons civil rights; or more commonly, for such "hate groups" it means groups that routinely engage in crimes of various sorts, including violence, with the fact that the same group may also hold extreme political views. Early scholars like Puffer, Furfey, and Thrasher did not include adult gangs such as the Ku Klux Klan, or vigilante groups. Rather, early scholars focused on youth groups who tended to go against the grain of mainstream society, its culture, its values, and its norms. That is, some sense of youthful deviance. The present analysis will show why we must also consider such groups like the Aryan Brotherhood, the Aryan Nation, the KKK, Neo-nazis, etc, also qualify as "gangs" for purposes of both criminological research and prosecution[16].

To be more specific, here the definition of gangs will be restricted to not simply involvement with or committing acts of deviance, but rather to crime. Crime is a special subset of deviance. In this sense, members of the Jonestown religious community could not be considered a gang even though they engaged in deviant practices and their behavior was deviant from our perspective[17]. The problem with using deviance as the key ingredient to define gang behavior is that it is far too encompassing.[18]

A group is a gang when it exists for or benefits substantially from the continuing criminal activity of its members. Some element of crime must exist as a definitive feature of the organization for it to be classified as a gang. That need not be income-producing crime, because it could also be crimes of violence.[19] Examples would include such extremist groups like the Ku Klux Klan, the Aryan Brotherhood, young white racist group equivalents, and others who engage not necessarily in well known income-producing crimes, but who still commit crimes along a dimension of "bias". Often these crimes involve violence to property or persons, as "hate crimes" or "bias crimes".[20] This is a legitimate aspect of the gang problem because it is criminal behavior that is approved of, and often planned, as such by a group[21].

Crime involvement of a group must not therefore be a sub rosa function about which few of the members have knowledge if we are to consider the group a gang. Members of many legitimate voluntary associations and civic groups are sometimes arrested for a variety of offenses. But these are not offenses committed on behalf of their group, these are not offenses even necessarily known to their full social network, these are not offenses condoned and approved of in advance by their organization, or which enjoy their acceptance or blessing. To be considered a gang, the criminal involvement of members must be openly known and approved of as such.

Conspiracy laws have some application here. To prove a conspiracy it is generally necessary to prove one or more overt acts in furtherance of the conspiracy. The key word is "overt". It must be open and clearly regarded as law violation behavior. That is, they know it is wrong, they know it is against the law, and they do it anyway. Some element of criminal conspiracy to avoid detection for law violation must therefore be present, whether the actual/objective/material skill/knowledge/ability to avoid or limit the probability of arrest actually exists.

Thus, from the perspective of the analysis advanced in this book, a group is not a gang simply because it is labelled as being in some sense deviant. A group is a gang if and only if it meets the higher requirement of having a known involvement with crime. It can therefore include the Crips, Bloods, Folks, Peoples, Posse, Vice Lords, Latin Kings, motorcycle gangs (Pagans, Hells Angels, etc), and a host of others whose primary occupation is income-producing crime or who benefit substantially from it, and as well it can include those engaged in a mixture of traditional crime and political crime involving rightwing and leftwing extremism (e.g., Aryan Brotherhood, Supreme White Power, KKK, and others versus leftwing groups like the Symbionese Liberation Army, and others). Such crime patterns, particularly of more organized gangs who have been able to accumulate economic assets, can also include a mixture of legitimate income (small businesses, hustling, etc) and criminal pursuits.

A semantic problem that needs to be clarified here is that we can effectively use the phrase "youth gangs" in a logical and rigorous analysis of the gang problem. If there are youth gangs, then logically there are "adult gangs" as well; and any student of human development will recognize that there are many possible gradations along the life span in terms of age-categories. First, the term "youth" is not easily operationalized in social policy. Secondly, there is no level one or higher "gang" known to this author which in its code of conduct or its charter or its written constitution or in its informal norms restricts membership to simply "youths"[c]. Groups like the Crips and the Bloods, the Vice Lords and the Disciples, etc, cannot simply be regarded as "youth gangs": it is more accurate to say these level three gangs have many youthful members. Youths are the easiest to exploit, particularly in drug-trafficking.

Analysts who continue to use the phrase "youth gangs" find their results hard to apply to the real world of criminal justice: there are no "youth laws", there are juvenile laws, and adult criminal codes. Anyone 17 or older in Illinois, for example, is an adult under law; and their behavior in violating the law is not regarded as "juvenile delinquency", it is "adult criminality". It is also a data problem: we do not have any census of all gang members in the United States, so we cannot accurately say that the majority are "juveniles", or even "youths" --- whatever we interpret "youths" to mean operationally. Stephens, in quoting a police chief on gangs, says it is a myth that the majority of street gang members are juveniles, that is, in Los Angeles juveniles may constitute only about a fifth of the gang membership (Goldstein and Huff, 1993: p. 224)!

The problem, then, with using the term "youth gang" is that it inaccurately describes the social reality of American gangs. Further it implies that such gangs have no adult leaders whom they are accountable to. It mistakenly implies that just because they are "youths" they are therefore not culpable nor responsible for their acts: as if by compulsion to join a gang this would be any defense in committing violence against another citizen. No matter what their age, gang members young or old must be held accountable for their actions.

A level one gang is the most elementary form of a real "gang". At level four in the classification system advanced in this book, such a group is really "organized crime". A level zero gang is not really a gang at all, it is a play group, a peer group, call it anything you want: we have all been members of such groups who engage in many behaviors, but essentially not that of violating criminal laws over time in a context where the group knows and approves of such law violation behavior and in fact benefits from it.

---

[c] The notable exception are engineered gangs: those created by adult hate groups (e.g., neo-nazis) such as were created by the NSPA nazi movement in southwest Chicago in the mid-1970's. These were specifically age-graded "sects" of the larger adult neo-nazi organization.

Finally, many students of criminology today ask "what is the difference between prison gangs and street gangs?", and here some answers are now known. Previously it was thought that many prison gangs like the Aryan Brotherhood existed only in prisons and were not reported to be a problem for local law enforcement, or for other criminal justice personnel (probation or parole officers, etc). Clearly, we now know that gangs like the Aryan Brotherhood and their youth counterparts DO EXIST outside of the context of correctional institutions. And prison gang membership will be in most cases equivalent to gang membership on the outside of the correctional environment as well. Although, obviously, there are situations such as in our county jails and other institutions where confined persons "ride with" or temporarily show an allegiance to a gang simply while in custody and somehow reduce --- perhaps to its absolute minimum --- any such post-release gang affiliation. There are few if any "prison gangs" that do not represent if not by the same name then by proxy a similar gang problem on the "street".[22]

The language of this book is not limited to what some authors call "street gangs". We cannot define gangs simply in terms of those who "hang out on the streets", or "use the streets", or "claim the streets as their turf". The kind of gangs studied in this book are those who commit crime. Too often the casual reader about crime comes to think of "street crime" as a code word for crimes by minority persons. This book demonstrates that all ethnic groups, all races have gangs today; or had them in the past. If our social science vocabulary is so limited that we have to use the layman language of "street gang", then minimally and logically there must also exist "suite gangs" as well: those groups and organizations who commit their crimes from offices.

In sum, it is not where the gang operates, it is how it operates and functions that distinguishes it in terms of its sophistication and its objective crime threat.

THE BURNING QUESTION: How Much Crime in America is Gang-Related?

The study of gangs is justified as a portion of all curricula in every criminal justice, delinquency, criminology, sociology, psychology, etc program: if and only if gangs and their members constitute a significant portion of the overall American crime problem. This gets directly to the issue of what is a "gang-related crime". Or, alternatively, when can we count the value of "gang-impact" in assessing the overall threat that a gang or several gangs may pose in terms of their contribution to crime statistics in the United States? Some would have us believe that just because little Johnny robs someone, even though he was a member of a gang, as long as the gang did not order him to rob or as long as the robbery did not occur along with several other confederates who were members of the same gang, that this individual crime by a gang member should not be counted as "gang crime". The position advanced here is comparable to the Los Angeles law enforcement definition discussed later: if the crime was committed by a known gang member, it was a gang-related crime.

The reason is good logic: the offender in this instance has a larger more encompassing influence, the gang. Bad behavior while alone as a gang member may bring a violent punishment to the gang member from his/her own gang. Good behavior (i.e., defending the nation) would similarly --- as a lone person --- be behavior honored and perhaps even rewarded by the gang. Either way, there is little escaping the implications of behavior from the viewpoint of a larger social entity the offender belongs to: the gang. One is a gang member in some gangs 24 hours a day. Gang life in more organized or violent gangs is not a part-time commitment. It is more comparable to being a member of a cult or a total institution. One acts as a "gang member", and one may feel as a gang member he or she has greater protection for any individual acts. Thus, it is comparable to a police officer on duty taking a bribe: it is a police-based crime, whether the officer did it alone or as a member of a corrupt group. It should not be necessary to say that in the case of gang crime that the gang had to know and approve of the crime in advance before we consider it gang-related crime; for that could be considered gang legislated crime. We are far from having the nationwide facts about gang crime. Until we do it is best to have the widest possible definition until we know what that yields. When we are at the stage of adequately coming to grips with the scope and extent of this national problem, then we might be able to partial out those crimes which were known and approved of in advance by the gang itself, or authorized, or directed by gang leaders. It is a moot point at this time in history, because no one has the data. In this situation, your author elects to accept the definition of gang-related crime as any crime committed by a gang member.

So, back to the issue: do the facts currently justify the study of gangs in the sense that gangs and gang members tend to account for a sizable portion of the American crime problem? Yes, is the answer argued here. But sadly, all parameters of the answer are not completely known. Some attempts to estimate youth crime portions of national crime statistics suggested that about half of all such crimes were gang-related. The problem here is very complex and needs some explanation.

First, it is widely known that there are generally three sources of data for crime statistics. There is the FBI's Uniform Crime Report (UCR), but it does not ask local law enforcement agencies to "double-tag" offense reports so that we could even know nationally what the scope and extent of gang crime in America is. There is also the victimization survey, but it does not ask respondents if they believe the crimes that they were the victims of were gang-related. Finally, there are self-report surveys and these come closest, at present, to giving an indication, at this stage of social science, of what role gangs play in criminal law violation in America. None of these three sources are as of yet adequate to provide all of the answers needed regarding the problem of gang crime. By way of comparison, "hate crime" is something that became officially tracked only in relative recent history. This is not to say that America only had "hate crime" in its recent history only. This means that our official policy was to simply recognize it, like child abuse, as a new social problem worthy of systematically tracking and reporting. No state and no federal government agency is required by law to monitor and report all known gang-related crimes, or crimes committed by gang members at this writing. This can be expected to change in the future, because like "hate crime" or bias crime, or like child abuse crimes, crimes committed by gang members appears to be taking on the role of the new national bogeyman in America.

There is reason to believe, however, that gang-related crime constitutes a significant portion of all crime in America. It is for that reason that this study represents both a challenge and a knowledge development need for the future. Many of the gangs studied by Thrasher would probably not be considered gangs at all in this analysis. Indeed, the gangs which exist in America today represent a much more formidable challenge to law enforcement, corrections, and public safety. The "gangs" that Thrasher studied were lucky to have pocket knifes and baseball bats. Some gangs today have at their disposal fully automatic weapons and even military ordnance.[23]

Gangs are a national problem and are now reported to be a problem to some extent in nearly all states. The Camp and Camp (1985: p. 11) study showed only a few states not reporting a gang problem in their prison system (Alabama, Alaska, Delaware, Kansas,

New Hampshire, North Dakota, Oregon, Rhode Island, South Carolina, South Dakota, Vermont, Wyoming and missing data on New Jersey and Tennessee).

Recent data on correctional institutions, described in later chapters, shows the list of states with no gang problem behind bars to now be reduced to: New Hampshire, South Carolina, Vermont, and Wyoming. But from other sources we knew Alaska does have Filipino gangs (Jackson and Mc Bride, 1990: p. 50), and the Hell's Angels have been reported as far north as the North Pole. From the author's research, data is now emerging which shows that Alabama and Kansas have many gangs, Delaware, New Jersey and South Carolina have the Posse and others. Rhode Island has the Red Dragons (Cambodian) and others (Posse, Aryan Brotherhood, etc), Oregon has Crips and Bloods, Wyoming has the Mexican Mafia and more, and New Hampshire has skinheads at least. From the law enforcement surveys, we now know that the Dakotas are no longer completely without any reported active gangs. That leaves only Vermont[d] --- one state --- with no reported gangs. And if we looked much closer, perhaps we would find some gang activity there. We are rapidly approaching the point where those who do not report gangs at the correctional or law enforcement level are the exception to the rule.

One of the most fascinating criminological research needs regarding gang crime is how much crime and violence committed by gangs is simply never recorded in our national crime statistics. Routine "drive-by" shootings and rival-gang shoot-outs in many inner city areas, while being well known to the residents, are simply never recorded as "real crimes" by the police. Kotlowitz (1992: p. 18) reports the case of a large-scale shoot-out between rival gangs at the Henry Horner Homes public housing complex on Chicago's near west side that when a reporter called the next day for a copy of a police report, the reporter was told no such police report existed! Many such crimes in Chicago are routinely "unfounded", that is: not listed as real crimes, and therefore never reported to the FBI for its national crime statistics: rather the police radio messages tell us what happens, because no "complainant" exists to sign a complaint, the police officer responding to the call (if a call is ever made) simply radios back it is a "nineteen Paul", the code for "no problem", "no complainant", "no arrest", "no report". Anyone with a police scanner can listen to these police radio frequencies to hear of anonymous calls from "citizens" and actual complainants throughout the City of Chicago about such daily gang shootings, most of which get handled the same way "19 Paul".

What we have now as valid and reliable information is not sufficient to answer several basic national questions: how much crime committed in the United States is gang related, or committed by gang members? We don't know, all we have are estimates. How many gangs exist in the United States and how many gang members exist in the United States --- again all we have are estimates. The FBI's criminal division did recently estimate that there may be 400,000 gang members in the United States.[24]

HOW EASY IT IS TO OVER-GENERALIZE ABOUT GANGS

Some authors have sought to systematically root out the "myths" about gangs in America today (Sanchez-Jankowski, 1991). This generates far too much attention,

---

[d]   Research now shows (Nov., 1994) Vermont is no longer on the list of states "Having No Gang Problem". Vermont now has gangs in its Adult Correctional System.

because the problem is really empirical, not theoretical. Theoretically, gangs can vary in terms of a wide number of characteristics, functions, structures, and behaviors. Some gangs sell drugs, some may not. But generally, if it is a real gang (one that engages in crime), given the opportunity it is certainly capable of the crime. The reason this is an issue is that some studies may have focused on the strong linkage to either drug use or drug sales and such studies may seek to generalize their findings to the entire American gang problem.

The term "myth" is not used here (e.g., It is a myth that all gangs sell/use drugs). It is rather and more accurately called a logical fallacy that overgeneralizes from a specific instance to the larger scene. The phrase "All gangs use/sell drugs" is therefore just that: an over-generalization. Just finding an exception does not mean we do not have strong evidence of the role of gangs in selling drugs, nor does it diminish the general behavioral profile showing that gang members abuse drugs more than other offenders, or than non-offenders.

Some of these types of discussions are "straw-man" techniques to raise issues. While they are not unimportant issues, there is no limit to the logical number of such issues: the family's role, the role of single-parent families, the role of educational failure, the role of being stigmatized/labelled, etc. What we need are statistics: numbers that will help to clarify the parameters of such issues. Variation in illegal groups is to be expected in the same way that such variation is to be found in lawful groups. The global factors that vary with gangs are clearly: who, what, when, where, why and how. The variations in factors which help us to classify gangs are potentially endless.

Another common error made frequently by some newcomers to the gang issue in criminology is to assume that anything that applies to juvenile delinquents (e.g., treatment) automatically applies to "gangs". As stated earlier, we lack information over time on what percent of all American juvenile delinquents are in fact gang members, or even what proportion of all crimes committed by juveniles arrested represent such gang members. Thus, it is criminologically naive to think that simply because a "therapy" program that had some application to juvenile delinquency years ago may be of value for intervention with gang members today. All juvenile delinquents are not gang members, and not all gang members are juvenile delinquents. It is possible for a gang member to technically never be arrested for a crime and grow up as an adult with no "rap sheet" at all; perhaps even get hired as a police officer.

In the search for a honest view of gangs, the goal of this book has been to provide a holistic, interdisciplinary, and historical analysis covering the main issues. It is not easy to provide an overall theme that integrates material that has never before been provided in such a format. Indeed, some experts in the field when they heard of this plan for a textbook on gangs said that "it could not be done". They believed that viewpoints in the gang literature are so different and the research methods are so diverse, that it is "premature" to have the basis for a textbook on gangs. Actually, there are a number of commonalities in the literature as will be shown.

It is no easy task to organize into a coherent whole all of the extensive gang literature. The reader is strongly encouraged to closely follow the footnotes provided. Other reading in areas of interest from the recommended readings and bibliography provided is also suggested.

Where the author digresses at various points in the book to discuss historical issues, or matters of research ethics, etc, these discussions are provided because the author felt the issues were important to raise. Please pardon some cliches to be found in the book as a deviation from a professional writing style. While the author has endeavored to provide a comprehensive analysis of gangs in America, this book by no means "covers everything". No single book could ever claim to "know it all".

In no sense does the amount of space or attention provided to specific gang authors imply any relationship to their overall contributions in the field. This means some prior authors who may have been only marginally connected to the field of gang studies could be discussed much more than prolific gang authors. This book does not try to establish such a "pecking order" of gang wisdom. New data is now emerging that will have much bearing on the analysis of gangs in America. It is, in short, a volatile field; partly because gangs are emerging as such a national problem.

Finally, not each and every "gang action program" in America is discussed here. Many are not known outside of their immediate area. There is no central "GANG CRIME INFORMATION AND REFERRAL SERVICE"[25]. The author therefore apologizes to the many local efforts not mentioned here, commends them, and hopes to hear from them[26]. Finally, "tone" in this book may vary at times. Some would say it could have been more dispassionate, perhaps softened, and much less sarcastic/argumentative/cynical in certain respects.

FOOTNOTES

1. "The Little Rascals" was a TV series produced by Hal Roach in the 1930s. The series involves neighborhood kids, with a clubhouse at times, who are not adult supervised. Because they are not adult supervised some authors today would still consider them a gang. The present author does not consider them a real gang. Only a group involved in crime or benefiting from crime, over time, is a gang in the authors definition.

2. A criminologist should be a social scientist --- someone who does not simply take an "official" definition as the gospel. In prisons today, some religious groups are classified by correctional administrators as "threat groups", essentially treated the same way gangs are.

3. Gangs represent a group, collective behavior, organizational patterns, and other features that have historically been the turf of sociology. However, other disciplines have much to add to this area of study --- and these include the perspectives from law, psychology, social service administration/social work, human development, urban studies, anthropology, corrections and criminal justice, and other areas of specialization in the social sciences.

4. Vigil and Yun (in Huff, 1990: p. 159) describe the uniqueness of Vietnamese youth gangs in not having a name even within their group "for fear that it would invite police recognition". Thus, a secret society with criminal functions would also be a gang in this sense.

5. Malcolm Klein's definition of gang is that the members "recognize themselves as a denotable group (almost invariably with a group name)". This is generally accurate and covers most of the gang problem.

6. Gorn (1987) reports the case of massive public attendance at a gang leader's funeral, involving 250,000 people back in 1855. What all gangs and those in the funeral procession seemed to have in common was their social class.

7. The informed reader will note that the tourist industry in Chicago has adapted itself to this problem. Bus tours now routinely take tourists through the city to show them where Al Capone conducted business, where mobsters were slain, etc. An "Al Capone" museum was recently opened as a tourist attraction in Chicago as well. A bar in Peotone, Illinois is locally referred to as "Capone's place" and features a large picture of Al Capone and a sign reading "Gangsters Hall"; again a kind of reverence shown to figures like Al Capone.

8. The bibliography for this book shows over 50 such contributions during the 1970s to the study of gangs or gang members. There was in no sense, then, a "black out" on gang studies.

9. Perhaps contrary to many of such author intentions, they have also communicated by their provincial analyses that the only gang threat in America is that by "persons of color". Or that, there is no problem with Ku Klux Klan members, right wing extremists, hate groups that commit bias crimes and engage in anti-semitism, etc. In fact, our data shows groups like the Ku Klux Klan and the Aryan Brotherhood, and others prone to engage in bias crimes and illegal acts of anti-Semitism are very much a current problem facing America today.

10. It is important to note, historically, that in spite of this problem there have been significant efforts that have induced much effect in terms of using criminal justice resources to target organizations as the focus of investigation. We need only recall how in the 1950s the American Communist Party was the target of an enormous investigation.

11. The research in Hyde Park by Shireman, et al showed adolescent versions of the street corner group (Liebow, 1967; Anderson, 1978), but which were faced with fearful adults in the area who were most prone to define them as a gang or "up to no good".

12. The State of California, in its penal code, sections 186.20 through 186.27 has the "Street Terrorism Enforcement and Prevention Act" which is addressed towards gang suppression. It has become an important tool for intelligence and prosecution.

13. See: "6 Abortion Foes Are 1st Charged Under New Law", Chicago Tribune, June 7, 1994, Section 1, p. 3. These were the six arrested in Milwaukee.

14. According to some sources, we might add to this list the case of Synanon. A drug treatment organization that for years was recognized as the best in the business. Then the press and mass media uncovered how the organization had controlled vast economic enterprises, operated with the use of firearms, and was less than a organization with a "wholesome" appearance.

15. Some states do not consider groups like the Aryan Brotherhood or Ku Klux Klan "gangs"; rather they are considered "hate groups". Presumably hate groups prone to crime.

16. It would appear to be somewhat discriminatory to consider group criminal behavior as "gang crime" when it is committed by groups who consist predominantly of racial minority group members, and not applying the same standard to white groups who also engage in such continuing criminal behavior patterns. This is particularly important in terms of the legal validity of enforcing gang abatement or gang crime statutes. Allowing groups like the Aryan Brotherhood to escape the investigative and prosecutorial thrust of anti-gang legislation may make such statutes unconstitutional (see Destro, 1993: p. 235).

17. The issue is: is it illegal to prepare for suicide or simulate it under the laws of the country in which this particular tragedy occurred? If they knew it was illegal to self-destruct, or encourage others to do so, then it is a criminal code violation behavior over time, a crime of violence, not income-producing crime.

18. Obviously, social scientists are always free to use some literary license here in defining what they think should be considered to be gang behavior, just as criminolo-gists rejecting the legalist definition of crime are free to declare what they think should be a crime. Such a list is potentially endless, particularly for youths given the tendency of adults to view with alarm any non-conformity among youths; and the historical tendency of each new adult generation to declare its youth population "gone to the dogs". The analytical focus here, to repeat, is on crime; not deviance; not "ill", "malo", or "immoral" behavior; and not even on what should be legislated as crime.

19. The Ku Klux Klan and related political extremist groups are clearly included in the definition of criminal gang. Obviously, like some of our more organized gangs to be discussed in later chapters, some may believe they are really emergent varieties of organized crime.

20. Typical examples of actual crimes committed involve: bombing business establishments and painting graffiti, such as anti-Semitic threats on synagogues. See: "Supremacist Guilty in Bombing, Vandalism", Chicago Sun-Times, Sept. 14, 1994, p. 19.

21. Some gang analysts see only three possibilities: youth gangs, hate groups, and organized crime. The problem is, this is not a classification system where logic is on our side. Youths can be members of hate groups, and of organized crime. Some groups loosely considered "youth gangs" may simply mean "youth members" of various types of gangs, indeed: gangs whose top leadership structure is not in any sense "youth controlled", but is rather driven by adults with long criminal records.

22. The chapter on gangs in the adult correctional institutions also addresses this issue: for example, two such gangs were felt to exist only inside prisons in Illinois (e.g., Northsiders, and the S.I.A.). However, recent additional research has now shown "Northsiders" to be an identification used at the jail inmate level as well.

23. Let us keep a historical perspective here on the armed offender in the gang context. Prior to 1968 anyone in America could readily acquire firearms over the counter, through the mail, etc. If Thrasher's gangs wanted them, at that time in history they could also purchase as much dynamite as they wanted in local hardware stores. Both explosives and weapons laws changed dramatically in 1968, making it somewhat more difficult for offenders to acquire these instruments of destruction.

24. See: "Feds Can Help Cities Fight Gangs, FBI Says", by Jerry Moskal, Chicago Sun-Times, Feb. 10, 1994, p. 8.

25. Shortly after the first edition of this book appeared in 1991, the National Youth Gang Information Center appeared as an information service on gangs similar to what the National Criminal Justice Reference Service does. But all it did was collect information on gang research, particularly federally funded projects on gangs. At the time of the second edition (1993), the NYGIC was under threat of closing and being absorbed by the NCJRS. It is now gone completely. A separate national clearinghouse on gangs and gang intelligence is still sorely needed. The fact that federal leadership on this has been lacking has resulted recently in correctional gang intelligence coordinators forming their own clearinghouse.

26. Actually, at this writing, such a national analysis of actual gang programs is underway; tracking all federal and foundation support to programs involving "gangs" or "gang members". The full and complete book on recent and contemporary gang programs has not yet been written. I am working on it now.

CHAPTER TWO
PRIMARY BIBLIOGRAPHY ON GANGS

Ackley, N.
1984 Gangs in Schools: Breaking Up Is Hard To Do, U.S. Dept. of Justice, Office of Juvenile Justice and Delinquency Prevention, Washington, D.C. Ackerley, Ethel G. and Beverly R. Fliegel

1960 "A Social Work Approach to Street-Corner Girls", Social Work (5)(4): 27-36.

Adams, Stuart
1967 "A Cost Approach to the Assessment of Gang Rehabilitation Techniques", Journal of Research in Crime and Delinquency (Jan.).

Adler, P.A.
1985 Wheeling and Dealing: An Ethnography of an Upper-Level Drug Dealing and Smuggling Community. New York: Columbia University Press.

Agopian, Michael
1991 "Evaluation of G.A.P.P. - Gang Alternative Prevention Project in the Los Angeles Probation Department", paper presented at the Annual Meeting of the Academy of Criminal Justice Sciences, Nashville, Tennessee.

Aiken, Carol; Jeffrey P. Rush; and Jerry Wycoff
1993 "A Preliminary Inquiry Into Alabama Youth Gang Membership", The Gang Journal: An Interdisciplinary Research Quarterly (1)(2): 37-47.

Amandes, Richard B.
1979 "Hire a Gang Leader: A Delinquency Prevention Program", Juvenile and Family Court Journal (30)(1)(Feb): 37-40.

Anderson, Elijah
1978 A Place on the Corner. Chicago: University of Chicago Press.

Anderson, James F.
1993 "Review Essay: A Methodological Critique of Islands in the Streets", The Gang Journal: An Interdisciplinary Research Quarterly (1)(2): 49-57.

Arnold, William R.
1965 "The Concept of Gang", The Sociological Quarterly (7)(1): 59-75.

Asbury, Herbert
1927 Gangs of New York. New York: Garden City Publishing Co.

1939 The Gangs of New York. New York: Alfred A. Knopf.

Austin, David M.
1957 "Goals for Gang Workers", Social Work (2)(4): 43-50

Axelson, Roland G.
    1984 "The Psychological Influence of Street Gangs on School-Aged Youth: A Case Study in Hartford, CT". The I.N. Thut World Education Center, Hartford, CT.

Bailey, William C.
    1969 "Educational and Occupational Experience, Perception, and Future Expectations of Lower Class Negro Gang Delinquents", Master's thesis, Washington State University.

Baird, L.H.
    1986 "Prison Gangs: Texas", Corrections Today (18)(July): 22.

Baittle, Brahm
    1961 "Psychiatric Aspects of the Development of a Street Corner Group: An Exploratory Study", American Journal of Orthopsychiatry (31)(Oct):703-712.

Barker, George C.
    1950 Pachuco: An American-Spanish Argot and Its Social Function in Tucson, Arizona. Social Science Bulletin No. 18 (Vol. XXI)(No. 1)(Jan), Tucson, Arizona: University of Arizona Press.

    1979 -----

Barrett, Leonard E.
    1988 The Rastafarians. Boston: Beacon Press.

Bartollas, Clemens
    1990 "The Prison: Disorder Personified", chapter 1 (pp. 11-22) in John W. Murphy and Jack E. Dison (Eds.) Are Prisons Any Better? Twenty Years of Correctional Reform, Sage Criminal Justice System Annuals, Newbury Park, CA: Sage Publications.

Beck, L.M.
    1962 Three Groups of Delinquents of the Family Court of East Baton Rouge Parish, Ph.D. dissertation, Louisiana State University.

Beier, Ernest G.
    1951 "Experimental Therapy With a Gang", Focus (30)(July): 97-102.

Bell, J. and D. Sullivan
    1987 Jackson, Mississippi Mayor's Task Force on Gangs: Final Report, Jackson, MS.

Bennett, James
    1981 Oral History and Delinquency: The Rhetoric of Criminology. Chicago: University of Chicago Press.

Bensinger, Gad J.
    1984 "Chicago Youth Gangs: A New Old Problem", Journal of Crime & Justice (VII): 1-16.

Bernstein, Saul
    1964 Youth on the Streets -- Work with Alienated Youth Groups. New York: Associated Press.

Bessant, Judith and Rob Watts
    1992 "Being Bag is Good: Explorations of the Bodgie Gang Culture in South East Australia, 1948-1956", The Gang Journal: An Interdisciplinary Research Quarterly (1)(1): 31-55.

    1994 "The American Juvenile Underclass and the Cultural Colonisation of Young Australians Under Conditions of Modernity", Journal of Gang Research (2)(1)(Fall): 15-33.

Bing, Leon
    1991 Do or Die. New York: Harper-Collins.

Blanchard, W.H.
    1959 "The Group Process in Gang Rape", Journal of Social Psychology: 259-266.

Bloch, Herbert
    1963 "The Juvenile Gang: A Cultural Reflex", Annals of the American Academy of Political and Social Science (347)(May): 20-29.

Bloch, Herbert and Arthur Niederhoffer
    1957 "Adolescent Behavior and the Gang: A Cross-Cultural Analysis", Journal of Social Therapy (3): 174-179.

    1958 The Gang: A Study in Adolescent Behavior. New York: Philosophical Press.

Block, Carolyn Rebecca and Richard Block
    1993 Street Gang Crime In Chicago. National Institute of Justice, Research in Brief. December.

Blumberg, Leonard
    1964 "A Possible Application of the Epidemiological-Public Health Model to Civic Action-Research", Social Problems (12)(Fall): 178-185.

Bobrowski, Lawrence J.
    1988 "Collecting, Organizing and Reporting Street Gang Crime", 82 pp., Chicago Police Department, Prepared for the 40th Annual Meeting of the American Society of Criminology, CPD: Special Functions Group.

Bogardus, Emory
    1943 "Gangs of Mexican-American Youth", Sociology and Social Research (28): 55-66.

Bolitho, W.
    1930 "The Psychosis of the Gang", Survey: 501-506.

Bookin, H.
1980 "The Gangs That Didn't Go Straight", paper presented at the Society for the Study of Social Problems, New York.

Bookin-Weiner, Hedy and Ruth Horowitz
1983 "The End of the Youth Gang: Fad or Fact?", Criminology (21)(4)(Nov): 585-601.

Bordua, David J.
1961   "Delinquent Subcultures: Sociological Interpretations of Gang Delinquency", Annals of the American Academy of Social Science (338): 119-36.

Born, Peter
1971 Street Gangs and Youth Unrest. Chicago: Chicago Tribune Educational Service Department.

Bowker, L.H. and Malcolm W. Klein
1983 "The Etiology of Female Juvenile Delinquency and Gang Membership: A Test of Psychological and Social Structural Explanations", Adolescence (18)(72)(Win): 739-751.

Brooks, William Allan
1952 Girl Gangs. A Survey of Teen-Age Drug Addicts, Sex Crimes, Rape, Kleptomania, Prostitution, Truancy, and Other Deviations. New York: Padell Book Company.

Brotman, Richard
1949 A Group Approach to the Treatment of the Aggressive Gang, Master's Thesis, City College of New York.

Brown, Waln K.
1977   "Black Female Gangs in Philadelphia", International Journal of Offender Therapy and Comparative Criminology (21): 221-228.

1978   "Black Gangs as Family Extensions" & "Graffiti, Identity, and the Delinquent Gang", International Journal of Offender Therapy and Comparative Criminology (22)(1): 39-48.

Brueckner, William H.
1960   "Corner Group Work with Teen-Age Gangs", Federal Probation (24)(Dec): 84.

Bryant, D.
1989 Community Responses Crucial for Dealing With Youth Gangs, U.S. Dept. of Justice, Office of Juvenile Justice and Delinquency Prevention, Washington, D.C.

Brymmer, R.A.
1967 "Toward a Definition and Theory of Conflict Gangs", (mimeo) paper presented at the annual meeting of the Society for the Study of Social Problems (August 26).

Buentello, S.
1986 Texas Syndicate: A Review of Its Inception, Growth in Violence and Continued Threat to the TDC, Texas Department of Corrections, unpublished.

Burns, E. and T.J. Deakin
1989 "New Investigative Approach to Youth Gangs", FBI Law Enforcement Bulletin (58)(10)(Oct): 20-24.

California Attorney General's Youth Gang Task Force
1981 Report on Youth Gang Violence in California. California: Department of Justice.

California Council on Criminal Justice
1986 Final Report: State Task Force on Youth Gang Violence. Sacramento, CA.

1989 State Task Force on Gangs and Drugs. Sacramento, CA: 95823.

Camp, George and Camille Graham Camp
1985 Prison Gangs: Their Extent, Nature, and Impact on Prisons. Washington, D.C.: U.S. Dept. of Justice.

Campbell, Anne
1984 The Girls in the Gang: A Report from New York City. New York: Basil Blackwell Ltd.

1984 "Girls' Talk: The Social Representation of Aggression by Female Gang Members", Criminal Justice Behavior (11): 139-156.

1987 "Self Definitions by Rejection: The Case of Gang Girls", Social Problems (34)(5)(Dec): 451-466.

Campbell, Anne and Steven Muncer
1989 "Them and Us: A Comparison of the Cultural Context of American Gangs and British Subcultures", Deviant Behavior (10)(3): 271-288.

Caplan, Nathan S.; Dennis J. Deshaies, Gerald D. Suttles, and Hans W. Mattick
1963 "The Nature, Variety, and Patterning of Street Club Work in an Urban Setting", pp. 135-169 in Malcolm W. Klein and Barbara G. Meyerhoff (eds), Juvenile Gangs in Context: Theory, Research, and Action, Confererence Report, August 25-26, 1963, Youth Studies Center, Los Angeles: University of Southern California.

1964 "Factors Affecting the Process and Outcome of Street Club Work", Sociology and Social Research (48)(Jan): 207-219.

Carey, Sean
1985 "I just Hate 'em, That's All", New Society (73)(1178)(July): 123-125.

Cartwright, Desmond S. and Kenneth I. Howard
1966 "Multivariate Analysis of Gang Delinquency: I. Ecologic Influences", Multivariate Behavioral Research (1)(July): 321-71.

Cartwright, Desmond S.; Kenneth I. Howard; and Nicholas A. Reuterman
1970 "Multivariate Analysis of Gang Delinquency: II. Structural and Dynamic Properties of Gangs", Multivariate Behavioral Research (5)(July): 303-24.

----- 1971 "Multivariate Analysis of Gang Delinquency: III. Age and Physique of Gangs and Clubs", Multivariate Behavioral Research(6)(Jan):75-90.

----- 1980 "Multivariate Analysis of Gang Delinquency: IV. Personality Factors in Gangs and Clubs", Multivariate Behavioral Research (15): 3-22.

Cartwright, Desmond S.; B. Tomson; and H. Schwartz
1975 Gang Delinquency. Monterey, CA: Brooks/Cole.

Cavanagh, Suzanne and David Teasley
1992 Youth Gangs: An Overview. Washington, DC: Congressional Research Service.

Cellini, Henry D.
1991 Youth Gang Prevention and Intervention Strategies. Albuquerque, NM: Training and Research Institute, Inc.

Chazal, J.
1964 "A Current Criminological Problem: Juvenile Delinquency in Gangs", Quebec Society of Criminology Bulletin (3)(2): 5-11.

Chicago Area Project
n.d. "Shaw's Thoughts".

1939 "Chicago Area Project", March, 1939.

n.d. Chicago Area Project: The Nation's First Community-Based Delinquency Prevention Program.

Chicago Police Department
1989 Murder Analysis. Richard M. Daley, Mayor. Leroy Martin, Supertindendent of Police. Chicago, IL.

Chin, Ko-Lin
1986 Chinese Triad Societies, Tongs, Organized Crime, and Street Gangs in Asia and the United States. Ph.D. dissertation, University of Pennsylvania.

1988 Chinese Gangs in New York City: 1965-1988. Baltimore, MD and Taipeh, Taiwan: Loyola College and National Taiwan University.

1990 Chinese Subculture and Criminality: Non-traditional Crime Groups in America. Westport, Conn: Greenwood Press.

1993 "Methodological Issues in Studying Chinese Gang Extortion", The Gang Journal: An Interdisciplinary Research Quarterly (1)(2): 25-36.

Clark, J.H.
        1981   A Report of the Gang Activities Task Force. Chicago Board of
        Education, Chicago, Illinois.

Cloward, R.A. and L.E. Ohlin
        1960   Delinquency and Opportunity. New York: Free Press.

Cohen, Albert K.
        1955   Delinquent Boys: The Culture of the Gang. Glencoe, IL: The Free
        Press.

Cohen, Bernard
        1970   "The Delinquency of Gangs and Spontaneous Groups", Chapter 4 in
        Delinquency: Selected Studies, Thorsten Sellin and Marvin E. Wolfgang
        (eds.), New York: John Wiley and Sons.

Cole, Juan R.I. and Moojan Momen
        1986   "Mafia, Mob and Shiism in Iraq: The Rebellion of Ottoman Karbala
        1824-1843", Past and Present (112)(Aug): 112-143.

Collins, H. Craig
        1977   "Street Gangs of New York: A Prototype of Organized Youth Crime",
        Law and Order (25)(1)(Jan): 6-16.

Collins, Jessie
        1993   "Joe: The Story of an Ex-Gang Member", Gang Journal: An Interdisci-
        plinary Research Quarterly (1)(3): 45-50.

Conrad, J.P.
        1979   "Who's in Charge? The Control of Gang Violence in California
        Prisons", in Correctional Facility Planning edited by Robert Montilla and
        Nora Marlow, pp. 135-147, Lexington, Mass: D.C. Heath.

Cook, James I.
        1993   "Targetting Gang Violence in the City of Westminister", Westminister
        Police Department, Westminister, CA.

Covey, Herbert C.; Scott Menard; and Robert J. Franzese
        1992   Juvenile Gangs. Charles C. Thomas Publisher: Springfield, IL.

Cox, V.
        1986   "Prison Gangs - Inmates Battle for Control", Corrections Compendium
        (10)(9)(Apr): 1,6-9.

Crane, A.R.
        1951   "A Note on Pre-Adolescent Gangs", Australian Psychology (3): 43-45.

        1958   "The Development of Moral Values in Children: IV; Pre-Adolescent
        Gangs and the Moral Development of Children", British Journal of
        Educational Psychology (28)(Nov): 201-208.

Crawford, Paul I.; Daniel I. Malamud; and James R. Dumpson
1950 Working With Teenage Gangs. A Report on the Central Harlem Street Clubs Project. New York: Welfare Council of New York City.

Crime Control Digest
1976 "Detroit Mayor Against City's Growing Youth Gangs: Citizen Involvement in Crime Prevention", Aug. 30, 1976, p. 5, (10)(35).

1980 "Gangs - Police, Community Relations", Mar. 30, 1980, pp. 7-8, (14)(9).

1984 "Police Community Relations: Gangs - Chicago Police Department: Citizen Involvement in Crime Prevention", Mar. 26, 1984, pp. 5-6, (18)(12).

1987 "Detroit Mayor Unveils Plan to Fight Youth Crime: Gangs and Crime Prevention", Jan 26, 1987, p. 6, (21)(4).

1987 "California's Vietnam Refugees Work on Their Own to Divert Teens from Street Gangs", June 8, 1987, pp. 9-10,(21)(23).

Crowner, James M.
1963 "Utilizing Certain Positive Aspects of Gang Phenomena in Training School Group Work", American Journal of Correction (25)(July-August): 24-27.

Cummings, Scott and Daniel Monti (eds.)
1993 Gangs: The Origins and Impact of Contemporary Youth Gangs in the United States. Albany, NY: State University New York Press.

Curry, G. David and Irving A. Spergel
1988   "Gang Homicide, Delinquency, and Community", Criminology (26)(Aug): 381-405.

Cusson, Maurice
1989 "Disputes over Honor and Gregarious Aggressions", Revue Internationale de Criminologie et de Police Technique (Geneva, SWITZ) (42)(3): 290-297.

Dahmann, J.
1981 "Operation Hardcore: A Prosecutorial Response to Violent Gang Criminality", interim report, MITRE Corporation, McLean, VA.

Daniels, S.
1987 "Prison Gangs: Confronting the Threat", Corrections Today (29)(2)-(Apr): 66,126,162.

Dart, Robert W.
1992 "The Future is Here Today: Street Gang Trends", The Gang Journal: An Interdisciplinary Research Quarterly (1)(1): 87-90.

David, J.J. and M.H. Shaffer
1988 Intelligence Gathering in the Investigation of Motorcycle Gangs, National Institute of Justice, NCJRS, Rockville, MD.

David, J.J.
1988   "Outlaw Motorcycle Gangs: A Transnational Problem", paper presented at the Conference on International Terrorism and Transnational Crime, University of Illinois at Chicago, August, 1988.

Davis, James R.
1978   The Terrorists: Youth, Biker and Prison Violence. San Diego, CA: Grossmont Press.

1982   Street Gangs: Youth, Biker and Prison Groups. Dubuque, Iowa: Kendall/Hunt Publishing.

Davis, Mike
1988   "War in the Streets", New Statesman & Society (1)(23)(Nov): 27-30.

Davis, R.H.
1982   Selected Bibliography on Publications Related to Outlaw Motorcycle Gangs, U.S. Dept. of Justice, FBI Academy, Quantico, VA 22134.

Day, D.
1987   "Outlaw Motorcycle Gangs", Royal Canadian Mounted Police Gazette (49)(5): 1-42.

Dawley, David
1973   A Nation of Lords: The Autobiography of the Vice Lords. Garden City, NY: Anchor Press.

1992   A Nation of Lords. Prospect Heights, IL: Waveland Press.

Delaney, J.L. and Walter B. Miller
1977   Intercity Variation in the Seriousness of Crime by Youth Gangs and Youth Groups, Report to the Office of Juvenile Justice and Delinquency Prevention.

Delaney, Lloyd T.
1954   "Establishing Relationships with Antisocial Groups and an Analysis of Their Structure", British Journal of Delinquency (5)(1): 34-42.

De Leon, Aleister
1977   "Averting Violence in the Gang Community", The Police Chief (44)(7)(July): 52-53.

Denisoff, R. Serge and Charles H. McCaghy
1973   Deviance, Conflict, and Criminality. Chicago: Rand McNally & Company.

Destro, Robert A.
1993   "Gangs and Civil Rights", pp. 227-304 in Scott Cummings and Daniel J. Monti (Eds.), Gangs: The Origin and Impact of Contemporary Youth Gangs in the United States. Albany, NY: State University of New York Press.

Dolan, Edward F. and Shan Finney
    1984 Youth Gangs. New York: Simon & Schuster, Julian Messner.

Donohue, John K.
    1966 My Brother's Boy: A Treatise on Criminology. St. Paul, MN: Bruce
    Publishing Co.

Douglas, Jack D.
    1970 Youth in Turmoil: America's Changing Youth Cultures and Student
    Protest Movements. Center for Studies of Crime and Delinquency, National
    Institute of Mental Health, Washington, DC: Government Printing Office.

Dumpson, J.R.
    1949 "An Approach to Antisocial Street Gangs", Federal Probation: 22-29.

Dumpson, James R., et al
    1952 "Gang and Narcotic Problems of Teen-Age Youth", American Journal
    of Psychotherapy (6)(Apr): 312-46.

Dunbar, Ellen A.
    1963 "How to Help the Gang Member Through His Family", Special Service
    for Groups, Los Angeles: unpublished.

Dunston, Leonard G.
    1990 Report of the Task Force on Juvenile Gangs. New York State Division
    for Youth. Albany, New York.

Dunston, Mark S.
    1992 Street Signs - An Identification Guide of Symbols of Crime and
    Violence. Powers Lake, WI: Performance Dimensions Publishing.

Duran, M.
    1975 "What Makes a Difference in Working with Youth Gangs?", Crime
    Prevention Review (2): 25-30.

Earley, Pete
    1992 The Hot House: Life Inside Leavenworth Prison. New York: Bantam.

Eisenstadt, S. N.
    1951 "Delinquency Group Formation Among Immigrant Youth", British
    Journal of Delinquency (2)(1).

Elliott, D.S.
    1962 "Delinquency and Perceived Opportunity", Sociological Inquiry
    (32)(Spr): 216-27.

English, T.J.
    1990 The Westies: The Irish Mob. New York: St. Martins Press.

Erlanger, Howard S.
    1979 "Estrangement, Machismo and Gang Violence", Social Science
    Quarterly (60)(2): 235-49.

Fagan, Jeffrey
1989   "The Social Organization of Drug Use and Drug Dealing Among Urban Gangs", Criminology (27)(4): 633-664.

Fagan, Jeffrey and Ko-lin Chin
1989   "Violence as Regulation and Social Control in the Distribution of Crack", in M. De la Rosa; B. Gropper; and E. Lambert (eds.), Drugs and Violence, National Institute of Drug Abuse Research Monograph, Rockville, MD: U.S. Dept. of Health and Human Services.

Ferrell, Jeff
1992   Crimes of Style: Urban Graffiti and the Politics of Urban Criminality. New York: Garland.

Fishman, L.
1988   "The Vice Queens: An Ethnographic Study of Black Female Gang Behavior", paper presented at the Annual Meeting of the American Society of Criminology.

Florida House of Representatives
1987   Issue Paper: Youth Gangs in Florida. Committee on Youth. Tallahassee, FL.

Fong, Robert S.
1987   A Comparative Study of the Organizational Aspects of Two Texas Prison Gangs: Texas Syndicate and Mexican Mafia. Ph.D. dissertation, Sam Houston State University, Huntsville, Texas.

1990   "The Organizational Structure of Prison Gangs: A Texas Case Study", Federal Probation (54)(1)(Mar): 36-43.

Fong, Robert S. and Salvador Buentello
1991   "The Management of Prison Gangs: An Empirical Assessment", paper presented at the Annual Meeting of the Academy of Criminal Justice Sciences, Nashville, Tennessee.

Fong, Robert S.; Ron Vogel; and Robert Little
1991   "Behind Prison Walls: Racially Based Gangs and Their Level of Violence", paper presented at the Annual Meeting of the Academy of Criminal Justice Sciences, Nashville, Tennessee.

Fossett, Christine A.
1974   Evaluation Report: North Central Youth Academy. Educational Management Associates, Consultants, Facilitators, Applied Behavioral and Management Sciences, Design, Development and Audit of Urban Programs, Philadelphia, PA (NCJRS# 09900.00.027469).

Fox, Robert W. and Mark E. Amador
1993   Gangs on the Move: A Descriptive Cataloging of Over 1500 Most Active Gangs in America. Placerville, CA: Copperhouse Publishing Company.

Frias, Gus
      1982 Barrio Warriors: Homeboys of Peace. Los Angeles: Diaz Publishing.

Friedman, C.J.; F. Mann; and A.S. Friedman
      1975 "A Profile of Juvenile Street Gang Members", Adolescence (10): 563-607.

      1976 "Juvenile Street Group: The Victimization of Youth", Adolescence, (44)(Winter): 527-533.

Fry, John
      1969 Fire and Blackstone. Philadelphia: J.B. Lippincott.

      1973 Locked Out Americans. New York: Harper and Row.

Furfey, Paul Hanley
      1926 The Gang Age: A Study of the Pre-Adolescent Boy and His Recreational Needs. New York: The Macmillan Company.

Furman, Sylvan S. (ed).
      1952 Reaching the Unreached. "Working with a Street Gang" (pp. 112-121) New York: New York City Youth Board.

Gandy, John M.
      1959 "Preventive Work with Street-Corner Groups: Hyde Park Project, Chicago", Annals of American Academy of Political and Social Science (323)(Mar): 107-116.

Gannon, Thomas M.
      1967 "Dimension of Current Gang Delinquency", Journal of Research in Crime and Delinquency (Jan)(4)(2): 119-131.

      1970 -----. Chapter 34 in Marvin E. Wolfgang, Leonard Savitz, and Norman Johnston (eds.), The Sociology of Crime and Delinquency, New York: John Wiley & Sons, Inc.

Geis, Gilbert
      1965 "Juvenile Gangs", President's Committee on Juvenile Delinquency and Youth Crime, Washington, D.C.

Gerrard, Nathan L.
      1964 "The Core Member of the Gang", British Journal of Criminology (4)(Apr): 361-371.

Giles, H. Harry
      1957 "Case Analysis of Social Conflict", Journal of Educational Sociology (30)(Mar): 289-333.

Giordano, P.C.
      1978 "Girls, Guys and Gangs: The Changing Social Context of Female Delinquency", Journal of Criminal Law and Criminology (69): 126-132.

Glane, Sam
    1950 "Juvenile Gangs in East Side Los Angeles", Focus (29)(Sept): 136-141.

Goldstein, Arnold P.
    1991 Delinquent Gangs: A Psychological Perspective. Champaign, IL:
    Research Press.

Goldstein, Arnold P. and Barry Glick, et al
    1994 The Prosocial Gang: Implementing Aggression Replacement Training.
    Thousand Oaks, CA: Sage Publications.

Gonzalez, Alfredo
    1981 Mexican/Chicano Gangs in Los Angeles. D.S.W. dissertation,
    University of California at Berkeley, School of Social Welfare.

Gordon, Robert A.
    1963 Values and Gang Delinquency, Ph.D. dissertation, University of
    Chicago.

    1967 "Social Level, Disability, and Gang Interaction", American Journal of
    Sociology (73)(July): 42-62.

Gordon, Robert A.; James Short, Jr.; Desmond S. Cartwright; and Fred L. Strodtbeck
    1963 "Values and Gang Delinquency: A Study of Street-Corner Groups",
    American Journal of Sociology (69)(2): 109-128.

    1970 "Values and Gang Delinquency: A Study of Street-Corner Groups",
    Chapter 33 in Wolfgang, et al (eds.), The Sociology of Crime and Delinquen-
    cy, New York: John Wiley & Sons, Inc, pp. 319-339.

Gorn, Elliott J.
    1987 "Good-Bye Boys, I Die a True American": Homicide, Nativism, and
    Working-Class Culture in Antebellum New York City", Journal of American
    History (74)(2)(Sept): 388-410.

Gott, Raymond
    1991 (Audio Training Tape) "Juvenile Gangs and Drug Trafficking",
    available through the National Juvenile Detention Association, 217 Perkins
    Bldg, Richmond, KY 40475-3127.

Greeley, Andrew and James Casey
    1963 "An Upper Middle Class Deviant Gang", American Catholic Sociologi-
    cal Review (24)(Spr): 33-41.

Hagedorn, John M.
    1987 Final Report: Milwaukee Gang Research Project, Milwaukee:
    University of Wisconsin-Milwaukee.

Hagedorn, John M. and Perry Macon
    1988 People and Folks: Gangs, Crime and the Underclass in a Rustbelt City,
    Chicago: Lakeview Press.

Hagedorn, John M. and Joan W. Moore
    1987 "Milwaukee and Los Angeles Gangs Compared", paper presented at the
    Annual Meeting of the American Anthropological Association, Oaxaca,
    Mexico.

Haire, Thomas D.
    1979 "Street Gangs: Some Suggested Remedies for Violence and Vandalism",
    The Police Chief (46)(7)(July): 54-55.

Hamm, Mark S.
    1990 "Dealing with Skinheads, the Ku Klux Klan and other Idiots with
    Ideology: Toward a Correctional Education to Reduce Racial Hatred in
    Prison", paper presented at the International Conference of the Correctional
    Educational Education Association, July 8-11, 1990, Burnaby, British
    Columbia.

    1993 American Skinheads: The Criminology and Control of Hate Crime.
    Westport, Conn.: Praeger Series in Criminology and Crime Control Policy.

Hanson, Kitty
    1964 Rebels in the Streets: The Story of New York's Gang Girls. Englewood
    Cliffs, NJ: Prentice-Hall.

Harding, J.
    1952 "A Street Corner Gang and its Implications for Sociological and
    Psychological Theory", In J.E. Hulett and K.R. Stagner (eds.), Problems in
    Social Psychology, Urbana: University of Illinois Press.

Hardman, Dale G.
    1963 Small Town Gangs, Ph.D. dissertation, University of Illinois, College
    of Education.

    1967 "Historical Perspectives of Gang Research", Journal of Research in
    Crime and Delinquency (4)(1): 5-27.

    1969 "Small Town Gangs", Journal of Criminal Law, Criminology and Police
    Studies (60)(2): 173-81.

Harris, Mary G.
    1988 Cholas: Latino Girls and Gangs. New York: AMS Press.

Harrison, F.V.
    1988 "The Politics of Outlawry in Urban Jamaica", Urban Anthropology
    (17)(2,3)(Sum/Fall): 259-277.

Haskins, James
    1974 Street Gangs: Yesterday and Today. New York: Hastings House.

Helmreich, W.B.
    1973 "Black Crusaders: The Rise and Fall of Political Gangs", Society
    (11)(1)(Nov/Dec): 44-50.

Hendry, Charles E., et al
      1947 "Gangs", John Dewey Society, Ninth Yearbook: 151-175, New York:
      Harper.

Hobsbawm, Eric J.
      1965 Primitive Rebels. New York: W.W. Norton & Co., Inc.

      1969 Bandits. Delacorte Press.

Hodge, Patricia
      1964 Self-Descriptions of Gang and Nongang Teen-Aged Boys, Master's
      thesis, Department of Sociology, University of Chicago.

Hoenig, Gary
      1975 Reaper: The Story of a Gang Leader. Indianapolis: The Bobbs-Merrill
      Company, Inc.

Hoffman, Paul
      1993 "A Nation of Lords: Book Review", The Gang Journal: An Interdisci-
      plinary Research Quarterly (1)(2): 71-72.

Hogrefe, Russell and John Harding
      1947 "Research Considerations in the Study of Street Gangs", Applied
      Anthropology (6)(Fall): 21-24.

Horowitz, Ruth
      1982 "Masked Intimacy and Marginality: Adult Delinquent Gangs in a
      Chicano Community", Urban Life (11): 3-26.

      1983 "The End of the Youth Gang", Criminology (21)(4): 585-600.

      1983 Honor and the American Dream. New Brunswick, NJ: Rutgers
      University Press.

      1986 "Remaining an Outsider: Membership as a Threat to Research
      Rapport", Urban Life (14)(4)(Jan): 409-430.

      1987 "Community Tolerance of Gang Violence", Social Problems (34)(Dec):
      449.

Horowitz, Ruth and Gary Schwartz
      1974 "Honor, Normative Ambiguity and Gang Violence", American
      Sociological Review (39): 238-51.

Houston, James G.
      1993 "An Interview with Lewis Yablonsky: The Violent Gang and Beyond",
      The Gang Journal: An Interdisciplinary Research Quarterly (1)(2): 59-67.

      1994 "National Policy Neglect and Its Impact on Gang Suppression", Journal
      of Gang Research (2)(1)(Fall): 35-62.

Howson, Gerald
1970 Thief-Taker General: Jonathan Wild and the Emergence of Crime and Corruption as a Way of Life in Eighteenth Century England. New Brunswick: Transaction Books.

Huff, C. Ronald
1988 "Youth Gangs and Public Policy in Ohio: Findings and Recommendations", paper presented at the Ohio Conference on Youth Gangs and the Urban Underclass, Columbus: Ohio State University.

---- "Youth Gangs and Police Organizations: Rethinking Structure and Functions", paper presented at the Annual Meeting of the Academy of Criminal Justice Sciences, San Francisco.

1989 "Youth Gangs and Public Policy", Crime & Delinquency (35)(4)(Oct.): 524-37.

---- "Gangs, Organized Crime, and Drug-Related Violence in Ohio", In Understanding the Enemy: An Informational Overview of Substance Abuse in Ohio, Columbus, OH: Governor's Office of Criminal Justice Services.

1990 Gangs in America: Diffusion, Diversity, and Public Policy. Newbury Park, CA: Sage Publications.

Hunsaker, A.
1981 "The Behavioral-Ecological Model of Intervention With Chicano Gang Delinquents", Hispanic Journal of Behavioral Sciences (3): 225-239.

Hunt, G.; S. Riegel; T. Morales; and D. Waldorf
1992 "Keep The Peace Out of Prisons: Prison Gangs, an Alternative Perspective". San Francisco, CA: Institute for Scientific Analysis, Home Boy Study.

1993 "Changes in Prison Culture: Prison Gangs and the Case of the Pepsi Generation". San Francisco, CA: Institute for Scientific Analysis, Home Boy Study.

Ianni, Francis A.J.
1974 Black Mafia: Ethnic Succession in Organized Crime. New York: Simon and Schuster.

Illinois Department of Corrections
1984 Gangs and Gang Awareness. Training Academy.

1988 Gangs and Gang Awareness. Training Academy.

Inciardi, James A.
1984 Criminal Justice. Orlando: Academic Press, Inc.

Intl. Assoc. of Chiefs of Police
1986 Organized Motorcycle Gangs, Gaithersburg, MO 20878.

Jackson, George
       1970 Soledad Brother: The Prison Letters of George Jackson. New York:
       Bantam Books.

Jackson, Pamela Irving
       1991 "Crime, Youth Gangs, and Urban Transition: The Social Dislocations
       of Postindustrial Economic Development", Justice Quarterly (8)(3): 379-397.

Jackson, Patrick G.
       1989 "Theories and Findings About Youth Gangs", Criminal Justice
       Abstracts (21)(2)(June): 313-329.

Jackson, R.K. and W.D. McBride
       1985 Understanding Street Gangs. Sacramento, CA: Custom Publishing.

Jacobs, James
       1974 "Street Gangs Behind Bars", Social Problems (21)(3): 395-408.

       1977 Stateville. Chicago: University of Chicago Press.

James, Don
       1963 Girls and Gangs. Derby, Conn: Monarch.

Jameson, S.H.
       1956 "Policeman's Non-Official Role in Combatting Gangs and Vandalism",
       Association for Professional Law Enforcement, Quartly Journal (3)(June): 1-
       3.

Jankowski, Martin Sanchez
       1991 Islands in the Street: Gangs American Urban Society. Berkeley:
       University of California Press.

Janowitz, Morris
       1970 Political Conflict. Chicago: Quadrangle Books.

Jansyn, Leon
       1960 Solidarity and Delinquency in a Street Corner Group: A Study of the
       Relationship between Changes in Specified Aspects of Group Structure and
       Variations in the Frequency of Delinquent Activity, Master's thesis,
       University of Chicago.

       1967 "Solidarity and Delinquency in a Street Corner Group", American
       Sociological Review (31): 600-14.

Jayasuriya, J.E. and Sundari Kariyawasam
       1958 "Juvenile Delinquency as a Gang Activity in the City of Colombo",
       Ceylon Journal of Historical and Social Studies (1)(2)(July): 202-215.

Jereczek, Gordon E.
       1962 "Gangs Need Not Be Delinquent", Federal Probation (26)(Mar): 49-52.

Joe, D. and N. Robinson
    1980 "Chinatown's Immigrant Gangs: The New Young Warrior Class",
    Criminology (18)(3)(Nov): 337-345.

Joe, Karen
    1980 "Kai-Doi's: Gang Violence in Chinatown". Paper presented at the
    Annual Conference of the Rho Chapter of the California Alpha Kappa Delta
    association. Los Angeles, CA: University of California at Los Angeles.

    1993 "Issues in Accessing and Studying Ethnic Youth Gangs", The Gang
    Journal: An Interdisciplinary Research Quarterly (1)(2): 9-23.

Johnson, Gwendolyn
    1949 The Transformation of Juvenile Gangs into Accommodated Groups:
    A Study of Eight Boys' Gangs in Washington. Master's Thesis, Howard
    University.

Johnson, Patrick
    1989 "Theories and Findings about Youth Gangs", Criminal Justice
    Abstracts (June): 313-327.

Johnson, W.C.
    1981 "Motorcycle Gangs and White Collar Crime", The Police Chief
    (47)(6)(June): 32-33.

Johnstone, John W.C.
    1981 "Youth Gangs and Black Suburbs", Pacific Sociological Review
    (24)(3)(July): 355-375.

Joselit, Jenna Weissman
    1983 Our Gang: Jewish Crime and the New York Jewish Community 1900-
    1940. Bloomington: Indiana University Press.

Juvenile Justice Digest
    1980 "Police Community Relations: Crime Prevention of Gangs", Feb. 22,
    1980, pp. 7-8 (8)(4).

Kantor, David and William Ira Bennett
    1968 "Orientation of Street-Corner Workers and Their Effect on Gangs", In
    Stanton Wheeler (ed.), Controlling Delinquents, New York: Wiley.

Karacki, Larry and Jackson Toby
    1962 "The Uncommitted Adolescent: Candidate for Gang Socialization",
    Sociological Quarterly (32)(Spr): 203-215.

Kasimar, Yale
    1971 "When the Cops Were Not 'Handcuffed'", pp. 46-57 in Donald R.
    Cressey (ed.), Crime & Criminal Justice, Chicago: Quadrangle Books.

Keiser, R. Lincoln
    1969 The Vice Lords: Warriors of the Streets. New York: Holt, Rinehart
    and Winston.

Kleeck, Mary van; Emma A. Winslow; and Ira De A. Reid
    1931 Work and Law Observance. An Experimental Inquiry into the Influence of Unemployment and Occupational Conditions Upon Crime for the National Commission on Law Observance and Enforcement, No. 13, June 26, 1931, pp. 163-333.

Klein, Lloyd
    1990 "Running on the 'Wild Side': The Central Park Jogger Case and Adolescent Criminal Activity", paper presented at the Annual Meeting of the American Society of Criminology, Baltimore, MD.

Klein, Malcolm W.
    1964 "Internal Structures and Age Distribution in Four Delinquent Negro Gangs", Youth Studies Center (Dec.), Los Angeles: University of Southern California.

    1965 "Juvenile Gangs, Police, and Detached Workers: Controversies About Intervention", Social Service Review (39): 183-190.

    1966 "Factors Related to Juvenile Gang Membership Patterns", Sociology and Social Research (51): 49-62.

    1967 Juvenile Gangs in Context. New Jersey: Prentice-Hall.

    1968a "Impressions of Juvenile Gang Members", Adolescence (3)(59): 53-78.

    1968b From Association to Guilt: The Group Guidance Project in Juvenile Gang Intervention. Los Angeles: Youth Studies Center.

    1968c The Ladino Hill Project. Los Angeles: Youth Studies Center.

    1969a "Violence in American Juvenile Gangs", in D. Mulvihill and M. Tumin (eds.), Crimes of Violence, National Commission on the Causes and Prevention of Violence, Vol. 13: 1427-1460.

    1969b "On the Group Context of Delinquency", Sociology and Social Research (54): 63-71.

    1969c "Gang Cohesiveness, Delinquency, and a Street-Work Program", Journal of Research in Crime and Delinquency (July).

    1971 Street Gangs and Street Workers. Englewood Cliffs, NJ: Prentice-all.

    1990 "Having an Investment in Violence: Some Thoughts About the American Street Gang", The Edwin H. Sutherland Award Address to the American Society of Criminology, Annual Meeting, November 9, 1990.

Klein, Malcolm W. and Lois Y. Crawford
    1967 "Groups, Gangs, and Cohesiveness", Journal of Research in Crime and Delinquency (4): 63-75.

Klein, Malcolm W.; Cheryl Maxson, and Margaret A. Gordon
    1985 "Differences Between Gang and Non-Gang Homicides", Criminology
    (23)(2): 209-20.

    1986 "The Impact of Police Investigations on Police-Reported Rates of Gang
    and Nongang Homicides", Criminology (24): 489-512.

Klein, Malcolm W.; and Cheryl L. Maxson
    1985 "Rock' Sales in South L.A.", Social Science Research (69): 561-565.

    1989 "Street Gang Violence", In Marvin E. Wolfgang and Neil A. Weiner
    (eds.), Violent Crime, Violent Criminals, Newbury Park, CA: Sage Publica-
    tions.

Klein, Malcolm W.; Cheryl Maxson; and Lea Cunningham
    1990 "'Crack,' Street Gangs, and Violence", Center For Research on Crime
    and Social Control, University of Southern California.

Klein, Malcolm W. and Barbara G. Meyerhoff (eds)
    1964 Juvenile Gangs in Context: Theory, Research, and Action, Conference
    Report, August 25-26, 1963, Youth Studies Center, Los Angeles: University
    of Southern California.

Klein, Malcolm W. and Neal Snyder
    1965 "The Detached Worker: Uniformities and Variances in Style", Social
    Work (10)(Oct): 60-68.

Klofas, John; Stan Stojkovic and David Kalinich
    1990 Criminal Justice Organizations: Administration and Management.
    Belmont, CA: Brooks/Cole Publishing Company.

Knox, George W.
    1976 The Urban Crisis in Southwest Chicago: A Research-Based Discussion
    of Racial Conflict, (Dec., 1976), unpublished monograph.

    1978 "Perceived Closure and Respect for the Law Among Delinquent and
    Non-Delinquent Youths", Youth and Society (9)(4)(June): 385-406.

    1978 "Determinants of Employment Success Among Exoffenders", Offender
    Rehabiliation (2)(3)(Spr): 204-214.

    1980 "Educational Upgrading for Youthful Offenders", Chidren and Youth
    Services Review (2)(3): 291-313.

    1981 "Differential Integration and Job Retention Among Exoffenders",
    Criminology (18)(4)(Feb): 481-499.

    1981 "A Comparative Cost-Benefit Analysis of Offender Placement
    Programs", LAE Journal of the American Criminal Justice Association
    (43)(1,2): 39-49.

    1984 "How Criminologists View Rehabilitation", Indian Journal of Criminol-
    ogy (12)(1)(Jan): 26-32.

1989 "Family Services in Corrections", The State of Corrections, Proceedings of the Annual Conferences of The American Correctional Association, pp. 179-182.

1991 An Introduction to Gangs. Berrien Springs, MI: Vande Vere Publishing, Ltd.

1991 "Gangs and Social Justice Issues", chapter 1 (pp. 1-19), in Sloan T. Letman (Ed.), Prison Conditions and Prison Overcrowding, Dubuque, IA: Kendall/Hunt Publishing Company.

1992 "Gang Organization in a Large Urban Jail", American Jails.

1994 The Unabridged Thrasher (Ed.). Berrien Springs, MI: Vande Vere Publishing, Ltd. (in press).

Knox, George W.; Benito Garcia; and Pat Mc Clendon
1983 "Social and Behavioral Correlates of Gang Affiliation", paper presented at the Annual Meeting of the American Society of Criminology, Nov. 10, 1983, Denver, CO.

Knox, George W.; Edward D. Tromanhauser; and David Laske
1992 Schools Under Siege. Dubuque, IA: Kendall/Hunt Publishing Company.

Knox, George W.; Edward Tromanhauser; and Thomas F. Mc Currie
1991 "Gangs in Juvenile Corrections: Training Issues", Journal of Correctional Training (forthcoming).

Knox, George W.; and Edward Tromanhauser
1991 "Gangs and Their Control in Adult Correctional Institutions", The Prison Journal (LXXI)(2)(Fall-Winter): 15-22.

1991 "Gang Members as a Distinct Health Risk Group in Juvenile Correctional Facilities", The Prison Journal (LXXI)(2)(Fall-Winter): 61-66.

1992 "Comparing Juvenile Correctional Facilities: A Brief Overview", Journal of Juvenile Justice and Detention Services (7)(1)(Spr): 7-13.

1993 "Gang Training in Adult Correctional Institutions: A Function of Intensity, Duration and Impact of the Gang Problem", Journal of Correctional Training.

Knox, George W.; Edward D. Tromanhauser; Pamela Irving Jackson; Darek Niklas; James G. Houston; Paul Koch; and James R. Sutton
1993 "Preliminary Findings from the 1992 Law Enforcement Mail Questionnaire Project", Gang Journal: An Interdisciplinary Research Quarterly (1)(3): 11-27.

Kobrin, Solomon
1959 "The Chicago Area Project - a Twenty-five Year Assessment", Annals of the American Academy of Political and Social Science (322): 19-29.

1961 "Sociological Aspects of the Development of a Street Corner Group: An Exploratory Study", Amerian Journal of Orthopsychiatry (31)(4): 685-702.

1964 "Legal and Ethical Problems of Street Gang Work", Crime and Delinquency (10)(2): 152-156.

Kobrin, Solomon and Malcolm W. Klein
1983 Community Treatment of Juvenile Offenders: The DSO Experiments. Beverly Hills, CA: Sage Publications.

Kobrin, S.; J. Puntil; and E. Peluso
1967 "Criteria of Status Among Street Groups", Journal of Research in Crime and Delinquency (4)(Jan): 98-119.

Kolender, W.B.
1982 Street Gangs (Revised). In-service Training. San Diego Police Department, Training Section.

Kornblum, William
1974 Blue Collar Community. Chicago: University of Chicago Press.

1987 "Ganging Together: Helping Gangs Go Straight", Social Issues and Health Review (2): 99-104.

Kornhauser, Ruth R.
1978 Social Sources of Delinquency. Chicago: University of Chicago Press.

Kotlowitz, Alex
1991 There Are No Children Here. New York: Doubleday.

1992 There Are No Children Here. New York: Anchor Books.

Krajick, K.
1990 "The Menace of Supergangs", Corrections Magazine (June): 11-14.

Kramer, Dale and Madeline Karr
1953 Teenage Gangs. Henry Holt and Co., Inc.

Krech, David; Richard S. Crutchfield; and Egerton L. Ballachey
1962 Individual in Society: A Textbook of Social Psychology New York: McGraw-Hill Book Company, Inc.

Krisberg, Barry
1971 Urban Leadership Training: An Ethnographic Study of 22 Gang Leaders. Ph.D. dissertation, University of Pennsylvania, Philadelphia.

1974 "Gang Youth and Hustling: The Psychology of Survival", Issues in Criminology (9)(1)(Spr): 115-131.

1975 The Gang and the Community. School of Criminology, University of California, Berkeley. San Franciso, CA: R and E Research Associates.

Lagree, J. and P.L. Fai
    1989 "Girls in Street Gangs in the Suburbs of Paris" (from Growing up Good: Policing the Behavior of Girls in Europe, pp. 80-95, Maureen Cain, editor), Newbury Park, CA: Sage Publications.

Landesco, John
    1929 Organized Crime in Chicago. Part III of the Illinois Crime Survey. Illinois Association for Criminal Justice, 300 West Adams Street, Chicago, IL. In Cooperation with the Chicago Crime Commission.

Lane, Michael
    1989 "Inmate Gangs", Corrections Today (51)(4)(July): 98-99, 126-128.

Lauderback, David; Joy Hansen; and Dan Waldorf
    1992 "Sisters are Doin' It For Themselves: A Black Female Gang in San Francisco", The Gang Journal: An Interdisciplinary Research Quarterly (1)(1): 57-72.

Law and Order
    1977 "Gangs: Police Community Relations", (25)(12): 20-23.

Leissner, Aryeh
    1969 Street Club Work in Tel Aviv and New York. London: Longmans, Green and Co., Ltd.

Lerman, P.
    1967 "Gangs, Networks, and Subcultural Delinquency", American Journal of Sociology (73): 63-72.

Liebow, Elliot
    1967 Tally's Corner: Study of Negro Street Corner Men. Boston: Little, Brown and Co.

Loo, C.K.
    1976 The Emergence of San Francisco Chinese Juvenile Gangs from the 1950s to the Present, unpublished Master's thesis, San Jose State University.

Los Angeles County Probation Department and Youth Studies Center
    1962 Progress Report, Study of Delinquent Gangs, July 1, 1961 - June 30, 1962. Los Angles and University of Southern California.

    1963 Second Annual Progress Report: Study of Delinquent Gangs, July 1, 1962 - June 30, 1963. Los Angeles and University of Southern California.

    1964 Third Annual Progress Report: Study of Delinquent Gangs, July 1, 1963 - June 30, 1964. Los Angeles and University of Southern California.

Lotter, J.M.
    1988 "Prison Gangs in South Africa: A Description", The South African Journal of Sociology (19)(2)(May): 67-75.

Lowney, Jeremiah
    1984 "The Wall Gang: A Study of Interpersonal Process and Deviance
    Among Twenty-Three Middle-Class Youths", Adolescence (19)(75)(Fall):
    527-538.

Lyman, M.D.
    1989   "Street Youth Gangs", (From Gangland: Drug Trafficking by
    Organized Criminals, pp. 95-111), Newbury Park, CA: Sage Publications.

Madden, Max
    1993 The NACGI Journal. Various Copyrighted Materials in the Institution
    Gang Investigator Series.

Majors, Richard and Janet Mancini Billson
    1992 Cool Pose: The Dilemmas of Black Manhood in America. New York:
    Lexington Books.

Malcolm, Dino.
    1981 "D To the Knee! Stone To the Bone!", Best of Hair Trigger: A Story
    Workshop Anthology, pp. 81-91, Chicago: Columbia College Writing
    Department.

Martin, Richard H.
    1993 "Gang Colors: Should Students Be Allowed to Wear Them in College?",
    The Gang Journal: An Interdisciplinary Research Quarterly (1)(2): 69. 69.

Mattick, Hans W. and Nathan S. Caplan
    1962   Chicago Youth Development Project: Street Work, Community
    Organization and Research, April, University of Michigan Institute for Social
    Research, Ann Arbor, Michigan.

    1964 The Chicago Youth Development Project, February, University of
    Michigan Institute for Social Research, Ann Arbor, Michigan.

Maxson, C.L.; M.A. Gordon; and Malcolm W. Klein
    1985 "Differences Between Gang and Nongang Homicides", Criminology
    (23): 209-222.

Maxson, Cheryl L. and Malcolm W. Klein
    1983 "Agency versus Agency: Disputes in the Gang Deterence Model", in
    James R. Kluegel (ed.), Evaluating Contemporary Juvenile Justice, Beverly
    Hills: Sage.

    1986 "Street Gangs Selling Cocaine "rock": The Confluence of Two Social
    Problems", Social Science Research Center, University of Southern Califor-
    nia.

    1989 "Street Gang Violence: Twice as Great, or Half as Great?", paper
    presented at the annual meeting of the American Society of Criminology,
    Reno, Nevada, November.

Maxson, Cheryl L.
1983 "Gangs: Why We Couldn't Stay Away", in James R. Kluegel (ed.), Evaluating Contemporary Juvenile Justice, Beverly Hills: Sage.

1993 "Investigating Gang Migration: Contextual Issues for Intervention", The Gang Journal: An Interdisciplinary Research Quarterly (1)(2): 1-8.

Mazon, M.
1985 The Zoot-suit Riots: The Psychology of Symbolic Annihilation, Austin: University of Texas Press.

McCaddon, Jeff
1993 "Jakes: Jamaican Posses, The Most Violent Crime Groups Operating in North America!", P.B.S.P, February.

Mc Carthy, J.E. and J.S. Barbaro
1952 "Redirecting Teenage Gangs", in S.S. Furman (ed.), New York City Youth Board.

Mc Connell, Elizabeth H.
1990 "Assessing Youth Gangs in an Urban High School", paper presented at the Annual Meeting of the American Society of Criminology, Baltimore, MD.

1994 "Youth Gang Intervention and Prevention in Texas: Evaluating Community Mobilization Training", Journal of Gang Research (2)(1)(Fall): 63-71.

Mc Guire, P.
1986 "Outlaw Motorcycle Gangs - Organized Crime on Wheels", National Sheriff (37)(2)(Apr-May): 68-75.

Mc Kay, Henry D.
1949 "The Neighborhood and Child Conduct", Annals of the American Academy of Political and Social Science (Jan): 32-41.

Mc Kinney, K.C.
1988 Juvenile Gangs: Crime and Drug Trafficking, U.S. Dept. of Justice, Office of Juvenile Justice and Delinquency Prevention, Washington, D.C.

1988 "Juvenile Gangs: Crime and Drug Trafficking", Juvenile Justice Bulletin, 2-7.

Mc Lean, Gordon
1991 Cities of Lonesome Fear: God Among the Gangs. Chicago: Moody Press.

Mc Pherson, James Alan
1966 "The Blackstone Rangers", The Atlantic (223)(5)(May).

Meyerhoff, Howard L. and Barbara G. Meyerhoff
1964 "Field Observations of Middle Class Gangs", Social Forces (42): 328-336.

Mieczkowski, Thomas
  1986 "Geeking Up and Throwing Down: Heroin Street Life in Detroit",
  Criminology (24): 645-666.

Miller, Walter B.
  1957 "The Impact of a Community Group Work Program on Delinquent
  Corner Groups", Social Service Review (31): 396-406.

  1958 "Lower Class Culture as a Generating Milieu of Gang Delinquency",
  Journal of Social Issues (14)(3): 9.

  1962 "The Impact of a 'Total Community' Delinquency Control Project",
  Social Problems (10)(Fall): 168-91.

  1963 "The Corner Gang Boys Get Married", Transaction (1): 10-12.

  1966 "Violent Crimes by City Gangs", Annals of the American Academy of
  Political and Social Sciences (364): 219-230.

  1969 "White Gangs", Transaction (6)(1).

  1976 Violence by Youth Gangs and Youth Groups as a Crime Problem in
  Major American Cities. Washington, D.C.:   U.S. Government Printing
  Office.

  1980 "Gangs, Groups and Serious Youth Crime", In D. Schichor and D.
  Kelly (eds.), Critical Issues in Juvenile Delinquency, Lexington, MA:
  Lexington.

  1981 "American Youth Gangs: Past and Present", Current Perspectives on
  Criminal Behavior: Original Essays on Criminology, 2nd edition, edited by
  Abraham S. Blumberg, New York: Knopf (also 1974).

  1982 Crime by Youth Gangs and Youth Groups in the United States, report
  prepared for the National Youth Gang Survey, Washington, DC: Office of
  Juvenile Justice and Delinquency Prevention.

  1983 "Youth Gangs and Groups", In Sanford H. Kadish (ed.),
  Encyclopedia of Crime and Justice. New York: Free Press.

  1985 "Historical Review of Programs and Theories of Work With Youth
  Gangs: 1920-1985", in D. Ingemunsen and G. Johnson, Report on the Illinois
  Symposium on Gangs, Springfield, IL: Illinois Department of Children and
  Family Services.

  1989 "Recommendations for Terms to Be Used for Designating Law
  Violating Youth Groups", paper presented at the Conference of the National
  Youth Gang Suppression and Intervention Project, Chicago.

Miller, Walter B.; Hildred Geertz; and Henry S.G. Cutter
  1961 "Aggression in a Boys' Street-Corner Group", Psychiatry (24)(4): 283-
  298.

Milner, John G.
1959 "Working With Juvenile Gang Members", California Youth Authority, Quarterly (12)(Spr): 3-7.

Mitchell, R.
1951 "Capturing Boys Gangs", Human Organization (Summer).

Molland, John, Jr.
1967 Cross Pressures: A Study of the Reconciliation by the Gang Boys of Perceived Expectations of Others, Ph.D. dissertation, University of Chicago.

Moore, Jack B.
1993 Skinheads Shaved For Battle: A Cultural History of American Skinheads. Bowling Green, OH: Bowling Green State University Popular Press.

Moore, Joan W.
1977 "The Chicano Pinto Research Project: A Case Study in Collaboration", Journal of Social Issues (33)(4): 144-158.

1978 Homeboys: Gangs, Drugs, and Prison in the Barrios of Los Angeles, Philadelphia: Temple University Press.

1983 "Residence and Territoriality in Chicano Gangs", Social Problems (31): 182-194.

1985 "Isolation and Stigmatization in the Development of the Underclass: The Case of the Chicano Gangs in East Los Angeles", Social Problems (33)(1)(Oct): 1-12.

1988 "Changing Chicano Gangs: Acculturation, Generational Change, Evolution of Deviance or Emerging Underclass?", In J.H. Johnson, Jr. and M.L. Oliver (eds.), Proceedings of the Conference on Comparative Ethnicity, Los Angeles: Institute for Social Science Research, UCLA.

1989 "Is There a Hispanic Underclass?", Social Science Quarterly (70)(2): 265-285.

1989 "Gangs, Drugs, and Violence", in M. de la Rosea, B. Gropper, and E. Lambert (eds.), Drugs and Violence National Institute of Drug Abuse Research Monograph, Rockville, MD: U.S. Department of Health and Human Services.

1989 "Gangs and Gang Violence: What we Know and What We Don't Know", paper presented at the California State University, Los Angeles, CA.

1991 Going Down to the Barrio: Homeboys and Homegirls in Change. Philadelpha, PA: Temple University Press.

Moore, Joan and Mary Devitt
1989 "The Paradox of Deviance in Addicted Mexican American Mothers", Gender & Society (3)(1)(Mar): 53-70.

Moore, Joan; J. Diego Vigil; and Robert Garcia
1983 "Residence and Territoriality in Chicano Gangs", Social Problems (31): 182-194.

Moore, Joan W. and J.D. Vigil
1987 "Chicano Gangs: Group Norms and Individual Factors Related to Adult Criminality", Aztlan (18)(2)(Fall): 27-44.

Moore, Mark and Mark A. R. Kleiman
1989 The Police and Drugs. Washington, D.C.: National Institute of Justice.

Moore, Winston; Charles P. Livermore, and George F. Galland, Jr.
1973 "Woodlawn: The Zone of Destruction", The Public Interest (30)(Winter): 41-59.

Morales, Armando
1963 "A Study of Recidivism of Mexican-American Junior Forestry Camp Graduates", Master's Thesis, Social Work, University of Southern California.

1982 "The Mexican American Gang Member: Evaluation and Treatment", in Mental Health and Hispanic Americans by Rosina M. Becerra, Marvin Karno, and Javier I. Escobar (eds.), New York: Grune and Stratton.

1989 "A Clinical Model for the Prevention of Gang Violence and Homicide", In A. Morales and B.W. Sheafor, Social Work: A Profession of Many Faces. Boston: Allyn and Bacon.

Morash, Merry
1983 "Gangs, Groups and Delinquency", British Journal of Criminology (23): 309-331.

1990 "Gangs and Violence", in A.J. Reiss, Jr..; N. Weiner; and J. Roth (eds.), Violent Criminal Behavior, Report of the Panel on the Understanding and Control of Violent Behavior, National Academy of Sciences, Washington, DC: National Academy Press.

Morici, J. and D. Flanders
1979 "Chinatown Youth Gangs - Past, Present and Future." California Youth Authority Quarterly (32): 19-24.

Mottel, Syeus
1973 CHARAS: The Improbable Dome Builders. New York: Drake Publlishers, Inc.

Muehlbauer, Gene and Laura Dodder
1983 The Losers: Gang Delinquency in an American Suburb. New York: Praeger Publishers.

Mundel, Jerome J.
1962 Differential Perception of Gangs. Master's Thesis, Social Work, University of Southern California.

Murphy, Suzanne
    1978 "A Year with the gangs of East Los Angeles", Ms. (July): 55-64.

Nash, Steven G.
    1984 Gang Crimes Study Commission. State of Illinois. Legislative Council
    Service Unit Order 841246 (May).

National Council of Juvenile and Family Court Judges
    1988 "Youth Gangs - A Special Problem", Juvenile & Family Court Journal
    (39)(4): 47-51.

National School Safety Center
    1988 Gangs in Schools: Breaking Up is Hard to Do. Malibu, CA: Pepper-
    dine University Press.

National Youth Gang Suppression and Intervention Program
    1989 Report of the Law Enforcement Youth Symposium.

    1990 Literature Review: Youth Gangs: Problem and Response. University
    of Chicago, School of Social Service Administration, Chicago, IL.

    1990 Survey of Youth Gang Problems and Programs in 45 Cities and 6 Sites.

    1990 Community and Institutional Reponses to the Youth Gang Problem.

    1990 Law Enforcement Definitional Conference - Transcript.

    1990 The Youth Gang Problem: Perceptions of Former Youth Gang
    Influentials. Transcripts of Two Symposia.

    n.d. Preventing Involvement in Youth Gang Crime.

Needle, Jerome A. and William Vaughan Stapleton
    1983 Police Handling of Youth Gangs. Washington, D.C.: American Justice
    Institute.

Neisser, Edith G. and Nina Ridenour
    1960 Your Children and Their Gangs. U.S. Children's Bureau. Publication
    No. 384. Washington, D.C.

New York City Youth Board
    1960 Reaching the Fighting Gang. New York.

Nieburg, H.L.
    1970 Political Violence: The Behavioral Process. New York: St. Martin's
    Press.

Oetting, E.R. and Fred Beauvais
    1987 "Common Elements in Youth Drug Abuse: Peer Clusters and Other
    Psychosocial Factors", Journal of Drug Issues (17)(1-2)(Win-Spr): 133-151.

O'Hagan, F.J.
    1976   "Gang Characteristics: An Empirical Survey", Journal of Child Psychology and Psychiatry (17): 305-314.

Oleson, Jim
    1988   Treating Street Youth: Some Observations. Community Research Associates, 115 N. Neil Street, Suite 302, Champaign, IL 61820.

Olivero, J. Michael
    1991   Honor, Gangs, Violence, Religion and Upward Mobility: A Case Study of Chicago Street Gangs During the 1970s and 1980s. Edinburg, TX: The UT-Pan American Presss.

Ontario Police Department
    1989   "Gangs, Move 'Em Out of Your Life", (video). Ontario, CA 91761.

Oppenheimer, Martin
    1969   The Urban Guerrilla. Chicago: Quadrangle Books.

Padilla, Felix
    1992   The Gang as an American Enterprise. New Brunswick, NJ: Rutgers University Press.

Padilla, Felix and Lourdes Santiago
    1993   Outside the Wall: A Puerto Rican Woman's Struggle. New Brunswick, NJ: Rutgers University Press.

Paramount Plan
    1988   The Paramount Plan: Alternatives to Gang Membership. City of Paramount, California.

Parrot, Philippe and Monique Gueneau
    1961   "Gangs of Adolescents: The History of Such a Gang", Excerpta Criminologica (1): 397-399.

Patrick, James
    1973   A Glasgow Gang Observed. Trowbridge, Wiltshire: Redwood Press Ltd., Great Britain.

Pennell, Susan and Christine Curtis
    1982   Juvenile Violence and Gang-Related Crime. San Diego: San Diego Association of Governments.

Perkins, Useni Eugene
    1987   Explosion of Chicago's Black Street Gangs. Chicago: Third World Press.

Pfautz, Harold W.
    1961   "Near-Group Theory and Collective Behavior: A Critical Reformulation", Social Problems (9)(2): 167-174.

Phelps, Roy David
1988 The History of the Eastside Dudes, a Black Social Club in Central Harlem, New York City, 1933-1985: An Exploration of Background Factors Related to Adult Criminality. Ph.D. dissertation, Fordham University, Bronx, New York.

Philobosian, R.H.
1986 State Task Force on Youth Gang Violence. Sacramento, CA: California Council in Criminal Justice.

Pleister, Margaret A.
1963 An Exploratory Study of Factors Influencing Nine Adolescent Girls in their Movement To and From Both School and the Gang. Master's thesis, Social Work, University of Southern California.

Poirier, Mike
1982 Street Gangs of Los Angeles County. Los Angeles: Self-published, P.O. Box 60481, Los Angeles, CA 90060.

Police Chief, The
1979 "Gangs, Violence, Vandalism: Citizen Involvement in Crime Prevention", (46)(7): 54-55.

Pope, Whitney
1962 Detached Workers, Delinquent Boys and the Theory of Exchange. Master's Thesis, University of Chicago.

Poston, Richard W.
1971 The Gang and the Establishment. New York: Harper & Row Publishers.

President's Commission on Organized Crime
1986 The Impact: Organized Crime Today.

Propper, Leonard M.
1957 "Juvenile Delinquency and the Gang Problem", Juvenile Court Judges Journal (8)(Mar): 24-28.

Puffer, J. Adams
1912 The Boy and His Gang. Boston: Houghton, Mifflin Co.

Quicker, John C.
1974 "The Chicana Gang: A Preliminary Description", paper presented at the Pacific Sociological Association meeting.

1983 Homegirls: Characterizing Chicana Gangs. San Pedro, California: International Universities Press.

1983 Seven Decades of Gangs: What has been done, and what should be done. Sacramento, CA: State of California Commission on Crime Control and Violence Prevention.

Quinn, James F. and Bill Downs
    1993 "Predictors of the Severity of the Gang Problem at the Local Level: An Analysis of Police Perceptions", Gang Journal: An Interdisciplinary Research Quarterly, (1)(3): 1-10.

    1993 "Non-Criminal Predictors of Gang Violence: An Analysis of Police Perceptions", Gang Journal: An Interdisciplinary Research Quarterly (1)(3): 29-38.

Rafferty, Frank T. and Harvey Bertcher
    1962 "Gang Formation in Vitro", American Journal of Orthopsychiatry (32)(Mar): 329-330.

Ralph, Paige H; James W. Marquart; and Ben M. Crouch
    1990 "Prisoner Gangs in Texas", paper presented at the 1990 Annual Meeting of the American Society of Criminology, Baltimore, MD.

Ranker, Jess E., Jr.
    1958 A Study of Juvenile Gangs in the Hollenbeck Area of Los Angeles, Master's thesis, University of Southern California, Dept. of Sociology.

Redl, Fritz
    1954 "The Psychology of Gang Formation and the Treatment of Juvenile Delinquency", pp. 367-377 in The Psycho-Analytic Study of the Child, Vol. 1, New York: International Universities Press.

Regulus, Thomas A.
    1994 "The Effects of Gangs on Student Performance and Delinquency in Public Schools", Journal of Gang Research (2)(1)(Fall): 1-13.

Reuter, P.
    1989 Youth Gangs and Drug Distribution: A Preliminary Enquiry. RAND Corporation, Paper prepared for the U.S. Office of Juvenile Justice and Delinquency Prevention, Washington, DC.

Ribisl, Kurt M. and William S. Davidson, II
    1993 "Community Change Interventions", Chapter 11 (pp. 333-355) in Arnold P. Goldstein and C. Ronald Huff (Eds.), The Gang Intervention Handbook, Champaign, IL: Research Press.

Riccio, Vincent and Bill Slocum
    1962 All The Way Down: The Violent Underworld of Street Gangs. New York: Simon and Schuster.

Richards, C.
    1958 "Can We Get a Focus For Our Working With Hostile or Hard To Reach Youth Gangs," Welfare Council of Metropolitan Chicago.

Ridgeway, James
    1990 Blood in the Face: The Ku Klux Klan, Aryan Nations, Nazi Skinheads, and the Rise of a New White Culture. New York: Thunder's Mouth Press.

Riley, William E.
1988 "Prison Gangs: An Introduction, Crips and Bloods", Washington State Penitentiary.

Rivera, Ramon J.
1964 Occupational Goals: A Comparative Analysis, Master's Thesis, University of Chicago.

Robert, Phillipe and Pierre Lascoumes
1974 Les Bands D'Adolescents: Une Theorie de la Segregation. Paris, France: Les Editions Ouvieres.

Robins, Gerald
1964 "Gang Membership Delinquency: Its Extent, Sequence, and Pattern", Journal of Criminal Law, Criminology, and Police Science (55): 59-69.

Robinson, N. and D. Joe
1980 "Gangs in Chinatown", McGill Journal of Education (15): 149-162.

Rodeheffer, I.A.
1949 "Gangdom: Fists to Reasoning", Journal of Educational Sociology (22)(Feb): 406-15.

Rodriguez, Luis J.
1994 Always Running: La Vida Loca, Gang Days in L.A.. Curbstone Press.

Rogers, Kenneth H.
1945 Street Gangs in Toronto. Toronto: The Ryerson Press.

Rosenbaum, Dennis P. and Jane A. Grant
1983 "Gangs and Youth Problems in Evanston: Research Findings and Policy Options", Center for Urban Affairs and Policy Research, Northwestern University, July 22, 1983.

Rothman, Edwin, et al
1974 The Gang Problem in Philadelphia: Proposals for Improving the Programs of Gang-Control Agencies. Pennsylvania Economy League (Eastern Division) in association with the Bureau of Municipal Research Liberty Trust Building, Philadelphia, Pa. 19107, Report No. 375; supported by a grant from the William Penn Foundation.

Rush, Jeffrey Paul
1993 "An Interview With Richard Cloward", The Gang Journal: An Interdisciplinary Research Quarterly (1)(3): 51-53.

Sale, R.T.
1971 The Blackstone Rangers. A Reporter's Account of Time Spent with the Street Gang on Chicago's South Side. New York: Random House.

Salisbury, Harrison E.
1958 The Shook-up Generation. New York: Harper.

Sanchez-Jankowski, Martin
1991 Islands in the Street: Gangs in American Urban Society. Berkeley: University of California Press.

Sanders, Willliam B.
1994 Gangbangs and Drivebys: Grounded Culture and Juvenile Gang Violence. New York: Aldline De Gruyter.

Santamaria, C; et al
1989 "Study of a Juvenile Gang in a High Risk Community", Salud Mental (12)(3)(Sept): 26-36.

Sato, Ikuya
1982 "Crime as Play and Excitement: A Conceptual Analysis of Japanese Bosozoku (Motorcyele Gangs)", Tohoku Psychologica Folia (41): 1-4,64-84.

Savitz, Leonard D.; Michael Lalli; and Lawrence Rosen
1977 City Life and Delinquency --- Victimization, Fear of Crime and Gang Membership. National Institute for Juvenile Justice and Delinquency Prevention. U.S. Department of Justice, Government Printing Office, Washington, D.C.

Scallan, J.H.
1987 Prison Gang Codes and Communications. Texas Department of Corrections, unpublished.

Scharr, John H.
1963 "Violence in Juvenile Gangs: Some Notes and a Few Analogies", American Journal of Orthopsychiatry (33)(1)(Jan): 29-37.

Schrag, C.
1962 "Delinquency and Opportunity: Analysis of a Theory", Sociology and Social Research (46)(Jan): 167-75.

Schwendinger, Herman and Julia
1967 "Delinquent Stereotypes of Probable Victims", in Malcolm W. Klein (ed.), Juvenile Gangs in Context, New Jersey: Prentice-Hall, pp. 91-105.

1985 Adolescent Subcultures and Delinquency. New York: Praeger.

Schwitzgebel, Ralph
1965 Street-Corner Research: An Experimental Approach to the Juvenile Delinquent. Cambridge, MA: Harvard University Press.

Schlossman, Steven and Michael Sedlak
1983 The Chicago Area Project Revisted. A Rand Note. Prepared for the National Institute of Justice. Santa Monica, CA: The Rand Corporation.

Scott, Peter
1956 "Gangs and Delinquent Groups in London", British Journal of Delinquency (7)(1): 4-26.

Shaw, Clifford R.
　　1929 Delinquency Areas. Chicago: University of Chicago Press.

　　1931 The Natural History of a Delinquent Career. Chicago: University of Chicago Press.

　　1939 "Group Factors in Delinquency Among Boys", Society for Research in Child Development, Proceedings of the Third Biennial Meeting: 14-26.

　　1951 The Natural History of a Delinquent Career. Philadelphia: Albert Saifer.

Shaw, Clifford R. and Jesse A. Jacobs
　　1939 Chicago Area Project, March, 1939. Chicago Area Project, Chicago, Illinois.

Shaw, Clifford R. and Henry D. McKay
　　1931 Social Factors in Juvenile Delinquency: A Study of Community, the Family, and the Gang in Relation to Delinquent Behavior. Volume II in the National Commission on Law Observance and Enforcement. U.S. Government Printing Office.

　　1942 Juvenile Delinquency and Urban Areas. Chicago: University of Chicago Press.

　　1956 Juvenile Delinquency and Urban Areas. Chicago: University of Chicago Press.

Shaw, Clifford R. and Earl D. Meyer
　　1920 "The Juvenile Delinquent", Chicago: The Illinois Crime Survey.

Shaw, Clifford R. and Maurice E. Morre
　　1931 The Natural History of a Delinquent Career. Chicago: University of Chicago Press.

Shaw, Clifford R. and Anthony Sorrentino
　　1956 "Is 'Gang-Busting' Wise?", National Parent-Teacher Magazine (50)(Jan): 18-20+.

Shelden, Randall G.; Ted Snodgrass; and Pam Snodgrass
　　1992 "Comparing Gang and Non-Gang Offenders: Some Tentative Findings", The Gang Journal: An Interdisciplinary Research Quarterly (1)(1): 73-85.

Sherif, Muzafer; O.J. Harvey; Jack White; William R. Hood; and Carolyn W. Sherif
　　1961 Intergroup Conflict and Cooperation: The Robbers Cave Experiment, Norman, OK: University of Oklahoma Institute of Group Relations.

Sherman, Lawrence W.
　　1970 Youth Workers, Police and the Gangs: Chicago 1956-1970. Master's thesis, University of Chicago.

　　1973 "Street Work History Includes Three Stages", The Forum (May): 17-24.

Sheu, Chuen-Jim
     1990 "Nonsyndicated Organized Crime in Taipei, Taiwan", paper presented
     at the 1990 Annual Meeting of the American Society of Criminology,
     Baltimore, Maryland: Nov. 7-10, 1990.

Shimota, Helen E.
     1964 "Delinquent Acts as Perceived by Gang and Nongang Negro Adoles-
     cents", Youth Studies Center, presented Dec. 12, 1964 before the California
     State Psychological Association; Los Angeles: University of Southern
     California.

Shireman, Charles H., et al
     1957 An Examination and Analysis of Technique Used by a Street Worker.
     Chicago: Hyde Park Youth Project.

     1958 An Analysis of the Dynamics of the Interrelationship of Agency, Group
     and Community in Providing Staff Service To A "Street Club". Hyde Park
     Youth Project. Welfare Council of Metropolitan Chicago.

Short, James F.
     1963 "Street Corner Groups and Patterns of Delinquency: A Progress
     Report", American Catholic Sociological Review (28): 13-32.

     1964 "Gand Delinquency and Anomie", pp. 98-127 in Marshall B. Clinard
     (ed.), Anomie and Deviant Behavior. New York: Free Press of Glencoe.

     1964 "Aleatory Risks Versus Short-run Hedonism in Explanation of Gang
     Action", Social Problems (12): 127-140.

     1965 "Social Structure and Group Processes in Explanations of Gang
     Delinquency", in M. and C. Sherif (eds.), Problems of Youth. Chicago:
     Aldine.

     1968 Gang Delinquency and Delinquent Subcultures. New York: Harper
     and Row.

     1968 "Comment on Lerman's 'Gangs, Networks, and Subcultural Delinquen-
     cy'", American Journal of Sociology (73)(4)(Jan): 513-515.

     1974 "Youth, Gangs and Society: Micro and Macrosociological Processes",
     Sociological Quarterly (15): 3-19.

     1975   "Gangs, Violence and Politics", In Duncan Chappell and John
     Monahan (eds.), Violence and Criminal Justice Lexington, Mass: Lexington
     Books.

     1976 "Gangs, Politics, and the Social Order", in J.F. Short (ed.), Delinquen-
     cy, Crime and Society, Chicago: University of Chicago Press.

     1989 "Exploring Integration of Theoretical Levels of Explanation: Notes on
     Gang Delinquency", in S.F. Messner, M.D. Krohn, and A.E. Liska (eds.),
     Theoretical Integration in the Study of Deviance and Crime: Problems and
     Prospects (pp. 243-259), Albany: State University of New York Press.

Short, James F., and John Molland
1976 "Politics and Youth Gangs: A Follow-up Study", Sociological Quarterly (17): 162-179.

Short, J.F.; R. Rivera; and R.A. Tennyson
1965 "Perceived Opportunties, Gang Membership and Delinquency", American Sociological Review (30)(Feb):

Short, James F., Jr. and Fred L. Strodtbeck
1965 Group Process and Gang Delinquency. Chicago: The University of Chicago Press.

1974. _____.

Shukla, K.S.
1981 "Adolescent Criminal Gangs: Structure and Functions", The International Journal of Critical Sociology (5): 35-49.

Sibley, James Blake
1989 "Gang Violence: Response of the Criminal Justice System to the Growing Threat", Criminal Justice Journal (11)(2)(Spr): 403-422.

Sifakis, Carl
1987 The Mafia Encyclopedia. New York: Facts on File Publications, Inc.

Sipchen, Bob
1993 Baby Insane and the Buddha. New York: Doubleday.

Skolnick, J.H.
1990 "Gangs and Crime Old as Time: But Drugs Change Gang Culture", Commentary, Crime and Delinquency.

Skolnick, Jerome H.; Blumenthal, Ricky and Theodore Correl
1990 "Gang Organization and Migration", Berkeley, CA: University of California at Berkeley, Center for the Study of Law and Society (2-18-90).

1993 "Gang Organization and Migration", pp. 193-217 in Scott Cummings and Daniel J. Monti (Eds.), Gangs: The Orgins and Impact of Contempoary Youth Gangs in the United States, Albany, NY: State University of New York.

Skolnick, J.H. Correl, T.; Navarro, E.; and R. Rabb
1989 "The Social Structure of Street Drug Dealing". Sacramento, CA: Office of the Attorney General, State of California.

Slack, Charles W.
1963 "SCORE -- A Description", in Experiment in Culture Expansion, Report of Proceedings, U.S. National Institute of Mental Health, Bethesda, MD.

Sleeman, Lieut.-Col. W.H.
1849 Report on Budhuk alia Bagree Decoits and other Gang Robbers by Hereditary Profession and on the measures adopted by the Government of

India for their Suppression. Calcutta: J.C.Sherriff, Bengal Military Orphan Press.

Snyder, P.Z.
1977 "An Anthropological Description of Street Gangs in the Los Angeles Area", prepared for the Department of Justice, Santa Monica, CA: Rand Corporation.

Song, John
1991 "Lost in the Melting Pot? The Causes of Asian Gangs in the United States", paper presented at the Annual Meeting of the Academy of Criminal Justice Sciences, Nashville, Tennessee.

Song, John Huey-Long and John Dombrink
1990 "Gangs, Groups and Organized Crime: Defining Asian Racketeering", paper presented at the Annual Meeting of the American Society of Criminology, Baltimore, MD.

Song, John Huey-Long; John Dombrink; and Gilbert Geis
1992 "Lost in the Melting Pot: Asian Youth Gangs in the United States", The Gang Journal: An Interdisciplinary Research Quarterly (1)(1): 1-12.

Spaulding, Charles B.
1948 "Cliques, Gangs and Networks", Sociology and Social Research (32)(July-August): 928-937.

Spergel, Irving
1960 Types of Delinquent Groups, D.S.W. dissertation, Columbia University. Dissertation Abstracts (21)(Jan): 2034-35 (1961).

1964 Racketville, Slumtown, Haulburg: An Exploratory Study of Delinquent Subcultures, Chicago: University of Chicago Press.

1966 Street Gang Work: Theory and Practice. Reading, MA: Addison-Wesley Publishing Company, Inc.

1984 "Violent Gangs in Chicago: In Search of Social Policy", Social Service Review (58): 199-226.

1985 The Violent Gang Problem in Chicago. Chicago: Social Services Administration, University of Chicago.

1985 Youth Gang Activity and the Chicago Public Schools. Chicago: Social Services Administration, University of Chicago.

1986 "The Violent Gang Problem in Chicago: A Local Community Approach", Social Service Review (60)(1)(Mar): 94-131.

1988 "The Youth Gang Problem: A Preliminary Policy Pespective", draft, Prepared for the Juvenile Gang Suppression and Intervention Research and Development Program, Office of Juvenile Justice and Delinquency Prevention, U.S. Dept. of Justice.

1989 Youth Gangs: Problem and Response: A Review of the Literature, Executive Summary. U.S. Dept. of Justice, Office of Juvenile Justice and Delinquency Prevention, Washington, D.C.

1989 Survey of Youth Gang Problems and Programs in 45 Cities and 6 States. Washington, DC: Office of Juvenile Justice and Delinquency Prevention.

1989 "Youth Gangs: Continuity and Change", In N. Morris and M. Tonry (eds.), Crime and Justice: An Annual Review of Research (12): Chicago, University of Chicago Press.

1990 "Youth Gangs: Continuity and Change", in Norval Morris (ed), Crime and Justice: Annual Review of Research, 267-371.

1990 "The Violent Gang Problem in Chicago: A Local Community Approach", Social Service Review (60)(1)(Mar): 94-131.

Spergel, Irving A. and Ron L. Chance
1990 Community and Institutional Responses to the Youth Gang Problem: Case Studies Based on Field Visits and Other Materials. National Youth Gang Suppression and Intervention Project, School of Social Service Administration, University of Chicago (Jan.).

Spergel, Irving A.; Glen David Curry; R.A. Ross; and R. Chance
1989 Survey of Youth Gang Problems and Programs in 45 Cities and 6 Sites (Technical Report, No. 2, National Youth Gang Suppression and Intervention Project), Chicago: School of Social Service Administration, University of Chicago.

Srivastava, S.S.
1981 "Problem of Dacoity in India - A Sociological Perspective" The International Journal of Critical Sociology (5): 23-34.

Stapleton, W. Vaughn and Jerome Needle
1982 Police Handling of Youth Gangs. Washington, D.C. Office of Juvenile Justice and Delinquency Prevention.

Steward, Samuel M.
1990 Bad Boys and Tough Tattoos. New York: Harrington Park.

Stinchcombe, Arthur L.
1964 Rebellion in a High School. Chicago: Quadrangle Books.

Strodtbeck, Fred L.; James F. Short, Jr.; and Ellen Kolegar
1962 "The Analysis of Self-Descriptions by Members of Different Gangs", Sociological Quarterly (24): 331-356.

Stover, Del
1986 "A New Breed of Youth Gang is on the Prowl and a Bigger Threat Than Ever", American School Board Journal (173)(8)(Aug): 19-24,35.

Stumphauzer, Jerome S; Esteban V. Veloz; and Thomas W. Aiken
    1981 "Violence by Street Gangs: East Side Story?", in Robert B. Stuart (ed.), Violent Behavior. New York: Brunner- Mazel.

Suall, Irwin and David Lowe
    1988 "Shaved for Battle - Skinheads Target America's Youth", Political Communication and Persuasion (5)(2): 139-144.

Sun, Key
    1993 "The Implications of Social Psychological Theories of Group Dynamics for Gang Research", Gang Journal: An Interdisciplinary Research Quarterly (1)(3): 39-44.

Sung, B.L.
    1977 Gangs in New York's Chinatown (Monograph No. 6), New York: City College of New York, Department of Asian Studies.

Suttles, Gerald D.
    1959 Territoriality, Identity, and Conduct: A Study of an Inner-City Slum with Special Reference to Street Corner Groups, Ph.D. dissertation, University of Illinois at Champaign.

    1968 The Social Order of the Slum Chicago: University of Chicago Press.

Swans, Bennie J., Jr.
    1985 "Gangbusters! Crisis Intervention Network.", School Safety, Winter, 1985, pp. 12-15, National School Safety Center.

Sweeney, T.
    1980 Streets of Anger, Streets of Hope: Youth Gangs in East Los Angeles. Glendale, CA: Great Western Publishing.

Takata, Susan and Richard Zevitz
    1987 "Youth Gangs in Racine: An Examination of Community Perceptions", Wisconsin Sociologist (24)(4)(Fall): 132-141.

    1990 "Divergent Perceptions of Group Delinquency in a Midwestern Community: Racine's Gang Problem", Youth and Society (21)(3)(Mar): 282-305.

Taylor, Carl S.
    1988 "Youth Gangs Organize Quest for Power, Money", School Safety (Spr): 26-27.

    1990 Dangerous Society. East Lansing, Michigan: Michigan State University Press.

Tennyson, Ray A.
    1966 Family Structure and Gang Delinquency. Ph.D. dissertation, Washington State University.

Thompson, Craig and Allen Raymond
    1940 Gang Rule in New York. New York: Dial Press.

Thompson, D.W.
    1986 Preventing Youth Membership in Urban Street Gangs: The Evaluation of a Behavioral Community Intervention. Dissertation Abstracts International, 47, 3987B.

Thompson, David W. and Leonard A. Jason
    1988 "Street Gangs and Preventive Interventions", Criminal Justice and Behavior (15)(3)(Sept): 323-333.

Thrasher, Frederic M.
    1927 The Gang. A Study of 1,313 Gangs in Chicago. Chicago: University of Chicago Press.

    1936 _____. 2nd revised eidition. Chicago: University of Chicago Press.

    1968 _____. Third Impression, Abridged and with a Introduction by James F. Short, Jr. Chicago: University of Chicago Press.

Tice, Lawrence Clinton
    1967 "The National Avenue 'Rebels': A Study of a Puerto Rican Gang in Milwaukee", M.A. thesis, Department of Social Welfare, University of Wisconsin-Milwaukee.

Toby, Jackson
    1957 "Social Disorganization and Stake in Conformity", Journal of Criminal Law and Criminology (48)(May-June): 12-17.

Todorovic, Aleksander
    1978 "Special Conditions and Causes That Influence the Forming of Juvenile Gangs", Socioloski Pregled (7): 27-38.

Toll, Joseph F.
    1944 "Converting the Gang into a Club", Probation (23)(Dec): 49-55.

Tompkins, Dorothy Campbell
    1966 Juvenile Gangs and Street Groups - A Bibliography. Institute of Governmental Studies, University of California, Berkeley.

Torres, Dorothy M.
    1979 "Chicano Gangs in the East Los Angeles Barrio", California Youth Authority Quarterly (32)(3): 5-13.

    1980 Gang Violence Reduction Project 3rd Evaluation Report. Sacramento, CA: California Department of the Youth Authority.

    1981 Gang Violence Reduction Project: Fourth Evaluation Report, July 1979-June 1980. Department of the Youth Authority, Sacramento, CA.

Toy, Calvin
    1992 "Coming Out to Play: Reasons to Join and Participate in Asian Gangs", The Gang Journal: An Interdisciplinary Research Quarterly (1)(1): 13-29.

Tracy, Paul E.
1984   "Subcultural Delinquency: A Comparison of the Incidence and Seriousness of Gang and Nongang Offensivity", University of Pennsylvania: Center for Studies in Criminology and Criminal Law.

Tracy, Paul E. and E.S. Piper
1984   "Gang Membership and Violent Offending: Preliminary Results from the 1958 Cohort Study". Paper presented at the Annual Meeting of the American Society of Criminology, Cincinnati, OH.

Tracy, Paul E. and M. Epstein
1979   Subcultural Delinquency: A Comparision of the Incidence and Seriousness of Gang and Nongang Member Offensivity. Center for Studies in Criminology and Criminal Law, Philadelphia: University of Pennsylvania.

Tracy, Paul E. and Elizabeth S. Piper
1982   "Gang Membership and Violent Offending: Preliminary Results from the 1958 Cohort Study", paper presented at the annual meeting of the American Society of Criminology, Cincinnati.

Tromanhauser, Edward
1981   "The Problem of Street Gangs", chapter IV in Chicago Safe School Study, Board of Education, City of Chicago.

Trostle, Lawrence Charles
1987   The Stoners: Drugs, Demons and Delinquency: A Descriptive and Empirical Analysis of Delinquent Behavior, Ph.D. dissertation, Claremont Graduate School, California.

Turner, Ralph H and Samuel J. Surace
1956   "Zoot-Suiters and Mexicans: Symbols in Crowd Behavior", American Journal of Sociology (62)(July): 14-20.

Useem, Bert and Peter Kimball
1989   "A Gang in Rebellion - Joliet (1975)", Chapter 4 (pp. 59-77) in States of Siege: U.S. Prison Riots, 1971-1986 New York: Oxford University Press.

Vaz, Edmund W.
1962   "Juvenile Gang Delinquency in Paris", Social Problems (10)(Sum): 23-31.

Vetter, Harold J. and Leonard Territo
1984   Crime & Justice In America: A Human Perspective. St. Paul, MN: West Publishing Co.

Vigil, J. Diego
1983   "Chicano Gangs: One Response to Mexican Urban Adaptation in the Los Angeles Area", Urban Anthropology (12)(1)(Spr): 45-75.

1987   "Street Socialization, Locura Behavior and Violence Among Chicano Gang Members", in J. Kraus et al (eds.), Violence and Homicide in Hispanic Communities, Washington, DC: National Institute of Mental Health, Office of Minority Health.

1988 "Group Processes and Street Identity: Adolescent Chicano Gang Members", Ethos (16)(4)(Dec): 421-445.

1988 Barrio Gangs: Street Life and Identity in Southern California. Austin, TX: University of Texas Press.

Vold, George B.
1958. Theoretical Criminology. Oxford University Press.

1981. Theoretical Criminology. New York: Oxford University Press.

1986. With Thomas J. Bernard. Third edition.

Wattenberg, William M. and James Balistrieri
1950 "Gang Membership and Juvenile Misconduct", American Sociological Review (15)(Dec): 744-752.

1959 "Gang Membership and Juvenile Misconduct", pp. 169-177 in Sheldon Glueck (ed), The Problem of Delinquency Boston: Houghton.

Watts, T.J.
1988 New Gangs: Young, Armed and Dangerous. Monticello, IL: Vance Bibliographies (P.O. Box 229, Monticello, IL 61856).

Webb, Margot
1991 Coping With Street Gangs. New York: Free Press.

Weiner, Arthur K.
1965 "C-r-a-c-k-i-n-g The Hard Core Area", Police Chief (32)(Jan): 27-31.

Weisfeld, Glenn and Roger Feldman
1982 "A Former Street Gang Leader Re-Interviewed Eight Years Later", Crime and Delinquency (28): 567-581.

Weissman, Harold (ed.)
1969 Community Development in the Mobilization for Youth. New York: Association Press.

Werthman, Carl
1964 Delinquency and Authority, Master's Thesis, University of California, Berkeley.

1966 "Police Action and Gang Delinquency", in D. Bordua (ed.), The Police, New York: Wiley.

Werthman, Carl and Irving Piliavin
1967 "Gang Members and the Police", in David Bordua (ed), The Police: Six Sociological Essays, New York: Wiley.

West, Pat and Tony Ostos
1988 Pilot Study: City of Paramount Alternatives to Gang Membership Program. City of Paramount, 16400 Colorado Ave., Paramount, CA 90723.

Whyte, William Foote
    1943 Street Corner Society: The Social Structure of an Italian Slum. Ph.D. dissertation, University of Chicago.

    1943 Street Corner Society. Chicago: University of Chicago Press.

    1981 Street Corner Society. Chicago: University of Chicago Press, third edition.

Williams, Hampton; Rex Leonard; and Phillip Terrell
    1991 "Students' Perceptions of Some Selected Conditions that Might Lead to Gang Membership: An Exploratory Investigation", paper presented at the Annual Meeting of the Academy of Criminal Justice Sciences, Nashville, Tennessee.

Wilner, Daniel M.; Eva Rosenfeld; Robert S. Lee; Donald L. Gerard; and Isidor Chein
    1957 "Heroin Use and Street Gangs", Journal of Criminal Law, Criminology, and Police Science (48)(4): 399-409.

Wilson, Everett
    1971 Sociology: Rules, Roles, and Relationships. The Dorsey Press.

Wilson, James Q. and George L. Kelling
    1989 "Making Neighborhoods Safe", The Atlantic Monthly (Feb): 46-52.

Wilson, William J.
    1987 The Truly Disadvantaged. Chicago: University of Chicago Press.

Wise, John M.
    1962 A Comparison of Sources of Data as Indices of Delinquent Behavior, Master's thesis, Department of Sociology, University of Chicago.

Wolfe, Tom
    1968 The Pump House Gang. New York: Farrar, Straus and Giroux.

Wooden, Wayne
    1989 "Profile of Stone Gang Members in the California Youth Authority", paper presented at the American Society of Criminology, Annual Meeting, Reno, Nevada, November.

    1990 "Contemporary Youth Identities: Problems and Issues", paper presented at the Western Society of Criminology, Annual Meeting, Las Vegas, Nevada (February).

Xu, J.
    1986 "Brief Discussion of New Trends in the Development of Juvenile Delinquent Gangs", Chinese Education (19)(2)(Sum): 92-102.

Yablonsky, Lewis
    1958 A Field Study of Delinquent Gang Organization and Behavior With Special Emphasis on Gang Warfare. Ph.D. dissertation, New York University.

1959 "The Delinquent Gang as a Near-Group", Social Problems (7): 108-117.

1962 The Violent Gang. New York: MacMillan.

Youth Gang Task Force (California)
1981 Report on Youth Gang Violence in California. State of California Department of Justice. Sacramento.

Zatz, Marjorie S.
1985 "Los Cholos: Legal Processing of Chicano Gang Members", Social Problems (33): 13-30.

1987 "Chicano Youth Gangs and Crime: The Creation of a Moral Panic", Contemporary Crises (11)(2): 129-158.

Zinn, Elizabeth
1959 "He Begged that Gang Violence End With His Life", Federal Probation (23)(Sept): 24-30.

CHAPTER THREE
SECONDARY BIBLIOGRAPHY ON GANGS

Auletta, Ken
    1983 The Underclass. New York: Vintage.

Bales, Robert F. and Fred L. Strodtbeck
    1951 "Phases in Group Problem Solving", Journal of Abnormal and Social Psychology (46): 485-495.

Bell, Daniel
    1953 "Crime as an American Way of Life", Antioch Review (XIII)(June): 131-54.

Bennett, James
    1981 Oral History and Delinquency: The Rhetoric of Criminology. Chicago: University of Chicago Press.

Bennis, W.G.; K. Benne; and R. Chin.
    1969. The Planning of Change. New York: Holt, Rinehart and Winston.

Benton, J. David
    1975 Denver - Southwest Youth Employment Service - Annual Report, Jan. 15, 1975. National Criminal Justice Reference Service # 09900.00.029808.

Bergmann, Barbara R. and David E. kaun
    1966 Structural Unemployment in the United States. The Brookings Institute, Washington, D.C.

Berk, Richard A.; Kenneth J. Lenihan; and Peter H. Rossi
    1980 "Crime and Poverty: Some Experimental Evidence from Exoffenders", American Sociological Review (45)(5)(Oct): 766-86.

Berkowitz, Leonard (ed.)
    1978 Group Processes. New York: Academic Press.

Bernardo, A.J.
    1977 Supported Employment for Adolescents - An Evaluation. NCJRS # 0990.00.061938.

Best, Joel and David F. Luckenbill
    1982 Organizing Deviance. Englewood Cliffs, NJ: Prentice-Hall.

Blalock, H.M.
    1965 "Theory Building and the Statistical Concept of Interaction", American Sociological Review (30): 374-80.

Bogen, David
    1944 "Juvenile Delinquency and Economic Trends", American Sociological Review (9): 178-84.

Bonn, Robert L.
 1984 Criminology. New York: McGraw-Hill Book Company.

Bowker, L.H.
 1977 "Helping Delinquent Dropouts to Cope - An Evaluation of An
 Innovative Project", paper presented at the National Conference on Criminal
 Justice Evaluation, Washington, D.C. (Feb.).

Burby, Raymond J. and William M. Rohe
 1989 "Deconcentration of Public Housing: Effects on Residents' Satisfaction
 With Their Living Environments and Their Fear of Crime", Urban Affairs
 Quarterly (25)(1): 117-141.

Burgess, Ernest W.
 1928 "What Social Case Records Should Contain to be Useful for Sociological Interpretation", Social Forces (6): 524-32.

Burns, Tom and G.M. Stalker.
 1968. The Management of Innovation. London: Tavistock Publications
 Limited.

Callahan, Daniel
 1987 Setting Limits: Medical Goals in an Aging Society. New York: Simon
 and Schuster.

Carey, James T.
 1975 Sociology and Public Affairs: The Chicago School. Beverly Hills: Sage.

Carter, Robert M.
 1972 "Dialogue With Daniel Glaser", Issues in Criminology (7)(2)(Fall): 21-
 33.

Chin, Robert and Kenneth D. Benne
 1972. "General Strategies for Effecting Changes in Human Systems", chapter
 18, pp. 233-254 in Zaltman, Gerald, et al (eds.), Creating Social Change, New
 York: Holt, Rinehart and Winston, Inc.

Clark, Ramsey
 1970 Crime in America. New York: Simon and Schuster.

Clemmer, Donald
 1940 The Prison Community. Boston: The Christopher Publishing House.

Cole, George F.
 1983 The American System of Criminal Justice. Third edition.   Monterey,
 CA: Brooks/Cole Publishing Company.

Coleman, James
 1954 Community Conflict. Twentieth Century Fund.

Cook, Thomas J.; L. Douglas Dobson; and Eva Lantos Rezmovic
 1979 Experimental Evaluation of the Challenge Program: Final Report. The
 Safer Foundation, Chicago, Illinois.

Cottingham, Clement (ed.)
    1982 Race, Poverty, and the Urban Underclass. Lexington, Mass: Lexington
    Books.

Crutchfield, Robert D.
    1989 "Labor Stratification and Violent Crime", Social Forces (68)(2): 489-
    512.

Curry, G. David
    1985 Sunshine Patriots: Punishment and the Vietnam Offender.   Notre
    Dame: University of Notre Dame Press.

Davis, James A.
    1980 General Social Surveys, 1972-1980 Cumulative Codebook.   National
    Data Program for the Social Sciences. National Opinion Research Center,
    University of Chicago.

Diamond, Shari, et al
    1977 Community Rehabilitation Programs.   Second Deliverable Product:
    Evaluation Designs. Chicago, IL: University of Illinois at Chicago.

DiRenzo, Gordon J.
    1984 Sociological Perspectives. Lexington, MA: Ginn Custom Publishing.

Duster, Troy
    1987 "Crime, Youth Unemployment, and the Black Urban Underclass",
    Crime and Delinquency (33): 300-16.

Dyer, William G.
    1984. Strategies for Managing Change. Reading, MA: Addison-Wesley
    Publishing Company, Inc.

Eisenstadt, S.N. (ed.)
    1968. Comparative Perspectives on Social Change. Boston: Little, Brown
    and Company.

Elliott, D.S.
    1962   "Delinquency and Perceived Opportunity", Sociological Inquiry
    (32)(Spr): 216-27.

Etzioni, Amitai
    1964 Modern Organizations. Englewood Cliffs, NJ: Prentice-Hall.

Etzioni-Halevy, Eva and Amitai Etzioni
    1973. Social Change. New York: Basic Books, Inc.

Etzioni-Halevy, Eva
    1981. Social Change: The Advent and Maturation of Modern Society.
    London: Routledge & Kegan Paul.

Farrington, David, et al
    1986 Understanding and Controlling Crime. Toward a New Research
    Strategy. New York: Springer-Verlag.

Fleisher, Belton M.
    1966 The Economics of Delinquency. Chicago: Quadrangle Books.

Ginsburg, Helen
    1975 Unemployment, Subemployment, and Public Policy. New York
    University, School of Social Work, Center for Studies in Income Maintenance
    Policy.

Glaser, Daniel
    1964 The Effectiveness of a Prison and Parole System. New York: Bobbs-
    Merrill Co., Inc.

Glaser, Daniel and Kent Rice
    1959 "Crime, Age and Employment", American Sociological Review (24):
    679-686.

Glasgow, Douglas G.
    1981 The Black Underclass: Poverty, Unemployment, and Entrapment of
    Ghetto Youth. New York: Vintage Books.

Glueck, Sheldon and Eleanor
    1952 Delinquents in the Making. New York: Harper and Brothers.

Gordon, David M.
    1972 "Class and Economics of Crime", in Allen and Bacon (eds.), Political
    Economy: Radical and Orthodox Approaches; see also David M. Gordon,
    (ed), Problems in Political Economy: An Urban Perspective, D.C.: Heath,
    1971.

Greenberg, David F.
    1978 "The Dynamics of Oscillatory Punishment Processes", Journal of
    Criminal Law and Criminology, no. 69.

Guttentag, Marcia
    1968 "The Relationship of Unemployment to Crime and Delinquency",
    Journal of Social Issues (24)(1): 105-114.

Hagan, Frank E.
    1987 Introduction to Criminology. Chicago: Nelson-Hall.

Hardt, R.H. and S.J. Peterson
    1968 "Arrests of Self and Friends as Indicators of Delinquency Involvement",
    Journal of Research in Crime and Delinquency (5)(Jan): 44-51.

Harris, Ramon I.; et al
    1975 The Practice of Oral History: A Handbook. Glen Rock, NJ: Microfilm-
    ing Corporation of America.

Inbau, Fred E. and John E. Reid
    1962 Criminal Interrogation and Confessions. Baltimore: The Williams &
    Wilknis Company.

Indik, Bernard P. and F. Kenneth Berrien (eds.)
        1968 People, Groups, and Organizations. New York: Teachers College Press.

Irwin, John
        1985 The Jail: Managing the Underclass in American Society. Berkeley: University of California Press.

Janis, Irving L.
        1972. Victims of Groupthink: A Psychological Study of Foreign-Policy Decisions and Fiascos. Boston: Houghton Mifflin.

Janowitz, Morris
        1970 Political Conflict. Chicago: Quadrangle Books.

Johnson, Richard E.
        1977 "The Relevance of Social Class to Delinquent Behavior: A New Test", paper presented at the 72nd Annual Meeting of the American Sociological Association, Sept. 5-9, Chicago, IL.

Kahn, Alfred J.
        1963 Planning Community Services for Children in Trouble. New York: Columbia University Press.

Kasimar, Yale; Wayne R. LaFave; and Jerold H. Israel
        1990 Basic Criminal Procedure: Cases, Comments, and Questions. Seventh Edition. St. Paul: West Publishing Co.

Keen, Sam
        1986 Faces of the Enemy. San Francisco: Harper and Row.

Killinger, George and Glen A. Kercher
        1974 Employment Assistance and Support for the Ex-Offender, Project E.A.S.E., Office of Youth Opportunities, Dept. of Community Affairs, State of Texas. Institute of Contemporary Corrections and Behavioral Sciences, Sam Houston State University, Huntsville, TX.

Kleeck, Mary van; Emma A. Winslow; and Ira De A. Reid
        1931 Work and Law OBservance. An Experimental Inquiry into the Influence of Unemployment and Occupational Conditions Upon Crime for the National Commission on Law Observance and Enforcement, No. 13, June 26, 1931, pp. 163-333.

Klofas, John; Stan Stojkovic and David Kalinich
        1990 Criminal Justice Organizations: Administration and Management. Belmont, CA: Brooks/Cole Publishing Company.

Knox, George W.
        1975 "A Critique of the Mertonian Typology of Deviant Behavior With Implications for a Post-Industrial Society", paper presented at the Annual Meeting of the Southwestern Sociological Association, March 27, San Antonio, TX.

1977   "The Rise of the NSPA Nazi Movement and the Urban Crisis in Southwest Chicago", paper persented at the Spring Institute, Society for Social Research, Department of Sociology, University of Chicago, April 30, Chicago, IL.

1977   "The Use of Cost-Benefit Analysis in the Evaluation of Manpower Service Programs", paper presented at the Criminal Justice Statistics Association, meeting August 11, Oklahoma City, OK.

1978 (a) "Offender Prediction Methodology: Suggestions For Improvement", paper presented, National Institute of Corrections, Screening for Risk Hearings, May 26, Denver, CO.

1978 (a) The Determinants of Employment Success Among Exoffenders, Ph.D. dissertation, Department of Sociology, University of Chicago, Sept., 1978.

1978 (b) The Impact of Manpower Services on Illinois Offenders, unpublished manuscript, June 30, 1978.

1978 (?) "Cultural and Structural Disjunction: The Concept of Differential Integration", paper presented at the Annual Meeting of the Midsouth Sociological Association, November 3, Jackson, MS.

1978 (?) "Differential Integration and Job Retention Among Exoffenders", paper presented at the Annual Meeting of the American Society of Criminology, November 10, Dallas, TX.

1978 (?) "A Comparative Cost-Benefit Analysis of Programs for Illinois Offenders", paper presented at the Second National Workshop on Criminal Justice Evaluation, Nov. 20, Washington, DC.

1980   "Employment and Exoffender Recidivism", paper presented at the Fall Conference of the Illinois Correctional Association, March 28, Chicago, IL.

1980   "Social Disorganization Models of Deviance", paper presented at the Annual Meeting of the American Society of Criminology, Nov. 5, San Francisco, CA.

1981   "Surplus Population Theory and Criminality", paper presented at the Annual Meeting of the American Society of Criminology, Nov. 14, Washington, DC.

1981   Educational and Vocational Upgrading for Juvenile Delinquents: The State of the Art in Community Based Programs. Center for the Study in Delinquency Prevention, School of Social Services Administration, University of Chicago.

1982   "How Criminologists View Rehabilitation", paper presented at the Annual Meeting of the American Society of Criminology, Nov. 5, Toronto, Canada.

1983 "Social and Behavioral Correlates of Gang Affiliation", paper presented at the Annual Meeting of the American Society of Criminology, Nov. 10, Denver, CO.

1984 "How Criminologists View Rehabilitation", Indian Journal of Criminology (12)(1)(Jan): 26-32.

1984 "Capital Punishment: Where's The Logic?", paper presented at the Annual Meeting of the Midwestern Criminal Justice Association, Oct. 4, Chicago, IL.

1985 "The Human Relations Factor in Field Research on Serious Offenders", paper presented at the Society for the Study of Phenomenology, Chicago, IL.

1985 "Oral History and Offenders: More on Method", paper presented at the Annual Meeting of the American Society of Criminology, San Diego, CA.

1985 "Recidivism Prediction: A Duel Between the Bellybutton and the Computer", paper presented at the Annual Meeting of the American Society of Criminology, San Diego, CA.

1987 "Nominal Measures of Rehabilitation in Relationship to Subsequent Arrests", paper accepted but not presented the Annual Meeting of the American Society of Criminology, Montreal, Canada (Not presented because none of the attributes by ASC members, See Knox 1984, were significant in differentiating subsequent arrests.

1988 "The Family Services Program: Findings from the Cook County Jail PACE Institute", paper presented at the First National Conference on Family and Corrections, April 26, Sacramento, CA.

1988 "Family and Crime: Theory and Findings", paper presented at the Annual Meeting of the American Sociological Association, Session 57, August 24, Atlanta, GA.

1988 "An Oral History Study of Felons: The Post-Release Religion Identity", co-author Tyrone Staggers, paper presented at the Annual Meeting of the Midwestern Criminal Justice Association, Oct. 17, Chicago, IL.

1988 "Changing Attitudes Toward the Death Penalty: A Mass Communications Experiment", co-authored with Leonel Campos and Chris Anaele, paper at the Annual Meeting of the American Society of Criminology, Chicago, IL.

1991 "The U.S. Gang Problem: An Analysis", paper presented at the meeting of the Illinois Academy of Criminology, Jan. 22, Loyola University of Chicago, Chicago, IL.

1991 "The Racism-Oppression Thesis in Gang Analysis", paper presented at the Annual Meeting of the Academy of Criminal Justice Sciences, Nashville, TN.

1991 "Gangs, Guerilla Warfare, and Social Conflict", paper presented at the Annual Meeting of the Academy of Criminal Justice Sciences, Nashville, TN.

1991 "Social Justice Issues and the American Gang Problem", paper presented at Purdue University, West Lafayette, IN, Criminal Justice at the Crossroads: Crisis in the Black Community Conference, March 15.

1991 "Gangs: A Chicago High School Revisited", paper presented at the Illinois Academy of Criminology, Loyola University of Chicago, Chicago, IL.

1991 "U.S. Gangs: An Analysis of Recent Data", paper presented at the Annual Meeting of the American Society of Criminology, Nov. 20, San Franciso, CA.

1991 "Beliefs About Police Brutality: A Study of African-Americans", paper presented at the Annual Meeting of the American Society of Criminology, Nov. 23, San Francisco, CA.

1992 "Gangs in Juvenile Institutions: Fighting, Drugs, and Other Health Risks", with co-author Edward D. Tromanhauser, paper presented at the Annual Meeting of the Academy of Criminal Justice Sciences, March 10, Pittsburgh, PA.

1992 "Teaching About Gangs: A Research and Policy View", paper presented at the Annual Meeting of the Academy of Criminal Justice Sciences, Pittsburgh, PA.

1992 "Gangs and Related Problems Among Asian Students: Preliminary National Findings", paper presented at the Annual Meeting of the National Association of Asian and Pacific Island Educators, May 15, Chicago, IL.

1992 "Translating Community Policing Theory into Practice: The Gang Problem", paper presented to the graduating class of the Executive Officer Corp Program, Oct. 9, University of Illinois at Chicago, Chicago, IL.

1992 "Gang Identification and Gang Interviewing", co-authored with Thomas F. Mc Currie, paper presented at the National Defense Investigators Association, Chicago, IL.

1992 "The Gang Problem Among Asian Students", paper presented at the Annual Meeting of the American Society of Criminology, Nov. 8, New Orleans, LA.

1992 "The Thrasher Temptation: Over Estimating the High School Gang Problem", paper presented at the Annual Meeting of the American Society of Criminology, Nov. 8, New Orleans, LA.

1993 "From Banana Stalks to M-60 Machine Guns: Weapons Acquisition and Usage Patterns Among Contemporary American Gangs", paper presented at the Feb. 7, COPEX - Contingency & Operational Procurement Exhibition, "New World Disorder - Operational & Tactical Responses to Transnational Crime and Urban Violence", Miami, FL.

1993 "Gang Issues for Illinois Juvenile Police Officers", paper presented at the Annual Meeting of the Illinois Juvenile Officers Association Training Conference, May 6, Matteson, IL.

Kraus, J.
1979 "Juvenile Unemployment and Delinquency", Aust. and New Z. Journal of Criminology (June)(12): 37-42.

Lamm, Richard D.
1984 "When Miracle Cures Don't Cure: Long Time Dying", The New Republic (Aug. 17): 20-23.

1989. "Public Policy in An Aging Society", 9 pp. unpublished MS for presentation at the Fourth Annual National Conference - April 14 & 15, 1989, De Paul University College of Law - Health Law Institute, Chicago, Illinois.

LaPiere, Richard T.
1965. Social Change. New York: McGraw-Hill.

Leiberg, Leon G.
1978 "Crime and Employment Issues", A Collection of Policy Relevant Monographs. The American University Law School, Institute for Advanced Studies in Justice.

Lerner, Daniel
1968. "Toward a Communication Theory of Modernization: A Set of Considerations", Chapter 9, pp. 133-155 in S.N. Eisenstadt (ed.), Comparative Perspectives on Social Change, Boston: Little, Brown and Company.

Lipsey, M.W.
1988 "Juvenile Delinquency Intervention", New Directions for Program Evaluation (37): 63-84.

Lipsey, Richard G.
1965 "Structure and Deficit-Demand Reconsidered", in Arthur M. Ross (ed), Employment and the Labor Market, University of California Press, pp. 210-55.

Lundman, Richard J.
1984 Prevention and Control of Juvenile Delinquency. New York: Oxford University Press.

Luthans, Fred and Robert Kreitner
1975. Organizational Behavior Modification. Glenview, IL: Scott, Foresman and Company.

Miller, M.J.
1972 "Future Employment Prospects and Vocational Training in Prisons", Georgia Journal of Corrections (1)(3): 103-111.

Mills, C.M. and T.L. Walter
 1979   "Reducing Juvenile Delinquency - A Behavioral-Employment Intervention Program". In Jerome S. Stumphauser (ed), Progress in Behavior Therapy with Delinquents, Springfield, IL: Charles C. Thomas Publisher.

Moore, Wilbert E.
 1963. Social Change. Englewood Cliffs, NJ: Prentice-Hall, Inc.

Newsweek
 1981 "How The Mob Really Works", Jan. 5, 1981.

Niehoff, Arthur H. (ed.)
 1966. A Casebook of Social Change. Chicago: Aldine Publishing Company.

O'Connor, James
 1973 The Fiscal Crisis of the State. New York: St. Martin's Press.

Olmsted, Michael S.
 1959 The Small Group. New York: Random House.

Oppenheimer, Martin
 1969 The Urban Guerrilla. Chicago: Quadrangle Books.

Paine, Frank T. and William Naumes
 1982. Organizational Strategy and Policy. Third edition. New York: CBS College Publishing.

Palmore, E.B. and P.E. Hammond
 1964 "Interacting Factors in Juvenile Delinquency", American Sociological Review (29): 848-54.

Parsons, Talcott
 1969 "Suggestions for A Sociological Approach to Theory of Organizations", pp. 32-46 in Amitai Etzioni (Ed.), A Sociological Reader on Complex Organizations, New York: Holt, Rinehart and Winston, Inc.

Payne, Roy and Cary L. Cooper (eds.)
 1981 Groups at Work. New York: John Wiley & Sons.

Petersilia, Joan and Susan Turner
 1988 "Minorities in Prison: Discrimination or Disparity", Corrections Today, Official Publication of the American Correctional Association, June.

Phillips, A.W.
 1958 "The Relationship Between Unemployment and the Rate of Change of Money Wage Rates in the United Kingdom, 1862-1957", Economica (25)(Nov): 283-99.

Pirog-Good, Maureen A.
 1979 "The Relationship Between Youth Employment and Juvenile Delinquency: Some Preliminary Findings", Philadelphia, PA: Wharton Management and Behavioral Science Center.

Pollard, Beatrice E.
1962. Social Casework for the State. London: The Pall Mall Press.

Popenoe, David
1983 Sociology. Englewood Cliffs, NJ: Prentice-Hall, Inc.

Pownall, G.A.
1969 "Employment Problems of Released Prisoners". Manpower Administration, U.S. Department of Labor, Contract 81-19-37 with the University of Maryland.

President's Commission on Law Enforcement and Administration of Justice
1968 The Challenge of Crime in a Free Society. New York: Avon.

Quinney, Richard
1977 Class State and Crime. New York: David McKay Company.

Radzinowicz, Leon and Marvin E. Wolfgang (eds.)
1971 Crime and Justice. Volume I. The Criminal in Society. New York: Basic Books, Inc.

Raper, Arthur F.
1933 The Tragedy of Lynching. University of North Carolina Press.

Reid, Sue Titus
1990 Criminal Justice. New York: MacMillan Publishing Co.

Revere, Virginia L.
1982 Applied Psychology for Criminal Justice Professionals. Chicago: Nelson-Hall.

Reid, William J. and Ann W. Shyne
1969. Brief and Extended Casework. New York: Columbia University Press.

Richmond, Mary E.
1922. What is Social Case Work? New York: Russell Sage Foundation.

Robison, Sophia M.; H. Cohen; M. Sachs
1946 "Autonomous Groups: An Unsolved Problem in Group Loyalties and Conflicts", Journal of Educational Sociology: 154-62.

Robison, Sophia M.
1960 Juvenile Delinquency: Its Nature and Control. New York: Holt, Rinehart and Winston.

Rosenberg, M.
1965 Society and the Adolescent Self-Image. Princeton, NJ: University Press.

Rulo, J.H. and D.M. Zemel
1979 "I Am the Proud Mother of a Yesterday Kid", Juvenile and Family Court Journal (30)(2)(May): 3-9.

Rumney, Jay and Joseph P. Murphy
    1952 Probation and Social Adjustment. New Brunswick, NJ: Rutgers
    University Press.

Schneider, Louis
    1976. Classical Theories of Social Change.   Morristown, NJ: General
    Learning Press.

Schrag, C.
    1962 "Delinquency and Opportunity: Analysis of a Theory", Sociology and
    Social Research (46)(Jan): 167-75.

Schwartz, Barry N. and Robert Disch
    1970 White Racism: Its History, Pathology and Practice. An anthology of
    historical and contemporary writings on a crucial social problem: the white
    American's bigotry and his deeply prejudiced view of the black man. New
    York: Dell Publishing Co., Inc.

Schwendinger, Herman and Julia
    1974 Sociologists of the Chair. New York: Basic Books.

Sedlak, K.M.
    1975 Employment Opportunities for the Released Prisoner in Relation to His
    Work History and Vocational Training and Work Experience in Prison.
    Master's thesis.

Sheffield, Ada E.
    1920. Social Case History. New York: Russell Sage Foundation.

Simpson, D. Dwayne, et al
    1976 DARP Data Book, Statistics on Characteristics of Drug Users in
    Treatment During 1969 - 1974. Institute of Behavioral Research, Texas
    Christian University, Fort Worth, TX.

Snodgrass, Jon D.
    1972 The American Criminological Tradition: Portraits of the Men and
    Ideology in a Discipline. Ph.D. dissertation, University of Pennsylvania.

Spear, Allan H.
    1967 Black Chicago: The Making of a Negro Ghetto, 1890-1920. Chicago:
    The University of Chicago Press.

Spergel, Irving
    1963 "Male Young Adult Criminality, Deviant Values, and Differential
    Opportunities in Two Lower Class Negro Neighborhoods", Social Problems
    (Winter)(10)(3): 237-50.

Stoner, J.A.F.
    1961 "A Comparison of Individual and Group Decisions Including Risk",
    Cited in Stephen Wilson, 1978. Informal Groups: An Introduction,
    Englewood Cliffs, NJ: Prentice-Hall.

Strasser, Hermann, and Susan C. Randall
    1981. An Introduction to Theories of Social Change. London: Routledge &
    Kegan Paul.

Swanson, Charles R.; Neil C. Chamelin; Leonard Territo
    1984 Criminal Investigation. New York: Random House.

Swift, Linton B.
    1928 "Can the Sociologist and Social Worker Agree on the Content of Case
    Records", Social Forces (6): 535.

Tannenbaum, Frank
    1938 Crime and the Community. Boston: Ginn and Company.

The Iron Fist and The Velvet Glove
    1975 The Iron Fist and the Velvet Glove: An Analysis of the U.S. Police.
    Center for Research on Criminal Justice, Berkeley, California: San Francisco:
    Garrett Press.

Thio, Alex
    1988 Deviant Behavior. Third edition. New York: Harper & Row Publishers.

Vetter, Harold J. and Leonard Territo
    1984 Crime & Justice In America: A Human Perspective.   St. Paul, MN:
    West Publishing Co.

Votey, Harold Jr. and L. Phillips
    1974 "The Control of Criminal Activity: An Economic Analyis", in Daniel
    Glaser (ed), Handbook of Criminology. Chicago: Rand McNally.

Wadsworth, M.
    1977   Colorado - Southwest Youth Employment Services - Final Report,
    1974-1977, Colorado Division of Criminal Justice, Denver, CO. NCJRS #
    09900.00.045993

Wallach, Michael A; N. Hogan; and D.J. Bem.
    1962. "Diffusion of Responsibility and Level of Risk Taking in Groups",
    Journal of Abnormal and Social Psychology, 68: 263-74.

White, Bernard J.; John H. Stamm; and Lawrence W. Foster
    1976 Cases in Organizations: Behavior, Structure, Processes.   Dallas, TX:
    Business Publications, Inc.

Whitney, Wilbur Montgomery, Jr.
    1974 An Evaluation of a Community Based Delinquency Program on the
    Basis of Group and Individual Employment. Ph.D. dissertation, Michigan
    State University.

Wilson, Everett
    1971 Sociology: Rules, Roles, and Relationships. The Dorsey Press.

Wilson, William Julius
    1987 The Truly Disadvantaged. Chicago: University of Chicago Press.

Wolf, Kurt H.
  1964 The Sociology of Georg Simmel. New York: The Free Press.

Woodside, Arch G. and Robert Fleck, Jr.
  1979 "The Case Approach to Understanding Brand Choice", Journal of Advertising Research (19)(2): 23-30.

Wrobleski, Henry M. and Karen M. Hess
  1987 Introduction to Law Enforcement and Criminal Justice. St. Paul: West Publishing Company.

Young, T.R.
  1978 "Crime and Capitalism", prepared for the 1978 meetings of the Western Social Science Association, Denver.

Zaltman, Gerald; Philip Kotler; and Ira Kaufman (eds.)
  1972 Creating Social Change. New York: Holt, Rinehart and Winston, Inc.

Zimbardo, Philip G.
  1972 "Pathology of Imprisonment", Society (9)(Apr).

CHAPTER FOUR
MAJOR GANGS' CONSTITUTIONS

Latin King Nation
Spanish Gangster Diciple Nation
Vice Lords
Brothers of the Struggle

WRITTEN CONSTITUTION AND BY-LAWS OF THE
ALMIGHTY LATIN KING NATION

CHAPTER CONSTITUTION
OF THE
ALMIGHTY LATIN KING NATION

IN THE SIXTH DECADE OF THE TWENTIETH CENTURY THE A.L.K.N. WAS FORMED. GENERATION AFTER GENERATION OF KINGS HAVE LIVED BY A CONSTITUTION OF PRINCIPLES BASED UPON THE IDEAS OF KINGISM. THOSE IDEAS, OUR LAWS AND PRINCIPLES WE NOW IMPACT TO ALL KINGS WITH THIS CONSTITUTION.

FROM THIS DAY FORWARD WE SHALL ORGANIZE OURSELVES UNDER CONSTITUTIONAL LAW TO INSURE THAT WE AS A NATION SHALL LEAD THE WAY TO PROGRESS AND NO LONGER STAND IN THE SHADOW OF IT: WE AS A NATION SHALL LEAD THE WAY FOR TRUE KINGISM.

DEVOTING YOUR LIFE TO THESE PRINCIPLES IMPLIES A LIFE OF SERVICE TO EACH OTHER AND TO THE ALMIGHTY LATIN KING NATION.

LOVE - HONOR - OBEDIENCE
SACRIFICE - RIGHTEOUSNESS

INCA

The Inca is the highest ranking officer in every chapter of the Nation. The Inca is elected by majority vote of his Chapter's membership. His term of office is indefinite. However, he must run in an election for a "vote of confidence" every two years in order to retain as position as Commander-In-Chief.

The Inca is responsible for the actions of his Chapter, its security, the treasury and the general well-fare of the membership. He is responsible for promoting academic and vocational skills and for providing the aid and way in our search for peace, unity and freedom.

The Inca must file a State of the Nation report every three months with Los Coronas concerning the affairs of his Chapter. Any action taken by the Inca shall be enforced through the Cacique.

CACIQUE

The Cacique shall be second in command of his chapter. He, like the Inca, is elected by majority vote of the membership of his Chapter and his term of office is indefinite. However, he too must run in a vote of confidence election every two years.

The Cacique is to work hand-in-hand with the Inca and assume the responsibilities of the Inca in case of the Inca's absence.

The Cacique is responsible for keeping the Inca informed on all actions taken by the Officers of his Chapter.

Any action taken by the Cacique shall be enforced through Chapter Enforzador.

ELECTIONS

The elections will be conducted by the Chairman of the Chapter Crown Council for both Inca and Cacique. Elections for these officer must be held within thirty days of their departure from office. However, if the Council Chairman has prior knowledge of an immediate or forthcoming departure of either the Inca or Cacique then he has the option of proceeding with an election thirty days prior to such departure.

The Crown Council members will each select five members as candidates of whom in their opinion are the most qualified to run for Office. The two candidates that receive the highest number of votes from the Chapter Crown Council members will automatically run for Office. The candidate that receives the highest number of votes from that Chapter's membership will be elected as Inca and the other candidate as Cacique.

In order to run for office a Brother must be a member of the Nation for a minimum of three years. This is the basic requirement. Other requirements include but are not limited to the following:

1. He must be a member in good standing and have some type of prior experiences an Officer of the Nation with the rank of Chairman of the Crown Council, Chapter Enforzador and/or previous Inca and Cacique.

2. He must also have been in the chapter for a period of six months so that he has gained experience and knowledge in understanding the policies and principles of the Almighty Latin King Nation.

Every two years the Inca and Cacique must run for re-election. This is called a Vote of Confidence and is to assure that the membership is satisfied with the leadership. A vote of confidence is not an election of new officers but a vote by the Chapter's membership to determine if the Inca and Cacique have fulfilled the responsibilities of their Office.

If the majority of the Chapter's membership is dissatisfied with their elected Officers, the People's will shall be manifested by a vote of NAY - one who votes no. If the majority of the Chapter's membership is satisfied with the rule of their Inca and Cacique they shall cast a vote of YEA - one who votes yes.

LAS CORONAS

Las Coronas are the highest ranking Officers of the Nation. Their term of office is indefinite. Las Coronas are responsible for seeing that all Officers of the Nation abide by the Constitution and respect the rights of our membership.

Las Coronas have the power to bring justice where the abuse of power or corruption has occurs by the Inca and Cacique in any Chapter. In the event the Inca and Cacique violate the Laws of this Constitution, Las Coronas have the power to place all rank on hold pending investigation and appoint temporary positions of rank until a new Inca and Cacique have been elected.

Las Coronas have the power to give Crowns to new members of the nation without them being required to be voted in by the Chapters' Crown Councils.

Any member seeking re-entry into the Nation must be approved by Las Coronas.

Once a proposal has been put to a vote and approved by the Chapter and Council, the Inca and Cacique, final approval must be given by las Coronas before it is added to the Constitution and Law.

EL CONSEJADOR

The Inca's advisor shall serve as an consejador and Cacique. This position is usually reserved for members who have served as past Inca and have been in the nation for a long period of time with a record of having served wisely.

All members reaching the age of fifty (50) years, who are members in good standing and have during their years in the Nation held the rank of Inca, Cacique, Chapter Crown Council Chairman and Chapter Enforzador shall, with the approval of Las Coronas, hold the title of National Consejador and are to be treated with the respect of an Officer.

The name of this association shall be the ALMIGHTY LATIN KING NATION.

An organization of international brotherhood with exists for the purpose of:

1. Promoting prosperity and freedom through love and understanding to all oppressed people of the world.

2. To train our People to become aware of our social and political problems and of the conditions we are subjected to live under as a Third World People.

3. To provide the aid and way in our search for peace and unity.

4. To promote and encourage education and vocational learning in order to train our People in the art of survival.

MEMBERSHIP

Membership shall be available to anyone who is willing to change their life-style for the doctrine of Kingism.

Membership shall be denied to anyone who has willfully taken the life of a Latin King or a relative of a member of the Nation.

Membership is forbidden to anyone addicted to heroin and denied to rapists.

Membership is forbidden to anyone who is expelled from Nation unless his re-entry is approved by Las Coronas. Anyone seeking re-entry into the Nation must find an Officer with the rank of Chapter Enforcer, Chapter Crown Council Chairman, Inca or Cacique, to sponsor him before las Coronas will even consider him for re-entry.

CHAPTER ENFORZADOR

The Enforzador will be in charge and responsible for the security of every member Chapter. He shall be appointed by the Inca and Cacique and report to them directly. The Enforzador shall see that the Laws are enforced and the orders of the Inca and Cacique are obeyed.

CHAPTER TESORERO

The Tesorero will be appointed by the Inca and Cacique. It shall be his responsibility to collect and invest Chapter funds. However, members of each Chapter shall determine by majority vote, the amount of dues they pay monthly and how their Chapter funds are to be spent.

The Tesorero shall file a report with the Inca and Cacique at the first of every month on his Chapter's financial status. Brothers who are delinquent in payment of dues are not members in good standing and are not allowed to vote in how Chapter funds are to be spent.

CHAPTER SECRETARIO

The Secretario will be appointed by the Inca and Cacique. His duties shall consist of the following:

1. Collection and distribution of Nation literature.

2. Keeping records of all business conducted by the Chapter Crown Council. Although the Secretario sits in all matters of business conducted by the Crown Council, he may not interfere with the proceedings and must abide by the Rules of the Council.

3. Keep Communications open to all Chapters through the Secretario of every Chapter.

CHAPTER INVESTIGATOR

The Chapter Investigator shall be appointed by the Inca and Cacique. He shall conduct an investigation of all new members. All prospective new members shall be placed on hold until the investigation is completed.

The Investigator shall also conduct all investigations requested by the Inca, Cacique, Chapter Crown Council, Enforzador, Tesorero and Secretario. A report of all investigations, no matter what Officer makes the request, must be filed at the completion with the Inca and Cacique.

CHAPTER CROWN COUNCIL

The Chapter Crown Council shall have its powers delegated to it under this Constitution. Council members do not maintain any power outside the Council. However, Council members shall be recognized as Officers of the Nation. Council members shall be responsible to the Council Chairman, the Inca and Cacique.

The Chapter Crown Council shall be the Law making body of the Chapter and guardian of the Constitution. The Council shall the authority to make their own Rules and Regulations concerning the procedures they are to follow in order to function effectively as a Council.

The Council shall be composed of not more or less than seven of most qualified members of the Chapter.

The Chapter Crown Council shall have the absolute power of holding trials for everyone in the ALMIGHTY LATIN KING NATION regardless of who they are or their position of rank, this includes the Inca and Cacique.

Thee Chapter Crown Council has the prerogative of asking for the resignation of the Inca and Cacique but only a majority of the entire Chapter can remove either of them from Office.

The Council, under the leadership of the Chairman, shall automatically take control of the Chapter in the absence of the Inca and Cacique.

The Council shall have the power, by majority vote, to dismiss a member of the nation under the recommendation of the Inca and Cacique or Las Coronas.

Once the seven members of the Council have been selected and approved it will then become the Council's responsibility; to choose any new members whenever a seat has been vacated. A new member of the Council can be selected by majority vote from the remaining members of the Council.

Whenever the Chairman's seat is vacant, the Inca, Cacique and remaining Council members shall, by majority vote, select a new Chairman.

A council member can be removed from office by the Inca or Cacique's vote along with the majority vote of the remaining Council members.

ALTERNATE COUNCIL MEMBERS

Members of the Chapter Crown Council, by majority vote and with the approval of the Inca or Cacique, shall select members of the Chapter to serve as alternate Council members. Alternate Council members may be selected for the following purposes:

1. In order to form a full quorum.

2. In the event a member appearing before the Council requests that a Crown Council member be excused for possible prejudice.

3. In order to train new members as prospective permanent Council members.

The Chapter Crown Council shall have the power, by majority vote, to accept an individual as an Almighty Latin King or reject him from membership. All individuals seeking membership shall be screened by the Council. The Council shall also interview any member that wishes to make any comments in support of or against any person seeking membership.

The Chapter Crown Council shall try all cases that involve Constitutional violations. The Council may also try cases where an infraction has been committed outside the Constitution but only under the recommendation of the Inca, Cacique or Las Coronas.

Council members are not allowed to discuss any issues or business before it with any members outside the Council until the procedures are completed. This or course does not include their investigative work.

The Chapter Crown Council Chairman shall have no vote in the proceedings but may vote in case of a tie vote among Council members. It is the Chairman's duty to conduct the proceedings and make recommendations on all actions taken by the Council. The Chairman must also keep records of all proceedings conducted by the Council.

If the Inca and Cacique issue an order or implement a Rule that the Chapter Crown Council feels is detrimental to the Chapter, the Council by majority vote, has the authority to null and void such rule or order. However, Las Coronas must be informed in the event of such action is taken by the Council.

CHAPTER CROWN COUNCIL MEMBERS

The first Council member will be appointed by the Inca and Cacique and he shall be the Chapter Crown Council Chairman. The Chairman will then select six other members to complete the quorum of the Council. The members chosen by the Chairman must be approved by the Inca and Cacique.

Council members will be referred to ass Council members and never as "Crown" member. Only Nation Crowns of this rank will be recognized by this title.

Every member of the nation shall honor, respect and protect with his life the lives and reputations of all members of the Almighty Latin King Nation.

When a member gives another member the Nation Salute it should always be returned.

There shall be no stealing inside the Nation and proliferation of the community by acts of vandalism, destruction of property and graffiti is strongly discouraged.

No member shall use his membership or position in the Nation to exploit anyone inside or outside the Nation.

No member shall incur debts with other members that he cannot afford to repay.

Nation affairs are to be kept within the Nation and are not be discussed in the presence of anyone outside the Nation.

No King shall strike or disrespect another King unless it is in self-defense. And any Officer that strikes another member (with the exception of the Inca and Cacique) will automatically lose his rank and may be subjected to further disciplinary action pending an investigation and hearing before the Chapter Crown Council.

Any member found guilty of being a traitor or police collaborator shall automatically lose his position (if he has one) and be expelled from the Nation.

No member shall take the Law into their own hands especially when he knows that what he does will reflect upon the Nation and jeopardize the health and well-being of every member of the Chapter.

No member shall take a lie detector test without the approval of the Inca and Cacique.

No member shall conduct an interview with any person from the news media concerning Nation affairs without the approval of the Las Coronas.

Any member accused of rape shall be put on hold pending investigation by the Chapter Crown Council and subject to approval by the Inca and Cacique.

No member shall bring false charges or statements against another member of the Nation.

Any member or group of members caught disrespecting the Inca and Cacique in public, or conspiring against them or any other member of the Nation shall be brought before the Council on a charge of conspiracy and treason.

No King shall stand idle while another King is in need of assistance.

The use of what is commonly known as angel dust (tick, tack or animal tranquilizer), glue, L.S.D. (acid), heroin, downers and free-basing is unlawful, and cannot be sold in our communities.

Those who are known to have previously used heroin for the purpose of addiction cannot obtain a position of rank without the approval of Las Coronas.

Nothing which can be construed as an emblem of another organization can be worn by a member of the Almighty Latin King Nation.

In recognition of our culture, each January the 6th will be recognized as Kings Holy Day - a day dedicated to the memory of our departed Brothers and Sisters; a day of sacrifice in which each and every member of the nation will observe by fasting.

The first week in the month of March of each and every year is a Nation holiday. This holiday is known as King's Week or Week of the Sun. This holiday is the nation's anniversary and is week of celebration.

TRIAL PROCEDURES

Any member that violates a Law shall be brought before the Chapter Crown Council within a reasonable time to stand trial for his offense. If he is unable to appear he may present a written defense.

Any member that violates a Law must be presented with a copy of the charges as soon as possible so that he may be allowed adequate opportunity to prepare his defense.

Every member of the Nation has the right to have another member of the Nation represent and assist him at his trial. They shall also be allowed the privilege of one continuance for the purpose of presenting witnesses on their behalf and to give them an opportunity to gather information to prove their innocence. If the Chapter Crown Council feels that further investigation is necessary in order to assist them in their work, then they may order a continuation for such purpose. The Chapter Crown Council also maintains the right to call witnesses.

When an Officer of the Nation must stand trial, the Inca or the Cacique must be present. However, the Inca nor the Cacique has the right to vote in such matters as their responsibility is to review the decision of the Chapter Crown Council.

If a member if found guilty of an offense by the Council, the Council will determine the punishment, subject to the approval of the Inca or Cacique. If the member is an officer, the Inca and Cacique, with the recommendation of the Chapter Crown Council, will determine the punishment.

In order to try the Inca or Cacique, any charges brought against either one of them must be brought before the Chapter Crown Council. Any member has the right to bring charges.

If the Council feels the charges are valid, the Council must immediately inform Las Coronas before proceeding with a hearing. If the charges are serious enough to warrant a public trial, the Inca and/or Cacique has the option of abdicating their throne or submitting to the trial.

If the Inca and Cacique do not receive approval of their performance by a majority of their Chapter's membership, a new election of Officers shall be held according to Constitutional law.

HOW LAWS ARE MADE

Any member of the Almighty Latin King Nation has the right to make a proposal, requesting that said proposal be made a part of our Law. A proposal is introduced first to the Chapter Crown Council by any member of the Chapter.

Once the proposal has been submitted, reviewed and debated by the Council, the majority vote will then decide whether or not the submitted proposal has been approved or denied. Once the proposal has been approved by the Chapter Crown Council it will be presented to the Inca and Cacique for their approval.

If the proposal is approved by the Inca and Cacique it will be submitted to Las Coronas. The proposal cannot be Chapter Law without the approval of Las Coronas.

LAWS

Rules and regulations may vary from Chapter to Chapter but the laws of all Chapters are the same. Rules and regulations implemented by the Inca and Cacique falls under their jurisdiction and they will handle all such infractions. The violation of a Law falls under the jurisdiction of the Chapter Crown Council and they will handle all such violations.

The first and most Law of the Almighty Latin King Nation is "Once a King, always a King", unless he is expelled from the Nation for violation of its Laws.

AMENDMENTS

As of this date,_____,
passage of the following proposal has been enacted into the Constitutional Law as the
First Amendment to the Constitution of the Almighty Latin King Nation.

AMENDMENT I.

AMENDMENTS

An amendment is an amelioration of the Constitution without involving the idea of any
change in substance or essence.

For the purposes of continued growth, the modification or alteration proposed under
an amendment is, as of this date, given its force and effect in the following manner:

> Once the passage of a proposal to amend is given by a Chapter Inca
> and Cacique and approved by Las Coronas it shall be added
> hereunder as Constitutional Law. Amor!

APPROVED:

_____

DATED: _____

MANIFESTO
OF THE
ALMIGHTY LATIN KING NATION

THE KING MANIFESTO

ALMIGHTY LATIN KING NATION

He who knows, and knows that he knows, is a wise man,
Listen to him!

He who knows, and does not know that he knows, is asleep,
Wake him up!

He who does not know, and knows that he does not know,
Wants to learn... Teach him!

He who does not know, and does not know that he does
Not know, is a fool... Avoid him!

Confucian

ALMIGHTY		LATIN	KINGS		NATION
OENRAOA		AMRLA	NNOLT		ALONNU
VA ERWH	TEILT		ODBOR		TLG EC
ES AMAV	IRBUU	WEIWE	UIE L		
U TORE	NIEMR	LSLIN	RET E		
R ND	C IA		ETING	ASH U	
E YS		A NL	DRTGT		L E S
D		N A	GUY H		R
		T	EC		
		I	T		
		N	I		
		G	B		
			L		
			E		

A LOVE MEASURED IN GREAT HARMONY TOWARDS YAHVE
LATIN AMERICAN TRIBE ILLUMINATING NATURAL
KNOWLEDGE, INDESTRUCTIBLE NOBILITY and GLOWING STRENGTH
NATURAL ALLIES TOGETHER IN ONE NUCLEUS

HOLY PRAYER

Almighty Father, King of Kings, Maker of the Universe and Foundation of Life, bring
peace to our souls, to the here present, to those not present, to the young and to the old.

As an Almighty Nation under one Sun protected by thine love and guidance we bring our right fist upon our heart for sincerity, love, wisdom, strength, knowledge and understanding. Three hundred-sixty degrees of Strong King Wisdom.

Illuminate our minds and our hearts. Guide our thoughts with thine righteousness. Guide and protect the thoughts of our Coronas and all those holy and righteous lovers and followers of our beloved family and tribe - the Almighty Latin King Nation.

Let the manifestation of our departed Brothers be the path to thee and let it be as it was in the beginning - Strong King Wisdom on both continents, Peace in Black and Gold.

King love! Yesterday, Today, Tomorrow, Always and Forever.

KINGS AND QUEENS PRAYER

Oh King of the Universe, Supreme maker of all things, We the Almighty Latin King and Queen Nation ask you, Almighty King, to bring peace our cause. As an Almighty Nation under the Sun, protected by your love and guidance, we bring our right fist upon our hearts for love, honor, obedience, sacrifice and righteousness.

We ask you Almighty King to bless our departed Brothers and sisters, members of our beloved and mighty Nation, who on this very day rest in the bosom of your sanctuary. May they rest in your care and may they have found the peace and freedom they sought. In our critical moments bring us comfort and guide us through those days of confusion and oppression. May the blessings of the ancients and the wisdom of the ages guide us and keep our Nation strong as we battle the forces that seek to deny us.

We, the Almighty Latin King and Queen Nation, are entrusted with a divine mission, one that transcends personal gains and recognition. As Kings and Queens we pledge ourselves ever faithful to that mission. Make us all aware that others look to us for guidance, and let us always prove ourselves worthy of providing it. For, though we are of different Nationalities, we all share the same cultures of our ancient ancestors whose every word is law throughout the world. It is our destiny to lead rather than to be led.

We, the Almighty Latin King and Queen Nation, have the blood of royalty in our veins. We are the guiding light of our People. Place wisdom in our minds love in our hearts, and fortitude to withstand the trials of time. Guide and protect our Coronas so that they may lead us to our ultimate goal - the awakening of our People to their oppressed state that they may lift our heritage to its rightful place among the thrones of Kings and Queens,

LET THE MANIFESTATION OF OUR SACRIFICED BROTHERS AND SISTERS
BE THE PATH SO THEE, AND LET IT BE AS IT WAS IN THE BEGINNING: STRONG KING AND QUEEN WISDOM - PEACE IN BLACK AND GOLD....

ALMIGHTY LATIN KING NATION

The Almighty Latin King Nation is a religion which gives us faith in ourselves, a national self-respect, power to educate the poor and relieve the misery around us.

It is the Brotherhood of man, blending like the waves of one ocean, shinning as the Sun, one soul in many bodies bearing fruit of the same tree.

It creates in us a thirst like the heat of earth on fire, a thirst for knowledge, wisdom, strength, unity and freedom.

It is the Sun glowing in the essence of our being, the brightness in our eyes that cast reflections of its rays spitting fire in all directions.

It is the unshakable spirit and the nobleness of our hearts, the limitless power of the mind, the unrelentless will to be free.

It is pride, ambition, love, sacrifice, honor, obedience and righteousness, all our powers and all our desires thrown into the mission of human service and united into one Single Gold Sun.

If you want to find Yahve serve the Almighty Latin King Nation. Put on the Gold Sun - Black and Gold colors, place your right fist upon your heart and pledge devotion to the Almighty Latin King Nation, to Yahve and all oppressed people. This is the Nation of Kingism....

BEHOLD KING LOVE!

ICONA

The history of all hitherto existing gang feuds is the History of label struggles for the sake of "click" recognition. It is thin egotistical force for recognition which leads to rivalry and senseless disputes which often cost the high price of human life. The life of our People, the oppressed Third World People.

With the intentions of changing this social and oppressive phenomena the King Manifesto is written; to serve as a guide and enlighten our deplorable conditions under the existing order of things. With this thought in mind we proceed to create the New King, the Moral King, the King of Others, the lover of men and the Turning Wheel of Change.

Devoting your life to the principles of Kingism implies a life of service to your fellow man. We can be of service in no other way. If you turn your back on your Brother simply because of a label you are turning your back on the Almighty Latin King Nation.

One who does not know the Almighty Latin King Nation and its Laws is like a plant growing in the shade. Although it knows not the Sun, it is nevertheless absolutely dependent upon it.

The Nation is in your hands. If you turn your back on the Nation you are denying yourself the sole purpose of your existence - the right to be free!

BEHOLD LATIN KING

KINGISM

Kingism is the doctrine of the Almighty Latin King Nation. There are three stages or cycles of Nation life that constitutes Kingism. They are:

> PRIMITIVE STAGE
> CONSERVATIVE STAGE
> THE NEW KING STAGE

In order for one to grasp a good understanding of each stage and its development, one must understand and consider the social factors surrounding each stage.

THE PRIMITIVE STAGE is that stage in life where the King Warrior acts on impulse, executing his actions without giving them the serious thought that they demand. A stage of immaturity where the King Warrior's time is spent "gang-banging", getting high and being recognized as big and bad.

This can also be classified as the wasteful stage to a certain extent; to the extent that what is being done is being done unconsciously. Yet it is not wasteful in the sense that the environment conditions this type of behavior in order for one to survive the hardships of ghetto life - that undesirable level at the lowest plane of social existence. It is wasteful in that energy is being misused. There are no objectives for one's actions except for the factual phenomena that the entire affair is centered around recognition, label recognition and personal recognition. This egotistical tendency often leads to a blind alley.

Regardless of how senseless one's nations may seem at this level, this is the original stage of Kingism and from the roots of the Primitive Stage emerges the second stage. It is at this level where one either breaks or becomes strong. True lovers of the Nation develop at this stage.

THE CONSERVATIVE STAGE (also known as the Mummy Stage) is the stage of so-called maturity. At this level the King Warrior becomes tired of the Primitive Stage. He no longer wishes to participate in the senseless routine of gang fighting, hanging on the corner or being recognized as big and bad. Most often at this level the King Warrior gets married and retires, alienating himself from the boys and the Nation, concentrating his energies and devotion to his Queen, his children and his responsibility to them; ignoring the fact that he has unconsciously been neglecting his main responsibility to them and himself i.e., to make himself and his loved ones free!

It is inappropriate to call this stage the maturity Stage due to the fact that the King Warrior at this time does not really become mature in the true sense of maturity. Instead he becomes mummified or reaches a level of mummified maturity. He, in his conservative role, lives with no future, accepting life as it has been taught to him by the existing system that exploits all People of color - dehumanizes them and maintains them under the economic and social yoke of slavery.

True members of the Nation do not quit at this level, they do not cease to identify themselves with the Kings, instead they alienate themselves from them. They do not cease to be who they are, they conserve what they are; they become conservative. There are more Kings at this level than at any other level. And, although this stage has all the characteristics of a regressive stage, it is really the stepping stone into the third stage of Kingism - the New King Stage.

THE NEW KING is the stage of awareness and decision. The Primitive and Conservative stages are a compliment to the third. They go hand-in-hand with this stage of maturity, it does not keep the King Warrior in the limbo state of being i.e., the mummy like stage. At this level there is a stage of awareness, an awareness of one's self as a subject of decision.

Under the New King stage the world takes a completely new form. One no longer continues to visualize the street corner as his turf or being tough as a man of survival as in the Primitive stage nor does he remain in the mummy stage. Instead he learns to appreciate the values of organizational work, the values of life and Brotherhood. One no longer views the rival warrior as the cause of one's ills, instead his vision broadens to the extent of recognizing himself as a subject of decision. He learns that his ills lie at the roots of a system completely alien to his train of thought and his natural development due to the components of dehumanization that exist therein.

This stage is what determines righteousness, for it is at this stage where awareness leads to the point of decision, that point where one must decide one's future. This is where he either becomes an accomplice to that anti-King system or a subject of decision - A New King!

The New King recognizes that the time for revolution is at hand. Yes, revolution - a revolution of the mind! The revolution of knowledge! A revolution that will bring freedom to the enslaved, to all Third World People as we together sing and praise with joy what time it is - it's Nation time! Time for all oppressed People of the world to unite. The young warriors and future leaders look at the New King with the hope of someday being free. We shall not destroy the faith they have in us, for in doing so we destroy ourselves.

The New King is the end product of complete awareness, presieving three hundred-sixty degrees of enlightment. He strives for world unity. For him there are no horizons between races, sexes and senseless labels. For him everything has meaning, human life is placed above materialistic values. He throws himself completely into the battlefield ready to sacrifice his life for the ones he loves, for the sake of humanization.

The New King is endowed with the supreme natural powers that surpass the human scope of comprehension. This highly complexed energical entities separate him from the abstract world and all those who surrender themselves to vanity and idleness and place materialistic values above and beyond human principle.

The New King sees himself as a subject of decision, a Sun that must glow forever to enlighten those not so fortunate as he. He feels the rays of the Sun glowing in the essence of his being, giving him life, energy and strength - the strength of his unshakable spirit and the nobleness of his heart. The hypnotizing profundity of his gaze reflects the limitless power of his mind and the unshakable will to be FREE.

THE CODE OF KINGISM

Every member of the Nation shall honor, respect and protect with his life the lives and reputation of all members of the Almighty Latin King Nation.

Stand up for those who stand up for themselves in their quest for peace, justice, freedom, progress and prosperity.

Never exploit or bring harm to any member of the most righteous Tribe - The Lion Tribe - the Almighty Latin King Nation or any other oppressed person or nation.

Respect and protect with your life Brown Women for they are the mothers of our beautiful color the life of the future Suns of the Universe.

Love and respect children of all races, sexes, cults and religions. Protect them with your life for they are the leaders of tomorrow's Nations.

Honor and respect the Nation Salute for it means. "I DIE FOR YOU; the Sacred Colors for they represent the People we love and live for - the memory of those who rest in peace in the sanctuary of the Almighty Father, King of Kings.

Educate yourself, for an illiterate King is a weak King and a weak King has no place in a Strong Nation.

Learn your King Manifesto and live by it for it shall lead to Peace - Freedom - and Justice.

BEHOLD LATIN KING

NATIONAL EMBLEM

The Crown is the National Emblem of the Almighty Latin King Nation. It displays our royalty among men; our sovereignty and our Kingdom among Nations. The Crown is a symbol that is recognized all over the world and although there are many different types, the two that the Almighty Latin King Nation identify with the most are the Imperial and the Coronet.

The Imperial is the one most generally used to represent our beloved Nation because of its very meaning and magnificence.

Each of the Coronet's five points has a special meaning. They represent Love, Honor, Obedience, Sacrifice and Righteousness. The Crown enthrones our idealism, our belief and attitudes towards a better way of life in the universe....

SACRED COLORS

BLACK represents the solid dominant color of the universe, the brave and the bold, the darkness of the immense night. It represents People of one idea, one body, mind and soul, the Alpha and the Omega.

GOLD represents the fabulous brilliant Sun at its highest peak; the splendoring glow of hope in oppressed People, the brilliance of the mind and the solid unity in strength, love and sacrifice.

Two colors of natural creations existing since the beginning of time and enduring forever.

NATIONAL SALUTE

A fist upon our heart.... it means, "I DIE FOR YOU" for you are flesh of my flesh, blood of my blood, son of my mother who is the Universal Nature and follower of Yahve who is the Almighty King of Kings; it also means Love - Strength - Sacrifice.

BEHOLD LATIN KING

Glory to the Queens and Power to the Kings
Almighty Latin King Love, Yesterday, Today, Tomorrow, Always and Forever!

FEARLESSNESS

To the Almighty Latin King Nation, fearlessness implies absence of all kinds of fears. It is the freedom from such fears as hunger, humiliation, wrath and criticism of others. It is also the freedom from the fear of resistance, the freedom from the fear of loss of courage and the freedom from the fear of physical death. It is a necessity for a true Latin King because cowards can never be moral. Fearlessness is indispensable for the growth of other noble qualities.

How can one seek liberation, truth, or cherish love without fearlessness? Moral Bravery is, for the Nation, the highest heroism. And it consists in the readiness to

sacrifice patiently and fearlessly, everything, including life for the good of other members of the Tribe of Righteousness out of love for them....

BEHOLD LATIN KING

NATION FLAG

The Flag shall consist of either two stripes - one Black and one Gold - running horizontally with a circle in the upper left corner of the top color with a Crown in the center of the circle or the Flag may consist of three stripes running vertically with a circle in the center stripe and a Crown in the circle.

The Flag shall never touch the floor or be placed where dishonor may fall upon it.

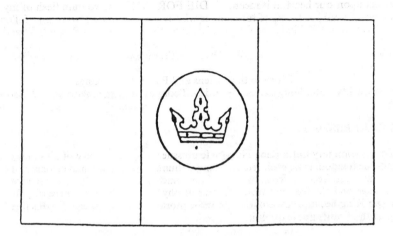

BEHOLD LATIN KING

The New King is the turning wheel of change, he recognizes what time it is - It's Nation time! He sees the rulers of our present system lavishing their treasures freely on the means of destruction, then towards that which would promote the happiness of mankind. These strifes and this bloodshed and this discord must cease and all oppressed People unite as one Nation, as one kindred, as one family.

The New King is aware of the fact that in the Almighty Latin King Nation all are servants, Brothers and Sisters - natural allies together in one nucleus. As soon as one feels a little better than the other, a little superior to the rest, he is in a dangerous position and unless he casts away the seed of such evil thought, he is not an instrument for the service of the Nation. Just as calamity is due for disobedience, so deliverance form calamity can be obtained by obedience. Turning from the Nation brings inevitable disaster and turning to the Nation brings blessings.

In order to establish the Kingdom of freedom in the world, it must first be established in the hearts of men. The King that lives the life according to the teachings of this Nation is the True King. A King who loves his Nation, his People and freedom; one who works for universal peace, universal freedom and universal Brotherhood. A man may call himself a King just as an ugly man may call himself handsome, yet if he does not live the life of a True King, he is not a King, and a ugly man deceives no one.

He who would be a New King needs to be a fearless seeker and lover of freedom. If his heart is pure and his mind is free from prejudice he shall not fail to recognize freedom from slavery. The call of the New King to mankind is that men should open their eyes and use their reason, not suppress it. It is seeing and free thinking, no servile credulity that will enable the True King to penetrate the clouds of prejudice, to shake the fetters of blind imitation and attain from the realization of truth a new revelation.

The New King will not only believe in the teachings of his Nation but will find in them the guide and inspiration for his life and joyfully impart to others the knowledge that is the well-spring of his own being. Only then will he receive the full measure of power of the Almighty Latin King Nation.

When a man becomes a New King the will of the nation becomes his will, for to be at variance with the Nation is one thing that cannot endure. The Almighty latin King Nation requires while-hearted and compete devotion.

How can divine King Love be demonstrated to an unbelieving world its capacity to endure to the utmost blows of calamity and the treachery of seeming friends; to rise above all t his undismayed and unembittered, still to forgive, bless and unite? The light of King Love irradiates his foggiest days, transmutes his suffering into hope and martyrdom itself into an ecstatical bliss. The New King longs to see believers of freedom shouldering the responsibilities of the cause. Now is the time to proclaim the Kingdom that is rightfully ours. Now is the time for union and concord. Now is the day of unity because it's Nation time!

The New King recognizes that the day of resurrection is here. A time for the appearance of a new manifestation of truth. The rising of the dead means the spiritual awakening of those who have been sleeping in the graveyard of ignorance. The day of the oppressor must now be judged by the oppressed.

BEHOLD LATIN KING

THE ALMIGHTY EYE

When a King Warrior accepts Kingism as described in the King Manifesto, his life takes a complete turn. For him everything changes. His vision is no longer limited to narrow horizons, instead he is gifted with the power of the Almighty Eye - a Sun that glows to enlighten, through the sense of sight, the New King and the Nation.

The eyes of the Nation are everywhere there is a Nation man, a True King. His perceptions, viewed in the concept of universal human progress, is the reflections of his soul, his ideology, his quest for freedom and his desire for unity among his People. His observations are free and independent; his thoughts are not clouded by any form of prejudice and his actions are based on common sense and knowledge.

Seeing, perceiving and observation by all Kings is the network of the Nation - the eyes of the Almighty Latin King Nation are everywhere.

BEHOLD LATIN KING

KING AM I

> Whether in front or profile I stand
> On that finished form let glory bestow
> Black its midnight shadow, Gold its morning glow
> In precision clear, a vision ever so bright
> That over the rest the domineering light
> Spreads the extensive vigor of its rays
> Any yields to me the power they praise

That majesty, that grace, rarely given
To remove the restraints with which they confine
To pass before the turning wheel of change
With supreme perfection my aim
Love, truth and knowledge my claim.
Below the thunderous lofty arch of light
The whole in loveliest harmony unites
For a True King the brightest glories soar
The King of Kings applauds him and the world adores
Let then each be firm allied
And let no one separate or divide
United in strict decorum, time and place
An emulous love and genuine faith
Be Grace, Be Majesty thy constant strive
That majesty, that grace - King Am I.

Be it always remembered that the original Manifesto was written and dedicated to all oppressed people of the world, to the People and the Nation and to all our beautiful Sisters by the Brown Prince of Darkness. Amor!

BEHOLD LATIN KING

BROWN FORCE

The Latino can draw additional strength from another force too if he has the will and the faith.

Anonymous millions of Brown Men and Women have given their life in the fight for liberation. They have fought against colonialism, hunger and ignorance and for the human dignity of our People. They have drawn from one another, through unity, a force of fortitude - Brown Force - the force which provides the splendoring glow of hope in oppressed people. The seed they cast into the founding of a Nation - the Almighty Latin King Nation - has withstood the trials of time.

Drawing upon the endurance and fortitude of Brown Force, we continue our quest to unify and insure free political and culture expression among the Third World People and among the commonwealth of individuals. We are the People's liberating force - Brown Force - the foundation of the Nation.

BEHOLD LATIN KING

NATION MEN

Who is a Nation man and who is not? The difference lies in what they do, how they carry themselves and how they talk. But in order for one to really understand the contrast one must know and understand the principles of the King Manifesto and Modern Kingism.

One of the clearest contrastive examples is when the so-called Nation Man claims to be a Latin King, a member of the Almighty Latin King Nation, and by the same token says, "I am a Little; A Coulter King; A Pee Wee; I'm from such and such a branch or chapter, etc." He might be a Latin King, that is true, but he definitely is not a Nation Man.

This clearly testifies that this so-called Nation Man is really a demagogue, a preacher of a false philosophy, an agent of confusion and disunity. His mind is broad only to the scope of where his particular "click" is concerned. Outside of that click mentality his mind meets with the brick-wall of prejudice and individualism.

Nation Men on the other hand are devoted followers and believers of unity, supporters of the harmonious whole. For Nation Men there are no horizons between clicks and branches for they identify only with the Nation, not with a particular click, branch or section - natural allies together in one nucleus, one Nation, the Almighty Latin King Nation.

BEHOLD LATIN KING

**WRITTEN CONSTITUTION AND BY-LAWS OF THE
SPANISH GANGSTER DISCIPLE NATION**

**CONCEPT'S
OF THEE
20th CENTURY**

TABLE OF CONTENTS

(1)   GREETING'S

(2)   INSIGNIA

(3)   CROSS

(4)   PREAMBLE

(5)   CODE OF S.G.D.N.

(6)   A BROTHER'S OATH TO THE NATION

(7)   ADMINISTRATORS OF OUR NATION

(8)   ORGANIZATIONAL STRUCTURE

(9)   COMMUNICATION AND MEETING'S

(10)   AMENDMENTS OF S.G.D.N.

(11)   AMENDMENTS OF THEE INCATCERATED

(12)   EDUCATION AND EMPLOYMENT

(13)   SECURITY

(14)   DISCIPLE'S HISTORY

(15)   GANGSTER'S HISTORY

(16)   MOTTO - IDEALOGY - GOALS

(17)   LOVING MEMORIES OF OUR BROTHER'S & SISTER'S

(18)   GLOSSARY

(1)

GREETING'S TO OUR COMRADES

Greeting's Comrades

Before I proceed any futher into this letter, I would like to extend our nation's love to all our family members who in their time of incarceration have served our distinguished organization faithfully and effectively.

My sole purpose is to speak to our comrades in arms through these unspoken words, in order that I may convey the basic information that you may need to function effectively in our dignified organization. It also gives me great pleasure to acquaint you with our new ideology and some of the needed changes that have taken place within our nation. To begin with, changes in our nation will continue, it's through these changes that our nation will grow to it's height. Changes come through the new ideas proposed by any family member. Each individual who is an active member of this supreme nation, is given the opportunity to grow and develop along with it.

To further the growth of our nation, I have proposed an idea that will advance the unification of all our allies. My presentation to our allies is for us to go under one name, not only in these penal institutions, but also in the free world.

I discussed my proposal over with Mad-Dog, in respect that he is looked upon as a leader among his peoples organization, and with some of our other allies, and they all endorsed my proposal. So our strength of minds were mutual.

We will assume the name of - Spanish Gangster Disciple nation, those of you who oppose our proposal will just have to step to the side and let our nation lunge forward and gain ground.

Mad-Dog and I, have dispatched word to the free world informing our comrades of the S.G.D.N. movement. All of us as a whole are obligated to spread the word to our comrades who are in different penal institutions, and to those who are in the free world. Through full and total participation we shall achieve the development and growth of our nation, and thereby stimulate the personal development of each of our members. Those members who show leadership potentials should be prepared to assume leadership roles in our organization.

A symbol had to be thought up, one which would characterize and represent our newly founded nation, and we came up with the idea to devise a cross that will symbolize the Spanish Gangster Disciple Nation. So Sach-Mo and I designed it. The cross bares five(5) stones, with the colors of each of the original organizations that came together to form the S.G.D.N., the cross is a process by which the "whole nation" can offer it's member's, a total experience, personal development, and not to forget, effective service to the S.G.D.N. These functions are absolutly essential for the "total S.G.D.N." to be a reality.

We must all be aware that in the history of anyone of our organizations, we have shown failure in many ways, and we have also accomplished some achievements, as for instance, the 60's for us was not a decade of many accomplishments, and the same applies for the 70's, but the 80's will be a new day for us, and not to mention a more successful decade. "No other success can compensate for failure in our Nation".

Here is something we must all acknowledge! The S.G.D.N. makeup is a composite of all the organizations that came together to form it. If we all play active roles, the S.G.D.N. will become a strong nation. And if we don't all agree to participate, our nation will become weak. "It's that simple". We can all make a difference.

Your position of leadership requires that you become totally knowledgeble in planning projects and conducting our nations business, we can make being members of the S.G.D.N. a beneficial and meaningful experience. Remember that our objective is to give our family members tools through which they can personally benifit and apply to their lives.

I urge you brothers to put in all your heart and mind, and participate in helping our nation have years of pride and accompishments. I bid you peace love an loyalty and deep respect for our fallen comrades.

> Our deeds will travel
> with us from afar, and
> what we have been,
> makes us what we are"'

VICTOR

(2)

INSIGNIA

The Spanish Cross derives from our heretic ways, the first word in our Nations name, in which we find our race, our creed, our essential belifs and our faith.

These guiding principals unite us closer together and bound us as one. The circular disc behind the cross represents the highest degree of unity, unity being the reason for which we have constructed the S.G.D.N.

To unionize and coordinate the structure of all our branches under one foundation of S.G.D.N.

The disc behind the cross is to be carved on edge with "WREATH" type circles, for our loving memories of our dead.

Each stone on the cross will represent the color of our branches, the middle stone is to be the color of your original branch, all colors on the insignia are there to show respect and tribute to each of our affiliate organizations, which secure peace, praise, and credit to the foundation of our Nation.

This "Insignia" is to be worn proud, with a constant loyalty shown to the people of thee:

S.G.D.N.

(3)

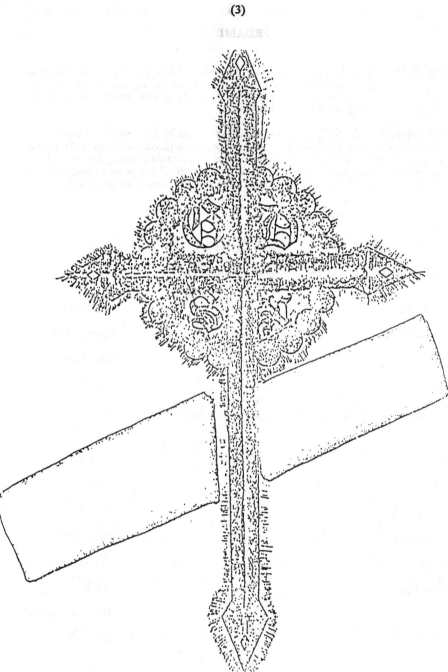

(4)

PREAMBLE

We, of thee: S.G.D.N. grateful to all our brothers for thier participation in our years of struggle, for our brothers with thier years of loyalty to our nations life. Through our nations decades we've enjoyed providing security, a sure safety and domestic tranquillity amoung the lives of our people.

We, brother's of the S.G.D.N. must ordain and abide by the nations constitution, to eliminate poverty and inequality amoung our people, to provide a structure of potential developments for the individual of our nation, to maintain a liberty for our children and a more gratifying style of social living. We bless all our people along with our families and we will constantly obtain a future for the descendants of our nation.

(5)

CODE OF S.G.D.N.

"All code word's must be in a set of quotation's."

Stateville	"Vic's Crib"
Pontiac	"Imoky's Crib:
Manard	"Slim's Crib"
Administration	"Neek's"
Police	"Pig"
S.G.D.N.	"Folk's"
Familia Disciple's	"Gente"
Cobra's	"c"s"
Gangster's	"Division"
Disciple's	"Rockwell"
Satan Disciple's	"Taylor's"
B.G.D.N.	"Allies"
B.D.N.	"Discipulo Negro's"
King's	"Corona"
S.C.R.	"Peaches"

Joliet	"Angel's Crib"
Mail	"Carta"
Nation	"Nasióa"
Segragation	"Pit"
Parole Board	"Tabla de Violar"
Law's	"Leyes"
Constitution	"foundation"
Literature	"Fact's"
Organization	"La Unión"
Incarcerated	"Pared"
Penal Institution's	"Cháteau"
Figa	"Old Spice"

Add words as needed -

(6)

A BROTHER'S OATH TO THE NATION

A sworn oath to the nación in sound form from each of our hearts, a oath to the people, for the people and accepted by the people. As a brother of the Spanish Gangster Disciple nación, I, in belief of the nación's ideology and teachings of the constitution, swear to uphold the honor and protect the nación, to show love and endure 100% loyalty toward the people of our nación.

To maintain silence in our nación, in respect to abiding by the law's of our constitution, giving my life to my brother's; never to betray a brother in code of *Death*Before*Dishonor*, securing our rights to love, to carry life, and to pursue the loyalty we share.

As this statement to be truth I, swear to our beloved insignia to carry the name Spanish-Gangster-Disciple-Nación-, and to serve as a prophet to the faith of our Nación until my death...

(7)

ADMINISTRATOR'S OF OUR NACIÓN

Governor:

Our Governor is the chief executive of our Nación. Our Governor's responsibility is to maintain and oversee his administrator's functions toward the people of the Nación.

****

Lt. Governor:

There is one Lt. Governor in our Nación while incarcerated, his function is to exercise and perform duties handed down to him by the Governor.

****

Ambassador's:

Ambassador's are officials appointed by the Lt. Gov.- an ambassador's functions are to carry out duties handed down to them by the Lt. Gov.; an appointed ambassador must carry himself in form as follows:

1. A) Our ambassador's must carry a positive and firm attitude, this be mentally as well as physically. He has to maintain a strick discipline upon himself in which those of our Nación can see and recognize: "A Explicit Character".

1. B) Our ambassador is an official appointed in position of commands, but the ambassador is not to constantly impose his position upon our brother's of the Nación.

2. A) Ambassador must have a wide understanding along with patience to relate to any situation that may arise. To be able to comprehend all information before making the decision to make a move, the ambassador must consult with the Lt. Governor before he makes the move in question.

2. B) An ambassador has to approach and speak to all brother's of our Nación in a manner in which all the brother's understand what has been said, and to make sure all brother's comprehend the idea at hand.

3. A) A ambassadors mental attitude must be to maintain peace at all times, this is amoungst our Nación; we are to bare arms after all avenues have been exhausted.

3. B) A ambassador must realize for faulty decisions he is to expect the same penalty as any brother in transgression.
****

VICEROY- Appointed by the ambassador to maintain a cell-house!

(8)

ORGANIZATIONAL STRUCTURE

There is no ideal organizational structure that fit's the needs of every single S.G.D.-member, but there is one that is right for your's, which is, "The Board Of Directors", the board of directors merely figures out all the job functions and activities that are needed. The board sensibly and fairly distributes them to certain officers on the board.

Fortunately we have been in existence long enough to assist you with the assignment. As you design your structure there are a few guidelines that will assist you, they are:

****

1.) No one person should be required to manage more than six (6) to ten (10) member's.

2.) The workload should be balanced between the Board Member's.

3.) The system must be flexible so that additional people and programs can be added during the coming years. It must also be flexible enough to handle a reduction in the number of people and programs.

4.) Each Ambassador must know what is expected of him, the importance of his role in achieving the overall objectives, and the standards by which his performance will be judged.

****

SAMPLE OF OUR ORGANIZATIONAL STRUCTURE

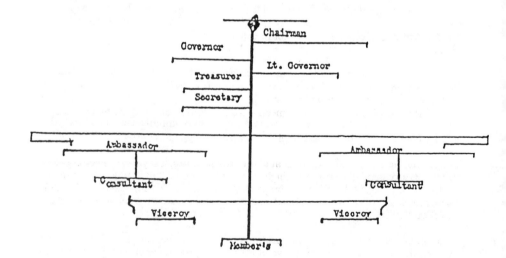

These are examples of how you can shift workloads to a new officer when it is necessary. Whatever structure you finally choose, let it be flexible enough to accommodate the growth of your section. As you grow, al the management functions of your section increase. It's far better to add new positions to alleviatae some of the new burdens than to let the present Board members become overworked. Don't be afraid to change your structure when it is necessary.

****

(9)

COMMUNICATION AND MEETING'S

If you don't communicate effectively, you won't lead effectively. Leadership involves getting things done through people. How well you do this, this will be determined by your ability to communicate. You have to look upon communication as your most valuable asset, other than your own personal communication methods there is one primary way that a section can comunicate with it's member's. Thee primary way is through:

Meeting's!

****

MEETING'S

Board meetings are the single most important time where all aspects of the management of your section should be reviewed and discussed. Items that should be discussed are such items as follows:

1.) The status of all projects.

2.) Attitude of older and younger member's.

3.) Whose dues are due next month.

4.) Budget review and your sections plan of action.

5.) Review of last membership meeting's, the good point's and the bad point's.

6.) Plan for next Board meeting!

You should be an active participant at all Board meeting's, it is your elected responsibility. Regular membership meeting's are equally important. It is during these meeting's that several things are accomplished. Direction for your section is decided, the member's are informed, motivated, and the opportunities available in your section are on display.

Even though it is the direct responsibility of your Governor, Lt. Governor, or Ambassador to insure that you have effective and productive meeting's, it is your responsibility to assist them in several areas. Areas such as:

1.) You should actively participate in the planning of the next membership meeting at each Board meeting.

2.) You should insure that your reports, and reports of your Directors and committee chairman are always short, clear, and concise. (To the Point)- Nothing turns off members more than long and unprepared committee reports.

3.) If the meeting or an individual becomes unruly you should assist the Governor in getting the meeting back to order as soon ass possible. Or Chairman -
****

NOTE:

Always arrive at Board meetings one half hour before starting time of the meeting. You can help with any last minute set ups. Be sure that you also review the basics with all members so that they can more effectively participate in meeting's.

Speaking of Board meeting procedures, you should have a basic idea of how it works and it's importance in conducting the affairs of our organization. You don't have to be a lawyer to understand the Board's procedure. All you must do is realize that it is merely a tool to shorten meeting's, conduct business and ensure fairness to all our member's.

(10)

AMENDMENTS OF S.G.D.N.

1.) All members must respect and participate in maintaining a code of silence within our family, and at all times conduct themselves in accordance with our family's laws. All members must display faithful allegience to the family's organization and to thier appointed superiors.

2.) Discourtesy, rude, or impolite remarks will not be tolerated, absolutley no fighting amoung family members.

3.) No family members shall at anytime consume any addictive drugs, or encourage the use of drugs to any family member.

4.) All family members will acknowledge authorative commands handed down to them by thier appointed superiors. Insubordination, will not be tolerated from any member towards thier superiours.

5.) "At No Time" - will any member put up with, or tolerate any offensive critisizm towards this organization - by those non-affiliated with our family, nor shall we see any members outrage the moral feelings of any righteous family member.

6.) All members of this family are expected to sacrifice and devote thier lives for this family's cause.

7.) All members will be at any aid to the members of thee B.G.D.N. - and to this family, in any difficulty or problem that they may have, be it mentally or physically.

8.) Misrepresentation of this family, or of any appraisales, flags, embloms, or colors will not be tolerated.

9.) All members- regardless of rank or position must strive to assist each other, not to compete with one another.

10.) All members must make a solemn declaration to uphold all commands handed down to them, and to make a oath from thier heart and soul to this family- that all members will be a part, even if there are times of depression.

11.) All members will experience and undergo the same penalties imposed on any member of this organization who breaks or goes beyond the limits of our set laws. "No exceptions will be made!" Regardless of rank or position.

12.) The penalty for any transgression made against this organizations laws- will be left up to the discreation of your superiors, considering the nature of the law that was broken, then the member in the wrong will be dealt with according to the law broken.

13.) Ignorance of our laws are of no excuse, all members shall make it thier initiative to come and know each and every law, and percieve to understand the full meaning to our laws, and also apply yourselfs to them.

(11)

AMENDMENTS OF THEE INCARCERATED

1.) In each place of where you are confined, there is a box... All family members who are able must contribute to help others in the family who are not as fortunate as other members. (This includes for the people of orientation).

2.) At no time shall we disrespect any member of another nation - all grudges from the street are to be held until you return to the streets. We as a nación, are in no position to participate in meaningless struggles which will only prolong our stay in these confinements. If any problems occur, a decision will be made by high authority.

3.) We shall not play with any officer of the jail, they have a job to do. It is to keep us here. Unless you can gain off the situation, leave it alone. Our struggle is to show love to each other, and one day be set free. The administration holds us. So consider them off limits, unless it benifits you, or any other member of this family.

4.) We are allies of the B.G.D.N., but we are an independant nación, we are our own ruler, we take orders from our own organization only... Give the members of the B.G.D.N., all due respect at all times.

5.) Attend to your personal needs, ask one another for what you lack, we shall not hold back on anything that will make one of our people be without...

6.) All members shall take orders from thier appointed superiours of any cellhouse. Disrespect in any form is an immediate violation of King Vic's laws.

7.) We shall represent with (2) fists across the chest. We all have an original way of representing. Either way will be proper. We all understand the love and meaning behind representing.

8.) We all know who we are, and what we stand for. If in any place or situation you cannot represent, well, we know one doesn't have to hit his chest to be 100% loyal to this almighty family.

9.) We are Gangsters, Disciples, Cobras, Eagles, all united into one familia de amor, We are Disciples of each other-we are King Vic's Disciples. We be about the latino organization, so spread out the laws and the teachings of our supreme Nación.

(12)

EDUCATION + EMPLOYMENT

This section is specifically for all our fellow familia members to gain as much knowledge in these two areas as possible. Education and Employment are two essential needs throughout your confinement and also in todays society.

During ones confinement, if an individual has not yet obtained his diploma, he should take advantage of the educational system. We find in our confinement areas that there are two types of educational programs. 1.) One is the school for individuals to obtain a G.E.D. The other educational program is the vocational school, a place where a individual can learn a trade. Actual learning experiences in trades such as: welding skills, electrical training, small engines, computer programing, and a print shop trade. Of these mentioned vocational skills an individual can obtain a verified certificate of his achievement. An individual can further the achievement into becoming a "Journey Man" in one of these specific field's.

Members of our organization with these achievements are important assets to our daily progress, but also as an individual with these skills you can become financially stable. Employment is most important to our people's needs, whether it is employment while incarceration, or in society. But a structure of development must be set to raise our peoples standards and classification.

While in confinement there are jobs where a individual can learn a specific skill, such as; tailoring, cooking, barbering, electrician skill, plumbing or even legal aid's. Our ideas toward our people are; not letting thim sit around to let time pass by, each of our people must take a day in life to make the decision of what he or she wants out of life, and to set the structure of obtaining the set goal, whether it be through Education or Employment.

(13)

SECURITY

In maintaining security of the lifestyle we live, one must have eyes that memorize and see at the same time. The importance of memory can be vital to you and any brother around you. Communication amoung our brothers is our greatest virtue, for what one brother misses in his sight, another brother can carry the blind to see the light of a situation; as in understanding, teach our brothers understanding until they are capable of being the prophet.

In maintaining security of a organization; all information that is kept within one brothers mind can be vital to other brothers who are left in the dark of a situation. Our guard is to be up at all times and we are to strike first if need be, because for our people to be struck at first is a sure sign of being lax.

It is always best to be in the pressance of another brother at all times, if not, for best results let another bother know of your whereabouts, in case of any occurrance that may come about. When the question is asked about a brothers whereabouts, someone should know at all times. In case of any unusual happening it is a brothers first obligation to notify others, a brother is always to handle the situation at hand, any revengious act of a brother is not tolerated, especially a act alone- consult other brothers in the surrounding's to make the wisest decision as a whole, never leaving any brother in the dark.

As a individual in a organization, to maintain personal security it is wise to be properly clothed at all times, and also to have showes on instead of "Thongs", or slippers. When returning from a shower it is best to put on shoes, never lounge around - especially in jail where a incident may occur at any given time.

In maintaining personal security it is wise to sleep with the door locked, never sleep with the door open. Then again in parable form, "Never Sleep"...

(14)

WORDS OF HISTORY

The history and concepts of thee: Maniac Latin Disciples. The current slogan "You've come a long way baby" certainly applies to the "Maniac Latin Disciples".

We have evolved from the dream of a small group of youths in the late part of the sixties into a vital, effective organization.

When the scope of the Spanish Gangster Disciple Nation, of today is considered, it is difficult to concieve it's beginning as the Latin Scorpions of Rockwell and Hirsch.

The Maniac Latin Disciples, are not of recent vintage, of course. The organization had been built exactly a decade and a half ago, and it's purpose, the social elevation of it's members, a goal the organization rapidly attained. By the mid-seventies it was the most outstanding organization in the vicinity and it prepared to merge with several other similar groups to form the federation of the Maniac Latin Disciples.

During the early years of our emergence, followed a series of clashes with our rivals, a wawr that to this day is still in existence. Where upon we lost a great number of our comrades, our members pride themselves on dealing with the enemy in thier terms, I could describe hundreds of episodes that relate to the wars we've had, but it would take me forever. Also, during the early years of our existence the Maniac Latin Disciples gained support from many of it's members, but none was greater and more valuable than the support gained from our allies.

This history culminates today into what we now term "The Spanish Gangster Disciple Nation Concept". It, then, can be understood as a convenient label pinned to a whole way of life, a living system that develops and changes in the course of time.

(15)

WORDS OF HISTORY

The life of a common street gang, a historical document manufested for future purposes of: Our descendants having questions of how we as a people came about, and how we as a people still progress in todays era, as well as the yesterdays.

Speaking vividly as a original member of the Imperial Spanish Gangster's, I can only try to put over 15 years of events on paper in a brief menner, many events here with will remain known only to those of the Imperial Spanish Gangsters who lived through the history of the Nation.

To bring out the reason why we as a people became a Nation; our first lable was not Gangsters, we were just a bunch of young kids attending school, but being that the school was dominated by the white, as Latino's, we fought against the white almost every day- never having intentions of being any specific group, so as time went by more Latino's attended the school, thus giving the Latino's more power and making survival easier.

In the year 1969 a section of Imperial Gangsters had became known in the area of Armitage and Drake, by people like; Pito a said leader as well as Jabar, Lil Mexico, Lil Bug's, Goyo, and Killer, not having any real goal in mind but to be as a defense to the white street gangs.

At the end of the same year another section of people came about which added another name to the already - Imperial Gangsters, being that most members were of latin origin the second section became -- Imperial Spanish Gangster's, the section was labled the dividion and grand people, or Cameron Gangster's. In that same year a sweater was brought about by one- Jesse Rodreguez, or known as "Lil Bug's" R.I.P., the sweater being black with baby pink cuts and trim. The first sweater thought of by the people of Cameron was to be black and white, but this unballanced the two sections so to unite the two sections Cameron people accepted the pink and black, for a emblom which was a Imperial crown- it is always to be a rounded crown at the top, with 5 head band diamonds to distinguish the crown from the three point crown of the latin kings, a later enemy to the Nation.

As Imperial Spanish Gangsters, the two sections decided to have thier leader's, which was a president, a vice president and a war chief. The first leaders started to live thier personal lives with wives and from that the people of armitage and drake had to take a step of advancement, the section of armitage and drake had to move the section to a different place and vote on we leadership.

The Imperial Gangsters of armitage and drake had the business on armitage tied up in thier favor, resturants, a theator, a cleaners, and parshally a liquor lounge. These businesses were important because of the donated money handed to the people of armitage and drake. As a street gang many shootings took place, shootings against the white gangs who just didn't like the latino, and the shootings against a street gang of latinos who wanted all latins to became latin kings. But the two sections of Imperial.

Gangsters held thier ground and kept what was thier's.

A meeting took place in 1972 for the section of Armitage people to move because they were to open for target and to open for the enemy of the law. The meeting was held in the Armitage theator which was a known place of the Gangster people. During the meeting it was known that the leaders of the new section was to be Lil Mexico as president, Goyo as vice president, and the move was to be on Palmer and Drake.

Lil Bug's was considered for position, but because of his military involvment, he "Lil Bug's" didn't want position.

For positions of the Cameron people, the first leader was Spanky as president, Tito as vice president-the people of Cameron had a change in leadership after a year or two, and the leadership was in one man known as; Godfather, he was the president and instead of a vice president, or war chief, the people of Cameron had thier "main" people. People like; Tiny, Casanova, Jauquin, Mr. Doc, M.D.Ron, Cisco, "secret squarral James", Caveman R.I.P., Lil man, Alberto, Tomo, Modesto, Fingers, Lil Joe, and Miguel "Chulito", White Boy.

The Cameron people had a section of future's who were; Sinbad, Cat, Milton Juni, Speedy, Armondo "Chico", and moreno, Moreno with his aggressive style and attitude became one of the main people and participated in the Gangster Nation with his life. A credit to the future's for being young and having the heart of survival.

With Cameron being the back bone to the Nation of Gangster's and with Armitage people having thier money businesses, more sections were formed, as Palmer and Drake became larger, a section of people came about, being the Sawyer and Armitage people, stemming from the help of people like- Lil Bug's and Lil Mexico, as for other factions of Gangster's, there were- Continental Gangsters- originated by the minister, Ghetto Gangsters originated by Mijo and the newest section of Imperial Spanish Gangster's on North & Hamlin.

Two brother's by the name of Smokey and Ellio are the ones who came up with the name Gangster's. The Supreme Gangster's, turned into the Imperial Gangster's.

There were always the lady Gangster's to each section, ladies being mostly latin and dedicated in our ways; ladies like; Morena R.I.P., Miss Lee R.I.P., Flac, Goofie, Bozo,

Jeanie, Liz, Luz, Anita, Chiqueta, Happy, Smiley, Troubles, Peanut, Tita Maria, Elsa, Patty, Cateyes, Mary, GiGi, Herliena and Gym shoes. These ladies being a important part in our life, being mother to our peoples children and mostly by getting bonds together for thos who found themselves in jail.

As jail became part of the Nations life it brang about different ideas and made the members of the Nation smarter with sophisticated acts instead of openly-where jail was the next step.

Jumping to the year of 1976, this was the year the Imperial Spanish Gangsters had thier share of dealing with the law, until 1976 members were going in jail and finding it hard to get out, so the next thing to do was deal with the jail system because there were more Gangster's coming in jail then leaving the jail. In the jails the people of the Imperial Spanish Gangster's found other allies that they've dealt with on the street, by allies I speak of; Maniac Latin Disciple's, Satans Disciple's, Latin Eagle's, Spanish Cobra's, O-A;S, Milwalkee Kings and the Y.L.O. DISCIPLE'S.

In the jail wa've found the enemy still existed so a merge was constructed and these Nations became silently united in the struggles of the jail, we found ourselves fighting just to go to court in peace, to be able to get the proper share of food, or because of what you belonged too and to survive in jail as a whole was a duty you had to plan, there were only a hand full of people; Vic, M.D.R., Sach-Mo, Pito, Moreno, Bad-Boy, Aggie, Slim-D, Beaver, Mustang, Killer and Lucky plus Chino. We were never able to put our guard down against the whole system and the only people who could be trusted was these members of the silently put together Nation.

After years of seperation from these people because of convictions and seperated joints the silent Nation was at a stand still, but during the past year steps have been taken to unite and foundate all the Nations under one main title, never to forget your originating people, and instead of all the different titles and beliefs, a structure was set up by leaders of these Nations for all the people to understand one way in one belief as a whole. In this one way we all have to follow a pattern to survive, to prosper in our growth, and to set forth a accomplishing goal.

We as a Nation have to have morals, to teach our young in every subject, to abide by our set of laws, to carry our Nations oath in our heart, to accept our prayer for our desceased and accept our constitution to keep our "Families" and "Nation" in a state of peace and well being.

-- Constantly in Thought --

Always a special tribute to our ladies,
and to our families for putting up with
our chaotic ways, to all the people who
have suffered in making our Nation possible, all the goods and bads we've dealt
with and we still live. My special love
too two aggressive brothers of the Nation.

Moreno-- and TopCat.

(16)

MOTTO OF S.G.D.N.

Motto being a structure of words to express ones beliefs, ones conduct; a phrase suitable to it's character;

> "Our deeds will travel with us from afar, and what we have been, makes us what we are".

****

IDEOLOGY OF S.G.D.N.

: INGREDIENTS :

1. LOYALTY

2. SECURITY

3. PROGRESS

****

GOALS

1. Freedom for our confined brother's

2. Enbetterment of our people, and our children.

3. Unity-North and South - Harmony within the Latino Barrios.

(17)

LOVING MEMORIES OF OUR BROTHER'S & SISTER'S

:   Please, with a powerful unseen faith, with a meaningful trust and for the sake of loving memory, let us combine our hearts in a true moment of silence for our Brother's & Sister's who have lost thier lives in being part of our Nation's struggle...

:   A mere moment is vaguely enough to show tribute for the feelings we have. With this dedicated thought to you of our desceased, we will carry you in our hearts for the peace we have had in our daily lives...

:   We feel you through music we hear, we feel you through things we see, we feel you through our conversations, and most of all we have a hold on each other's heart...

:   At times we have a picture in our hand, at times we have a vision in our mind, and at this time we praise what you be rested in your peace...

: In Loving Memory
of our's who --:
REST IN PEACE

(18)

GLOSSARY

A's

1.) Accomodate - To make fit or suitable, adapt.

2.) Accordance - Agreement, conformity.

3.) Affiliate - To connect closely often as a member, branch, or associate.

4.) Allegience - Devotion or loyalty to a person, group, or cause.

5.) Alleviate - To remove or correct in part.

6.) Ambassador - An authorized representative of the government.

7.) Appraisals - The value so determined.

8.) Aspects - A particular status or phrase in which something appears of may be regarded.

9.) Asset - Advantage, recourse.
****

C's

1.) Compensate - To be equivalent to in return to.

2.) Composite - Made up of distinct parts or elements.

3.) Comrade - An intimate friend or associate.

4.) Concise - Marked by compactness of expression or statement.

5.) Convey - To impart or communicate or serve as a means of poparting or communicating.

6.) Coordinate - To bring into a common action, movement, or condition.

7.) Creed - A set of guiding principals or beliefs. Of a certain racial background.
****

D's

1.) Descendants - Proceeding from an ancestor or source.

2.) Disciples - A pupil or follower who accepts and helps to spread his master's teachings.

3.) Distinguished - To recognize one thing from other things.

4.) Domestic Tranquillity - Of or relating to the family, having no agitation free from problem.
****

E's

1.) Endorsed - To give one's support. Express approval of.

2.) Essential - Important in the highest degree.

3.) Explicit - So clear in statement that there is no doubt about the meaning.
****

G's

1.) Goals - The end toward which effort is directed.

2.) Govenor - An official elected or appointed to act as ruler. Chief executive.

3.) Lt. Govenor - An officer empowered to act for a higher official.
****

H's

1.) Heritic - Ways of the forfather.

2.) Honor - A keen sense of ethical conduct. Integrity, "respectful reputation".
****

I's

1.) Ideology - A manner or the conduct of thinking characteristic of an individual, group, or culture.

2.) Impose - Exploiting a relationship.

3.) Initiative - An introductory step or movement.

4.) Insignia - Something distinguishing, mark - emblem-badge - etc. "In our cause the Spanish cross".

5.) Insubordination - Un willing to submit to authority, disobedient.
****

L's

1.) Lax - Slack, loose - to open. Not being strict or stringent. (Rigid)

2.) Loyalty - Faithful to a cause or ideal.
****

M's

1.) Member - One of the individuals or units belonging to or forming part of a group or organization.

2.) Moral - Expressing or teaching a conception of right behavior. Moral conduct. Teaching's or beliefs.

3.) Motto - A sentence, phrase, or words to express one's beliefs.
****

O's

1.) Oath - A solmen appeal to some revered person or cause to bear witness to the truth of one's word or having sacredness in one's promise.

2.) Obtain - To gain or attain by planning or offer's.
****

P's

1.) Parable - A short simple story illustrating a moral or truth.

2.) Potential - Something that can develop or become actual. Possible -

3.) Poverty - The state of being poor.

4.) Preamble - An introductory statement.

5.) Prophet - An effective or leading spokesmen for a cause, doctring, or group. Teacher-
****

R's

1.) Righteous - Acting rightly: upright.
****

S's

1.) Solemn - Done or made seriously and thoughtfuly. Sacred -

2.) Status - Condition, situation.

3.) Structure - Something constructed, a definite pattern of organization.
****

T's

1.) Transgression - Violation of a law, command, or duty.
****

U's

1.) Unification - The state of being unified.
****

V's

1.) Vaguely - Not felt, grasped, or not enough.

2.) Viceroy - An official in government who rules as the representative of the chief executive. "In our cause - an underBoss of the executive".
****

W's

1.) Wreath - ('R_th) - Something intertwined into a circular shape: Garland, chaplet.

CONSTITUTION OF THE VICE LORDS

Amalgamated Order Of Lordism
Lah Via Va Va Illilaha Halaliil, Allah Akbun
Supreme Chief, Al-Ugdah

Salutations my brothers I greet you in the name of V/L, With dedications to V/L, And sincerity of V/L. My brothers I greet you under the master sign.

This literature is a revelation of the nature of V/L, It's principals and its superiority.

It is manifested at this time to steer this nation to its proper course and to unify V/L the world over into and Amalgamated Order Of V/L dedicated to V/L's and Lordism.

There also is another reason for the manifestation of this revelation. there is a demonstration in our midst that has confused, misled and divided V/L's. This demonstration is called the (L.O.I. Lords Of Islam Nation. V/L's have been led to believe that this is the literature and or law of the V/L's. IT IS NOT! The Supreme Chief Of V/L's is Al-Ugdag, And he has not order or give consent to V/L's being govern by the dictate of L.O.I. Every true V/L is a V/L by choice. The V/L Nation is comprised of various branches of V/L's, This has always been and will be. Every V/L has personalize roots in any particular branch and those will not be uprooted. So awaken brothers and remember from whence you came that loi is not V/L. It is a chartered motorcycle club with bylaws and laws of already set stipulations. Law governs all events. Justice is Supreme.

We leave you as we came, In Peace, In Love, and in Lordism. As the wind shall blow the whole world shall know we come as we are, We are as we come, In the name of Almighty most glorious V/L.

Behold the truth and the Law Nov, 17, 1989 Chief Al-Ugdah.....

Why we chose the name Amalgamated Order Of Lordism because we as V/L's are a diverse people, Meaning we are people with a choice, And are autonomous in our same representations of Lordism. We have different precinct preference, And yet the same principals, And Concept. These precincts, And autonomous in nature, And in essence for us the core of versatility, Such fundamentals sameness, And different are the ingredients necessary for the continuity, development, And prosperity of the Amalgamated Order Of Lordism. Question; Is that a contradiction?

Answer;NO!

Explanation; That sameness that we experience together that we are all expressing and practicing, And living Lordism as true V/L'.

The difference is that we all belong to different precincts, Our Unifying, Common Denominator is summed up in one word, Amalgamated; Draw Brothers, Amag means that we are a conglomeration of people, A family. For clarification. (And elaboration see key 14 of keys to the throne of power).

Lah Via Va Va Illilaha Halaiil, Allah Akur.....

Amalgamated Order Of Lordism.....
Supreme Chief, Al Ugdah.....
Chair of Command.....

Supreme Chief King Of Kings.....

The Supreme Chief holds the reigns of the nation in his hands. He has the power, And the authority to delegate responsibility and make law to and for all representatives of V/L. His decree shall keep the nation moving in an organize and constructive manor down the golden path of Lordism. He was, Is, And will be the choice of the consensus of the kings of V/L's, And in effect is the king of kings of V/L's, And the precepts, Of V/L's, And in effect is the king of kings is V/L. The precepts, Policies, And laws set down by his administration are absolute. The Supreme Chief does not indulge in precinct policies, He allows all precinct to be autonomous, Thus self govern. (Note: The price to appeasing certain people is total subjugation). I'm determine not to setup to any level that will compromise my manhood, Or principals in any shape fashion Or form. I will never become subservient to the wills, And expectations of others especially when such projections conflict with my own.

Prince Of The Nation.....

This brother is second only to Supreme Chief, He is to be held in high regards. In the event of Unforeseen absence of the Supreme Chief, The Prince is responsible for keeping the nation on the golden path, And is to keep a line of communications open with the Supreme Chief, And other Kings. In the event of death of this Supreme Chief (may Allah forbid) the Kings of V/L will convene to reestablish a King of Kings, And a Prince from the Amalgamated Order from their own ranks, The selections of the Nation Prince is manifested in the same fashion as the Supreme Chief (King Of Kings), Is selected, By the panel of Kings.

Minister Of Justice.....

He is to be both respected, And honored by all representatives of V/L. His functions is to make sure orders and laws directed by Supreme Chief are put into manifestation in an orderly, Prompt, Effectively fashion, He is also to advise the Supreme Chief as to the need of modification, Amending of any existence of oppose laws. He is also responsible for balancing justice within our nation, And making sure that the law and principal are adhered to.

Kings Of Nation.....

These individuals are few. They are the distinct leaders of precinct. Kings of each precincts have universal appeal, And influences, And are to be respected and honored by all precincts, And all V/L's period. In the history of V/L every branch (Precinct) head has been traditionally recognized and respected as kings. This tradition will continue to be in effect.

Universal Elites.....

In the not to distant pass, Without the express consent or authorization of the Supreme Chief, Universal Elite were appointed. That practice as is of now terminated! The Supreme Chief alone has this authority. Recommendation for brothers to be appointed will be accepted from any king, Universal status, And some circumstances from representative. All existing Universal Elites will continue to be honored, And carried in highest regard by the Supreme Chief, And all representatives of the Amalgamated Order Of Lordism, That status, Contributions, And sincerity to V/L is reviewed by the Supreme Chief, And or whomever he may appoint to an elite review committee, Which such committee will be establish in the near future, And will consist of representatives from each precinct.

Ambassador.....

The brothers, Or sisters that are blessed with the position of Ambassador have a great responsibility to undertake. They act as missionary. They are to propagate, And promote Lordism in any area designed which lack organizational structure. They will spread. And correctly expound on the way of life as V/L. And Ambassador is appointed by the Supreme Chief, And is to inform him weekly of the progress, Problem, Needs, Ect., Of the designated area which he/she has been sent. And Ambassador has Universal appeal, And require a Universal star upon his/her appointment. (Note: Kings of precincts can appoint precinct ambassadors at there own discretion., However, They will not be a Universal nature but are to be respected by all representatives.

Minister Of Command.....

These brothers will be chosen by the kings of there respected branches. There function are to insure that Laws, Orders, And directed issue by the Supreme Chief, By way of the minister Of Justice, Or issued by there respected Kings, Are being adhere to in there respected precincts. It is there responsibility to communicate with the Minister Of Justice to insure that they have the proper understanding of the letter spirit of any Laws, Orders, or directives of the Supreme Chief. They also serve as sounding post for there administration as to any difficulty do to circumstances, Or environment surrounding any particular precincts regarding effective manifestation of Laws, Orders, Or directives. (Note: In the past there has been manifestation, And demonstration of abusiveness).

(Due to display of ignorance from one Lordself to another who apparently lacks the knowledge that one branch part, Or precinct constitute in nature one nation whole. The continuity, And self reliance dictate that we adopt this new measure of identity once referred to as branches, And now precincts. This has a two fold affect. One, being the inextricable ties of precinct, And to All precincts inherently, An intrinsic relationship with the Amalgamated Order Of Lordism, So in this literature from here out branches are referred to, And indeed are precincts.

Precincts Elite.....

These brothers are to be respected, Honored, And carried high by all representatives, As it there due, And our nature. A Precinct Elite authority is to be restricted to his particular precinct, And his appointment is left to the discretion of the king of his precinct. Precinct Elite may require stars based on having a particular number of representatives in his following, And or, Meritoriously. His functions include assuring the overall effectiveness of his particular precinct, And can be viewed as a trouble shooter for his precinct.

Lieutenant.....

Appointment of Lieutenant is left to the discretion of the respective administration of each precinct. Its function is also left to the same discretion.

Minister of Literature.....

This position is a very essential position in our nation. The brother holding this position in any precinct must be respectful as well as respected at all times. His functions include teaching of the Amalgamated Order Of Lordism literature As well as any precinct literature, To his brothers, And making sure that they know the meaning behind the words. He would also help representatives to acknowledge and understand there spiritual selves.

(Note: In the past their has been disrespect from one precinct to another under the Amalgamated Order Of Lordism, Such display, Reflection, Or infractions will no longer be intolerated justice is the call today, And in this event justice will be swift).

(Note: All Universals appointed will move under the sign of the Amalgamated Order Of Lordism. Although they still have there precinct roots in there heart, As they should be, But there promotions of Lordism will encompass the totality Of Lordism. Such expression must be express thru the Amalgamated Order Of Lordism to insure proper adherence, Unity, And Respect.

Summation.....

This Chair Of Command is a structure that is in the tradition of V/L. Time, As circumstances as time dictate change. As we move into the 90's we have the opportunity to realize past mistakes, That we now put them behind us as we travel on the golden path. Gone are the days of many chief, And few indians, Gone are the days of fractured Unity, Gone of the days of selfish motives. With the strength of lions and wills of ants we will move forward for a better tomorrow for every V/L present, And future. Every V/L has a moral, And Lordly obligations to work both within, And outside of this nation to bring about a nation of V/L truth. Every position of leadership whether of a Universal Nature, Or a precinct Nature is to be honored, And Respected. We must, And will work together for the common good of all, For only together are we a nation, Lord to Lord, Precinct, And all into the Amalgamated Order Of Lordism.

Lah Via Va Va Illilaha.....
Amalgamated Order Of Lordism.......

Code Of Conduct.....

(A)   Respect: This is a very essential ingredient of a V/L character. Every V/L will at all times give proper respect to every representative in our organization, And to representatives of other organizations. We will demand by conduct, Character, Demeanor, Actions, Deeds, Respect in return. We will always give respect to persons who are not representatives of any organization also. Disrespect is a very serious violation of the principals of law of our Amalgamated Order, And will be judge according. Therefore it will not be tolerated.

(B)   Discipline: Discipline has a multiple faceted character. It must, And will be maintain in all it aspects for the successful function of the nation. Discipline does not only entail efficiency in following orders. Representatives must also be discipline mentally as well as spiritually. Lack of discipline in any area could very easily be detrimentally to a representative, "Other Representatives" Or the whole nation as a whole. For those reasons one understands discipline is of the utmost importance. Every order you receive pertaining to nation business has a specific reason, And will not question unless a representative does not understand the specific order being given, failure to be a discipline representative will result in discipline actions that will be taken.

(C)   Meetings: General meetings of the Amalgamated Order Of Lordism are held for the purpose of the nation business, And will be conducted accordingly. During all meetings the highest ranking representative will be first to start business of the meeting, (Unless someone else has been designed for that purpose). That representative will be followed by administration representative if they have input at that time. Then each representative will be given the opportunity to speak about matters in relation to those being discussed at that time. When any representative is speaking at meetings all other representatives will be quite, And Attentive, Failure to do so constitute disrespect and will result in immediate disciplinary action. Any problem relating to any particular precinct will be discussed once the business of the nation as a whole is resolved every one will uphold the character, And demeanor of V/L while meetings are in progress.

(D)   Fighting: While it is the unspoken obligation of every V/L to defend himself and every other V/L to the extent of giving his life if necessary, No representative of the Amalgamated Order Of Lordism will place his or herself or other representative in any situation where he is needlessly involve in fights over trivia matters. If any V/L is attacked it is the sworn duty of every V/L to overcome his or her attacker by whatever means is necessary. If any representative regardless to his or her authority within the nation, take it upon themselves to fight with another representative it is a violation of all our laws of the Amalgamated Order of Lordism, And will be addressed immediately. Therefore no representative of the Amalgamated order Of Lordism will ever fight with another representative unless authorized by someone with the authority to do so.

Amalgamated Order Of Lordism
Lah Via Va Va Illilaha Halaliil, Allah Akbun
Supreme Chief, Al-Ugdah

Dues.....

It is understood that every organization in existence needs a financial foundation in order to sustain itself, Our organization is no exception. There is an economic program establish for the Amalgamated Order Of Lordism, However it will not be manifested at this time. Interim representation of the order are to continue with the existing program relating to dues that are establish in there respected precinct.

Lah Via Va Va Illilaha Halaliil.....
Amalgamated Order of Lordism.....

Rules and Laws.....

(1)   Each and every representative of the Amalgamated Order Of Lordism will be aware of, An Knowledge of these precise Chain Of Command. (Supreme Chief, Prince Of The Nation, Minister Justice, Kings, Universal Elites, Ambassador, Minister Of Command, Precinct Elite, Lieutenant, And Minister of Literature.)

(2)   Every member of the Amalgamated Order Of Lordism will at all times maintain him or herself within the Code Of Conduct Chain Of Command, And the Principals of law in the highest manor. In the past representatives have failed to honor parts of the code, The change, And the laws due both to ignorance, And lack of enforcement. These laws and bylaws of the Amalgamated Order Of Lordism Will be enforce, And adhered to.

(3)   It is the responsibility of the kings of each precinct to revise a plan within there precinct to keep and accurate account, And are census of the representatives and elites in his precinct.

(4)(5) The king of each precinct must have a way of communication with each other, As well as with the Supreme Chief and the Minister Of Justice. This is to assure readiness, And the alertness in the event that assistance is needed in another precinct. If not directed by the Supreme Chief, Prince, Or the Minister Justice, The Kings of the Precinct involve are the only ones that have the authority to call on another precinct and its representatives for assistance. No representatives can take it upon him or herself to deal with a problem that arises. He or she shall always use the proper chain with in his of her precinct. Taking things in your hands is taking the chance of making a bigger problem, And is out of accord with the chain.

(6)   All precinct problems and altercations will stay within the precinct. No representative will ever take a from one precinct to another. Pertaining to the Amalgamated Order Of Lordism, Unless the problem in that particular precinct cannot be handle in that precinct due to extenuating circumstances.

(7)   Representatives of the Amalgamated Order of Lordism will be nobly respected because as V/L's we demand respect by our actions, And deeds and give respect in the same matter as we demand it. Representatives disrespecting each other will not be tolerated.

(8)   Every representative upon given the laws, And Principals of the Amalgamated Order Of Lordism will never stray from this principals that we stand by, And die for. The guidelines established thru out our Laws, Principals will be strictly adhered to by all representatives.

(9)   All representatives are expected, And encouraged to strive for self development this include but it is not limited to acquiring high school diploma or its equivalence,

College Course, Vocational training, And especially the study of Laws, And Principals of Lordism.

(10) Upon attending Religious services or nation meetings all drugs, And alcoholic beverages will be left outside the particular place. Everyone will carry themselves respectfully, And orderly at these function. Because we need not promote anything but the higherself, And to be in the right frame of mind.

(11) No V/L should ever overlook our main purpose, Which is to be a organization thru out these times, Our objective is to be sincere about what we believe in, And what we will die for. We aim to show the world what we stand on, And that is Lordism.

(12) If a representative fail to realize to meet the high standard of V/L by continuing expression of the lowerself thru continuing misuse of our divine principals, And concept, It will be incumbent on the kings of the particular precinct (Or his representative) to make the decisions as to whether that representative should be placed on hold, Or worse. We have no time for individuals who threatening to stunt our growth.

(13) As a representative of the Amalgamated Order Of Lordism we will continually seek solutions for the betterment of all our people.

(14) As a representative of the Amalgamated Order Of Lordism we must learn to live with and respect other representatives, Including those before us who paved the way for us to walk the golden path of righteous. We must also learn to with, And respect other representatives life principals, And Religious denomination, Even if they defer from our own.

(15) We the representatives of the Amalgamated Order Of Lordism should not worry about possing threat to each other person prestige, But should concentrate our united effort, And thoughts upon solving the hurt, And injustice done daily to our representatives, And our Nation as a whole.

(16) We as representatives must understand, And highly respect that instead of arrogance that will be humility among each other, As oppose to being drunk with power, There will be stronger realization to serve our nation in the spirit of Lordism.

(17) Representatives of the Amalgamated Order Of Lordism will be guided by tenants of morality, And the divine principals of love that governs Lordism, And will show the world that we are Lords of the world.

(18) All representatives of the Amalgamated Order Of Lordism will be fair, Straight Forward, And Honest in his dealings. He or she at all times uphold the truth, And justice, Even at the cost of his or her life.

(19) We of the Amalgamated Order Of Lordism will accent our youth. The young seeds essential. They can, And should provide New Ideas, New Methods, And New approaches. Your representative following the truthful teaching of Lordism that have potentials to be in any position to benefit the nation will not be overlook because of there youth.

(20) Every representative of the order will be conscious of there appearance at all times, And will always appear neat and clean.

(21) Every representative should make it his her sworn duty to uphold the Laws, And Principals of Lordism wherever they may be where other representatives are present.

(22) If at anytime a representative of the Amalgamated Order Of Lordism wishes to remove his or herself from the nation it will be upon the king of that particular precinct or (His Representatives) to grant the request of the representatives.

Note: We are not making anyone by force be a part of the Amalgamated Order Of Lordism. We became V/L's by choice, And the choice is ours.

Principals Of Laws.....

(1) I as a representative of the A/V/L/N swear with my life never to dishonor our most high Chief, All appointed of the A/V/L/N.

(2) I as a representative of the A/V/L/N will teach our people, Protect our people, Love our people, And if is the will of Allah die for our people, So that one day they will walk the golden path of V/L as free people, As productive people progressing in the love of V/L, The knowledge of V/L, Wisdom of V/L, Understanding of V/L, And the future of V/L.

(3) I as a representative of the A/V/L/N will never go astray from the truthful teachings of our most wise, And beloved high Chief.

(4) I as a representative of the A/V/L/N will help my people with any problem that they may have, Be it mentally, Or Physically, For there problems are my problems and my problems are there problems.

(5) I as a representative of the A/V/L/N will never take word of another before that of any representative of the V/L Nation without placing the burden of proof on there accusers.

(6) I as a representative of the A/V/L/N swear with my life never to put anything or anyone before most high and beloved Chief, Any appointed Chief, Or any representative of the V/L nation.

(7) I as a representative of the A/V/L/N swear that I will never deny any V/L Materially, Apiritualy, Mentally, Financially or Physically, My help under any circumstances at all or be denied.

(8) I as a representative of the A/V/L/N swear with my life that I will never lie on any representative of the A/V/L/N or V/L from another precinct or take anything from any representative of the A/V/L/N. I swear by my life to live by these laws under any circumstances.

Flag: The flag is the national identification for any nation of people. It is what the people represent and live for. This flag is a symbol of the entire order of the Amalgamated Order Of Lordism and consist of the following:

(1) Circle: The circle means 360 degrees of knowledge and what was will always will be, That Black people once ruled the world and will once again rule.

(2)   Fire: The circle is surrounded by fire. The fire means and represent our nation true knowledge of themselves as being suppressed. The flame prevent our reaching 360 degree of knowledge because of the heat (Rome or Europeans).

(3)   Darkness: Inside the circle is darkness (Jet Black) and represents that universaly Black people are a majority of people, Not a minority.

Note: If we were not brainwashed into thinking that we are different from other Blacks around the world, We would have a population of over 700 Million! There are 400 Million Blacks in mother land (Africa) alone, The darkness that we have been kept in so long.

(4)   Moons: Inside the darkness are (Two) crescent moons. They represents the splitting of one nation into two. One in the east (Asia And Africa) and the other in west our nation. They also represents entity of the male and female factor.

The Flag: When these two moons come together they represent the marriage between the Lord and his Lady a union which is mandatory if we are to acquire 360 degrees of pure Knowledge, Wisdom, And Understanding.

(5)   Star: Also in this darkness is a golden star. This is the eye of Allah keeping watch over his people, A just and justice seeking people.

(6)   Pyramid and Triangle; The darkness also engulfed the Pyramid Triangle which is our strength. It is the phenomena that puzzle the white world today. There is still no knowledge of Pyramids building today, Even with all this technology of the white man's world, This society cannot even begin to build or understand how to build the Pyramid., Yet the pyramid was build by Black people many centuries ago. We V/L's are sheltered by this pyramid of strength, Until we are able to cleanse our minds. There are three aspects to the formation of the might puzzling pyramid. The are Physical, Mental, And Spirit. He must decide now how we want to live. Are we going to let our physical cravings take control of our minds? Or are we going to control our bodies as it is suppose to be? As V/L's, We have one choice.

(7)   Sun: Inside the pyramid is the sun. This represents the raising truth in our nation. Once our minds have gained control over our physical body, We will then think as men and be able to understand and to respect one another life position. Then we can move men (One in a righteousness direction_ We, Like all Black people who are living within the shelter of the pyramid and under the watchful eye of Allah, Are guided down the proper path.

(8)   Hat: The Hat represents the shelter of our heads until we can get them together.

(9)   Cane: The Cane is our staff of strength. As we need the cane to help us walk when we are old, The cane represents the need for us to support one another in these trying times.

(10)   Glove: The glove represent purity., That we keep our hands clean of any acts that cause division among our people. This is also the reason for representing the way we do now. Our palms out and upward, showing each other that our hand are clean and that we mean no harm.

Lah Via Va Va Illilaha Halaliil

Supreme Chief, Al-Ugdah

A Message To My Muslim Brother.....

To my brother in Islam, I greet thy with the high sign of Love, In **Peace I come,** In tune I am. For what is Islam but Lordism, And Lordism but Islam? Each when served properly will give the people a different flavor of the same thing. "Almighty" is Allah, "Allah is Almighty."

Chocolate, Strawberry, and Vanilla is purposely design to meet the critera of the people taste, Yet the flavor doesn't subtract from the substance, Or change the ingredients that make up the ice cream. That which is righteous under any other name will turn out right.

I am as you are a true believer of Allah traveling the same pass you are own, But in a different vehicle adhering to the same law of caution.

I am the true V/L self and you are the true Muslim, But by virtue of our seeded part we are brother's under Allah's influence. We represent two establishments, Yet stand upon one stone, Our house built on the same foundations, "Brother," Islam, Or Lordism is just the umbrella we walk under, That Allah is the rainmaker, And sense we both acknowledge him we can walk in warmth, And confidence without the fear of getting drench, For our intentions are good, And our steps are righteous inclined.

Lah Via Va Va Illilaha Halaliil

The Keys Of V/L.....

(Key1)   What is Lordism?

It is a Philosophy. Ideology, And Guidelines of a chosen way of life. A lodestone made manifest through the primitive teaching of it first teacher, The Honorable "Pep Pillow," And chiseled by devoted believers from various schools of thought into a structure of today.

(Key2)   What is the philosophy of Lordism?

We believe in its authenticity in the sight of God, But we don't believe that any one person can have a monopoly on God, Or any one religion can claim Him exclusively. We believe all men are equal in the sight of God and that righteous V/L will be recipients of God's grace, The same as any other religious person regardless of their religion persuasion. The Quran says that man was put here as Vicegerents. We take that as man was put here to be V/L's in this physical world.

(Key3)   The meaning behind the name:

Vice means one having faults. (The Human Being) and being of second importance, Second only to God, God being the ruler of all the worlds and the universe and man was elected by him to his "Vice Lord" Or Vice Ruler, We see ourselves as God's highest creation, His custodians of the physical world. So whether you address yourself as a

Baptist, Christian, ect., By the definition of that which just been defined, You are still "Vice Lord" the only difference is interpretation and acceptance.

(Key4)   What is the religion of V/L?

Lordism is the religion, Yet we are not religious fanatics. The Quran and all religion books tell men to "Take the bounties of the earth" We interpret this as a sign that man should always strive to improve his life's condition. The A/V/L should strive to balance himself Physical, Mentally, Spiritual, and materially. Man seeks to promote himself in the sight of God, But also has concerns and needs here in the physical world.

(Key5)   About Religion:

A Lord is a seeker of truth and Lordism encompasses every facet of life. It acknowledge the existence of God in people and it acknowledge every person's right to communicate with him. It is a complete way of life, A life of involvement with both God and state and the belief in one true God whose proper name is (Allah) and associate no partners with him.

(Key6)   What is the Religion book of V/L?

A Lord will study any Religious book and use them selectively as reference points and guidelines as long as it will contribute to his development, But always in the frame of mind that man and not God is the author of such books. Everything in print deals with relative truth and not absolute. Absolute truth are the things that only the mind of God knows, While the relative truth are the things that the highest reason man understands them to be, But still, Of all the religious people tend to favor the Quran.

(Key7)   Why does the Lord tend to favor the Quran?

We believe that there is knowledge to be gained even from the Bible, But only after tedious process of shifting through its maze. On the other hand, Regardless of the fixation of relative truth that we automatically apply, We still find The Holy Quran the best book for our people, It corresponds with our way of thinking and supportive to our way of life, But still, we are Vice Lords and not Muslims, There exist that degree and that difference.

(Key8)   What's the difference between a Vice Lord and a Muslim since both acknowledge the Quran?

The difference is our guidelines, names, application and interpretation of faith.

(Key9)   Explain the difference a Lord and a Muslim:

Our names and Prayers, And the belief that all religious books deal with the relative and not the absolute truth. And that the righteous "Lord" will be made manifest in this physical realm of creation and we see ourselves as Allah's temple and that God exists in that temple.

(Key10) A Lord do not pray in the conventional style of a Muslim. A Lord making prayer bring his fingers to fingers, Making a pyramid over his head (A symbolic Gesture) and says, "O Allah, I seek shelter from the forces of evil and schemes and threatening plans of my enemies," And then brings his hands down to the palms up position and recites the "Al-Fatiha" The Universal Prayer.

(Key11) Greetings!

It would not subtract any degree from you if you would greet your Muslim brother as he would greet you, But when greeting one of our brothers, Greet him under the master sign of Lah Via Va Va, Illilaha Halaliil With your palms up and he should return that greeting with "Via Va Va Lah, Halaliil Illilaha.

(Key12) The meaning behind the greeting:

Lah (Love), Via (vice), Va Va (Lord), Illilaha (My Sword), Halaliil (My Shield).

(Key13) What are the master signs?

Palms up and all greets of V/L's, The flag Of V/L, The Emblem Of V/L, The Meaning of V/L, And the righteous representation, These are the master signs of V/L.

(Key14) Why the various schools of thought?

Because the A/V/L/N is symbolic to the real blood line family, It represents the highest principals of the real blood line family: Love, Truth, Peace, Freedom, Justice, Harmony, and Understanding.   As every family the Lord (Father) and the Queen (Mother) upon producing life have bestow a name of their favor upon that life, For every life they produce they honor that life with a first name for distinguishing proposes, And the child automatically inherit the last which will affirm his identity. Such is the composition of the various precincts or fractions that make up the A/V/L/N that have been granted autonomy and have form the various schools of thought according to their father, The brother of our father who share the family name.   No matter what the first name the child or parents call that child, As long as that adheres to the dictated of his parents ads accept the family name, One must remember the root of its existence is in the family.

The teachings as administered by Chief Al-Ugdah, From the unknown school of thought.

Statement Of Love...

To you my Brother, Sister, My love for you began at birth, has manifested through out our Heritage. Because of my Black skin, which is yours, My Blood and Flesh, Which is us I am you, And you are me. Our minds are for the same goal, Our effort is for the same cause, Our souls are bound by the same determination. To this nation I give my unity, And all my vitality. To you my Brother, And Sister, I give my love.

Oath.....

In the name of the almighty, I do solemnly swear, That I as a representative of the Amalgamated Order Of Lordism will not dishonor my most sacred weapon meaning Lord unity, Nor under the threat of death will I deny those that stand beside me. I as a representative of the Amalgamated Order Of Lordism will listen well to the truthful teachings of our king, And Elites. I will use my time constructively, I will become, And remain useful to my Nation, My community, And Myself as a whole. Let the Almighty God (Allah) bear witness to this oath by birth in the Spirit, And to, And thru the heart core. I come as I am, I am as I come, Almighty Vice Lord. Lord love means I have a undying love for this Nation, And I'll die for it. Lah Via Va Va, Illilaha Halaliil.

The Warning On Treason.....

Treason is a act by no less than a life of misery. The nature of such punishment constitute by its very nature one of two extremes. The above prescription is in order when circumstances, And events dictates (So as not to jeopardize the life, Or freedom of the righteous) That we spare the most serious extreme out of consideration. And preservation for our most truest, And righteous representative. Under no circumstances will treason Or disrespect be tolerated against the crown. The crown represents the embodies of V/L world wide. This is true regardless to which king sit on the crown. The crown is the glorious representation of the V/L. Speak on it with unrighteous intent, And you speak against the nation whole. Pain will come to you as a consequence of speaking on the crown with indignation. Scheme clandestinely against it, And such scheme will be made manifest at your own expense.

The crown has the resiliency of the people support. Those who will be in grievous error head this warning. There is a boomerang around the crown. Test it at your own risk. Lah Via Va Va Illilaha Halaliil.

Knowledge Of V/L Existence.....

Let our enemies take heed to these words, we shall pay any price for V/L, Bear any burden for V/L, Meet any hardship for V/L, And support and friend for V/L, Condemn any person that tries to upset the tranquility of V/L, To assure the survival, And success of this Nation.

Faith Of V/L.....

I am a V/L, In my possession I take pride, But without vain glory. To it I owe solemn obligations that I am eager to fulfill. As a V/L I will participate in none but honest enterprise. To him that has engage my service as soldier or warrior, I will give the utter most of perfection and fidelity. When needed my skills and knowledge they will be given without reservations for the (Nation) good. From special capacity springs obligations to use it well in the service of humanity, And I accept the challenge that this implies jealousy of the high repute of my callings, I will strive to protect the entrance and good name of any V/L that I know to be deserving, But I will not shrink should duty dictate from disclosing the truth regardless anyone that unscrupulous act has shown himself unworthy of the profession. Since the age of stone human progress has never been condition by the genius of my professional forebearers by them have been rendered usable to mankind nature resources of the material and energy. By them have been vitalize, And turn to practical account of principals, Science, And Revelations of technology. Accept this heritage of accumulate experience, My Efforts will feeble, I dedicate myself to dissemination of Lordism knowledge, And especially to the instructions of younger members of my profession in all is art and tradition. To my Lord brother I pledge in the same full measure I acts of them, And interpreted, Dignify

of our profession. With the consciousness always that our special expertise carries with it the obligation to serve humanity with Lords. I am proud to live, This place, And love V/L with the highest Devotion, Loyalty, And Honor.

Lordism In Focus.....

The Amalgamated Order Of Lordism is built on the laws and principals that govern everyday activities, And life of V/L. If followed properly these laws, And principals will guide our people on a path which is straight, And progressive. These codes of law is based on external principals of righteousness, And Fair Dealings, Sobriety, Cleanliness, Helpfulness, And Honesty to one another, Yet shaped into concrete form suites, And circumstances. Our goals are to abolish blood feuds, Help the weak, And the need, And harness wrong doing. Lordism is design to appeal our intellect so that we'll be able to make the best of our lives. We must not waste, Nor misuse our life for individually and indeed together we have a lot to offer. Lordism is more than just a religion of faith. It is the sewing together of knowledge, And logic, This a cooperative expression, A fraternal order which allows men as Lords of various religions the nominations to come together and the common denomination of Lordism, Thus enjoy true meaning of Lords.

Putting It In Perspective.....

We the members of the Amalgamated Order Of Lordism will continue to represent our beloved nation with Sincerity, Love, Commitment. Those who are pure in heart will no doubt be overcome by the common enemy which is rome. We as members of the Amalgamated Order Of Lordism will devote our time, Energy, And resources to advance, And uplift not only our nation, But all poor, And oppressed people with in our reach. We of the Amalgamated Order Of Lordism will greet, And honor each representative with greetings of the master sign, Not with the sign of our precinct. This is to identify with the fraternity of which we belong, And the cause that we all share. This greeting signify the meaning of poor nature, And is automatically a sign of our love, One together will cause nor show division among the members of the Amalgamated Order Of Lordism. We take not our oath to practice deceptions among ourselves, Nor should we attempt to promote discord. Time thru the ages bear's witness that nothing remains but faith, Good Deeds, And the teachings of Truth, Patience, And continuity. Do not slip off the golden path of Lordism my beloved brother, And for sure do not cause another brother foot to slip, You surely will experience the consequences of having rendered men from the path of God, And a mighty wraith will descend on you.

The Movement Mandates.....

We are under obligation to our nation, Our Supreme Chief, Our Elites and all the righteous representative, Of the master sign. We encourage our Elites, For its through their support for our Supreme Chief that our Supreme Chief is able to reach out, And grow it into us, And we into him, And together into the movement. But most of all we encourage ourselves, For we are the soldiers of growing nation, We are the architect for a better tommorrow. For we through our dedication, And total commitment shall build out of nothing, Something of great apprizal. We shall take an old nation and make a new movement dedicated to upliftment of our people. We shall take the name of the Amalgamated Order Of Lordism and like the world take seasons, And nature leaves her mark on man, We shall leave ours on the world.

Steps To Live By.....

In the name of the Almighty. I greet thy, All of you with the honorable thump of the thumping V across my chest. And with palms.

Greetings Righteous Seed.....

I want to spend some time on a paramount importance "What do we, You and I do as members of A/V/L/N? First, Or more directly, You must at one time or another ask yourself this question. What do I do now that I am V/L? As Ruler, Protector, And Teacher of the people, We have a really profound test ahead of us. One that cannot be viewed as being easy. How do you let other people know the beauty of your dreams of a new nation? How do you teach people, Reeducate the people to the philosophy of Lordism? Simple "By your example, By your reflective character. You my brothers and sisters are manifestations of V/L. If you profess to be about all its sublime beauties and grace, Then live it," There should never be any defamation of the V/L character. There will be acceptance and forgiveness for your fault and error. These can be corrected and improved upon. However willful Injury. Insults, Stealth, Deception, and Defamation of the V/L character shall not be condoned or tolerated. It will result in Fines, Restrictions, Or Expulsion. Your image should always be one of Love, Dedication, And Sincerity. The golden beam of Lordism should always Radiate, And Reflect from the glow of your presence. That will be the true indication of your sincere and pronounce devotion and dedications to the reconstruction of t his V/L Nation. Your conduct should be one that is full of confidence but yet not arrogance, "Respectful and yet not ostracizing. We should be on top of our knowledge, Sounding our knowledge, But not to the point that we talk to people. We are rulers, Protectors and Teachers of the people. Thus, We must be able to reach those that we need to tach and raise up to a level of awareness. We can b certain that we will have a very difficult time if we take on the air of better that thou. How many people at all times and among all nations close there heart to any distinction of knowledge or spiritual influence because of some little fragment which they have got and which they think is the whole of God's truth? Such an attitude shows really want of faith and a blasphemous limitations of Gods unlimited spiritual gift to his creatures. (Commentary 92 H.Q.).j

The times are over where we don't have to prove anything to anyone. The great fact that the longevity of our existence is a sign that we are here to stay. We have survived the necessary physical aspect of our formation. We have involve into the mental stages. This development dictated the focus on Revising, And Reconstruction from point one. We have to be professional. We are talking about a securing a future for our children. About a place in the future where the proper recognition will be giving to V/L. This will never come into existence without expertise and know how. It will never materialize without mind, And the proper effort motoring it. Obviously the present system is not *at all concerned about realistic educating our children. They are still systematically destroying them. "Force Busing". That is a illusion, Why are we so short on qualified teachers? Black Teachers? Why not upgrade the school facilities? We as a people are responsible for the teaching of our children. That and itself is the answer to this illusion.

If we qualify ourselves there will be no need to bus our children anywhere. We can teach them ourselves. But first we must feel our own heads with the necessary knowledge. Or groom and cultivate our own people so that they may fill the void. Yet that they shall never reach the thresh hole of reality unless we qualify ourselves first. We're gonna have to make a few adjustments in order to qualify ourselves from a mental perspective. We must cease being old fashioned, And modernize our ideas, And way of thinking to better serve us, All of us older Lords have or are down for game. We can do that very good. Let us put as much emphasis into seriously tightening up our knowledge and applying that knowledge to our everyday life. Lets do this so that our mere presence can demand it's respect. Its time we raise from the dark and ignorance, Into the light and knowledge of who we truly are. Its time we exhaust our energy and exploit our ability by building, Not to do so will surely reflect a cripple image of V/L's? May Allah bless and protect us in our infancy, And grant us the Strength, Desire, Dedication, And Preserverance that is needed in order to build our character and thus our nation.

Trichinosis.....

All products made of pork are forbidded to representatives of the Amalgamated Order Of Lordism. The pig was put here for medicinal, And is unfit for human consumption. There is a worm know to medical science, As the trichinosis worm. Its a parasite that attacks, And infests the organ structure of pigs. Our bodies became contaminated by these poisonous parasites whenever we eat pork. Ironically, The deterioring effect it has on us is intricately masked by the staking of times, In essence creating genetics disease. People tend to under estimate the actual danger that exist in our health. Pork is synonymous to dope. Its a gun pointed in the direction of the Black community. Every time we eat pork, The trichinosis worm penetrate our intestine and muscle tissue. Once this process begin our health slowly begin to deteriorate. The affect of pork on our health is devastating. It will inedibility induce a cycle of illness, And forgetfulness. No not immediately, Nevertheless no one really escape this parasite. Hypertension is the number one killer amongst Blacks. Why? Trichinosis! Its a killer that takes its dwelling in pork. No matter what you read about curing pork, The only solution to trichinosis is abstinence. You can smoke it, Burn tar baby black, Freeze it, Ect., But trichinosis will remain in its poignant, And deadly state. The pig have no veins, If bitten by a poison snake it will just turn around, And gobble the snake up. The pig is the world filthiest animal. Its a combination of the Cat, Rat, and Dog. Examine it microscopically if you like. It has the tail of a rat, The eyes of a cat, And the snout of a dog.
Yet most people love it. Biblical scripture has Jesus casting demons into pigs, And then driving them over a cliff.

The same scripture tells us not to eat the meat of the hoofed animal. Most religious leaders fail to mention this. Jews, Muslems, Buddist, ect., All obey Gods law when it comes to abstinence from swine, That is all about the Christian World. Most Black people state out of ignorance that their Mother, Father, Grandparents, Ect., Ate swine, and lived to be Sixty, Seventy, Or even 100, But none ever ask themselves how much older they have been if they had not consumed swine. Think about that. How can you love someone on one hand, And then turn around, And feed them that metamorphic swine?

Destiny From The V/L Point Of View.....

Being V/L mean we are in control of own destiny. If we who represent the true Lordism because victims at all or conquers, We have done it in our minds and wills, Or without faulty judgement and or illusion. If a Lord permit others to exploit him in private life, Or government he chooses it, Or he has made the fatal error of acquiescence and he should be condemned. The world forgives everything except weakness and submission. Universally men have been known to take advantage of these two traits. A V/L have no fear of battle, Even if it means a Lords death. In any event death come's to all men. How you die is your own choice. The Lord know that life is full of battles, On various levels and stages, In various forms, Which by law dictate battles that take shape by various means. Fighting or Submitting out of options, There is no halfway station in between offering supplementary premium, Lordism demands that we chose the warrior choice. Some men are born free even under the adversity of unfavorable times. Even under persecution. Even in slavery. It is strictly a matter of man's spirit on whether not man is free. V/L's are free at birth, In the spirit, And thru the heart core. If not at the birth of his mother, So at the birth of his chosen nation, For is not the master teachings of Love, Truth, Peace, Freedom, And Justice? The choice is ours that we wish to be.... No one impels us or compel us.... We may delude ourselves that is so but it is not! (Quote) "The same wind which blow a ship on the rock can blow it into a safe harbor just as well.... In short it is not the wind it is the set of the sail. (Unquote) A man who denies, That is a weakling who wishes to blame others for his life. V/L you are what you are by choice, And you have given some deliberation to the parts you have played and play in life. Move with the conscious that you can affect the outcome of many things, And cause many things to happen, Realize the two degrees of involvement, The direct and the indirect shoot of it, And set yourself up to take charge of every situation possible, For you posses the keys to do so. There are consequences involve with actions, Be man enough to accept the consequences of yours. Never say you are completely blameless without chewing on the two degrees of involvement. A V/L should strive to master total control over his life. A Lord knows he must pass away from this world some day and you have no control over this. In this sense his destiny is set. But in his dealings with the world what becomes of him will depend on his own efforts and state of mind. Allah gifted man with ability.

Thus place his destiny on earth outside of pasting away from this plan of being into his own lap.

A/V/L/N "Misrepresentation".....

In advocating the principals of this organization we find that we have been very much misunderstood, And very much misrepresented by men from within our organization, As well as others from without. Any reform movement that we seeks to bring about changes for the benefit of humanity is bound to be misrepresented by those who always taking it upon themselves to administer to and lead the unfortunate, And to direct those who may be place under temporary disadvantages. It has been so in all other movements whether social or political. Hence those of us in the "A/V/L/N" who lead, Do not feel embarrassed about this MISREPRESENTATION. About this misunderstanding as far as the aims and objectives of the "A/V/L/N" is concerned. But those who has taken timely notice of this great movement seeks not to develop the good nation within the nation, But to give expression to that which is most destructive and most harmful to society and the government. We desire to remove the misunderstanding that has been created in the minds of millions of people thru out the world in there relationship to the organization. The A/V/L/N stands for the bigger brotherhood. The A/V/L/N stands for human rights, Not only for the nation of V/L's, But all Black people world wide. We ask for nothing but the rights of all V/L's. We are not seeking to destroy or disrupt the society or the government. We of the "A/V/L/N" are determined to unite all V/L's for there own Industrial. Political, Social, And Religious Emancipation. Some have said that this organization seeks to create discord and discontent among the races. Some say we are organize for the purpose of hating other people. The A/V/L/N has no such intentions. We are organize for the absolute purpose for bettering our conditions, Industrially, Economically, Religiously, And Politically.

What Are The Master Teaching?.....

The master teachings are the master teachings of Lordism. The teachings of man as V/L second only to Allah in his relationship with the world. They are the teaching that places man in charge of his/selves and the world he live in.

"On The Selves Of (Mind) Man".....

Truth and falsehood are two absolutes, Personified they represents the develop man (Minds) and the deform man (Mind) which signify the virtuous and unvirtuous state of man (Mind). Or the higher self in coexistence with the pigmy self. The self that control will depend on the feed of the man. There entire composition of the human being rotates from the axis of these two absolute. The selves of man are inextricable. Man can only subdue his lower self not separate himself from it entirely. Destractions or temptation can open the valves and allow the lower self to seep thru. The Lord Man, Lord Father, The V/L every action, Every Reflection, Every deed spring from the balcony of the mind (His Virtuous Self) Or the basement of it. (His Virtuous Self). All the selves of man (Mind) are tied to these absolutes. This axiom is universal, Each of the three dimension of V/L spin from this fundamental truth.

The Spin Off From The Selves Of Man (Mind).....

Lord Man: The Lord man is V/L in his infancy not yet developed into the maturity of the true Lord self. His is the physical manifestation of the character of keys. He have been impress by the physical aspects of the nation, But is not yet cemented in the faith do to his lack of spiritual and mental reinforcements. He is either a new representative that the teachings have not had a chance to take firm of, Or a old unrighteous deceptor that will never graduate from the caterpillar state and in fact whole appearance and representation is false. The Lord Man is in his most vulnerable stage, He will either fall to external influences and pressures and forfeit his V/L self, Allow himself to be suspended in the stagnant caterpillar state, Or open his mind and heart to the teachings and love of V/L Thus growing into a true crowning glory.

Lord Father: The Lord Father signifies a harmonious balance of the physical and mental aspect of V/L, And a growing awareness and acceptance of the spiritual nature of it. He is one mindful of his responsibilities to his family and nation, And goes about interrupted, He knows the nation is not here to infringe upon the privacy or disrupt the order of the family but enhance the quality of the family life thru its teachings. His is the image of a righteous supporter and provider. Of love, And undying determination. He is not a stranger to trials and tribulations of life, Or the external and internal pressure and influences, Still his strength and constancy is unfaltering. His strong Lord father self bears witness to the splendor of V/L.

The V/L Developed: The fully formed V/L is in the ethereal state of the selves of man. Here the character keys are all balance and being a V/L is a state of euphoria. Lordism is a unconflicting way of life for him. A natural expression and thought form. He is V/L in his weakest moment as well as his strongest, And will die a pure state of Lordism. He have elected out of faith to carry the nation high and not to let the golden light be extinguish by the dark deeds and deception clock work by those of the caterpillar persuasion, Or the other debilitating and evenly subversive forces of men. He is loyal to his brothers and sisters and will cut his own heart out before he would betray a righteous believer. He upholds and enforces the principals of laws and articles of faith. None of the selves of man can pass hie righteous manifestation of his true Lord self because he superiorly demonstrate all the selves of man. He is the true crown and glory.....He forever V/L...., Shining!!!!!

Who Are The True Believers.....

The true Lord self is the true believers. The Lord that is not self servant or pertinacious in his representation so as to gain advantages. A true believer is one that do not falsify our love. One who has unshakable Faith, Confidence, And Trust in the nation. A true Crown And Glory.

Crown And Glory.....

A believer that exemplifies good Personal Hygiene, Good Habits, Self Discipline, Strength Of Character, Pursues Knowledge, Upholds The Principals Of Laws, And the Articles Of Faith, And truly has committed the nation to heart, Is indeed a Crown And Glory to V/L.

The Glory Of The Sisterhood And Brotherhood Of V/L.....

The sisterhood to V/L's are our biggest inspiration. Every dedicated and righteous sister is available and precious gem to us. As a jewel throws forth a light that is magnified by the light of the sun, So does the V/Lady throw forth life, And sustain life, Thus light up the sole and life of V/L. The Lord is a sun unto her, Magnifying the spirit of her soul, And given warmth to her as the sun give warmth to everything under its scope. Like the sun aid the vegetation in its growth, The Lord and Lady aid the vegetation in its growth, The Lord and Lady aid each other in there needs development. For whatever struggle or endeavor they undertake, Its done with each other in mind. Thus is the glory of the sisterhood and brotherhood of V/L.

What do A/V/Lady Represents.....

She represent the diversified transition of queen woman, to queen mother, To V/Lady. A cherish his woman and think of her and refer to her as his queen, To him every V/Lady is majestic and occupy a seat on his heart throne. This three dimensional view of our vision of beautiful also symbolizes the three character keys in the human being that every believer should be striving to develop. They are Spiritual, Physical, And Mental composition of the believer. (Referral to what a righteous represent).

Different Selves Of The Vision Beautiful.....

Queer Woman..... And The First Level of Development.....

Queen Woman is V/Lady unpredictable. Her primary entrance is in a specific V/L and not necessary the master teachings. Its the first level of development that is really responsible for her coming under the master sign, Her physical attractions to a particular Lord. If by chance things don't work out for her Lord Man she may decide to fall out of tune with the master teachings. She may develop a certain amount of spiritual and mental strength but not nearly enough to maintain fer faith. However (All praise to Allah) there are those that due come into the nation under the physical and enticement of a Lord Man and gained the spiritual and mental prowess necessary to embrace the master teachings and if there relationship with there Lord Man fail they will still exalt the master teachings, For they to are the vision beautiful.

Queen Mother..... And The Second Level Of Development.....

Queen Mother symbolizes the mental aspect of the Lord Child and also there responsibilities of being a good homemaker. Although she is dutiful in the her contributions to the life and the nation transcend beyond. Queen Mother is V/L as exemplifying the highest qualities of motherhood. Her image is Love, Concern, And Devotion to the family. Here is a true portrait of strength and a good balance of the three character keys that enhance the beauty of the human being. No mistakenly her for anyone else when you see her for she to is the vision beautify.

Different Selves Of The Vision Beautiful Cont.....

Queen Lady.....And The Third Level Of Development.....

Queen Lady is V/Lady in her highest manifestation of the teaching of Lordism. Because of the high esteem V/L holds for V/Lady the noble title of queen is granted, However whether the principal is called queen or V/Lady the substance remain, Either one is still the highest tribute a Lord can pay to the vision beautiful. The spiritual level of development is attached to her because as a true V/Lady her faith is unshakable, Given her a deeper spiritual sense of God in relationship to the master teachings and how it realistically comes together. She is dedicated to the principals of laws and the articles of faith. She honestly believes in V/L and will never forsake the faith. She respects all V/L's and is jealous of none for she know they are truly her brothers. She is well adjusted Spiritual, Physical, And Mentally. She is one concerned with the development of the nation and will sacrifice the best of her efforts for it. She is the true vision beautiful!!!!!

Oh Righteous Believers Never Forget.....

The V/Lady is a confinement and good manors. She is a pillar of strength to V/L. She is most ardent advocate and supporter, A buffer making him shine. She is second only to Allah in importance but most important after Allah to V/L. She is always the lady of the house, Always second in command to V/L. She is the vision beautiful!!!!!

The Collected Forces Of The Character Keys Made Manifest.

The V/L and Lady should always strive to enhance their Spiritual, Physical, And Mental state of being to draw the maximum benefits such conditioning has to offer. The proper collective force of these once balanced can open up the doors and secrets of life and help shape the believer into that righteous and harmonious self. These keys are essential to our development for they will allow for a smooth transition into this beautiful way of life. These are the keys that offer Security, Truth, Prosperity, And True Love.

The Queen Power.....

Article 1: Queenship is the highest status a V/Lady can achieve. A number of factors must determine this course of action. Sometimes emotions dictate under the guise of rational, Often times group appeal without the full season, In Essence, Dedication, Preseverance, Cultivation, Refinement, Commitment, And a Diligent application of Faith, And efforts towards the way of V/L. Because the autonomous set of order (Precinct) there can be several queens. However only one Supreme Queen. Know one can grant such a royal title, Or suspend, revoke or rescind, Other than the crown king. It is not only a expectation of the crown, But law! And law governs all events. Alternatives or Altercations: If due to circumstances beyond the crown king control dictates so, Appointment of queenship can be decreed by his prince, Or special elected committee consisting of all his elites. Under the existence circumstances the decree will be at most temporary, And subject to the capriciousness, Whims, And judgement of the crown king. Only he can pronounce with certainty, and surety (Which translate into law) the true crowning of his queen.

Article 2: The queen may appoint who ever she pleases to office, Including, But not limited it to princess. Her system of ranking, And organization take own the same structure of her kingship. Only the crown can dictate measure of law to her. She must always be studious and loyal to the (His kingship) crown. The queen can call meetings of the sisterhood at random, Or schedule fashion. All V/Ladies are to honor, And protect there queen. They must adhere to all the Precepts, Principals, And Articles of law in the same fashion, and fortitude exhibited by there brothers. V/Ladies, You have a obligation to yourself, And your nation to be morally conscious of your Hygiene, Appearance, Grooming, Conduct, Living Conducts, And Food Consumption, As well as your vocal output. ; You should always strive to exhibit these traits, And attributes that are distinguished by Refinery, Cleanliness, Sobriety, And Dedication

Article 3: The queen power is such in scope that it encompass the whole, Or part of the Amalgamated Order. Influence: If a precinct queen, Her influence will be categorize by, And limited to her precinct. On the other hand the supreme queen influence will be pervasive, Acknowledge and respected thru out our entire order. She will be carried highly and honored always, Whether precinct, Or not, by the entire order of V/L. Conduct in her presence must be one of Protectiveness, Sobriety, And Discipline. To dishonor or disrespect her image is a descration of our faith, Its a insult, And fragment disrespect to both crowns. Honor, Respect, And Protect her always! For such is law and law governs all events!

The V/L Manifesto.....

In The Name of Allah, We the righteous people of the Amalgamated Order give honor to our king Al-Ugdah, And all pioneers, Lords Of The Amalgamated Order Of Lordism. There has been tears, Bloodshed, Trials, Tribulations, And Trauma, By the pioneers of our most beloved order, We have witness the continue surfacing, And resurgence of a dedicated Ideology, And pedigree that refuses to die. We honor Prince Dank, And all the other countless Lord pioneers. For the dedicated pioneers with there Love, Knowledge, Wisdom, And Understanding, Have given Strength, Beauty, And a sense of direction, And purpose to our people. We honor our pioneers, And may Allah blessing forever be upon them for there sacrifices have been our gain. There dedication, Understanding And Tenacity has given birth to a new breed of V/Ladies, And Lords, The engineer. The engineers who strive to make a past ideology a present reality. The engineers who strive to be righteous, And productive in accordance to the vision that the pioneer held dearly. The pioneer have given the engineers a seed to nourish. And with a Love knowledge, Wisdom, And understanding even comparable to that of the pioneers, These engineers will design and perpetuate a flourishing nation second to none!!! May Allah forever bless, And Strengthen the sisterhood, And brotherhood, And inspire them to uphold the laws, And principals of the master sign, For we realize the difficult task ahead for all.

Foremost, We give the highest praise to Allah for blessing the Amalgamated Order Of Lordism with our most beloved, And dedicated pioneers, For it is thru perseveration that we are here today representing V/L..... We give the highest to Allah from blessing the Amalgamated Order Of Lordism with support, And love of our beautiful sisterhood, For they are the Delight, Love, And glory of the V/L nation.... They, And the lord child are our most precious treasures. We give high praise to Allah for blessing the V/L nation with you. The people of the most persecuted of faith, For it is thru dedication that we prevail Vice Omnipotent, For you are the engineers! Some of the pioneers are gone, Maybe some of the engineers will stray, But we rest assured with the knowledge That V/L is here to stay!!!!!

A/V/L/N "Righteous Sons".....

Almighty Righteous Sons, Of the most High, Reflecting true Lordism is not easy, Nor is it a righteous reflection displaying unrighteous acts. V/L is not sometimes, But always. Every moment, Every hour, Every week, Every month, Every year, Every breathe we take is V/L, Every step we take is V/L, Every thought we have is V/L, And know, V/L is not easy!!!!!

But each moment of our lives we righteous lords strive toward a deeper conscience of ourselves and what we are about. Knowing who and what we are give courage to stand temptation and reflect who and what we are in our weakest moment! The righteous for those who die fighting for the cause of V/L and every fallen lord spirit in the heart of us all!

We the righteous sons of the "Almighty" will never retrogress from our righteous principals and concepts. We the righteous sons of the most highest, Will defend these "Principals and Concepts" With our lives and discipline anyone found in violation of them!

In The Name of Allah, In The Name of our most High Chief, In the name of all appointed Chiefs, In The Name of all the righteous representatives of V.L.'s, We vow to uphold these truth's!

Lah Via Va Va Illilaha

Creed of the V/L.....

We the younger generation especially must feel a scared call to that which is before us. I go out to do my little part in helping my untutored brother. We of this less favorite race realize that our future lies chiefly in our hands, And we are struggling on attempting to show knowledge can be obtain under difficulties, That neither the old time slavery, Nor continued prejudice need extinguish self respect, Crush manly ambitions, Or paralyze effort. We know that neither institution, Nor friends can make a race stand unless it has strength in its own foundation, And that racist like individuals must stand, Or fall by there own merit, And for that to fully exceed they must practice the virtues of self reliance, Self respect, Industry, Perseverance, And Economy.

The Classifying of the young seeds.....

A young seed is a new member, Or young V/L. They are referred to as young seeds because the message (seed) of faith is being planted with in the rich soil of there fertile mind.

(A) The Way.....

Young seeds you are caterpillars not yet transformed into a butterfly (The True Believer). The possibility for such a transformation, But You must put your heart, And honest efforts into this nation.

(B) The Warning.....

There are older seeds around older seeds around that have been confined to being caterpillars, They are cripples missing the righteous attributes that are necessary in order to reach the butterfly state. They will l never become a CROWN AND GLORY, They are simply Teaches just hanging on to bleed us But one day they will be examine.

(C) Treachery of the old caterpillar seed.....

The old seed that have been confined to the caterpillar stage are like stagnant water, They collect bacteria, And its unfit to drink. They will poison your mind. If you wade in there water, Weak in your faith in the first place.

(D) The personification of V/L's at its. beset.....

Study, Be for real when you fly the love. Learn to discipline yourself, Learn patience, And Understanding.   Fight against the negative influences of the unrighteous pretender, They will inevitably let there own action trip them up. They stand before a mirror, And lack the sense to know it. Don't just settle for being a caterpillar, Be a butterfly. There are degrees to everything in life even to being a V/L.....

In The Search Of The Golden Path Or Righteous.....

In the silent of the night bountiful spoke to hunger, His voice was very vibrant, And his message touched his spirit, His soul, His heart core, There was no introduction necessary for bountiful, For the golden light of knowledge was a trademark to his degree of pureness. As hunger stared intently into the eye's of bountiful, The golden rays of compassion betook bountiful. Bountiful said I am here as a sign of what can be. I have witness your affliction. Behold hunger, For I can be of great comfort to you. I bring with me a mirror of your inner most desire's, Look into me, Now what do you perceive? Hunger answered said, "I see all the things I ever wanted out of life, I see an altruistic concern for your brother man, The flying of two great flags in the iris of your eye's. I see the coming of a new nation, A new way of life. I see a strong masculinity tide and a similar femininity one, They symbolizes the coming together of a King and Queen, They also symbolizes one purpose in life. I see little children who take pride in what they are as they adjust their golden sun's upon their heads. I see a multitude of happiness, A lack of poverty. I see a very proud people, A real display of unity, Vitality, And love, Oh bountiful, How can I be as you are? Surely all of this is merely a state of mind? Bountiful Replied.

Hunger I came you in the form of inspiration you had little hope, Little direction in life, And as you are now, Little meaning, Now I'll represent myself as truly am, So open your minds eye, Look around you, For I am a Vice Lord, A new way of life, And hunger replied "You deceived me, For I knew of you," And bountiful replied "No hunger, You only deceive yourself, As in the beginning, So shall it be in the ending, Vice Lord."

Introspection.....

Yesterday I was alone in the world, A flower growing in the shadows whos existence, Life was not aware of, And who was not aware of life. But today my soul has awakened, And I beheld V/L. I rose to my feet, And rejoice in the love of V/L, The knowledge of V/L, The wisdom of V/L And the understanding of V/L. All praise unto Allah, Today I am A V/L, And may Allah the Lord And master continue to lead me in the righteous path of V/L. Yesterday the touch of the frolicsome breeze seen breeze harsh, And the sunbeams seem weak. A mist hid the face of the earth, And the waves of the ocean roared like a tempest. All praise unto Allah, I am V/L. Yesterday I look all about me, But saw nothing but my own suffering self standing by myself, Wild pandoms of darkness rose, And fail around like ravenous vultures. All praise unto ALLAH, The Lord, And master, Today I am V/L. Whenever I look I see life's secrets lying open before me. Yesterday I was soundless word in the heart of the night. Today I am a song on the lips of time. All praise unto ALLAH, The Lord, And Master, I am V/L.....

All Praise.....

All praise to the kings and Elites, Sons of the Almighty and righteous warriors and prophet of the Amalgamated Order Of Lordism. All praise to the kings and Elites, Lord of Lords, Lord the World. All praise to the kings and Elites who have died in the name of V/L. All praise to the kings and Elites who suffered thru all the enemy had and will now lead there people to victory thru the truthful teaching of Lordism. All praise to the kings and Elites, The Way, The truth, The light. And thru them comes knowledge, Wisdom, and understanding of Lordism. All praise to the kings and Elites, who teach us to love one another, To become strong in one another, And to become one in Body, And Souls, In the true meaning of V/L. All praise to the kings And Elites, Nation builders, Builders of Nation, Mighty Nations under the golden banor that lets all righteous people walk in he golden light of 360 degrees of Lordism.....All praise to the Kings and Elites of V/L.....

Allah Akbur!!!!!

Deeper Revelations.....

Allah is the ominpotent, The Almighty, Second to none first to all. He is the face of sublimity in the appearance of the creation that exhales the holy breath of life, And hale that life by recall at the point of his readiness. He is uninfluence by the plans men have for he knows the rotation of everything that move from square to circumference, That is seen, And Unseen, of jiins, And of men for all that moves does so by his consent. His body extends, And overlaps all in creations, for his is the realm of all worlds, And nothing exist beyond him in any state, The ethereal, or material, For all that exist is thru him. He is the circle engulfing all spheres, The key that unlock all doors. His thought is beyond minds compactsity For the mind itself only coputes by his decree. He is the mind in man and far beyond the portion he receives as a result of his grace. Even if we could unite all our minds into one it would still retain its shadowness in comparison to Allah, For his depth unmeasureable. Almighty is Allah, Master of the world both seen, And unseen Thought, And behold Thought did manifest. Man he did create in his own image, And made him subservient to his will. Allah did give to ability, And capability, And it is unmatched. For by Allah design man as V/L, second to him, Lord of all fears of matter. Yet do they know? No! Indeed a sad affair. It was not Allah that reduce men to negro, Or caucasian, A Chinaman, A Mexican, Or A Romanian, Or Hulgarian, A Jew, Or even Native American. All never reduce man into a slave, Or referred to him by color simply because of the geographical conditioning of his skin. No he created men, And made him his servant, His custodian, His Vicegerent, His V/L, Second only to himself. Man took being in Allah's favor for granted and was punished, And made to scatter. Because of their shame they cloaked themselves in the garment of funny names, And cloaked every people in every direction with a differentiate between themselves in hope of vanishing blame for there Holy infractions committed in the garden of eve.

Allah did create man, And made him V/L. Man distort it, And disfigured himself. It was man that gave names to the multitude of religion, Each claiming there's to be the one true religion. But Allah put his presence in every man unchristian, And all man has to do to communicate with him is to mediate. And call within himself. Allah created man, And gave him the rank of V/L. Man created confusion, And his subself, And every atrocious act against his bother, And they tell a notorious lie by saying Allah sanction such extremities ALLAH is the ALMIGHTY, ALMIGHTY IS ALLAH, And we that are subservient to him hurl his honorable attributes before us his people

A/V/L/N. Vice which signifies that we are a people weak in the flesh who submit themselves only to a higher authority of ALLAH, And lord to affirm our position as his Vicegerent, And rulers of the physical world. ALLAH sign is the master sign, Although not exclusively, For no people have monopoly on ALLAH, And wherever truth, And righteous dwells so does he.

LAH VIA VA VA ILLILAHA HALALIIL, ALLAH AKBUR

Almighty Vice Lord Prayer.....

In the name of Allah, The Beneficient, The Merciful..... We the righteous people of the Vice Lord Nation seek thy understanding and thy blessing, As we commit ourselves to our chosen way of life.

We pray that you strengthen us Allah, And bestow upon us your favor. And that you help us in our strive to turn from wrong into right. We seek thy guidance and assistance in every phase of our development. And thy patience with us as a striving people.

We pray here in convenient form. YOUR SERVANTS AND VICE AGENTS, VICE LORDS OF THIS PHYSICAL WORLD. We pray for the good of our nation, And our people. And that you help us overcome our faults. We ask that you grant us the strength to carry this burden, For being V/L is not easy!

We thank you for the gift of life, And the glory of your love. And offer our gratitude for the potential and ability you have granted us as a people.

We pray that you will help us better utilize these keys, So that we may unlock the secrets and doors of both this life and the mystery after. We ask that you bless those who have died and lived in the name of V/L. And that you help us make this work if for none, Than for the Believers...........................Amen............................Amen

Almighty Vice Lord Prayer.....

In The Name of Allah, We the righteous of the Almighty Vice Lord Nation give praise to our Supreme Chief, righteous son of the Almighty and a divine prophet of V/L.

Behold, Here our prayers O'Lord of lords, And give us your people of the A/V/L/N the continuous courage to represent our nation, So that the world will know that we are V/L, And as such will never stray from our divine principals and concepts, The laws by which we the most righteous of your people live by.

By your divine grace and generosity, You have instilled with us thy divine seed of love, Knowledge, Wisdom, And Understanding. And as a representative of this Almighty Vice Lord Nation, It is our responsibility to apply these precious gifts to the interest of our beloved nation And all poor and oppressed people of color world wide.

It is known that if we retrogress from our divine principals and laws the wrath of this A/V/L/N will surely fall upon us. For we pledge our life, Love And Loyalty to this Nation.

..........This Almighty Vice Lord Nation..........

Let our conduct O'Lord of Lords be judged by you according to our deeds.....By Birth .....In The Spirit.....And Through the heart core.....Behold, Behold, We come as we are.....V/L.....Ar

Quranic Justice.....

The man of faith holds fast to his faith, Because he knows it is true! The man of the world rejecting faith, Clings hard to worldly interests, But let him not force his interest on men/women, Sincere, And true by Favor, Force, Or fraud. Let not men/women be intoxicated with power, Or material resources. To each is a goal to which Allah turns him/her, Then strives together as in a race towards all that is good where ever ye are. Allah will bring you together, For Allah has power over all things. Mankind was one single nation, And God sent messages with Glad Tidings, And with them he sent the book and the truth to judge between people where they differed, But the people of the book, After the clear signs came to them they did not differ among themselves, Except through selfish contumely. God by his grace guided the believer to the truth concerning that where in they differed, For God guides whom he will to a path that is straight Draw Brothers!

Ingredient of 360% Of Lordism.....

In order to obtain 360 degree's of Lordism, We as striving Lords must give fully of ourselves from ourselves.....We must apply the supreme degree of determination in all our endeavors, For through this all shall be accomplished..... Our level of conscience must be most high or life will pass..... We must incorporate all the essentials of a blood line family and from the hardcore give our support, And our Love, And if a situation dictates so. Our life..Thurst, Respect, Discipline, And Loyalty must be our appetizer, As for the main course, We through in our commitment, Our Queen should be taught of the Lords, For it is through them that our growth is finalized. With proper guidance and understanding a sister can reach 120% of pure Lordism...When a person lives it, Love it, Dream it, Eat it, Speak it, And Die in it, Then and only Then can they be called a righteous Lord to and through Hard Core. This and only this is the essence 360% of pure Lordism.

A/V/L/N Economic Program.....

1.   It will be incumbent on every representative of the A/V/L/N to pay membership dues on a regular and basis.

2.   The initial dues shall be fifty dollars per year each year there after shall be thirty dollars.

3.   A workable timetable shall be set up to accommodate each individual to alleviate and eliminate the crush of a financial strain.

4.   All monies will be placed in the subnations account in the following manner fifty percent goes to general account, forty percent subnation account.

5.   All monies will be under the authority of treasure(s): National Headquarters treasure in Chicago will be the paramount treasure and must be afforded a

monthly treasure report from all Subofficers.   These reports shall be submitted to the Chief or his appointed representative.

6.   No monies will be drawn from accounts without approval of Chief and representing office of SubNation. (1) NOTE, Other necessary funds for upkeeping and daily functioning of nation, In essence Rent, Salaries, Expenses.

7.   Each SubNation acting in accordance with this economic program shall be recipients of all the benefits and advantages that this entails.

One of our economic goals: Set a work program based on commitment and a work pledge. With a two hundred minimum given for the building and buying of a Lords center. Our goal will be to raise a million settling for no less than five hundred thousand dollars. Each Elite must donate five hundred dollars. Our Center/House of Lords, will be constructed from the ground once we gain the necessary funds for such a project, But initially we will settle for a building of comfort and conviency.

The National Athem.....

Throw your palms to the sky, Fly your Love most high, Be forever proud, forever real, And dedicated to the cause. Whether you be man, woman, Or Child it make no difference which one are thou. All that believe are the same. A fruit from (a) tree from which the nation sprang. Be V/L, And forever real. Oh precious people always strive to excell, Build upon your dreams, our faith, But don't let that stand in your way. We too are a living people of life with every right to be. Oh fruit from the tree which the Nation sprang, Beautiful, sweet bearing the V/L name, Throw your palms to the sky, Fly your love most high, be forever proud..........

(Note): THE CONSTITUTION OF THE UNITED STATES OF AMERICA GRANTS US THE RIGHTS TO ASSERT OUR RIGHT TO AN IDEALIZED WAY OF LIFE. LORDISM IS OUR CHOICE, AND ANY BELIEVER HAVE A RIGHT TO GIVE EXPRESSION TO IT..........

Conclusion.....

This Code Of Conduct, Chain Of Command, Principals Of Law, And all the other material containing this revelation has been designed, And arranged with great care, And consideration of every representative of the Amalgamated Order Of Lordism. It is the Law, Philosophy, And Structure of a great nation. It is established so that every V/L will know who he/she is, And who his/her Brother and Sisters are. This literature also serves to maintain a Security, Discipline, Safety, And Integrity of the order. This literature contains some of the truthful teaching of Lordism, But as Lordism literature a way of life, And the righteous truth seeking V/L cannot help but learn more truth as he/she travels the golden path of Lordism. You as V/L & V/Lady are expected to know, Respect, And Honor the Code, The Chain, And the principals of laws of this Almighty Amalgamated Order Of Lordism, And also know what Lordism is about, For in no other way can we sincerely represent V/L. Behold V/L, The Truth has now been revealed, Hold fast to it, And you will surely walk the golden path of Lordism as a true V/L.

Via Va Va Lah Halaliil Illilaha

INTERNAL DOCUMENTS AND OFFICIAL MEMORANDA
OF THE BROTHERS OF THE STRUGGLE (B.O.S.)

(typed Memo dated July 14, 1982: From an
Illinois Prison; reproduced here "as is" in
the original style, spelling, and syntax)

Date: July 14, 1982

From: The Chairman and Board of Directors

To: All Brothers of the Struggle

Subj: Awareness Session

The Movement

It is a fact, without contradiction that the success of any movement depends largely upon the participation of the mass of people involved in that particular struggle. Leadership without active support, is as useless as spitting in the winds to aid in putting out a major fire. (The fire in this case is the burning effects of povery, lost direction, and progressive states of self-destruction.) The same is true with the lack of Leadership for the people. The two must combine to coordinate the movement, and each part must do it's share in reaching the goals of the group. What is more important is that the directions of the Organization be set forth, and that each concerned member adher to those directions, making the necessary sacrifices required to accomplish the objectives.

The Objectives

A group of people organized around the idea of reaching common objectives is called an Organization. Without that Unity that comes from having a common purpose, the same group of people qualifies as a Mob, Gang, etc., Therefore it is essential that each member realize the objectives of the group. Know what it is that inspire the need for Unity, and what it is that binds them One to the Other. Otherwise, their membership becomes questionable.

One of the basic objectives of the Black Gangster Disciple Nation is: "To obtain the means to Self-Determination for our People." We can not possibly determine anything without being AWARE of our situation, as well as our alternatives.

This AWARENESS does not come from acting foolish, nor from beng lax in your efforts to learn. Therefore the Leadership has opened up avenues for you to gain a perspective on life, our situation, and all aspects of progressive AWARENESS. One such avenue is the AWARENESS SESSIONS, conducted by the Legal Arm of the Organization.

Awareness Session

The interest of our members are many, therefore the subjects of the Awareness Sessions are many. Listed below are the objectives of the Awareness Session.

1. Bring a vast range of Intelligence to the availability of the   people.

2. Promote an environment of creativity among the people.

3. Practice the art of debate.

4. Inspire dignity in our people, by introducing them to a Black   History, as well as a Black Heritage.

5. To in general, uplift the mental, emotional, and spiritual   growth of our people.

All sessions shall be in accordance with the six points of the Star of David, signifying the six principles upon which our Organization is founded. These principles are: Love, Life, Loyality, Knowledge, Wisdom & Understanding.

The goals we have set to reach in these AWARENESS SESSIONS are valid goals. We expect to range from Politics to Stock Markets. We shall speak of wars and cultures, as well as the law.

Rules of the BGDN

1. **Silence and Secrecy**. No member shall give any information or discuss any matters that concerns any member or the function of the organization to any individual that is not a standing member.

2. **Drugs**. No member shall consume or inject any drug that is addictive.

3. **Stealing**. No member shall steal from any convict, inmate, or resident.

4. **Respect**. No member shall be disrespectful to any member or non member. Being disrespectful to others only entices others to become hostile and disrespectful to you which leads to unnecessary and stilly confrontations. Always be respectful, dignified, honorable, loyal and thoughtful.

5. **Breaking and Entering**. No member shall break in or enter any building that will cause unde heat and pressure to others making moves that cause institutional lock-ups and shake-downs is prohibited.

6. **Gambling**. No member shall gamble in any games unles all parties have their money up front.

7. **Guards**. No member shall engage in any unnecessary confrontations with any officer's or administrative personnel.

8. **Sportmanship**. No member shall engage in any heated arguments or fights while participating in any sport or games. Use good sportmanship at all times.

9. **Personal Hygiene**. All members must look presentable at all times and all living quarters should be kept clean.

13. **Exercising**. All members are required to jog three times around the yard and do fifty jumping jacks together at the beginning of each yard period except on Saturday, Sunday and night yard.

14. **Exploiting**. No member shall use his membership, staff or office to exploit funds or favors from any member.

15. **A.R. 804**. All members are required to read and become familiar with the D.O.C. A.R. 804 administration discipline.

16. **Rape**. No member shall use threat or force to make any one engage in homosexual acts.

July 23, 1983

TO   : ALL BROTHERS OF THE STRUGGLE

FROM : THE CHAIRMAN AND THE BOARD OF DIRECTORS

 RE   : MIRANDA WARNINGS

FELLOW BROTHERS OF THE STRUGGLE

"Nothing hurts a duck, but its Bill (MOUTH)." The leadership is sure that you all are familiar with this old and truthful saying, because if any one of you have ever had the opportunity to go on a hunting trip (in the free world) before being locked up, then you know full well that if the duck had kept his mouth shut, instead of quacking, he wouldn't have given his position away, and naturally, would'nt have been our dinner.

This comparison with the duck, our Brothers, is used to stress home to everyone the value and importance of keeping your mouths shut, especially when you are confronted by investigators of the D.O.C., police, Counselors, med techs, even the ministers and others.

As you are all aware, situations occur where it may be necessary to take care of organizational business. Naturally it should be understood that there will be steps taken by D.O.C. messengers to find out who, and how the business was taken care of.

Not all business can be taken care of in a smooth way without a large mass of people actually seeing what has taken place, but they are in the immediate area., naturally, you should know that there will be a general round up of everyone in the vicinity.
Lets recount these steps very briefly, because they are very important. First some business is taken care of., Second, some one saw what occurred, but due to the amount of people in the vicinity at the time of discovery, everyone is detained and checked out.

Third, Whether your name was given by a notorious messenger, or you are being checked out by a group of investigators, state police, state's attorney, etc., due to the fact that the group you're in at the time (recreation period etc)., is being questioned, etc. The main question is "How do you handle yourslef at this time? What will be your reaction while you and maybe two, three, four, or more (B.O.S.) are being singled out as the persons to allegedly took care of the business, what would you say to these investigators who you know are tying to pin something on you with hopes of getting you the electric chair?

If, for whatever reason, you said you would talk to them in any way, (regardless of the exchange of words) you have just made the biggest mistake of your life, why? because, you are not, or were not to say anything at all to them. Let us explain further, here is the situation, the police, investigators etc, don't have enough information to go on that would give them a better than average chance to obtain a conviction., The only hoe they have is that they can make you convict yourself by breaking, thus implicating others, and making confessions etc. Say for instance that those of you being charged or investigated, were separated from one another and placed in different rooms, or different joints so you could'nt communicate with each other to find out what the other is saying or has said so far.

While you are in separate rooms, by yourselves for awhile, in comes two, three, or more investigators with a pen, pad or tape recorder. One of them offers a cigarette, coffee, food, or whatever, you accept it, or you Don't, its up to you. If, however, you take their offerings, then, you have implicated by your acceptance that the possibility of you breaking is very great, because, not everyone has the strong will to accept their offerings and turn around and say, "Go to hell", or "I have nothing to say".

Before any questions have been asked, you were supposed to have been given or read your rights, formerly known as the Miranda Warnings.

These warnings come from a 1966 case, (Miranda vs. Arizona), Under these wardings yu must be informed of the following:

1. You have the right to remain silent under the due process of law, 5th and 14th amendments, and that anything you say can and will be held against you in a Court of law.

2. You have the right to have a lawyer present and to consult with a lawyer during questioning., If you cannot afford one, a lawyer will be supplied by the government.

3. You are entitled to make one free telephone call so don't waste it, contact a lawyer or somebody who can obtain one for you.

While this is going on and afterwards, it is extremely important that you don't sign anything, papers, etc., without the advice of your lawyer.

Our Brothers, all of the above must be remembered, as well as, all that you say, if you made a statement or statements to the investigators in the presence of others, but did not sign it, it may still be used against you, so it is best to just remain silent, its as simple as that.

The investigators, police, state's attorney, etc., use a number of techniques to get a person to tell on himself and implicate others.

That which seems natural our brothers, is often times unatural, let us explain. Say for instance you were on your way to take care of some business and the cop stopped you, asking you for your pass but you don't have one and he tell you to return to your cellhouse, then somebody, member, non-member, etc, came passing by you and the cop, but the cop said nothing to them as he had you, and you blurt out to the cop "you let them go by why did you stop kme, and he call them back and ask for a pass, but they don't have one, this may appear to be a natural quesiton, but, what yu have done is told on someone and kept them from taking care of their business because of your big MOUTH.

This is called dry snitching and will not be tolerated from anyone, what one do reflects on the whole which you all know., To say that you let so and so do this or that, or they are doing this why can't we do it seems a natural question to ask the authorities but it clearly is not and cannot be justified, and most certainly will not be tolerated.

SINCERELY

YOUR CHAIRMAN AND BOARD OF DIRECTORS

(undated typed document)

Preface

Our governing body has decided to take on a New Concept of Organization. A concept that will bring us into the 80's and prepare us for the political and economical realities of Black America. Our Leadership feels that we must take advantage of our imprisonment; we must learn what's necessary to be a productive and disciplined organization while we're confined. If we are successful here in this inferior situation, there's no limitations on our potential in the outside world.

The Leadership doesn't expect miracles from the people in our new undertakings. We are aware of the fact that it took us eighteen (18) years to get into this shape. The Leadership also realizes without the full support of the people, it will take another (18) years or more to make this New Concept of Organization a reality. Unfortunately we don't have that kind of time to waste. Therefore, the Leadership is requesting that all qualified members help us make this transition in to the New Concept. We have wasted enough time dwelling on insignificant matters. Let's prepare ourselves for the World.

In the process of going from the Old to the New, we will have a few complications. It must be understood from the outset that we are not forgetting our past, (as some of you know, we have had good moments as well as bad moments in the past) we're putting our past where it belongs, behind us. Our past will serve as a motivating force that will enable us to have a glorious future. It's a necessity that we go through changes. You're either growing or dieing. To stand still is to Die, our Leadership has decided that we will live and flourish into something great.

All Organizations have Discipline. Discipline is a necessity in all things pertaining to development. Our organization is in transtion. Discipline is essential and must be enforced. All members will adhere to all laws governing the organization. The governing body has updated the laws. We want our laws to reflect our intelligence as well as our strength. These will be absolutely No!!!! exception or exemption from the laws.

Our governing body will be invested with the power to make policies and laws. Our Chairman will have final say on all policies and laws. Our governing body will be called board of directors. All board members will be appointed by the Chairman.

Organizational Structure

1. When it comes to the organization; the individual is subordinate to the organization.
2. The minority is subordinate to the majority.
3. The entire membership is subordinate to the Chairman and the governing body. Whoever violates these articles of organizational structure will be charged with disrupting organizational unity and dealt with in that fashion as an enemy   of the people.

We have witnessed what comes from a lack of Unity and Discipline. Now, observe what comes from Unity and Discipline.

If we are to become a power to reckon with, We must take on the concept of organization. Everyone must do their share. Everybody has a responsibility. For we make up the organization as individuals who have come together as a collective.

THE COMMON SENSE APPROACH

Notations: To be rememberd at all atimes:

Because of inadequate prevention against organization, organizing exist, a new engineering solution must be introduced for the present and future goals of this nation. In composing these solutions to the problems that deeply stagnates the body of this organization, the solutions to eradicate these problems will be given in a self-explanatory and compehensive dialogue, so that everyone may better understand the goals and concepts of our nation:

(Dialogue)

There seems to be a syndrome orientation of negativism, meaning an attitude or system or thoughts characterized by doubt and question, rather than approval and acceptance. An attitude characterized by ignorning, resisting, or opposing suggestions and orders coming from people that are in a position of authority......

(Findings)

A majority of our people are guility of this negativism, reasons are, "most people are unaware of the definition of organization, "therefore it will be spelled out as followed: (Organization is a unified & consolidated group of people, with an executive structure that deals with the well-being of all it's people. It's an executive structure of business & enterprise for individual growth and collective excelleration of the body as a whole. It does not mean a bunch of disorganized, wild radicals who have trouble in distinguishing the 80's from the 60's. Or feel they must hate and fight other organizations because their concepts are different from their own.

THere is also this attitude that some members think they have to be around the executive staff that governs the nation to be recognized. "All members will be judged on their character, loyality and ability to think; and above all, your ability to function as part of the organizations structure we have built, and is continuing to build." If we are to ascertain our success, security and endurance in this world, or the free world;

It has been noted that quite a few of our members have this attitude that they will rebel against decisions or judgement that has been made by the executive staff of this nation:

(Understanding)

It will be written here, and it will be UNDERSTOOD, "That the actions above will in no-way be tolderated by anyone, nor will we accept any group of people to disrupt the laws, the goals, and concept of progress of thils Nation:"

(Dialogue)

For effective functioning of this and other solutions, all persons with governing authority must be sincere about his responsibility, and sincere to the people the executive staff gave him authority to govern. Sincere means being sincere enough to step down from a spot if you feel that you are not capable of fulfilling it to its full capacity. Don't forsake the nation for your own personal faults, because only you can correct you, and as your people we are behind you in all that's positive and for the betterment of all. One must radiate a vibe that will let the people know that you are for the whole of our nation. With this attitude, you will generate a vibe that will let the young people of this nation know that we are for each other and about helping each other excell. Our cause is to have a successful "COSMOLOGY", which means - "the world for which we will make and live in, will be organized".

(Ignorant Outburst)

It has long been recognized that some of our people seem to have a problem in controlling the things they say out of their mouths. It should be first stipulated that the word "IGNORANT" does not mean that a person is stupid, it means a person having little knowledge, or education and experience in a particular area, subject, or matter. When a person makes a statement without first weighing it's value or logic, his outburst in most cases become harmful to the management of this nation. When someone does this, he is being ignorant without having knowledge of it. THis kind of attitude should be eradicated to ensure that there will be no stupid rumors formulating out of our organization. This stupidity has in the past, and will in the future get people hurt unnecessarily. It also causes confusion and sometimes spookism among people that are not involved. This should be acknowledged by all the people. It is extremely necessary and important to check and evaluate all information before you spread something you only got a part of, or heard somebody else say;. If a person in authority is not around during a period in which some vital information has been passed to you, then you must begin to think about the best decision or judgement to render the situation. THis is done by simply weighing the value of the information, and the credibility of the source from which it came. 8 out of 10 times, a person in authority will be around.

(Hand written, printed, document)

We the Brothers of the Stuggle pledging whole heartedly our live, life, loyalty have embraced the teaching of our "Chairman", are covenet until fully chance, teaching laws and policy set forth by our Chairman, and Executive staff. The Doctrine of New Concept, will be a guiding light that will for ever burn in our heart and mind. This light will serve as a constant reminder and motivating force with each of us. Also it will instill in us dedication and discipline. We standing firmly in our six point stance. Concepts of Organization, Politic, Economics, Serenity, Eduction, Unity.

1) Head - life
2) Right shoulder - love
3) Left shoulder - loyalty
4) Right elbow - knowledge
5) Left elbow - understanding
6) Heel of feet - wisdom

I agree to as long as I stand proudly under the blue sky to serve this glorious organization and its every cause aid and assist my fellow Brothers of the Struggle in our righteous endeavors. I will do that I can can to help us both to reach our fullest potential as the organization grows. I know that I will for our goals are inter-related. Positive organization produces poxitive productive people. That which we are, my every action and behavior, and attitude will vividly reflect the positive, dignified principle that the organization is built upon I will never do anything that would cause embarrassment or disrespect to the integrity of our organization. Standing strongly upon our six point stand I shall utilize knowledge wisdom & understanding as I strive in our Struggle for education, economical, political, social development, I will learn, look, and listen to anything that may be conductive towards the excelleration and never abandon our struggle, as in all struggles I realize that sacrifices must be made. I will not be selfish but for the sake of the preservation of our organization; I am willing to endure my share, I believe in the goal of the organization and its honor, to aid and assist in our struggle for success. We are with a great leader. Together we shall see the vision. May His visions become our vision. For his visions are for us to grow into a productive successful people with the consolidation and diligent efforts of everyone, our visions will be manifested into a reality.

(Undated typewritten document)

KEEP-UP NOT CATCH-UP

The affairs of these modern times are designed for the thinking man, the rational logical man, the man that contemplates beyond a 24 hour span of time. We as a organization are not thinkers that only realize their existence of today, but we are men of vision with foresight with future objectives of growth and development. My brothers this is a fast-pace competitive world where the pace isn't won by those that are just trying to catch-up, but is wond by those that keep up. The term (catch-up) signifies not up to a general or expected level of development. The key word is behind and behind is a place or time and here again I state, this is a different era of time now, the modern age of existence, an age in which races arent won by the behinders, and we all know what a behind is dont we? And we dont want to be a continuous ass, a Beast of Burden. My brothers, the Preface of our Organization is a clear sign of the timesk our Preface is a Beckoning Light of Knowledge, Wisdom, and Understanding of the Concept of Unity.

This concept has....anization can win this race, its not an easy race, the strenght to endure the trials and tribulations of this world. Whats to be gained by winning this race? The realization of the Growth and Development of a nation.
Remember a wise man changes his mind often, but a fool never does...
Keep Up With The Times My Brother

BOS PRAYER

Looking out the window as far as I can see,
All my BOS brothers standing around me,
GD's and BD's has combined,
As we both unite our star will shine,
King David he recuted gave the (G)
Strength on the street,
He recuted the (D) on the history of our G
will last forever,
As the Brothers of the Struggle
Struggle together.

GD PRAYER

All GDs must use the knowledge on the six point star, 360 base on the life we belive and the love we have for one another. Wisdom is what we use to grow knowledge on the six point star in our nation flag in order to be real you must be willing to appear in front of Larry Hoover.

G.D. Creed

We believe in the teaching of our Honorable Chairman; in all laws and polices set forth by our Chairman and Executive Staff.

In the concept of ideology of the organization in aid and assisting our fellow brother of the struggle in all righteous Endeavors.

And standing strongly upon our six points utilizing Knowledge, Wisdom, and Understanding as we strive in our struggle for Education, Economical, and Political and Social Development that we are a special group of people with Integraty and Dignity.

In the vision of our great leader and throuh his vision we can be come a reckoning power of people beyond Boundaries without measures.

INTERNAL RULES OF THE B.O.S.

1. SILENCE AND SECRECY. No member should give any Information or discuss any matter that concerns any member or function of the organization to any individual that is not an outstanding member.
2. DRUGS. No member shall consume or inject any drugs that are addictive.
3. STEALING. No member shall steal from any convict inmate or resident.
4. RESPECT. No member shall be disrespectful to any member or non-member being disrespectful only intices other to become hot-stely and be disrespectful to you which leads to unnecersery silly confrontation. always be respectful, dignified, honorable; loyal and thoughtful.
5. BRAKEING AND ENTERING: No member shall breake in or enter any building that cause un-due heat and presure to other. Making institutional move that leads to lock-up and shake down is prohibited.
6. GAMBLING. No member shall gamble in any game unless all parties have there money up front.

7. GUARD. No member shell engage in any unnissery confrontation with any officers or administrative personnel.

8. SPORTMANSHIP. No member shell engage in heated arguments or fights while participating in any sports or games. Use good sportmenship at all time.

9. PERSONAL-HYGENE. All member must look presenable at all times and livin quarters should be kept clean.

10. INCIDENTS. All incidents minor or major concerning the health and well being of any member or members should be reported to the coordinatorors.

11. AID AND ASSISTING. All member shell Aid and assisting one another in all righteous endeavors.

12. DUES. All member are required to give 2 pack a month if able.

13. EXERCISING. All member are required to job three times around the yard and do fifty jumping jacks together at the beginning of each yard period except Saturday, Sunday and night yard.

14. EXPLOITING. No member shall use his membership, staff, or office to exploit or favor for any member.

15. A.R. 504. All member shall read and become familiar with the D.O.C. A.R. 504 Administrative disaplene.

16. RAPE. No one should use threat or force to make anyone engage in any homosexual act.

Disciplinary Report Form Used by The B.O.S.

MINOR:_____

MAJOR:_____

TIME:_____
DATE:_____
INCIDENT:_____

WE BELIEVE IN THE TEACHING OF OUR HONORABLE
CHAIRMAN; IN ALL LAWS AND POLICIES SET FORTH BY OUR
CHAIRMAN AND EXECUTIVE STAFF.

INCIDENT:_____

_____

_____

_____

_____

GD:_____   _____

BD:_____   _____

NAME:_____   _____

_____

IN THE CONCEPT OF IDEOLOGY OF THE ORGANIZATION IN
AID AND ASSISTING OUR FELLOW BROTHERS OF THE
STRUGGLE IN ALL RIGHTEOUS ENDEAVORS. IN THE
VISION OF OUR GREAT LEADER AND THROUGH HIS VISION
WE CAN BECOME A RECKONING POWER OF PEOPLE BEYOND
BOUNDARIES WITHOUT MEASURE.

WITNESS:

_____

_____

_____

CHAPTER FIVE
NATIONAL GANGS DIRECTORY[1]

RESTRICTED USE: Note that this is a confidential and copyright protected document. It cannot be shared with the public. It cannot be quoted in anyway.

Legend of Information Sources[2]:
JU = Juvenile Correctional Institutions survey (1990)
PC = Police Chief survey (1990)
AI = Adult correctional Institution survey (1991)
PP = Probation and Parole officer survey (1991)
JI = Juvenile Correctional Institution Survey (1991)[3]
CS = County Sheriff's survey (1991)
JD = Juvenile Detention facilities survey (1992)[4]
W2 = 1992 Adult Corrections survey (1992)
AS = 1992 National Asian Student Survey
LE = 1992 Law Enforcement Survey (Chiefs/Sheriffs)
JA = 1993 National Jail Survey[5]
W3 = 1993 State Prison Warden Survey

---

[1] These are either gangs reported as a problem, or as gangs being reported as being active in any capacity in the area. This is self-reported information from public officials. Some respondents, for example, indicated "no current problem", but also indicated such gangs were "active in their area".

[2] Some of these data sources are from the survey research projects described in the book by Knox (1991), An Introduction to Gangs, Berrien Springs, Michigan: Vande Vere Publishing. Some are projects undertaken since the release of the book.

[3] The 1990 Juvenile Corrections data is provided in aggregate form at the end. The citations that appear within states and are identified by city are from the 1991 Juvenile Corrections Survey.

[4] This national survey used a much larger checklist of alphabetized gang names; the respondent was asked to "please examine this list and place a check next to each such gang that has been active in any capacity in your facility".

[5] Format: "what are the names of the top three major gangs that are represented among inmates in your facility", semicolon (;), then the checklist of "gangs that have been active in any capacity in your area".

L4 = 1994 Illinois Law Enforcement Survey[6]
RESTRICTED USE: Copyright 1994. No maps, Graphics, or Illustrations are permitted based on this data; nor are other summaries permitted for public use or dissemination to the public. This data is released for the restricted use of reading and reference only to specifically authorized users. Any reproduction of this document without the permission of the National Gang Crime Research Center is strictly prohibited. 3/94.

ALABAMA:

Atmore (AI[7]):   Black Gangster Disciples, Bloods, Crips, Aryan Brotherhood, Five Percenters

Autauga Co. (PP):   Disciples

Baldwin Co. (PP):   Disciples, Skinheads, Bloods, Crips, KKK

Birmingham (LE):   Disciples, Crips, Bloods, Aryan Brotherhood, BGD's, BD's, B.O.S., GD's, Ghost Shadows, Insane Crips, KKK, Miami Boys, Neo-nazis, Skinheads, Vice Lords

Barbour (PP):   Disciples, Bloods, Crips

Bay Minette (LE):   Disciples, Raiders, Kings,Bloods, Crips, Folks,

Bibb Co. (PP):   Bloods, Crips, Disciples, KKK

Birmingham (JI):   Bloods, Crips, Vice Lords, Disciples, Folks, Peoples, Black Gangsters, KKK, Miami Boys[8], White Gangster Disciples

Calhoun (PP):   Crips, Bloods, Disciples, Neo-Nazis, Mad Dogs, Four Horsemen of the Apocalypse[9], Vice Lords

Childersburg (W2):   Aryan Brotherhood, BGD's, Bloods, Crips

Childerburg (W3):   Disciples, Crips, Bloods; Aryan Brotherhood, BGD's, Eight Balls, Hell's Angels, KKK, Skinheads, Sons of Samoa (SOS), White Knights

Dothan (LE):   BGD's, Insane Gangster Disciples, Crips groups, BG's, Disciples, Down By the Laws (DBL's), Folks, Gangsters, GD's, Lynch Mob, Miami Boys, Piru, White Gangster Disciples

Elmore (AI):   Bloods, Crips, Aryan Brotherhood, Skinheads, Neo-nazis, Ku Klux Klan

Elmore (AI):   Black Gangster Disciples,

Elmore (AI):   Bloods, Crips, Disciples

---

[6]Data listing provides typically provides only the names of the largest three gangs in their area.

[7]"AI" and any other TWO ALPHA/NUMERIC DIGITS in parentheses after a City listing indicates the Data Source (see the Legend Above). AI signifies the data source of "Adult Correctional Institution survey".

[8]The "Miami Boys" are identified as a gang in many different jurisdictions; but do not according to a source in Miami exist as a gang by that name; rather this appears to be the residential identity factor at work; persons from Miami identify and "clique up" with their "homies" from the same area. The same phenomenon applies to other groups as well.

[9] A white gang.

Elmore (W3):   Black Gangster Disciples, Black Disciples, Aryan Brotherhood; Crips, Vice Lords, White Knights

Gadsden (LE):   Bloods, Crips, Disciples, BGDs, BDs, B.O.S., Four Horsemen of the Apocalypse, Folks, Lynch Mob, Insane Vice Lords, White Gangster Disciples

Huntsville (PC):   L.A. Kings, Black Gangster Disciples, Miami Heat, Bloods, Crips, Disciples, Aryan Brotherhood, Folks, Skinheads, White Gangster Disciples

Huntsville (LE):   L.A. Kings, BGD's, Vice Lords, Aryan Nation, Bloods, Disciples, Dukes, Hilltop Hustlers, Hoods, Lynch Mob, Miami Heat, Raiders, Skinheads, Vice Lords, White Gangster Disciples

Jefferson Co. (LE):   Disciples, Aryan Nation, BGD's, BD's, BG's, Bloods, Crips, GD's, KKK, Vice Lords

Madison Co. (LE):   BGD's[10], Insane Gangster Disciples (IGD's)[11], Ghost Gangster Disciples (GGD's)[12], Aryan Brotherhood, Aryan Nation, Brothers of the Struggle (BOS), Folks, GD's, L.A. Kings, Peoples, Tiny Rascal Gang (TRG), White Gangster Disciples, X-Men, Young Boys Inc, Zulu

Mobile (JI):   Bloods, Disciples, Folks[13]

Montgomery (PC):   Disciples, Bloods, Crips, Vice Lords, Folks, Peoples, Skinheads, Brothers of the Struggle, Posse, Neo-nazis, Black Gangsters, Ku Klux Klan, Insane Crips, White Gangster Disciples

Montgomery (JI):   Bloods, Crips, Vice Lords, Disciples, Folks, Peoples, KKK

Montgomery (W2):   BGD's, Bloods, Cobras, Crips, Disciples, Folks, Get Money Gang, Knights, Miami Boys, Satans Disciples, Vice Lords, White Gangster Disciples, 8-Balls

Montgomery (W3):   Black Gangster Disciples, Bloods, Crips; Aryan Circle, Aryan Nation, Bikers, Disciples, Five Percenters, Folks, Gangster Disciples, Insane Crips, Insane Vice Lords, KKK, Knights, Neo-nazis, Warlords

Montgomery (JD):   Black Gangsters, Crips, Disciples, Folks, Gangster Disciples, Satans Disciples, Vice Lords, Bloods, C Street, Insane Crips, L.A. Kings, Hoods

Moulton (LE):   Bloods, Kitchen Crips, KKK

Mt. Meigs (AI):   Bloods, Crips, Disciples, Aryan Brotherhood, Skinheads, Ku Klux Klan

Mt. Meigs (JI):   Bloods, Crips, Vice Lords, Disciples, Folks, Skinheads, Brothers of the Struggle, Black Gangsters, KKK

Phenix City (JA):   Crips, Miami Boys

Springville (AI):   Black Gangster Disciples, Bloods, Crips, Vice Lords, Aryan Brotherhood, White Gangster Disciples

Springville (W3):   Skinheads, Aryan Brotherhood; Crips, Bloods, BGD's; Aryan Nation

Troy (PC):   Blue Hats, Down By Laws,

---

[10]Black males.

[11]Black and white males.

[12]White males.

[13] Folks indicated as a white gang.

Troy (JI)[14]:   Bloods, Crips, Vice Lords, Disciples, Folks
Union Spring (W3):   Aryan Brotherhood; Disciples, Bloods, Crips; Aryan Nation,
  BGD's, BD's, BG's, El Rukns, Folks, GD's, KKK, Vice Lords

ALASKA:
Anchorage (AI):   Bloods, Crips, Aryan Brotherhood, Neo-nazis, Bikers
Anchorage (PP):   Bloods, Crips, Neo-nazis, Mexican Mafia, Insane Crips
Anchorage (CS):   Bloods[15], Crips, Skinheads, Hells Angels
Anchorage (W2):   Aryan Brotherhood, Bloods, Crips, Hell's Angels
Anchorage (LE):   Crips, Bloods, Hells Angels, Aryan Brotherhood, Aryan Nation,
  Skinheads
Anchorage (W3):   Aryan Brotherhood, Tiny Rascals, Hamo, Bloods; Aryan Nation,
  High Rollers, Hoods, KKK, La Familia, Mexican Mafia, Piru, Rolling 60, Vice
  Lords, 8-Balls
Eagle River (AI):[16]   Bloods, Crips, Aryan Brotherhood
Fairbanks (AI):   Skinheads
Fairbanks (JD):   Bloods, Crips, L.A. Kings, Raiders
Juneau (JI):   Crips, Bloods
Kenai (AI):   Aryan Brotherhood
North Pole (PC):   Bikers (Hells Angels)
Palmer (AI):[17]   Bloods, Crips, Aryan Brotherhood, Skinheads, El Rukns, Mexican
  Mafia, Bikers
Seward (W3):   Bad Boys of Alaska[18], Aryan Nation, Bloods, Crips, Neo-nazis, Posse
  Comitatus, Satanic Cult Gangs, Skinheads

ARIZONA:
Cochise Co.(PP):   Crips
Coconino Co. (CS):   Bloods, Crips, Aryan Brotherhood, Posse, Bikers
Douglas (AI):   Bloods, Crips, Disciples, Aryan Brotherhood, Skinheads, Posse, El
  Rukns, Mexican Mafia, Black Guerilla Family, Nuestra Familia, Pagans
Douglas (W3):   Aryan Brotherhood; New Mexican Mafia, A.A.C., Aryan Nation,
  BGD's, Black Guerilla Family
Florence (AI):   Aryan Brotherhood, Mexican Mafia, New Mexican Mafia, Bloods,
  Crips
Florence (AI):   Aryan Brotherhood, Mexican Mafia, Crips, Bloods, El Rukns, Black
  Guerilla Family, Blue Rags, Red Rags, Warrior Society

---

[14] Not local to Troy, but as gangs from the city of origin of youths confined at the
Troy facility.

[15] Gangs that occasionally migrate to the area but which are not organized there.

[16] Indicated no gangs in the institution, but these were active in the area.

[17] Known activity in State, not in this institution.

[18] An all white gang in the institution.

Goodyear (AI):   Bloods, Crips, Aryan Brotherhood, Skinheads, El Rukns, Neo-nazis, SUR, SWP, Mexican Mafia, Bikers, Black Guerilla Family, Nuestra Familia, Insane Crips, PYRU, SUR 13, L.V.L., F.T.W.[19], 19th Street Gang, NWK 14

Graham Co. (PP):   Bloods, Crips, Aryan Brotherhood, Skinheads, Neo-nazis, Mexican Mafia, Bikers

Jonesboro (JD):   Crips, Folks,

Maricopa (W3):   Aryan Brotherhood, Mexican Mafia, New Eme

Maricopa Co. (LE):   Wet Back Power, West Side City Crips, Wedge Wood Chicanos, West Side Chicanos, Aryan Brotherhood, Aryan Nation, Avondale Crack Monsters, Banditos, Barrio Chicano Locos, BGD's, Bikers, Black Guerilla Family, Bloods, Cononia Chiques, Crips, Disciples, El Rukns, E.M.E., F-13, Hell's Angels, Hollywood, Insane Crips, Kitchen Crips, KKK, Latin Kings, La Familia, La Raza, L.C.M., Mexican Mafia, Neo-nazis, Nortenos, Nuestra Familia, Nortenos, Outlaws, Pagans, Piru, Rolling 60, Santana Block, Scorpians, Skinheads, Sons of Silence, SUR 13, Vice Lords, Warrior Society, White Fence, Young Boys Inc, F-13, 18th Street Gang, 106 Watts

Mesa (LE):   West Side Mesa (WSM), South Side Mesa (SSM), Mesa Varrio Locos (MVL), Aryan Brotherhood, BGD's, Black Mafia, Bloods, Boot Boys, Crips, E.M.E., F-13, Folks, Insane Crips, Latin Kings, L.C.M., Los Hermanos, L.V.L., Lynch Mob, Neo-nazis, Nuestra Familia, Piru, Rolling 60, Santana Block, Sharps, Skinheads, Stoners, SUR 13, Tongan Crip Gang (TCG), White Power, White Pride, F-13

Navajo Co. (CS):   Bloods, Crips, Aryan Brotherhood, Mexican Mafia, Los Casados

Phoenix (PP):   Skinheads, Bloods, Crips, Southside Posse, Aryan Brotherhood, Mexican Mafia, Nuestra Familia

Phoenix (JI):   The Fourth Reich[20], Bloods, Crips, Aryan Brotherhood, White Pride, Skinheads, Posse, Neo-nazis, VHB, LCM, HHB, SWP, Mexican Mafia, Raiders, La Raza

Phoenix (W2):   Aryan Brotherhood, Aryan Nations, Biker gangs, Banditos, Black Guerilla Family, Bloods, Crips, F.T.W., Insane Crips, KKK, La Raza, Mexican Mafia, SWP, Warrior Society, White Power, White Pride

Phoenix (W3):   Aryan Brotherhood; Mexican Mafia, Crips; Aryan Nation, Aryan Warriors, Banditos, Barrio Chicano Locos, BC Boys, BGD's, Bikers, Black Disciples, Bloods, Black Guerilla Family, Bloods, Brown Gangster Disciples, Cobras, Crips, Dirty White Boys, Disciples, Eight Balls, F.B.I., The Fourth Reich, F.T.W., Gangsters, Ghost Riders, Hammer Gang, Gypsy Jokers, Hell's Angels, Hollywood, Imperial Gangsters, Insane Crips, Insane Vice Lords, Jokers, King Cobra, KKK, Latin Kings, L.A. Kings, La Familia, La Raza, L.C.M., Lil Locos, Mexican Mafia, Miami Boys, Montellos, Neo-nazis, Nortenos, Nuestra Familia, NWK 14, Outlaws, Pagans, Party Players, Pit Bull Posse, Piru, Rolling 60, Santana Block, Satanic Cult Gangs, Scorpians, Skinheads, Sons of Samoa, South Side Boys, S.S.G., Stoners, SUR 13, SWP, Texas Mafia, Vice Lords, Warrior Society, West End Rockers, West Side Posse, White Power, White Pride, 9th Street Dawgs, 14th Street Gang, 18th Street Gang, 19th Street Gang, 29th Street gang, 79th Street Gang

Picacho (AI):   Aryan Brotherhood, Crips, Bloods, Mexican Mafia

---

[19]F.T.W. is reported as also meaning Fuck The World, a stoner group, described in a section covering "satanic cults" in Gangs in School: Breaking Up is Hard to Do, National School Safety Center, 1988. Some other reports indicate these initials mean "Forever Truly White".

[20] White gang.

Picacho (W3):   Aryan Brotherhood, Mexican Mafia, Crips; Hell's Angels, High
   Rollers, Hollywood, La Familia, La Mafia, Warrior Society, 98 Posse
Prescott (PC):   Skinheads
Prescott Valley (PC):   Homeboys, skinheads, NIC
Safford (AI):   Aryan Brotherhood, SWP, Bloods, Crips, Skinheads, Mexican Mafia,
   Bikers, Black Guerilla Family, Nuestra Familia
Safford (W3):   Aryan Brotherhood, Brown Society, Mexican Mafia; Aryan Nation,
   Eight Balls, E.M.E., Five Percenters, Hell's Angels, Crips, Bloods, Bikers, La Familia,
   Nuestra Familia, Posse, Texas Mafia
Scottsdale (LE):   Wet Back Power, 108 St. Extension, Aryan Brotherhood, Bikers,
   Bloods, Crips, Skinheads
South Tucson (PC):   Bloods, Crips, Aryan Brotherhood, Mexican Mafia
Tucson (PC):   Bloods, Crips, Aryan Brotherhood, Skinheads, Neo-nazis, Posse, SUR,
   Black Gangsters, Mexican Mafia, Bikers, Nuestra Familia
Tucson (JI):   PJ's[21], Bloods, Crips, Vice Lords, Skinheads, Posse, Mexican Mafia,
   Bikers, Outlaws, PYRU, F.T.W., La Raza, Satanic Cult Gangs
Tucson, AZ (W3):   Aryan Brotherhood, Mexican Mafia (New), Mexican Mafia
   (Original); Aryan Nation, BGD's, Barrio Chicano Locos, Black Guerilla Family,
   Bloods, Crips, Crazy White Boys, Dirty White Boys, E.M.E., Hell's Angels,
   Hollywood, Insane Crips, La Raza, La Familia, Nuestra Familia, P.J.'s, Piru, Rolling
   60, Santana Block, Skinheads, S.S.G., Warrior Society
Tucson (W2):   Aryan Brotherhood, Barrio Chicano Locos, BGD's, Bikers, Black
   Gangsters, Black Mafia, Bloods, Crips, F.T.W., Hammer Gang, Hell's Angels,
   Hollywood, KKK, La Raza, La Familia, Mexican Mafia, New Mexican Mafia, neo-
   nazis, Nuestra Familia, Outlaws, Rolling 60, Satanic Cult Gangs, Satans Disciples,
   Skinheads, SWP, Warrior Society, White Pride
Youngtown (PC):   Barrio Chicanos Locos, West Side Posse, Avondale Crack
   Monsters
Winslow (PC):   Bloods, Crips
Winslow (W3):   Aryan Brotherhood; Mexican Mafia (old & new), Crips, Bloods,
   AAC; Bikers, KKK, La Familia, La Mafia, skinheads, Warrior Society, White Power
Yuma (PC):   West Side, Hollywood, Pagans
Yuma (LE):   Okie Town, West Side, Soma, Bloods, Crazy White Boys, Crips, Hells
   Angels, Mexican Mafia, neo-nazis, White Fence

ARKANSAS:
Bull Shoals (PC):   Aryan Brotherhood, Skinheads, Neo-nazis(W), Ku Klux   Klan
El Dorado (LE):   Hoover Folks
Eureka Springs (PC):   KKK, Aryan Nations, Neo-nazis
Faulkner Co. (CS):   Black Gangster Disciples, Aryan Brotherhood, Posse
Fayetteville (PC):   Arkansas Skinheads, Crips, Lobos, Jesters, Hard Tail Riders,
   Posse, Bloods, Skinheads, Neo-nazis, Mexican Mafia
Grady (AI):   Bloods, Posse, Aryan Brotherhood, Skinheads, Posse, KKK, Crips
Grady (W2):   Aryan Brotherhood, Posse
Grady (W3):   XIV[22]; BGD's, Crips, Bloods; Black Gangsters, Black Disciples, Folks,
   Four Corner Hustlers, Fruits of Islam, Gangster Disciples, Insane Crips, Insane Vice
   Lords, KKK, Piru, Shorty Folks, Vice Lords

---

[21] A white gang.

[22] A white gang.

Grady (W3)[23]:   New Aryan Empire; BGD's, Crips, Bloods; Aryan Brotherhood, Aryan Nation, Brothers of the Struggle (BOS), El Rukns, Folks, Fruits of Islam, Insane Crips, Insane Vice Lords, Posse, Vice Lords

Hope (PC):   Folks, Bloods, Crips, Disciples, PYRU[24] Jonesboro (LE): Two Hype, Pharoahs

Littlerock (AI):   Aryan Brotherhood, Posse, Bloods, Crips, Skinheads, KKK

Little Rock (LE):   Southwest King[25], BGD's, 21st Street Posse[26], Banditos, Crips, Eight Balls, Folks, Hilltop Hustlers, Insane Crips, Insane Vice Lords, La Mafia, Neo-nazis, Piru, Rolling 60, Shorty Folks, Vice Lords, West Side Posse

Pine Bluff (JI):   Dirty White Boys[27], Bloods, Crips, Vice Lords, Disciples, Folks, Peoples, Black Gangsters, Shorty Folks, Boomie Black Gangsters, Brothers of the Struggle

Star City (PC):   Folks

Tucker (AI):   Bloods, Crips, Disciples, Aryan Brotherhood, Folks, Posse, Shorty Folks, Posse

Tucker (AI):   Aryan Brotherhood, Bloods, Crips, Folks, El Rukns

Tucker (W3):   XIV, Brave Brotherhood, Aryan Brotherhood[28]; Black Gangster Disciples, Crips, Bloods; Aryan Nation, BD's, BG's, Boomie Black Gangsters, Brothers Behind Bars (BBB), Brothers of the Struggle (BOS), Down By the Law (DBL), El Rukns, Five Percenters, Folks, Four Corner Hustlers, GD's, G-Boys, Insane Crips, Insane Vice Lords, KKK, Latin Kings, NWA, Piru, Rolling 60, Shorty Folks, Skinheads, Two-Sixers, West Side Posse, White Power

Wrightsville (W3):   Vice Lords, Bloods, Crips; Aryan Brotherhood, BGD's, Brothers of the Struggle (BOS), Dirty White Boys, Folks, Shorty Folks

CALIFORNIA:

Alameda Co. (LE):   A St. Locos, S.B. ("Strictly Business"), D.G.F. ("Don't Giva Fuck"), All Brothers Together (ABT[29]), Aryan Brotherhood, Black Guerilla Family, Bloods, Border Brothers, Born To Kill (BTK), Crazy White Boys, Crips, Hell's Angels, Hua Ching, KKK, La Familia, Mexican Mafia, Neo-nazis, Nortenos, Nuestra Familia, Piru, Skinheads, Sons of Samoa (SOS), Surenos

---

[23]Cummins Unit.

[24] 6th Judicial District.

[25]Non-aligned white gang.

[26]Blood aligned gang.

[27] White gang.

[28]All white gangs.

[29]ABT in these data sources refers specifically to "All Brothers Together". The initials "ABT" can also refer to "Ayran Brotherhood Texas". The AB's of Texas are not designated by "ABT".

Anaheim (LE):   Folks - Fraternal Order of Latin Kings, W.S.A. - West Side Anaheim, Jeffrey Street, Aryan Brotherhood, BGDs, Black Guerilla Family, Crips, Hell Raisers, Latin Kings, La Familia, Mexican Mafia, Nuestra Familia, Tiny Rascal Gang (TRG), White Peoples Party

Bakersfield (PP):   White Knights, Dukes, White Pride Gangsters[30], North Side Boys, My Only Brothers (M.O.B.), Mexican Rap Mafia (MRM), Bloods, Crips, Aryan Brotherhood, Skinheads, SUR, SWP, Mexican Mafia, Nuestra Familia, Ku Klux Klan

Bakersfield (LE):   Colonia Bakers, Varrios Bakers, Eastside Crips, Aryan Brother hood, Aryan Nation, Aryan Warriors, Banditos, Bikers, Black Guerilla Family, Bloods, Border Brothers, Crips, E.M.E., F-13, Gypsy Jokers, Hells Angels, Insane Crips, King Cobra, Kitchen Crips, KKK, Knights, L.A. Kings, Neo-nazis, Nortenos, Nuestra Familia, Rolling 60, Santana Block, Shotgun, Skinheads, Sons of Samoa (S.O.S.), Surenos, SUR 13, Stoners, SWP, Tiny Rascal Gang (TRG), White Fence, 18th St. Gang

Bell (LE):   Playboys, Bratz, B.G. Locos, Aryan Brotherhood, King Cobra, La Familia, Mexican Mafia, Nuestra Familia, White Fence, White Power

Blythe (AI):   Aryan Brotherhood, White Peoples Party, Bloods, Crips, Skinheads, SUR[31], Mexican Mafia, Bikers, Black Guerilla Family, Nuestra Familia, Border Brothers[32],

Blythe (W2):   Aryan Brotherhood, Barrio Chicano Locos, Black Guerilla Family, Bloods, Border Brothers, Crazy White Boys, Crips, F-13, F.T.W., Insane Crips, Kitchen Crips, Mexican Mafia, Neo-nazis, Nuestra Familia, PYRU, Quo Vo, Rolling 60, Santana Block, Skinheads, SUR 13, West Side Boyz, White Power, White Pride, 14th Street Gang, 18th Street Gang, 39th Street Gang

Butte Co. (LE):   Oroville Mono Boys (O.M.B.), Chico Kings, Brown Pride Locito, Aryan Brotherhood, Bloods, Crips, F-13, Freight Train Riders of America, Hell's Angels, King Cobra, KKK, La Familia, Mexican Mafia, Neo-nazis, Nortenos, Nuestra Familia, Outlaws, Skinheads, SUR 13, White Pride

Chula Vista (LE):   VCV (Varrio Chula Vista), Otay (Otay community of Chula Vista), OTNC (Old Town National City), Bloods, Crips, CUBO, Insane Crips, Mexican Mafia, Nuestra Familia

Claremont (PC):   Bloods, Crips, Skinheads, SWP, PYRU, Clara Monte[33]

Compton (LE):   Crips, Bloods, Varrio Setentas, Santana Block, Sons of Samoa (SOS)

Concord (LE):   XIV-EBN (East Bay Nortenos), B.I.C. (Boys In Crime), T.M.K. (The Mad Kings), Bloods, Crips, Hells Angels

Corcoran (AI):   Aryan Brotherhood, Bloods, Crips, Neo-nazis, Mexican Mafia, Bikers, Black Guerilla Family, Nuestra Familia, 39th Street Gang, 19th Street Gang

Corcoran (W2):   Aryan Brotherhood, Barrio Chicano Locos, Bikers, Bloods, Blue hats/Blue rags, Border Brothers, Colonia Chiques, Crazy White Boys, Crips, Hell's Angels, Insane Crips, Latin Kings, La Raza, Mexican Mafia, My Only Brothers

---

[30] All three are white gangs.

[31] SUR's or 13's, Los Angeles, Mexicans.

[32] Mexican aliens from San Diego.

[33] A Hispanic gang.

(M.O.B.), neo-nazis, Nortenos, Nuestra Familia, Pyru, Rolling 60, Skinheads, South Side Tracy, Stoners, SUR 13, White Power, White Pride, 18th Street Gang

Costa Mesa (LE):   Varrio Little Town (VLT), Shailmar Street, skinheads

Covina (LE):   West Covina Mob (Crips), Baldwin Park North Side, Azusa Rifa, Bloods

Crescent City (AI):   Bloods, Crips, Black Gangster Disciples, Aryan Brotherhood, Skinheads, Posse, El Rukns[34], neo-nazis, Latin Kings, Mexican Mafia, Bikers, Black Guerilla Family, Nuestra Familia, Ku Klux Klan, Insane Crips, PIRU, 39th Street Gang, SUR 13, F.T.W.

Crescent City (W2):   Aryan Brotherhood, Black Guerilla Family, Bloods, Crips, Gypsy Jokers, Hell's Angels, Mexican Mafia, Nortenos, Nuestra Familia, Pyru, Skinheads

Downey (LE):   Dog Patch, Forencia 13[35], Kansas Street, Aryan Brotherhood, Bloods, Crips, F.T.W., Insane Crips, La Raza, P.J.'s, Piru, Rolling 60, Santana Block, SWP, 18th St.

El Centro (JI):   Bloods, Crips, SUR, Insane Crips, PYRU, SUR 13, Nortenos, Blue Rags, Red Rags

Escondido (DHHS):   Westside Gang, Diablos, CXL's, 9th Street Gang, South Locos[36]

Eureka (JD):   Red Hats/Blue Hats, Satanic Cult Gangs, 14th Street Gang

Fremont (LE):   Fremont (FMT), Tunay Na Pinoy (TNP), All Brothers Together (ABT), Aryan Brotherhood, Black Guerilla Family, Crips, H.T.C.G., KKK, Lynch Mob, Mexican Mafia, Nortenos, Nuestra Familia, NWK 14, Skinheads, Sons of Samoa (SOS

Fresno (PC):   Fresno Bulldogs, Crips, 209 Asian Crips, Aryan Brotherhood, Skinheads, Neo-Nazis, Latin Kings, SUR, SWP, Mexican Mafia, Bikers, Black Guerilla Family, Nuestra Familia, Insane Crypts[37], SUR 13, Bloods

Frontera (W2)[38]:   Aryan Brotherhood, Bikers, Black Guerilla Family, Bloods, Crips, Diamond Street, Insane Crips, KKK, Mexican Mafia, Neo-nazis, Nortenos, Nuestra Familia, NWA, Rolling 60, SUR 13, SWP, White Power, White Pride, 18th Street Gang

Fullerton (LE):   Fullerton Tokers Town (FTT), Baker Street (B St.), Luzon Visayan Mob (LVM), All Brothers Together (ABT), E.M.E., Hua Ching, Insane Crips,

---

[34] Black P. Stone nation.

[35] AKA: "F-13".

[36] All Hispanic gangs. Source: DHHS Report.

[37] Some gang writers/researchers somewhat naive to the the national picture on gangs first thought that some groups using this spelling "CRYPT" or "CRYPTS" were simply a matter of police and others not being able to correctly spell "CRIP". This is not the case. More recently, well after the compilation of this gang tracking data began, newspaper reports began to appear such as those in Monroe County, Indiana where gangs were clearly and intentionally using the "Crypt" spelling.

[38] Indicates no major gang problem, "associates only, no actual members validated".

Kitchen Crips, Mexican Mafia, Rolling 60, Santana Block, Skinheads, Tiny Rascal Gang (TRG)

Glendale (LE):   Tres Locos, West Side Locos, South Side Locos, Crips, Posse Comitatus

Glendora (LE):   Aryan Brotherhood, Aryan Warriors, Born To Kill (BTK), C.I.A. (Criminals In Action), Hell's Angels, White Power, White Pride, K-9 Posse, 18th Street Gang

Huntington Beach (LE):   South Side Huntington Beach (SSHB), Aryan Brotherhood, Aryan Nation, Bikers, Born To Kill (BTK), E.M.E., Bikers, Mexican Mafia, Skin heads, Sons of Samoa (SOS), Tiny Rascal Gang (TRG)

Indio (JA):   American Nazi Party, AB's, Peckerwoods[39], EME, AB's, NF; Aryan Brotherhood, BBMF, Black Guerilla Family, Bloods, Gypsy Jokers, Nuestra Familia, Piru, Skinheads

Kings Co. (JA):   Crips, Aryan Brothers, Aryan Circle, Cross Suns

La Habra (LE):   Campo, Monos, Loco's

La Mesa (LE):   Momz, East San Diego, Casa de Oro Bloods (C.O.B.), Aryan Brotherhood, Bikers, Bloods, Crazy White Boys, Crips, F.B.I., Hells Angels, KKK, Mexican Mafia, Neo-nazis, Nuestra Familia, Outlaws, Piru, Satanic Cult Gangs, Skinheads

Livermore (PC):   Skinheads, LVB (Livermore Valley Boys), Nortenos, Bloods, Crips, Aryan Brotherhood, Neo-nazis

Livermore (LE):   Livermore Bad Boyd Gang (LBG), Arroyo Vista Crew (AVC), Sons of Samoa (SOS)

Lodi (LE):   Vario Central Lodi (Norte), Playboy Surenos, Supreme White Power, Bloods, Border Brothers, Crips, Hell's Angels, KKK, Latin Kings, Nortenos, Skinheads

Lompoc (LE):   VLP, Tini-Locos

Long Beach (LE):   East Side Longos, Rolling Twenty's Crips, Insane Crips, Aryan Brotherhood, Banditos, Bikers, Black Guerilla Family, Bloods, Border Brothers, Fruits of Islam, Ghost Shadows, Hells Angels, Hua Ching, Madados, Mexican Mafia, Neo-nazis, Nuestra Familia, O.L.B., Piru, Red Dragons, Santana Block, Skinheads, Sons of Samoa (SOS), Stoners, Sun Downers Posse, SWP, Termites, Tiny Rascal Gang (TRG)

Los Angeles (PP):   Skinheads, FTW (Forever Truly White), Bloods, Crips, Aryan Brotherhood, Mexican Mafia, Bikers, Nuestra Familia, Insane Crypts

Los Angeles (LE):   18th Street[40], Rollin 60 Crims[41], Mara Salva Trucha (M.S.)[42], Aryan Brotherhood, Aryan Nation, Black Guerilla Family, Born To Kill (BTK), Crips, Diamond Street, E.M.E., Hell's Angels, Hua Ching, Insane Crips, Kitchen Crips, Mexican Mafia, Nuestra Familia, Piru, Sons of Silence, Stoners, White Fence, 14th Street Gang, 106 Watts

Merced (JD):   Bloods, Crips, My Only Brothers (M.O.B.), Nortenos

---

[39]White gangs.

[40]Hispanic.

[41]Black.

[42]Hispanic.

Merced (LE):   Black Dragon, Black Guerilla Family, Dukes, KKK, Skinheads, SWP, White Tigers

Modesto (LE):   West Side Boyz, Asian Gangs, All Brothers Together (ABT), Aryan Circle, BIkers, Black Mafia, Bloods, Boston Boys, C.I.A., Crips, E.M.E., F.T.W., Hells Angels, Wah Ching, KKK, Latin Kings, Mexican Mafia, Lynch Mob, Nortenos, NWA, Piru, Skinheads, SWP, Tiny Rascal Gang (TRG), West Side Boyz

Monrovia (LE):   Duroc Crips, Monrovia Nuevo Varrio, Duarte Eastside

Montebello (LE):   Varrio Nuevo Estrada (VNE), South Side Montebello (SSM), Vail Street Locos (VSL), E.M.E., King Cobra, Mexican Mafia, White Fence, 18th Street Gang

Monterey Park (LE):   Lomas (Hispanic youth), Wah Ching, United Bamboo, Black Dragon, Crips, Eight Balls, E.M.E., Flying Dragons, Ghost Shadows, Mexican Mafia, O.L.B., 18th St. Gang

Napa (LE):   X-13 (XIII), X-14 Nortes (XIV) Nortenos, Vigilantes (S.A.P.), Hells Angels, Neo-nazis, SUR 13

Nevada City (AI):   Bloods, Crips, Aryan Brotherhood, Skinheads, White Pride, Neo-nazis, SUR, SWP, Mexican Mafia, Bikers, Outlaws, Black Guerilla Family, Nuestra Familia, Hell's Angels, KKK, Insane Crypts, PYRU, SUR 13, Nortenos, F.T.W., La Raza, Blue Rags, Red Rags

Nevada Co. (JA):   Crips, Bloods, White Pride, Aryan Brotherhood, Crazy White Boys, Gypsy Jokers, Hell's Angels, KKK, Posse Comitatus, Satanic Cult Gangs, Skinheads

Norwalk (JI):   Bloods, Crips, Disciples, Aryan Brotherhood, White Pride, Skinheads, Neo-nazis, SUR, SWP, Mexican Mafia, Bikers, Outlaws, Black Guerilla Family, Nuestra Familia, Hell's Angels, KKK, Pagans, Kuang Le, Insane Crips, PYRU, G-Street, NWA, SUR 13, Nortenos, La Raza

Novato (LE):   18th Street, MS13 (Mara Salva Truchas), 415's, Surenos, White Fence

Oakland (LE):   Wo Hop To, Border Brothers, BGF, All Brothers Together (ABT), Black Guerilla Family, Bloods, Born To Kill (BTK), Crips, E.M.E., Hell's Angels, Hua Ching, La Familia, Mexican Mafia, Nuestra Familia, Sons of Samoa (SOS)

Oakton (PC):   NWK 14, Blue Rags, Red Rags, Mexican Mafia, Nuestra Familia

Oceanside (LE):   Posole Locos, Center Street Locos, Mesa Locos[43], Bloods, Crips, Dirty White Boys, La Familia, Rolling 60, Sons of Samoa (SOS), 18th Street Gang

Ontario (JI):   Bloods, Crips, Aryan Brotherhood, Skinheads, Neo-nazis, SUR, SWP, Bootboys, Bomber Boys, Two-Sixers, Black Guerilla Family, Cobras, Assassins Inc, Insane Crypts, PYRU, G-Street, Raiders, Knights, BBMF, 39th Street Gang, SUR 13, Nortenos, Blue Rags, Red Rags

Orange (LE):   Orange Varrio Cypress, Varrio Modena Locos, Pearl St., Aryan Brotherhood, Mexican Mafia

Orange Co. (LE):   Big Stanton, Crow Village, San Juan Boys, Aryan Brotherhood, Bikers, Black Guerilla Famly, Bloods, Crips, E.M.E., F.B.I., Hell's Angels, Hua Ching, Neo-nazis, Outlaws, Pagans, Skinheads, Sons of Samoa (SOS), Tiny   Rascal Gang (TRG)

Pacifica (LE):   Criminal Zone, P-Town, RPB

Paso Robles (JI):   White Power, SWP, Skinheads, Stoners, Bloods, Crips, Aryan Brotherhood, Neo-nazis, SUR, Mexican Mafia, Black Guerilla Family, Nuestra Familia, SUR 13, F.T.W., Blue Rags, Red Rags

Pismo Beach (PC):   Punk group, Bloods, Crips, Skinheads, Bikers

---

[43]All three are Hispanic street gangs.

Placer County (PP):   Bloods, Crips, Aryan Brotherhood, Skinheads, Posse, Neo-nazis, Mexican Mafia, Bikers, Black Guerilla Family, KKK, PYRU, SWP

Placerville (JA):   Nortenos, Surenos, SWP, AB's, White Pride; Black Guerilla Family, Bloods, Border Brothers, Crips, E.M.E., Hell's Angels, Nuestra Familia, SUR 13

Plumas Co. (CS):   Aryan Brotherhood, Mexican Mafia, Bikers, Ku Klux Klan

Rancho Dominguez (PC):   891 gangs, many over 1,000 strong. Bloods, Crips, Aryan Brotherhood, Skinheads, Posse, SUR, Mexican Mafia, Bikers, Black Guerilla Family, Nuestra Familia, etc.   .

Redding (JD)[44]:   Aryan Brotherhood, Bloods, Crips, C Street, F.T.W., Mexican Mafia, Neo-nazis, Nortenos, Raiders, PYRU, Satanic Cult Gangs, Skinheads, Stoners, 14th Street Gang

Redwood City (PC):   Skinheads, Mexican Mafia

Rialto (LE):   South Side Rialto[45], 357 (Pamona Crips), I.E. Mob[46], Aryan Brotherhood, Aryan Nation, Black Guerilla Family, Bikers, Black Mafia, Bloods, Dukes, El Rukns, E.M.E., Fruits of Islam, Gangsters, Hell's Angels, High Rollers, Insane Crips, Kitchen Crips, KKK, Latin Kings, Latin Locos, La Familia, Lil Locos, Mexican Mafia, Neo-nazis, Nuestra Familia, Nortenos, Piru, Rolling 60, Santana Block, Satanic Cult Gangs, Skinheads, Stoners, SUR 13, T.C.G. (Tongan Crip Gang), Termites, Tiny Rascal Gang (TRG), Warlords, 106 Watts

Riverside (PP):   Stoners[47], Crips, Gateway Posse, Barrio Dream Homes, Barrio Cathedral City, Bloods, Skinheads, Mexican Mafia, Black Guerilla Family, Nuestra Familia, KKK, SUR 13

Riverside (LE):   1200 Block Crips, Tiny Dukes, 2800 Block Crips, Aryan Circle, Aryan Nation, Black Guerilla Family, Bloods, Hells Angels, KKK, La Familia, La Raza, Mexican Mafia, Neo-nazis, Nuestra Familia, P.J.'s, Piru, Rolling 60, Satanic Cult Gangs, Satans Disciples, Skinheads, White Fence

Sacramento (JI):   Bloods, Crips, White Pride, Skinheads, Neo-nazis, SUR, SWP, Black Guerilla Family, Nuestra Familia, Hell's Angels, Piru, Nortenos, La Raza, Asian+Filipino gangs

Sacramento (JD):   Aryan Brotherhood, Bloods, Crips, Neo-nazis Sacremento Co. (LE): Varrio Franklin Boys[48], Oak Park Bloods, Del Paso Heights Bloods, BGD's, Black Guerilla Family, Border Brothers, Born To Kill (BTK), Crips, El Rukns, F.T.W., Hells Angels, Hua Ching, King Cobra, KKK, Mexican Mafia, Neo-Nazis, Nortenos, Piru, Rolling 60, Santana Block, Sharps, Sons of Samoa (SOS), Surenos, SUR 13, SWP, Tongan Crip Gang (TCG), Tiny Rascal Gang (TRG), White Fence, 18th Street Gang

San Benito Co. (PP):   Bloods, Crips, Aryan Brotherhood, Skinheads, SUR, Mexican Mafia, Nuestra Familia, SUR 13

---

[44]These are gangs that the kids identified themselves as, but no major activity is reported inside the institution.

[45]Hispanic gang.

[46]Bloods.

[47] White gang.

[48]Hispanic group.

San Bernardino (LE):   Inland Empire, Mount Vernon Rifa (MVR), ES 13th Street, Aryan Nation, Bikers, Bloods, Crips, Diamond Street, E.M.E., Hells Angels, Kitchen Crips, La Familia, Mexican Mafia, Piru, Rollin 60, Santana Block, Skinheads, Tiny Rascal Gang (TRG), SUR 13, 18th Street Gang, 106 Watts

San Diego (PP):   Skinheads, Bloods, Crips, Neo-nazis, Ku Klux Klan, PYRU, Blue Rags, Red Rags

San Diego (AI):   Bloods, Crips, Aryan Brotherhood, Skinheads, Neo-nazis, Black Gangsters, Mexican Mafia, Bikers, Black Guerilla Family, Nuestra Familia

San Diego (W2):   Aryan Brotherhood, Black Guerilla Family, Bloods, Crips, Mexican Mafia, Nortenos, Nuestra Familia, Pyru

San Diego Co. (LE):   Vista Home Boys, Imperials, Encinitas/Totrilla Flats, Bikers, Bloods, Boot Boys, Border Brothers, Crips, Hell's Angels, KKK, Mexican Mafia, Nuestra Familia, Piru, Rolling 60, Skinheads, Sons of Samoa (SOS), SWA's, Tiny Rascal Gang (TRG)

San Francisco (LE):   Wo Hop To (Asian), Swampy Desert (Black), Trece (Hispanic), Aryan Brotherhood, Aryan Nation, Black Guerilla Family, Bloods, Born To Kill (BTK), Crips, E.M.E., Ghost Shadows, Hells Angels, Wah Ching, Insane Crips, La Familia, Mexican Mafia, Nuestra Familia, 14th Street Gang, 18th Street Gang

San Francisco (JA):   Out of Control Crew (OCC)[49], Page Street Posse, SFM[50]; Aryan Brotherhood, Aryan Nation, BD's, BG's, Black Guerilla Family, Bloods, Border Patrol, Brothers of White Supremacy (BOWS), Crazy White Boys, Crips, Dirty White Boys, Hell's Angels, Hua Ching, Jokers, La Familia, Mexican Mafia, Neo-nazis, Nortenos, Satanic Cult Gangs, Skinheads, Sons of Samoa (SOS), SUR 13, Texas Mafia, White Peoples Party, 18th Street Gang, 25th Neighborhood, 34th Street Players

San Jose (JA):   Aryan Brotherhood, Black Guerilla Family, Bloods, Crips, Hua Ching, Mexican Mafia, Nuestra Familia, Skinheads, Sons of Samoa (SOS)

San Leandro (LE):   Davis Street Locos, East 7th, West Side Family, All Brothers Together (ABT), Aryan Nation, Hell's Angels, Nortenos, Sons of Samoa (SOS), SUR 13

San Louis Obispo (JI):   Crips, Bloods, SUR 13, White Power, SWP

San Luis Obispo (AI):   Aryan Brotherhood, Crips, Bloods, Surenos, Skinheads, SUR, Mexican Mafia, Bikers, Black Guerilla Family, Nuestra Familia, PIRU (A Blood), Nortenos[51]

San Luis Obispo (W2):   Aryan Brotherhood, Bikers, Black Guerilla Family, Bloods, Blue hats/Blue rags, Border Brothers, Cobras, Crips, C Street, CUBO, Eight Balls, F-13, Five Percenters, Gangsters, Hell's Angels, Insane Crips, Jokers, Kitchen Crips, KKK, Latin Kings, La Raza, Mexican Mafia, Neo-nazis, Nortenos, Nuestra Familia, PYRU, Red hats/Red rags, Rolling 60, Santana Block, Satanic Cult Gangs, Satans Disciples, Skinheads, Sons of Samoa (S.O.S.), Stoners, SUR 13, SWP, Upland Ghost Town (UGT), White Peoples Party, White Power, White Pride, 8-Balls, 14th Street Gang, 18th Street Gang, 19th Street Gang, 106 Watts

---

[49]AKA: "Space Age Gangster".

[50]San Francisco Misson.

[51] Blue Rags include Crips and Surenos (SUR); red rags include Bloods and Nortenos; PIRU and PYRU are bloods; Insane Crypts are the same as crips.

San Quentin (W3):   Aryan Brotherhood, Nuestra Familia, Northern Structure, Black Guerilla Family; All Brothers Together (ABT), Aryan Nation, BGD's, Bloods, Border Brothers, Crips, Dirty White Boys, E.M.E., Hell's Angels, Insane Crips, King Cobra, Kitchen Crips, KKK, Mexican Mafia, Neo-nazis, Nortenos, Nuestra Familia, Piru, Rolling 60, Sons of Samoa (SOS), Surenos, S.S.G., White Fence, 18th Street Gang

San Rafael (LE):   18th Street, Mara Salvatruchas (MS13), Aryan Brotherhood, Black Guerilla Family La Raza, Nortenos, Sons of Samoa (SOS), Surenos

Santa Ana (LE):   F-Troop, Middleside, Lopers (undocumented aliens), Crips, Hua Ching, Mexican Mafia, Skinheads, Sons of Samoa (SOS), Tiny Rascal Gang

Santa Cruz (JI):   Bloods, Crips, Aryan Brotherhood, White Pride, Skinheads, Neo-nazis, SUR, SWP, Mexican Mafia, Black Guerilla Family, Nuestra Familia, Hell's Angels, Insane Crypts, SUR 13, Nortenos

Santa Cruz (JD):   Bloods, Crips, Hell's Angels, Mexican Mafia, Neo-Nazis, Nuestra Familia, Sons of Samoa (S.O.S.), SUR 13, SWP, White Pride, PSL Boys, Skinheads

Santa Monica (LE):   Santa Monica 17 Pee Wee Locos, Santa Monica 13 Lil Locos, Graveyard Crips, Bloods, E.M.E., Insane Crips, Rolling 60, Sons of Samoa, 18th Street Gang

Sebastopol (PC):   Aryan Brotherhood, Skinheads, Posse, Bikers, Nuestra Familia

Shasta Co. (LE):   XIV, XII, Brothers of the Wind (motorcycle), Aryan Brotherhood, Bloods, Crips, F.T.W., Hell's Angels, Hua Ching, Insane Vice Lords, Latin Kings, La Familia, Lynch Mob, Mexican Mafia, Nortenos, Rolling 60, Santana Block, Skinheads, Tiny Rascal Gang, SUR 13, White Pride

South Gate (LE):   MLS = Marijuana Locos, GVL - Garden View Locos, Kansas Street (K-St.), F-13, King Cobra, White Fence, 18th Street

S. San Francisco (PC):   South City Boys, C Street, DWH

Stockton (JI):   Bloods, Crips, White Pride, Skinheads, Neo-nazis, SUR, SWP, PYRU, SUR 13, Nortenos, Asian Gangs

Stockton (LE):   S.S.G. (Sixth Street Gangsters, 110), N.S.G.C. (North Side Gangster Crip, 140), B.N.G. (Bahala HNA Gang, 120), A.B.T. (All Brothers Together), Aryan Brotherhood, BGD's, Bikers, Black Guerilla Family, Bloods, Border Brothers, Born To Kill (BTK), Crips, E.M.E., F.T.W., Hells Angels, Wah Ching, King Cobra, KKK, Latin Kings, La Raza, Mexican Mafia, Nortenos, Nuestra Familia, Posse Comitatus, Satanic Cult Gangs, Skinheads, Sons of Samoa (S.O.S.), South Side Tracy, Stoners, SUR 13, SWP, Tiny Rascal Gang (T.R.G.)

Tehama Co. (CS):[52]   Aryan Brotherhood, Posse, Mexican Mafia, Bikers, Pagans

Torrance (LE):   Centro Torrance 13, Eastside Torrance, Tortilla Flats, Aryan Brotherhood, Aryan Nation, Bloods, Crips, Dukes, Imperial Gangsters, Insane Crips, Kitchen Crips, L.C.M., NWA, P.J.'s, Piru, Rolling 60, Santana Block, Shotgun, Skinheads, Sons of Samoa, Surenos, SUR 13, T.C.G. (Tongan Crip Gang), Tiny Rascal Gang (TRG), White Fence, White Power, 18th Street Gang

Tracy (PC):   West Side Boyz, ABT (All Brothers Together), South Side Tracy, Posse, Nuestra Familia

Upland (PC):   Upland Los Olivos (ULO), Upland Ghost Town (UGT), Empire Villens (EVs), Bloods, Crips, Skinheads, El Rukns, Neo-nazis, SWP, Mexican Mafia, Bikers, Ku Klux Klan, PYRU, SUR 13, F.T.W.

Vallejo (LE):   XIV, XII, Vallejo Town Posse, All Brothers Together, Black Guerilla Family, Crips, Folks, Hells Angels, KKK, Nuestra Familia, Sons of Samoa (S.O.S.), Surenos, S.S.G., SUR 13, Tongan Crip Gang (T.C.G.)

---

[52]These gangs occassionally pass thru this county.

Ventura Co. (PP):   Pierpont Rats, EVIL[53], Crips, Colonia Chiques, Skinheads, Bloods, Mexican Mafia, Bikers, Nuestra Familia, SUR 13

Ventura (LE):   Ventura Avenue Gangsters, Ventura Mid-Town, Haoles, Bikers, Bloods, Born To Kill (BTK), Colonia Chiques, Crazy White Boys, Crips, E.M.E., Gangsters, Hell's Angels, KKK, Neo-nazis, Nuestra Familia, Pierpoint Rats, Rolling 60, Satanic Cult Gangs, Skinheads, SWP, Warlords

Visalia (LE):   Oriental Troops (O.T.'s), Mexican Gangster Boys (M.G. B.'s), North Side Visalia Boys (N.S.V.B.'s), Blue hats/blue rags, Border Brothers, Dukes, E.M.E., Nuestra Familia, Red hats/red rags, Tiny Rascal Gang (TRG)

Walnut Creek (LE):   Boys In Crime (B.I.C.), The Mad Kings (T.M.K.), XIV (14's), All Brothers Together (ABT), Aryan Brotherhood, Black Guerilla Family, Bloods, Crips, Hells Angels, Wah Ching, Skinheads, Sons of Samoa (SOS)

West Covina (LE):   NHC (Neighborhood Hustler Crips), EWF (Every Woman's Fantasy), WC13 (West Covina 13), Bloods, Crips, Mexican Mafia, Nuestra Familia, Rolling 60, Skinheads, SWP, White Fence

Westminster (LE):   West Trece, TRG, NIP Family, Aryan Brotherhood, Born To Kill (BTK), Hua Ching, Mexican Mafia, Nuestra Familia

Yuba City (PC):   Norte Bad Boys, Posse, Mexican Mafia, Nuestra Familia

Yuba City (LE):   Norte Bad Boys, V.L.O.L, Lake County Posse,Bloods, Crips

Walnut Creek (PC):   Boys in Crime, Crips

Watsonville (PC):   North Side Locos, City Hall Watson, Poor Side Watson, Nuestra Familia, SUR 13

Whittier (JI):   Stoners, Punks, SWP, Anarchist[54], Bloods, Crips, White Pride, Posse, SUR, Mexican Mafia, Black Guerilla Family, PYRU (Piru is correct spelling), SUR 13, Nortenos, Hustlers, WAR

Willows (PC):   O.B.'s, Humpty Crew Gang, Gypsy Jokers

Jolo Co. (LE):   Crips, Bloods, Outlaw Biker, Aryan Brotherhood, Aryan Nation, Banditos, Black Guerilla Family, E.M.E., Hells Angels, La Familia, La Mafia, La Raza, Mexican Mafia, Nuestra Familia, Nortenos, Pagans, Piru, Satanic Cult Gangs, Skinheads, White Pride, White Power

Yreka (JD):   Aryan Brotherhood, Bloods, Crips, SUR 13, SWP, White Power, White Pride

COLORADO:

Adams Co. (LE):   Crenshaw Mafia Gangsters ( ), North Side Mafia (NSM), Sons of Silence M/C Club, Aryan Brotherhood, Aryan Nation, Banditos, BGD's, Bikers, Bloods, Boot Boys, Crips, Gypsy Jokers, Hells Angels, Highway Men, Inca Boys, Insane Vice Lords, King Cobra, Latin Kings, KKK, La Raza, Lynch Mob, Mexican Mafia, Miami Boys, Neo-nazis, Outlaws, Pagans, Peoples, Posse Comitatus, Prison Motorcycle Brotherhood (PMB), Piru, Santana Block, Satanic Cult Gangs, Sharps, Shotgun, Sin City Boys, Stoners, Tiny Rascal Gang (TRG), Vice Lords, Warlocks, Warlords, White Pride, 98 Posse,18th St.

Arapahoe Co. (CS):   Bloods, Crips, Skinheads, Aryan Brotherhood, Posse, Mexican Mafia, KKK, Sons of Silence

---

[53] Both are white gangs.

[54] Along with skinheads, identified as white gangs.

Arvada (LE):   Crips (Tre Tre), Bloods (Crenshaw Mafia Gangsters), Northside Mafia[55], Tiny Rascal Gangsters[56], Banditos, BGD's, Bikers, Cholos, F.B.I., Inca Boys, KKK, Latin Kings, Lynch Mob, Miami Boys, Neo-nazis, NWA, O.L.B., Posse Comitatus, Rolling 60, Skinheads, Sons of Silence, Stoners, TRG, White Power, White Pride

Aurora (LE):   104th St. Crenshaw Mafia Gangster Bloods, Rollin 30 Crips, Compton Crips, Aryan Brotherhood, Aryan Nation, BGDs, Bloods, Eight Balls, El Rukns, Folks, Four Corner Hustlers, Inca Boys, Insane Crips, Insane Vice Lords, Kitchen Crips, KKK, La Familia, Lynch Mob, Mexican Mafia, Posse, Piru, Santana Block, Shotgun, Rolling 60, Six Pack Gang, Skinheads, Stoners, Tongan Crip Gang (TCG), Vice Lords, 8-Balls

Boulder Co. (LE):   Asian-TRGs, Skinheads, Aryan Brotherhood, Aryan Nation, Crips, Gypsy Jokers, Hells Angels, Inca Boys, KKK, Mexican Mafia, Outlaws, Pagans, Posse Comitatus, Sharps, Sons of Silence, Tiny Rascal Gang (TRG), Vice Lords, Warlords, White Power, White Pride, WOPS

Boulder (city of, LE):   Aryan Brotherhood, Aryan Nation, Bloods, Crips, E.M.E., F.B.I., Hells Angels, Inca Boys, KKK, La Raza, Mexican Mafia, Outlaws, Skinheads, Sons of Silence, Tiny Rascal Gang (TRG)

Brighton (JD):   Bloods, Crips, Kitchen Crips, KKK, Rolling 60, Satanic Cult Gangs

Burlington (PC):   Posse, Sons of Silence

Burlington (JA):   Bloods, Crips; All Brothers Together (ABT), Aryan Nation, Banditos, Cholos, Crazy White Boys, Neo-nazis, Posse Comitatus, Sons of Silence

Canon City (JA):   Crips, Bloods, Aryan Nation

Canon City (AI):[57]   Aryan Brotherhood, Skinheads, Bikers, Bloods, Crips, Neo-nazis, Mexican Mafia, Sons of Silence

Canon City (AI):   Bloods, Crips, Aryan Brotherhood, Skinheads, Mexican Mafia, Nuestra Familia, Sons of Silence

Canon City (AI):   Bloods, Crips, Aryan Brotherhood, Nuestra Familia

Cherry Hills (LE):   Skinheads, Crips, Bloods, BGD's, Boot Boys, Foul Play, Head Bangers, Hell's Angels, Inca Boys, The Kings Posse, KKK, Lynch Mob, Peoples, Posse Comitatus, Piru, Rolling 60, Sharps, Stoners, Sons of Silence, Tiny   Rascal Gang, Vice Lords, 18th Street Gang

Canon City (W3):   Bloods, Crips, Aryan Brotherhood; Aryan Nation, Banditos, Beirut Dogs, BGD's, Black Disciples, Black Guerilla Family, El Rukns, Hell's Angels, Inca Boys, Insane Vice Lords, Jokers, JVL Posse, Kitchen Crips, KKK, Latin Kings, La Raza, Mexican Mafia, Nuestra Familia, Outlaws, Prison Motorcycle Brotherhood (PMB), Skinheads, Texas Mafia, Vice Lords, Warlords, White Power, White Pride

Colorado Springs (JI):   Bloods, Crips, Skinheads, Hell's Angels

Colorado Springs (JD):   Bloods, Crips, Kitchen Crips, Rolling 60, Satanic Cult Gangs, Skinheads

Colorado Springs (LE):   Crips, Bloods, Four Corner Hustlers, Brotherhood, Aryan Nation, BGDs, Disciples, F.T.W., Banditos, Insane Crips, JVL Posse, Posse Comitatus, 18st. Gang, 19th St. Gang, 79th St. Posse

---

[55]Northside Mafia is Hispanic.

[56]Asians.

[57] Multiple observations from Canon City, or other cities, means only that there are multiple institutions in this area who responded to the survey.

Colorado Springs (LE):   Crips, Hustlers, Bloods, Aryan Brotherhood, Aryan Nation, Banditos, BGD's, Bikers, BD's, Bloods, Boot Boys, Four Corner Hustlers, Hells Angels, Inca Boys, Insane Crips, Kitchen Crips, KKK, La Raza, Neo-nazis, Posse, Posse Comitatus, Prison Motorcycle Brotherhood (PMB), Piru, Rolling 60, Skinheads, Sons of Silence, Vice Lords, West Side Posse, White Knights, 8-Balls

Crowley (W2):   Aryan Brotherhood, Supreme White Power (SWP), Banditos, Barrio Chicano Locos, BGD's, Bloods, Crips, Disciples, Gangster Disciples, Insane Crips, Insane Vice Lords, KKK, Knights, L.A. Kings, Mexican Mafia, Neo-nazis, Nuestra Familia, Rolling 60, Satanic Cult Gangs, Satans Disciples, Skinheads, Sons of Silence, Vice Lords

Crowley (W3):   Prison Motorcycle Brotherhood, A.B.'s, White Supremacists, G.O.D.S.[58]; Crips (all sets), Bloods (all sets); Aces, Aryan Nation, Barrio Chicano Locos, BGD's, Bikers, Black Disciples, Black Gangsters, Brothers of White Supremacy (BOWS), Cholos, Crazy White Boys, Dirty White Boys, Dukes, DWH, Eight Balls, E.M.E., Folks, The Fourth Reich, F.T.W., Gangsters, Gangster Disciples, Inca Boys, Insane Crips, Insane Vice Lords, KKK, Knights, Latin Kings, La Familia, La Raza, Mexican Mafia, Moors, Neo-nazis, Nortenos, Nuestra Familia, NWA, Outlaws, Pagans, Peoples, Posse, Piru, Santana Block, Satanic Cult Gangs, Satans Disciples, Skinheads, Sons of Silence, Sorenos, SUR 13, Vice Lords, Warlords, West Side Boyz, West Side Posse, White Power, White Pride, F-13

Delta (W2):   Aryan Brotherhood, Banditos, Bikers, Bloods, Crips, Mexican Mafia, KKK, Rolling 60

Delta (W3):   Prison Motorcycle Brotherhood; Crips, Bloods, Los Treces (Family 13); Aryan Brotherhood, BGD's, F-13 (aka: Family 13), Rolling 60

Denver (JI):   Bloods, Crips, Aryan Brotherhood, Skinheads, Latin Kings, KKK, 19th Street Gang, Posse Commitatus

Denver (LE):   Aryan Brotherhood, Aryan Nation, Aryan Warriors, Banditos, BGDs, Bikers, BDs, Bloods, Boot Boys, Brothers Speed, Crips, Disciples, Foul Play, Inca Boys, Insane Crips, Kitchen Crips, KKK, La Familia, Macomb St. Gang, Mexican Mafia, Neo-nazis, Nortenos, Peoples, Piru, Santana Block, Satanic Cult Gangs, Sons of Silence, Skinheads, Warlords, Vice Lords, White Power, White Pride, 8-Balls

Douglas Co. (LE):   Skinheads "Rocky Mountain Hammer Skins", Vendetta Knights, Posse, Bikers, Bloods, Boot Boys, Crips

Englewood (PC):   Crips, Bloods, Skinheads, Posse, Ku Klux Klan, Head bangers, Sons of Silence

Englewood (JA):   Crips, Bloods; Aryan Nation

Ft. Morgan (PP):   La Raza

Golden (PP):   Bloods, Crips, Skinheads, Neo-nazis, Bikers, Sons of Silence

Golden (JI):   Bloods, Crips, Vice Lords, Disciples, Aryan Brotherhood, Folks, Peoples, White Pride, Skinheads, Miami Boys, Posse, Neo-nazis, Latin Kings, Black Gangsters, Mexican Mafia, Hell's Angels, KKK, PYRU, Knights, Black Mafia, La Raza, Sons of Silence, G-Boys, Inca Boyz

Golden (LE):   Bloods, Inca Boys, Skinheads, Aryan Brotherhood, Banditos, Crips, Mexican Mafia, Neo-nazis, Posse Comitatus, Texas Mafia

Grand Junction (JI):   Bloods, Crips, Skinheads

Larimer Co. (LE):   Cherry Boyz, Northside Brownies, AK's, Crazy White Boys, Crips, Bloods, 8 Balls, KKK, Sons of Silence, Skinheads, Surenos 13, Tiny Rascal Gang (TRG)

---

[58]White gangs.

Littleton (LE):   Skinheads, Inca Boyz, Crips, Aryan Brotherhood, Aryan Nation, Aryan Warriors, Banditos, BGDs, C.I.A. (Criminals in Action), Insane Crips, Posse Comitatus, Piru, Sons of Silence, Skinheads
Milliken (PC):   Crips
Pueblo (JI):   Bloods, Crips, Los Carnales
Pueblo Co. (LE):   Los Carnales[59], Tre-Tre Duce, East Side Dukes (ESD) 13, Aces, Aryan Brotherhood, Aryan Nation, BGD's[60], BKU's, Bloods, Brown Gangster Disciples[61], Crips, Devastation Black Boys (DBB's)[62], Dukes, Eight Balls, Four Corner Hustlers, Freight Train Riders of America, Hell's Angels, Inca Boys[63], Insane Crips, Insane Vice Lords, KKK, L.A. Kings, La Familia, La Raza, Nuestra Familia, Skinheads, Warlords, 18th Street Gang, 106 Watts
Rifle (W3):   Bloods, Crips
Silverthorne (PC):   Bloods, Crips, Aryan Brotherhood, Skinheads
Walsenburg (PC):   Bloods, Crips, Aryan Brotherhood, Cobras
Wheat Ridge (LE):   Northside Mafia[64], Inca Boys, Crips, Bloods, Aryan Nation, Banditos, F.B.I., KKK, Posse Comitatus, Skinheads, Sons of Silence, La Raza
Yuma (PC):   The Kings Posse, Bloods, Crips, Skinheads, Posse, Sons of Silence

CONNECTICUT:
Bridgeport (AI):   Latin Kings, Latin Locos, Aryan Brotherhood, Skinheads, Posse
Bridgeport (JD):   Bloods, Latin Kings, Posse
Bridgeport (LE):   Latin Kings, Nation, Brotherhood, Born To Kill (BTK), Brothers of White Supremacy (BOWS), Hell's Angels, Latin Kings, Los Solidos, Neta
Bridgeport (W3):   B.O.W.S., Aryan Brotherhood; Latin Kings, Aryan Nation, BGD's, Black Guerilla Family, Brothers of the Struggle (BOS), Latin Locos, La Familia, Los Solidos, Monacillos (Neta), Sprangler Posse
Cheshire (W3):   B.O.W.S[65].; Latin Kings, Solidos, Elm; Aryan Brotherhood, Latin Locos
Enfield (AI):   Latin Kings, Savage Nomads
Enfield (AI):   Latin Kings, La Raza, Savage Nomads, Aryan Brotherhood, Skinheads, Bikers, KKK
Enfield (W2):   Latin Kings, Neta, Los Solidos
Enfield (W3):   Brothers of White Supremacy (BOWS); Latin Kings, Los Solidos, 20 Love

---

[59]Joined with Young Crowd.

[60]Denver, Colorado Springs.

[61]Denver, CO.

[62]Colorado Springs.

[63]Denver, Colorado Springs.

[64]Hispanic group.

[65]Said to also mean the Brothers of the White Struggle.

Fairfield Co. (PP):   Latin Kings, Posse, Neo-nazis, KKK
Glastonbury (PC):   Bloods, Skinheads, Ku Klux Klan
Hartford (AI):   Latin Locos, Latin Kings, Savage Nomads, Aryan Brotherhood, Skinheads, Posse, Neo-nazis, Bikers, Center City Locos
Hartford (PP):   Aryan Brotherhood, Latin Kings, Black Gangsters
Hartford (LE):   Los Solidos, Latin Kings, Twenty Love, Savage Nomads
Hartford (W3):   Brothers of the White Struggle (B.O.W.S.)[66], Latin Kings, Los Solidos, 20-Love; Aryan Brotherhood, Aryan Nation, Bikers, Black Guerilla Family, Brothers of the Struggle (BOS), Hartford Posse, Latin Locos, Neta, Savage Nomads, Posse
Litchfield (AI):   Latin Locos, Bloods, Aryan Brotherhood, Latin Kings, Bikers
Litchfield (W2):   Latin Kings
Meriden (LE):   Solidos, Latin Kings, Nation, Five Percenters, Hell's Angels, Imperial Nation, KKK, Latin Kings, Los Solidos, Posse
New Britain (LE):   Latin Kings, Los Solidos, Twenty Love, Hartford Posse
New Haven (AI):   Latin Kings, Latin Locos, Bloods, Aryan Brotherhood, Skinheads
New Haven (W3):   Aryan Brotherhood, B.O.W.S.; Latin Kings, Elm City Brothers, Neta; Black Guerilla Family, Latin Locos, Los Solidos, Monacillos (Neta)
Newtown (AI):   Aryan Brotherhood, Latin Kings
Niantic (W2):   Aryan Brotherhood, Hell's Angels, KKK, Latin Kings, Latin Queens, neo-nazis, Posse, Satanic Cult Gangs, Skinheads, Latin Locos, Neta
Plainfield (PC):   Skinheads, Ku Klux Klan, L.A. Posse
Somers (W2):   Brothers of White Supremacy (BOWS)[67], Aryan Brotherhood, F.T.W., Hell's Angels, Latin Kings, Latin Locos, Los Solidas, Posse, Savage Nomads
Storrs (W2):   Latin Kings, Brotherhood, Solidos
Wallingford (PC):   Bikers
Windsor Locks (AI):[68]   Bloods, Crips, Posse, Latin Kings, Bikers, Ku Klux Klan, Center City Locos

DELEWARE:
Claymont (AI):   Pagans, Warlocks, Thunderguards, Aryan Brotherhood, Black Gangsters, Ku Klux Klan, Knights
Georgetown (PC):   Bloods, Skinheads, Posse
Georgetown (W3):   Aryan Brotherhood, Black Junior Mafia; Aryan Nation, Five Percenters, Fruits of Islam, Pagans
Laurel (PC):   Posse, Ku Klux Klan, Pagans
Newcastle (PC):   Pagans, Bikers, Junior Black Mafia, Black Mafia, Skinheads, Neo-nazis, Cobras, Mad Dogs, BBMF
New Castle Co. (CS):   Aryan Brotherhood, Skinheads, neo-nazis, Ku Klux Klan, Pagans
New Castle Co. (LE):   Junior Black Mafia, Skinheads, New York Boys, 4th Street Gang, Aryan Brotherhood, Aces, Aryan Warriors, Black Mafia, Hells Angels, KKK, Warlocks
Selbyville (PC):   Pagans

---

[66]An all white gang.

[67]White gang

[68] Not in this facility, but in the State system.

Smyrna (AI):   Aryan Brotherhood, Vengeance[69], Fruits of Islam, Neo-nazis, SWP, Pagans, F.T.W.
Smyrna (W3):   Aryan Brotherhood, Fruits of Islam, Pagans, Latin Community
Wilmington (AI):   Aryan Nation, Aryan Brotherhood, Ku Klux Klan, Pagans

DISTRICT OF COLUMBIA (WASHINGTON, D.C.):
Wash., DC (JI):   Wheeler Road Crew, 5th & O Street Crew, LeDroit Park Crew
Wash., DC (JI):   8th & H Crew
Wash., DC (JI):   Bloods, Crips, Posse, Black Gangsters, Hell's Angels, KKK, Joe Louis Project, Simon City Royals, 5th & N O Crew, LeDroit Park Crew, R Street Crewt
Wash., DC (LE):   Aryan Nation, LeDroit Park Crew, Lynch Mob, Miami Boys, R Street Crew, Skinheads, Wheeler Road Crew, 5th & O Street Crew, 8th & H Crew

FLORIDA:
Alachua Co. (LE):   Village Green Posse, Oak Ridge Posse, Southside Posse, Aryan Brotherhood, Aryan Nation, Skinheads, White Peoples Party
Boco Raton (LE):   Northside Nation, Death Squad, World Wide Folk, Aryan Nation, C.I.A., Davie Boys, Eight Ball Posse, Folks, KKK, Latin Kings, La Familia, La Raza, Lynch Mob, Zulu
Bradenton (JI):   Skinheads, KKK
Bradford Co. (CS):   Posse, Head Bangers
Bushnell (AI):   Miami/Tampa/Jacksonville[70], Crips, Skinheads, Miami Boys, Bikers, Ku Klux Klan
Busnell (W3):   Aryan Nation, Odinists[71], Pagans; Five Percenters; Miami Boys
Chattahoochee (AI):   Bloods, Vice Lords, Disciples, Folks, Skinheads, Miami Boys, Latin Kings, Bikers
Chattahoochee (W3):   Miami based gang members (56th Street Gang)
Clearwater (JI):   Skinheads, Miami Boys, Posse, Black Gangsters, Bikers, Hell's Angels, KKK
Clearwater (JA):   Skinheads
Clermont (AI):   Latin Kings
Cross City (AI):   Bloods[72], Skinheads, Crips, Miami Boys, Folks, Latin Kings
Cross City (W3)[73]:   Tampa, Miami, Mariel Cubans East Palatka (W3): Miami Boys

---

[69] White gang.

[70] A common variation of "home boy" cliques, or gang groupings in the institution by their city of origin.

[71] White gang with religious theme.

[72] Indicated to exist as a separate white gang.

[73] Respondent's remark about white gangs in the facility is characteristic of the "most common denominator" function of gang formation (i.e., cliques "group up" or form along the lines of the most common denominator, e.g., color, language, city of origin, residential propinquity, etc). Respondent gave no specific names for the white gangs, but remarked they are organized "usually by the city they are from".

Fort Lauderdale (PC): Zulu, Davie Boys, Imperial Nation, Folks, Skinheads, Posse, Latin Kings, Bikers

Fort Lauderdale (LE):   Zulu, La Familia, World Wide Folk, BGD's, Crips, Davie Boys, DBL's, F.B.I., Folks, Imperial Nation, Insane Crips, Latin Kings, La Familia, La Raza, Lynch Mob, Peoples, Raiders, Skinheads, Spanish Cobras, White Fence

Ft. Lauderdale (JI):   Folk Nation, Zulus, Raiders, Davie Boys, Posse, Miami Boys, Outlaws, Skinheads, KKK, Neo-nazis, Latin Kings, Hell's Angels, 39th Street Gang

Ft. Myers (LE):   Raiders, Palmetto Ct. Posse, Ghetto Boys, Aryan Brotherhood, Aryan Nation, Bikers, Bloods, Imperial Gangsters, KKK, Latin Kings, La Familia, Skinheads, Sons of Silence, 8-Balls

Ft. Myers (JD):   KKK, Skinheads, Vice Lords

Hillsborough Co. (LE):   Romans, The Hood, Town N Country Posse, BGD's, Eight Balls, Hells Angels, Highway Men, Imperial Gangsters, KKK, Latin Kings, Miami Boys, Outlaws, Partners in Crime, Satanic Cult Gangs, Satans Disciples, Sharps, Skinheads, South Side Boys, Vice Lords

Hobe Sound (JI):   Posse, Latin Kings

Holly Hill (JI):   Skinheads, Outlaws, KKK, Airheads, Head Bangers

Indiantown (AI):   Aryan Brotherhood, Miami Boys, Bikers, Pagans

Jacksonville (JI):   Bloods, Crips, Skinheads, Miami Boys, Neo-nazis, Outlaws, Hell's Angels, KKK, Posse Commitatus, King 126

Lakeland (W2):   Aryan Brotherhood, KKK, Miami Boys, Neo-nazis

Lakeland (LE):   Miami Boys, Jamaican Posse, KKK

Lake Wales (PC):   Lincoln Avenue (L.A.) Posse, Skinheads, Miami Boys

Lawtey (AI):   Miami Boys, Hells Angels, Aryan Brotherhood, Skinheads, Ku Klux Klan

Lee Co. (LE):   Vice Lords, Imperial Gangsters, P.C. Posse, 8-Balls, Outlaws, Raiders, Skinheads, Zulu, Traveling Vice Lords, Latin Nation, Latin Disciples

Mayo (AI):   Outlaws, Hells Angels, Aryan Brotherhood, Miami Boys, Posse, Neo-nazis, Bikers, Ku Klux Klan, Pagans

Metro Dade Co. (LE):   International Posse, Latin Kings, Latin Force, Bloods, Davie Boys, Disciples, Folks, Four Horsemen of the Apocalypse, Imperial Gangsters, La Familia, Lynch Mob, Miami Boys, Skinheads, Spanish Cobras, TKK, Zulu, 34th Street Players

Miami (LE):   Latin Kings, 34 Street Players, Latin Force, Aryan Brotherhood, DBL's, Folks, Hell's Angels, Imperial Gangsters, La Familia, Miami Boys, Partners in Crime, Skinheads, TKK

Miami (AI):   Miami Boys, Ku Klux Klan

Miami (JI):   Folks, Peoples, Miami Boys, Posse, Latin Kings, Cobras, TKK (The King Killers), G-Boys, Bloods, Disciples Miami Beach (LE): Latin Kings, Latin Disciples, BD's, Davie Boys, Disciples, Imperial Gangsters, La Familia, Lynch Mob, Peoples, Spanish Cobras, TKK, Zulu, 34th Street Players

N. Miami Beach (LE):   Evil Nation, 10th Avenue Boys, Washington Park Boys, Davie Boys, EVIL, Folks, Imperial Gangsters, La Familia, Miami Boys, NWA, White Fence, Zulu

Okeechobee (JI):   Vice Lords, Latin Kings, Latin Disciples, West Side Posse, Play Boys, Mazda Boys

Olustee (W3):   Miami Boys, Jacksonville Boys, Tampa Boys[74]; Outlaws

---

[74]The respondent remarked that these are "not officially gangs, but are geographical groups that hang together".

Orange Co. (LE):   "B.C." Boys, "P.I.C.", Skinheads, Aryan Brotherhood, Aryan
    Nation, BC Boys, Beirut Dogs, BGD's, Crips, Disciples, GD's, Hua Ching, KKK,
    Latin Kings, La Raza, Knights, Lynch Mob, Miami Boys, Neo-nazis, Neta, Outlaws,
    Partners in Crime, Sharps, Tongan Crip Gang (TCG), Vice Lords, Warlocks
Orlando (AI):   Aryan Brotherhood, Miami Boys, Bikers
Orlando (PC):   Skinheads, Outlaw M.C. Gang, Beirut Dogs, Disciples, Miami Boys,
    Neo-nazis, Latin Kings, Ku Klux Klan
Orlando (JI):   Miami Boys, Outlaws, KKK, BC Boys, Skinheads, Pagans
Palm Beach Co. (LE):   Folk Nation, Latin Kings, Northside Nation, Aryan
    Brotherhood, Aryan Nation, Bikers, Born To Kill (BTK), C.I.A., Crips, Folks, KKK,
    La Familia, La Raza, Miami Boys, Neo-nazis, Skinheads, Spanish Cobras, White
    Peoples Party, Zulu, 8-Balls
Panama City (JI):   Miami Boys
Panama City (LE):   Aryan Nation, Crips, Eight Balls, Outlaws, Satans Disciples
Pasco Co. (LE):   The Family, The Irish, The Nightstalkers, Black/Hispanic Alliance
Pensacola (JI):   Brown Boys, Escambia Arms Posse, Foul Play, IVL (Insane Vice
    Lords)
Pinellas Co. (LE):   Lynch Mob, Clover Place Posse, Original Gangsters, KKK, Latin
    Kings, Macomb Street Gang, Outlaws, Skinheads, 8-Ball Posse
Polk City (AI):   Aryan Brotherhood, Skinheads
Polk City (W3):   Aryan Brotherhood
Polk Co. (LE):   Lincoln Ave. Posse, Highland Park Posse, Jack Boyz, Corner Boys,
    Aryan Brotherhood, Crips, Eight Balls, K-A Posse, Latin Kings, Peoples, Zulu
Punta Gorda (AI):   Aryan Brotherhood, Miami Boys, Ku Klux Klan
Raiford (JI):   G-Boys
Riverview (W3)[75]:   Aryan Brotherhood, Miami Boys, Outlaws, Skinheads
Sanford (JI):   Ku Klux Klan, Sanford Boys
Sarasota (LE):   8-Ball Posse, Hip-Hops, Miami Boys, Skinheads
Satellite Beach (PC):   Skinheads
Sharpes (AI):   Latin Kings, Posse
Sharpes (JI):   Skinheads, Miami Boys, Latin Kings
Stark (AI):   Aryan Brotherhood, Miami Boys, KKK
St. Johns Co. (LE):   Eight Ball Posse, Hell's Angels, KKK, Skinheads
St. Petersburg (PC):   Skinheads, Bikers
Tallahassee (PC):   Blook Killers, Kings, Raiders, Aryan Brotherhood, Ku Klux Klan,
    Macomb Gang, Basin Street Gang, Joe Louis Project
Tallahassee (JI):   Basin Street Gang, Joe Louis Project, Miami Boys, Macomb Gang,
    Basin Street Gang, Joe Louis Project, Miami Heat
Tallahassee (LE):   Basin St. - Raiders, Holton St. - Kings, Joe Louis St. - N.W.A.
    (Niggers With Attitudes), Folks[76], Lynch Mob[77], KKK, Macomb St. Gang, Miami

---

[75]Respondent remarked "No known gangs are represented among inmates in this
facility", but then checked off several from the checklist for "each such gang that has
been active in any capacity in your area".

[76]Graffiti only.

[77]Graffiti only.

Boys, NWA, Peoples[78], Raiders, Rat Pack, Skinheads, South City Boys, 34th St. Players[79]

Tallahassee (W3)[80]:   KKK, Skinheads, NWSSP,Aryan Brotherhood, Aryan Nation, WSG; Various "homeboy" groups: Jax Boys, Tampa Boyz, Miami Boyz; Banditos, BGD's,Bikers, Black Guerilla Family, Bloods, Born To Kill (BTK), Brothers of the Struggle (BOS), Cobras, Dirty White Boys, El Rukns, Five Percenters, Folks, The Fourth Reich, Gangster Disciples, Hell's Angels, Hell Raisers, Insane Vice Lords, Latin Kings, Miami Boys, Miami Heat, Nuestra Familia, Outlaws, Pagans, Posse Comitatus, Satanic Cult Gangs, Sons of Silence, Spanish Cobras, Texas Mafia, Zulu

Tampa (JI):   Skinheads, Latin Kings, Cobras, 34th Street Players (Miami), K-A Posse0

Vera Beach (AI):   Latin Kings

Vero Beach (W3):   Latin Kings, Folks

West Palm Beach (JA):   Folk Nation, Doo Rag Possee, Latin Kings; Folks, Mexican Mafia, Pagans, Skinheads, Thundercats

Zephyrhills (AI):   Skinheads, Miami Boys, Ku Klux Klan

GEORGIA:

Alamo (PC):   Hell Raisers

Albany (JI):   Skinheads, Miami Boys, EMC Rattler

Atlanta (PC):   Ku Klux Klan

Atlanta (LE):   Crips, Bloods, Jamaican Posse, Aryan Brotherhood, Aryan Nation, Banditos, BGDs, BGs, BDs, Black Guerilla Family, Born to Kill (BTK), Boyz of Destruction (BOD's), Chateau Boys, C.I.A., Cobras, Disciples, DBL's, Eight Balls, Ellenwood Boys, El Rukns, Five Percenters, Flying Dragons, Folks, Fruits of Islam, GDs, Ghost Riders, Ghost Shadows, Hells Angels, Highway Men, Hilltop Hustlers, Wah Ching, Insane Crips, Insane Vice Lords, The Kings Posse, Kitchen Crips, KKK, Latin Kings, Lynch Mob, Miami Boys, Neo-nazis, Outlaws, Pagans, Piru, Rolling 60, Skinheads, South Side Boys, Sprangler Posse, Twelve Gauge Posse, Vice Lords, West Side Posse, White Knights, K-9 Posse

Chattahoochee Co. (LE):   Posse

Clayton Co. (LE):   8 Ball Posse, Gangster Bloods, Fennokes, BGD's, Crips, KKK, Miami Boys, Skinheads, Twelve Gauge Posse

Columbus (AI):   Bloods, Crips

Cumming (LE):   KKK, skinheads

Decatur (JI):   Bloods, Crips, Miami Boys, Posse, KKK, DBL's

Decatur (JD):   Aryan Brotherhood, Bloods, Chateau Boys, Crips, Disciples, Down by the Laws (DBL's), Ellenwood Boys, Five Percenters, Miami Boys, Posse

Douglas Co. (LE):   Knox Brothers, Twins, X[81], Hells Angels, KKK, Miami Boys, Outlaws

---

[78]Graffiti only.

[79]Graffiti only.

[80]Response for the entire Florida Department of Corrections, from the Gangs/STG Intelligence Coordinator.

[81]From Malcolm X.

Forest Park (PC):   Down by Law, Twelve Gauge Posse, Rock Boys, Bloods, Crips, Aryan Brotherhood, Skinheads, Miami Boys, Posse, Ku Klux Klan, Pagans, Ellenwood Boys
Lawrenceville (JI):   Bloods, Crips, Skinheads, Miami Boys, KKK, Down By the Law (DBL)
Lawrenceville (JD):   Aryan Brotherhood, Crips, Down By the Laws, KKK, Miami Boys, Satanic Cult Gangs
Macon (JI):   Skinheads, Miami Boys, Posse
Macon (JD):   Airheads, KKK, Miami Boys
Macon (W2):   Aryan Brotherhood, Bikers, Miami Boys, Outlaws
Marietta (LE):   Jamaican Posse, Miami Boys, BGD's, Aryan Nation, Bloods, Crips, KKK, Outlaws MC, Skinheads, Vice Lords
Milledgeville (JI):   Bloods, Crips, Miami Boys, DBL's
North Metro (PC):   Ku Klux Klan
Rock Springs (AI):   Bloods, Crips, Aryan Brotherhood, Miami Boys
Savannah (AI):   Ku Klux Klan, Miami Boys, Aryan Brotherhood, Bloods, Black Gangsters, Insane Crypts, Mad Dogs
Savannah (JI):   Skinheads, Miami Boys, KKK
Savannah (W2):   Down By the Laws, Givens Drug Gang
Georgia Statewide(PP):   Miami Boys, Bloods, Crips, Skinheads, Neo-nazis, Bikers, Ku Klux Klan, Five Percenters
Webster Co. (CS):   Miami Boys, Bikers

HAWAII:
Hilo (AI):   Red rags
Hilo (CS):   Bloods, Crips, Bikers
Honolulu (PC):   Hawaii Brothers, Cross Suns, Palolo Valley Bloods, Skinheads
Honolulu (W2):   Sons of Samoa, PIRU, Hawaiian Brothers
Kailua (AI):   Bloods, Crips
Kailua (JI):   Bloods, Crips

IDAHO:
Ada Co. (LE):   Brother Speed (motorcycle club), Aryan Brotherhood, Bloods, Crips, La Familia, Mexican Mafia, MWA, Nuestra Familia
Blackfoot (PC):   BBP, 39th Street Gang
Boise (PC):   Bloods, Crips, Aryan Brotherhood, Neo-nazis, Mexican Mafia, Nuestra Familia
Boise (W2):   Aryan Brotherhood, Gypsy Jokers, Mexican Mafia, La Familia, Nuestra Familia, White Power
Boise (LE):   Crips, Bad Boy Posse, Punks/Skinheads, Aryan Brotherhood, Bloods, Eight Balls, F.B.I., Sharps, Sons of Samoa (SOS), Stoners
Boundary Co. (CS):   Aryan Brotherhood, Skinheads, Posse
Cottonwood (AI):   Bloods, 39th Street Gang, Texas Mafia, Crips, Aryan Brotherhood, Skinheads, Neo-nazis, Mexican Mafia, Nuestra Familia, Gypsy Jokers, Termites
Homedale (PC):   Warlords, Blades, Bloods, Aryan Brotherhood, Mexican Mafia, Ku Klux Klan, Brother Speed (Motorcycle gang)
Kootenai Co. (CS):   Crips, Skinheads, neo-nazis, Gypsy Jokers
Madison Co. (CS):   Crips, Aryan Brotherhood, Mexican Mafia, Bikers, Gypsy Jokers, 39th Street gang
Orofino (AI):   Aryan Brotherhood
Orofino (PC):   Skinheads, Satan Worshipers, Mexican Mafia, Aryan Brotherhood

Orofino (JI):   Bloods, Crips, Aryan Brotherhood, Skinheads, Neo-nazis, War Lords, Cholos
Orofino (W3):   Aryan Brotherhood
Pocatello (W2):   Aryan Brotherhood
Pocatello (LE):   Down Street Crips (D.S.C.), Varrios Locos St. Anthony (JI): Bloods, Crips, Aryan Brotherhood, Norwalk Barrio, MWA (Mexicans With Attitudes), 38th Gang

ILLINOIS:
Adams Co. (PP):   Vice Lords, Disciples, Latin Kings, Ku Klux Klan
Aledo (JA):   BGD's, Latin Kings, Vice Lords
Aledo Co. (L4):   Black Gangster Disciples, Vice Lords
Alexis (L4):   Vice Lords, Gangster Disciples
Algonquin (L4):   Gangster Disciples, Latin Kings, Vice Lords
Alton (LE):   Black Gangster Disciples, Crips (wannabes), Bloods (wanna-be's), GD's
Alton (L4):   Traveler Vice Lords, Gangster Disciples, Crips
Anna (L4):   Disciples
Arlington Hts. (LE):   Latin Kings, GDs, Spanish Cobras, Vice Lords, BGD's, BG's, Bloods, Cholos, Crips, Disciples, FOlks, Four Corner Hustlers, Gangsters, Imperial Gangsters, Insane Vice Lords, Peoples, Party Players, Satan's Disciples, Simon City Royals, Skinheads, Two-Sixers
Atlanta (L4):   Latin Kings, Vice Lords, White Supremicists
Aurora (PP):   Black Gangster Disciples, Vice Lords, Latin Kings, Aryan Brother hood, Folks, Peoples, Skinheads, Neo-nazis
Aurora (LE):   Latin Kings, Disciples, Vice Lords, BGD's, BD's, BG's, Crips, Folks, Four Corner Hustlers, GD's, Imperial Gangsters, Insane Vice Lords, Latin Counts, La Raza, Party Players, Peoples, Satans Disciples, Simon City Royals, Skinheads, Spanish Cobras, Two-Sixers
Aurora (L4):   Latin Kings, Black Gangster Disciples, Insane Dueces
Barrington (L4):   Disciples, Latin Kings, Black Gangster Disciples
Bartlett (PC):   Latin Kings, Black Gangster Disciples, Imperial Gangsters, Folks, Peoples
Bellwood (L4):   Vice Lords, Black Gangster Disciples, Black P. Stones, Four Corner Hustlers, Insane Vice Lords, Latin Kings, Maniac Latin Disciples, Spanish Cobras
Belvidere (L4):   White Gangster Disciples, Latin Kings, Vice Lords
Bensenville (L4):   Spanish Cobras, Latin Kings
Berkeley (L4):   Unknown Assassins, Black Gangster Disciples, Latin Kings
Blue Mound (L4):   Vice Lords, Gangster Disciples
Boone Co. (LE):   Latin Kings, GD's, BGD's, BD's, Disciples, Gangsters, Vice Lords
Bourbonnais (L4):   Gangster Disciples, Latin Kings, Vice Lords
Braidwood (L4):   Vice Lords, Latin Kings, Two-Sixers, Black Gangster Disciples, Chicago Outlaws, Insane Dueces, Latin Counts, Maniac Latin Disciples, Satan's Disciples
Brookfield (L4):   Latin Kings, Gangster Disciples, Two Sixers, Chicago Outlaws, Imperial Gangsters, Insane Popes, Simon City Royals, Two Two Boys
Brookport (L4):   Latin Kings, Gaylords, Black Gangster Disciples
Bunker Hill (L4):   Saddle Tramps MC, KKK
Bushnell (L4):   Gangster Disciples, Latin Kings, Vice Lords
Calumet Park (L4):   Gangster Disciples, Four Corner Hustlers, Latin Kings
Cambria (L4):   Kings
Cambridge (L4):   Gangster Disciples, Vice Lords
Carlinville (JA):   Aryan Brotherhood, Hell's Angels, KKK
Carol Stream (L4):   Latin Kings, Disciples, Vice Lords

Cary (L4):   Gangster Disciples, Latin Kings, Maniac Latin Disciples
Central City (L4):   Black Disciples
Champaign Co. (LE):   Hoods, Dawgs, Latin Counts, Vengeance
Cherry Valley (L4):   Black Disciples, Latin Kings, Vice Lords, Black Gangsters, Black Gangster Disciples
Chicago (City of, LE):   BGDs, Vice Lords, Latin Kings, BDs, GDs, Bloods, Born to Kill (BTK), Chicago Outlaws, Crips, Disciples, Latin Dragons, El Rukns, Four Corner Hustlers, Fruits of Islam, GD's, Imperial Gangsters, Insane Vice Lords, Latin Counts, Latin Eagles, Latin Locos, La Raza, Party Boys, Party Players, Satans Disciples, Simon City Royals, Spanish Cobras, Two-Sixers
Chicago Heights (LE):   GDs, Vice Lords, Latin Kings, Latin Counts,BDs, BGs, B.O.S., Disciples, Folks, Four Corner Hustlers
Chicago Heights (L4):   Latin Kings, Four Corner Hustlers, Gangster Disciples
Chicago Heights (L4):   Four Corner Hustlers, 11 Street Posse, Black Gangster Disciples
Chicago Ridge (L4):   Maniac Latin Disciples, Satan's Disciples, Two Sixers
Chillicothe (L4):   Gangster Disciples
Clinton (L4):   Bloods, Vice Lords, Gangster Disciples
Coles Co. (PP):   Aryan Brotherhood, Ku Klux Klan, Bikers
Colona (L4):   Vice Lords, Black Gangster Disciples, Gangster Disciples, Latin Kings
Colllinsville (L4):   Disciples, Vice Lords, Bloods, Crips
Country Club Hills(L4):   Gangster Disciples, Black P Stone Nation, Black Disciples, Four Corner Hustlers
Crystal Lake (L4):   Gangster Disciples, Latin Kings
Danvers (L4):   Latin Kings, Black Gangster Disciples, Simon City Royals
Decatur (LE):   BGDs, Vice Lords, Dime Boyz (local), BGs, BDs, B.O.S., Folks, Insane Vice Lords, Latin Kings, Simon City Royals
Dekalb (L4)[82]:   Ambrose, Bishops, Black Disciples, Black Gangster Disciples, Black P. Stones, Cobra Stones, Cullerton Deuces, Folks, Four Corner Hustlers, Gangster Disciples, Imperial Gangsters, Insane Vice Lords, Latin Kings, Maniac Latin Disciples, Two-Sixers, Vice Lords
Delavan (L4):   Latin Kings, Gangster Disciples, Vice Lords
Des Plaines (LE):   Latin Kings, Imperial Gangsters, Disciples, BGD's, GD's, Party Players, Simon City Royals, Spanish Cobras, Two-Sixers, Vice Lords, Spanish Lords
Downers Grove (LE):   Gangster Disciples, Vice Lords, Black P Stones, BGD's, Folks, Four Corner Hustlers, Insane Vice Lords, Latin Kings, Party Boys, Peoples, Spanish Cobras, Two-Sixers
DuPage Co. (PP):   Latin Kings, Disciples, Simon City Royals, Aryan Brotherhood, Brothers of the Struggle, Spanish Cobras, Black Gangsters, Outlaws MC, Harrison Gents, Maniac Latin Disciples, Kuang Le, Two-Sixers, Insane Dueces
Dwight (W3):   Disciples, Vice Lords, Latin Kings; BGD's, BD's, BG's, Chicago Outlaws, Cobras, Crips, El Rukns, GD's, Imperial Gangsters, Insane Vice Lords, Simon City Royals
Edwardsville (PP):   The Flannels[83], Skinheads, Vice Lords, Park Avenue, Black Gangster Disciples, Bloods, Crips, Hilltop Posse, Insane Crypts, F.T.W.
Effingham Co. (L4):   Damage Inc
Effingham (L4):   Damage Inc, Satan's Disciples, Latin Kings

---

[82]Some gang activity with 1 or more gang members in the past three years.

[83] A white gang.

Elgin (L4):   Latin Kings, Black Gangster Disciples, Maniac Latin Disciples
Elk Grove Village (L4):   Black Gangster Disciples, Black P. Stones, Gangster
  Disciples, Imperial Gangsters, Insane Unknowns, Latin Kings, La Raza, Orchestra
  Albany
Elmhurst (LE):   Latin Kings, Disciples, Vice Lords, BGDs, BDs, Folks, Four Corner
  Hustlers, GDs, Imperial Gangsters, Insane Vice Lords, Simon City Royals, Spanish
  Cobras, Two-Sixers
Evanston (PC):   Aryan Nations, skinheads, Aryan Brotherhood Posse
Evanston (LE):   BGDs, Vice Lords, Jamaican Posse, BDs, B.O.S., GDs, El Rukns,
  Insane Vice Lords, Simon City Royals
Evanston (L4):   Gangster Disciples, Vice Lords, Latin Kings
Evergreen Park (L4):   Gangster Disciples, Black Gangsters, B.O.S.
Ford Co. (L4):   Latin Kings, Vice Lords, Simon City Royals, Disciples, Gangster
  Disciples, Jamaican Posse, KKK, Northsiders
Fox Lake (L4):   Latin Kings, Gangster Disciples, Vice Lords
Frankfort (L4):   Satans Disciples, Ambrose
Franklin Park (L4):   Insane Gangsters, Latin Kings
Fulton Co. (PP):   Ku Klux Klan
Galesburg (PP):   Latin Kings, Black Gangster Disciples
Geneva (L4):   Latin Kings, Insane Deuces, Vice Lords
Gibson City (L4):   Latin Kings, Gangster Disciples
Glendale Heights (L4):   Latin Kings, Satan's Disciples, Black Gangster Disciples
Glenview (L4):   Latin Kings, Black Gangster Disciples
Grafton (JI):   Bloods, Crips, Vice Lords, Disciples, Posse, Latin Kings, Black
  Gangsters, Simon City Royals, Cobras
Grayslake (L4):   Latin Kings, Disciples, Vice Lords
Grundy Co. (LE):   Latin Kings, Two Sixers, Outlaws
Harrisburg (JI):   Vice Lords, Disciples, Folks, Peoples, Brothers of the Struggle,
  Latin Kings, Black Gangsters, Cobras, Simon City Royals, 4 Corner Hustlers
Harvard (L4):   Latin Kings, Bishops, Vice Lords, Gangster Disciples
Herscher (L4):   Latin Kings, Two-Two Boys
Hickory Hills (L4):   Satan's Disciples, Latin Kings, TAP Boys
Highwood (L4):   Spanish Gangsters, Latin Kings
Hinsdale (L4):   Two-Sixers, Maniac Latin Disciples
Hodgkins (L4):   Latin Kings[84]
Hoffman Estates (L4):   Gangster Disciples, Latin Kings, Vice Lords
Itasca (L4):   Latin Kings, Spanish Cobras
Jacksonville (L4):   Gangster Disciples, Vice Lords, Latin Kings
Joliet (AI):   Aryan Nation, Disciples, Vice Lords, Latin Kings, Crips, Aryan
  Brotherhood, Folks, Peoples, Skinheads, Brothers of the Struggle, El Rukns, Neo-
  nazis, Black Gangsters, Bikers
Joliet (LE):   Black Disciples, Vice Lords, Latin Kings, BGD's, B.O.S., Chicago
  Outlaws, El Rukns, Four Corner Hustlers, KKK, Outlaws, Simon City Royals
Justice (L4):   Gangster Disciples, Satan's Disciples, Vice Lords
Kane Co. (PP):   Darksiders, Latin Kings, MLK, Vice Lords, Disciples, Folks,
  Peoples, Black Gangsters, Ku Klux Klan
Kane Co. (LE):   BGD's, Latin Kings, Ambrose, BG's, Four Corner Hustlers, GD's,
  Insane Vice Lords, La Raza, Party Players, Satans Disciples, Two-Sixers, Vice Lords
Kankakee (PP):   Latin Kings, Vice Lords, Disciples, Crips, Ku Klux Klan

---

[84]Lenzi chapter.

Kankakee (LE):   BGD's, Latin Kings, Vice Lords, BG's, Disciples, Gangsters, GD's
Kewanee (L4):   Black Gangster Disciples, Vice Lords
Knox Co. (L4):   Gangster Disciples, Latin Kings, Vice Lords, Aryan Brotherhood,
  Aryan Nation, Bishops, Black P. Stones, Cobra Stones, Crips, Gaylords, KKK, Latin
  Jivers, Spanish Cobras, Two-Two Boys, White Gangster Disciples
Knoxville (L4):   Latin Kings, Vice Lords, Disciples
Lacon (L4):   Black Gangster Disciples, Latin Kings, Vice Lords
LaGrange (L4):   Black Gangster Disciples, Latin Kings, Two-Two Boys
LaGrange Park (L4):   Two-Sixers, 12th Street Players, Two Two Boys, Black
  Gangster Disciples, Latin Brothers
Lake Co. (PP):   Latin Kings, Maniac Disciples, Vice Lords, Disciples, Folks, Peoples,
  Brothers of the Struggle, Black Gangsters, Cobras
Lake Forest (L4):   Latin Kings, Gangster Disciples, White Gangster Disciples
Lake Zurich (L4):   Latin Kings, Vice Lords, Spanish Gangster Disciples
LaSalle Co. (PP):   Latin Kings, Disciples, Folks, Bloods, Crips, Vice Lords, Black
  Gangsters, Ku Klux Klan
LaSalle (JD):   Latin Kings
Lemont (L4):   Two-Sixers, Gangster Disciples
LeRoy (L4):   Latin Kings, Bloods, Gangster Disciples
Lincolnshire (L4):   Latin Kings, Gangster Disciples, Vice Lords
Lindenhurst (L4):   Gangster Disciples (8-Ball Posse), Insane Disciples, Vice Lords,
  Latin Kings
Lisle (L4):   Vice Lords, Gangster Disciples, Latin Kings
Livingston Co. (L4):   Black Gangster Disciples, Latin King Nation, Satan's Disciples
Lockport (L4):   Black Gangster Disciples, Two-Sixers, Latin Kings
Lombard (LE):   Latin Kings, GD's, Dueces, Assassins Inc, BGD's, Chicago Outlaws,
  Folks, Four Corner Hustlers, Imperial Gangsters, Insane Vice Lords, Outlaws, Satans
  Disciples, Spanish Cobras, Vice Lords, Two-Sixers
Lombard (L4):   Latin Kings, Insane Dueces, Black Gangster Disciples
Lyons (L4):   12 St. Players, Majestics, 22 Boys, 26 Boys
Grundy and Bureau Co.'s (PP):   Latin Kings
Macomb (L4):   Folks
Macoupin Co. (L4):   Back Doorsmen, Wind Tramps, Iron Sledge
Madison Co. (PP):   Crips, Black Gangster Disciples, Bloods, Vice Lords, Latin Kings,
  Posse
Manteno (L4):   Latin Kings, Black Gangster Disciples, Two-Two Boys
Maroa (L4):   Vice Lords, Latin Kings, Gangster Disciples
Mattoon (L4):   Vice Lords, Gangster Disciples
Maywood (LE):   Disciples, Latin Kings, Vice Lords, BGD's, BD's, BG's, Bloods,
  B.O.S., Crips, 8 Balls, El Rukns, Folks, Franklin Park Giants, Gangsters, GD's,
  Imperial Gangsters, Insane Vice Lords, King Cobra, Latin Counts, Latin Kings,
  Latin Locos, L.A. Kings, La Raza, L.V.L., Neo-nazis, Party Boys, Party Players,
  Peoples, Posse, Satans Disciples, Sharps, Simon City Royals, Sin City Boys,
  Skinheads, Spanish Cobras, 26-er's
Maywood (L4):   Vice Lords, Latin Kings, Black Gangster Disciples
McDonough Co. (L4):   Latin Kings, Disciples
McHenry (L4):   Gangster Disciples, Latin Kings
Merrionette Park (L4):   Latin Kings, Gangster Disciples, Skinheads
Metropolis (JA):   BD's, Northsiders[85]; Aryan Nation

---

[85]A white gang.

Metropolis (L4):   Gangster Disciples, Vice Lords, Party Boys
Midlothian (L4):   Gangster Disciples, Imperial Gangster Disciples, Black P. Stones
Milan (L4):   Vice Lords, Black Gangster Disciples, Latin Kings
Milledgeville (L4):   Latin Kings[86]
Millstadt (L4):   Disciples, Black Disciples
Minooka (L4):   Two Sixers, Vice Lords, Black Gangster Disciples
Mokena (L4):   Satan's Disciples, Ambrose, Latin Kings
Moline (LE):   Vice Lords, Black Gangsters, Latin Kings, BGD's, BD's, B.O.S.,
    Disciples, Folks, Four Corner Hustlers, GD's, Imperial Gangsters, Insane Vice Lords,
    KKK, Outlaws, Peoples, Spanish Cobras, Two-Sixers, White Gangster Disciples, 8-
    Balls
Moline (L4):   Gangster Disciples/B.O.S./S.O.S./, Vice Lords (7 sets), Latin Kings,
    Ambrose, Aryan Brotherhood, Bishops, Crips, 8 Ball Posse, Four Corner Hustlers,
    Imperial Gangsters, Insane Vice Lords, KKK, La Raza, New Breed, Satan's
    Disciples, Simon City Royals, The Lynch Mob, Two-Sixers
Momence (L4):   Two-Two Boys, Satan's Disciples, Black Gangsters, Latin Kings
Monmouth (L4):   Gangster Disciples, Vice Lords
Monticello (L4):   Latin Kings, Gangster Disciples, Vice Lords
Morton (L4):   Gangster Disciples, Crips
Moultrie Co. (L4):   Simon City Royals, Vice Lords
Mounds (L4):   Crips, Bloods, Disciples
Mt. Prospect (LE):   Latin Kings, Black Gangsters, Spanish Cobras, Simon City
    Royals
Murphysboro (L4):   Black Disciples, Gangster Disciples, Metro East, Vice Lords,
    Phantom's M.C., Bloods, Cobra Stones, Folks, Latin Kings, Northsiders, Simon City
    Royals, Aryan Brotherhood
Northbrook (L4):   Vice Lords, Latin Kings, Spanish Cobras
Oakbrook Terrace (L4):   Latin Kings, C-Notes, Insane Vice Lords
Oak Brook (L4)[87]:   Black Gangster Disciples, Insane Unknowns, Latin Kings, Two-
    Sixers, Two-Two Boys, Vice Lords
Oak Forrest (L4):   Latin Kings, Gangster Disciples, Ambrose
Oak Lawn (LE):   Satans Disciples, T.A.P. (The Arab Posse), Maniac Latin Disciples,
    BDGs, GDs, GDs, Chicago Outlaws, Folks, Four Corner Hustlers, Imperial
    Gangsters, Insane Vice Lords, Latin Kings, Outlaws, Party Boys, Party Players,
    Peoples, Simon City Royals, Skinheads, Spanish Cobras, Two-Sixers, Vice Lords
Ogle Co. (L4):   Latin Kings, Gangster Disciples, Vice Lords
Olympia Fields (L4):   Black Gangster Disciples, Latin Counts, Four Corner Hustlers
Onarga (PC):   Latin Kings
Oswego (L4):   Maniac Latin Disciples, Latin Kings, Latin Homeboys
Palatine (L4):   Latin Kings, Disciples, Vice Lords
Pana (L4):   Disciples[88], Vice Lords[89]

---

[86]Wannabes.

[87]Members of the gangs do not actually live there, they just work there.

[88]Indicates a source of Decatur.

[89]Decatur also indicated.

Park Ridge (LE):   Latin Kings, Simon City Royals, Black Gangster Disciples, Maniac Latin Disciples, BD's, Cholos, Cobras, Dragons, Folks, Flying Dragons, Four Corner Hustlers, GD's, Imperial Gangsters, Insane Vice Lords, Peoples, Skinheads, Spanish Cobras, Vice Lords
Park Ridge (L4):   Latin Kings, Simon City Royals, Gangster Disciples
Peoria ('V2):   Aryan Brotherhood, Bikers, Black Gangsters, Brothers of the Struggle (B.O.S.), Cobras, Four Corner Hustlers, Gangster Disciples, Latin Kings, Mexican Mafia, Neo-nazis, Spanish Cobras, Vice Lords, Northsiders (Bikers)
Peoria (LE):   Vice Lords, Disciples, Latin Kings, BGD's, BD's, BG's, GD's, Insane Vice Lords, Vice Lords
Piper City (L4):   Latin Disciples., Latin Kings
Pontoon Beach (L4):   Black Disciples, Vice Lords, Latin Kings
Prophetstown (L4):   Latin Kings, Vice Lords, Gangster Disciples
Prospect Heights (L4):   Spanish Cobras, Spanish Gangster Disciples, Imperial Gangster Disciples
Quincy (L4):   Black Gangster Disciples, Vice Lords, Black P Stone Nation
Richmond (L4):   Latin Kings
Richton Park (L4):   Gangster Disciples, Latin Counts, Latin Kings
River Forest (L4):   Vice Lords, Disciples, Two-Two Boys
Riverside (L4):   Latin Kings, 12th Street Players, Two-Two Boys, Neo-nazis, Skinheads, Two Sixers
Riverton (L4):   Simon City Royals, Vice Lords, Gangster Disciples
Robbins (L4):   Gangster Disciples, Vice Lords
Rochester (L4):   Latin Kings, Gangster Disciples, Vice Lords
Rock Falls (L4):   Latin Kings, Imperial Gangsters, Disciples, YANKs[90]
Rockford (JD):   BGD's, Gangster Disciples, Latin Kings, Vice Lords
Rockford (L4):   Gangster Disciples, Vice Lords (Insane, Conservative), Four Corner Hustlers, Latin Kings, Aryan Nation[91], Black Disciples, B.P.S.N., B.O.S., Cobra Stones, Crips, Gaylords, Imperial Gangsters, KKK, Maniac Latin Disciples, Northsiders, Satan's Disciples
Rock Island Co. (PP):   Black Gangster Disciples, Vice Lords, Latin Kings
Rock Island (PP):   Vice Lords, Disciples, Latin Kings, Brothers of the Struggle
Rock Island (LE):   Vice Lords, GDs, Latin Kings, BGDs, Bikers, BDs, BGs, B.O.S., Eight Balls, Folks, Four Corner Hustlers, F.T.W., Head Bangers, Imperial Gangsters, Insane Vice Lords, Peoples, Satans Disciples, Two-Sixers
Rock Island Co. (LE):   BGD's, Folks, Kings, BKU's, B.O.S., Five Percenters, Four Corner Hustlers, The Kings Posse, Peoples
Rock Island (L4):   Vice Lords, Black Gangster Disciples, Latin Kings
Round Lake Hts.(L4):   Latin Kings, Vice Lords, Low Lifes
Sandwich (L4):   Gangster Disciples, Latin Kings, Insane Gangster Disciples, Maniac Latin Disciples
Schaumburg (L4):   Black Gangster Disciples, Latin Kings, Vice Lords
Seneca (L4):   Gangster Disciples, Latin Kings, Two Sixers
Sheridan (AI):   Northsiders, Disciples, Vice Lords, Latin Kings, Brothers of the Struggle, El Rukns, Neo-nazis, Mexican Mafia, Bikers, White Gangster Disciples
Shorewood (L4):   Two-Six Nation, Latin Kings, Vice Lords
Silvis (L4):   Vice Lords, Latin Kings, Black Gangster Disciples

---

[90] A skinhead/white power youth gang (YANKs = Young American Nigger Killers).

[91] Subsequent listing: Indicates contact or influence in the city.

Skokie (L4):   Latin Kings, Gangster Disciples, Royals
Somonauk (L4):   Latin Kings, Maniac Latin Disciples
Sparta (L4):   Black Gangster Disciples, Gangster Disciples
Springfield (PP):   Suicide White Power, Black Gangster Disciples, Vice Lords, Latin Kings
Springfield (LE):   8 Ball Posse, Hammerskins, Latin Kings, BGDs, BDs, Simon City Royals
Springfield (L4):   Simon City Royals, Vice Lords, Gangster Disciples, Latin Kings, Hammerskins, KKK, Skinheads
Stark Co. (L4):   Disciples
Staunton (L4):   Iron Sledge
St. Charles (L4):   Latin Kings, Deuces, Ambrose
St. Clair Co. (LE):   Disciples, Vice Lords, Crips, Bloods, Aryan Brotherhood, Aryan Nation, Four Corner Hustlers, Hells Angels, KKK, Satanic Cult Gangs
Sterling (L4):   Gangster Disciples, Latin Kings
Stockton (L4):   Satanic Cult Gangs, Vice Lords
Streator (L4):   Black Gangster Disciples, Gangster Disciples, Latin Kings
Summit (L4):   Latin Kings, Gangster Disciples, Satans Disciples
Sycamore (JA):   Latin Kings, Disciples, Ambrose; Aryan Nation, Black Disciples, Bikers, El Rukns, Folks, Four Corner Hustlers, GD's, Insane Vice Lords, Peoples, Skinheads, Vice Lords
Sycamore (L4):   Black Gangster Disciples, Vice Lords, Ambrose
Tampico (L4):   Disciples, Folks, Latin Kings
Thomasboro (L4):   Latin Kings, Gangster Disciples
Thornton (L4):   Disciples, Vice Lords, Four Corner Hustlers
Toulon (L4):   Disciples
Vandalia (AI):   Black Gangster Disciples, Vice Lords, El Rukns, Aryan Brotherhood, Bikers, Brothers of the Struggle, Latin Kings, Ku Klux Klan, Cobras, Folks, Peoples
Venice (L4):   Vice Lords, Disciples
Vernon Hills (L4):   Latin Kings, Gangster Disciples, Two Sixers
Villa Park (L4):   Vice Lords, Gangster Disciples, Latin Kings
Warren Co. (L4):   Gangster Disciples, Vice Lords
Warrenville (L4):   Satan's Disciples, Gangster Disciples, Latin Kings
Washington (L4):   Gangster Disciples, Spanish Disciples, Latin Kings, Crips
Watseka (L4):   Latin Kings, Black Gangster Disciples, Two Two Boys
Wauconda (L4):   Latin Kings, Disciples
Waukegan (PP):   Latin Kings, Disciples, Vice Lords, Ku Klux Klan
Waukegan (LE):   Latin Kings, Maniac Latin Disciples, Disciples, BGD's, Four Corner Hustlers, GD's, Latin Locos, Vice Lords
Waukegan (L4):   Gangster Disciples, Latin Kings, Maniac Latin Disciples
Waukegan (L4):   Latin Kings, Vice Lords, Gangster Disciples, Black Disciples, Black P. Stones, B.O.S., Four Corner Hustlers, Insane Unknowns, Insane Vice Lords, Latin Lovers, Maniac Latin Disciples, Orchestra Albany, Satan's Disciples
Western Springs (L4):   Latin Kings, Black Gangster Disciples
Wheaton (L4):   Gangster Disciples, Latin Kings, Vice Lords
Will Co. (CS):   Disciples, Vice Lords, Latin Kings, Chicago Outlaws (bikers), Two-Sixers
Willowbrook (L4):   Black Gangsters, 2-2 Boys, Vice Lords, Latin Kings
Wilmington (L4):   Latin Kings, Vice Lords, Two Sixers
Winnebago Co. (L4):   Disciples, Vice Lords, Latin Kings
Winthrop Harbor (L4):   Latin Kings, Maniac Latin Disciples, Skinheads
Wood Dale (L4):   Latin Kings, Spanish Cobras, Playboys
Woodstock (L4):   Latin Kings, Disciples, II Down Posse*

Worth (L4):   Ambrose, Chicago Outlaws, Disciples, Hell's Angels, Insane Popes, Latin Kings, Maniac Latin Disciples, Orchestra Albany, Satan's Disciples, The Arab Posse (TAP), Two-Sixers, Two-Two Boys

Yorkville (JA):   Latin Kings, Skinheads; BGD's, B.O.S., El Rukns, GD's, Latin Counts, Party Players, Satan's Disciples, Simon City Royals, Two Sixers, Vice Lords

Yorkville (L4):   Gangster Disciples, Maniac Latin Disciples, Ambrose, Latin Kings

INDIANA:

Anderson (PC):   Black Gangster Disciples, Vice Lords, Crips, Folks, Peoples, Brothers of the Struggle, Miami Boys, Bikers, Ku Klux Klan, Hell Raisers, Sons of Silence

Bloomington (LE):   2-1, Vice Lords, Latin Kings, Crips

Fort Wayne (JI):   Bloods, Crips, Vice Lords, Disciples, Aryan Brotherhood, Folks, Peoples, Skinheads, Brothers of the Struggle, Posse, El Rukns, Latin Kings, Bomber Boys, Two-Sixers, Mexican Mafia, Cobras, Assassins Inc, Insane Crypts, Shorty Folks, Mad Dogs, La Raza, Lynch Mob, Aryan Knights, Trecherous Black Rose, City of Crazies, Comptons (CPT's)

Fort Wayne (LE):   BGD's, CPT's, Vice Lords, The Nation, BD's, BG's, Brothers of the Struggle, Crips, Eight Balls, GD's, Imperial Gangsters, Latin Kings, Skinheads

Greencastle (AI):   BBB (Brothers Behind Bars[92]), Kyklos Family[93], Vice Lords, Disciples, Latin Kings, Disciples, Aryan Brotherhood, Brothers of the Struggle, Posse, Neo-nazis, Ku Klux Klan, Bikers

Indianapolis (AI):   Ku Klux Klan, Outlaws

Indianapolis (JI):   Hell Raisers[94], Vice Lords, Disciples, Folks, Posse

Indianapolis (LE):   Ghetto Boys, Vice Lords, Disciples, BGD's, Bikers, BD's, BG's, Bloods, Crips, Folks, Four Corner Hustlers, GD's, Hells Angels, Hell Raisers, Imperial Gangsters, Insane Crips, Insane Vice Lords, L.A. Kings, Mad Dogs, Lynch Mob, My Only Brothers (MOB), Neo-nazis, Orchard Park, Outlaws, Posse, Skinheads, Sons of Silence, The Crew, White Knights, 8-Balls, 34th St. Players

Indianapolis (W3)[95]:   Aryan Brotherhood, Aryan Nation, Bloods, Brothers Behind Bars (BBB), Gangsters, Gangster Disciples, Hell's Angels, KKK, Satan's Disciples, White Gangster Disciples Kentland (JA): Disciples; BGD's,

La Porte (JD):   BGD's, Bikers, Bloods, Crips, Disciples, El Rukns, Hell's Angels, Hoods, KKK, Latin Kings, Mexican Mafia, Skinheads, Vice Lords

Marion (LE):   Vice Lords, BGD's, Dragon Right, Black Dragon, BG's, Bloods, Chicago Outlaws, Crips, Eight Balls, Folks, KKK, Latin Kings, Mexican Mafia, Two-Sixers

Marion Co. (LE):   Disciples, Vice Lords, 2-1, BGD's, BD's, Bloods, Crips, Eight Balls, Folks, Four Corner Hustlers, Gangsters, GD's, Hell Raisers, Imperial Gangsters, Insane Vice Lords, Mad Dogs, Outlaws, Posse, Skinheads, Sons of Silence

---

[92] A white gang.

[93] A white gang.

[94] White gang.

[95]Respondent indicated "no organized gangs function at this time" regarding the question of top three gangs among inmates in the facility; but checked off several gangs from the checklist.

Michigan City (AI):   KKK, Aryan Nation, Brothers Behind Bars, Outlaw motorcycle gang, Black Gangster Disciples, Aryan Brotherhood, One Way, Dragons, Latin Kings, Bloods, Crips, El Rukns, neo-nazis, Mexican Mafia, Black Guerilla Family, Pagans, F.T.W.

Monroe Co. (LE):   Hell Raisers[96], G.I. Boys[97], Vice Lords, El Rukns, Black Gangster Disciples, 3rd World Shotgun Crypts

Pendleton (AI):   Aryan Brotherhood, Bloods, Crips, Vice Lords, Disciples, El Rukns, Black Gangsters, Black Guerilla Family

Pendleton (W2):   Aryan Brotherhood, BGD's, Disciples, Folks, KKK, Moors, Satanic Cult Gangs, Vice Lords, White Gangster Disciples, 39th Street Gang

Pendleton (W3):   Aryan Brotherhood, Vice Lords, Disciples; BGD's, BD's

Plainfield (AI):   Aryan Brotherhood, Ku Klux Klan, Disciples, Vice Lords, Crips, Folks, Peoples, Skinheads, Brothers of the Struggle, Posse, El Rukns, Neo-nazis, Latin Kings, SWP, Bomber Boys, Black Gangsters, Bikers, Pagans, Miami Boys, Mad Dogs, Hell Raisers, White Gangster Disciples, F.T.W., Sons of Silence

Plainfield (JI):   Bloods, Crips, Vice Lords, Disciples, White Pride, Skinheads, Latin Kings, Black Gangsters, Raiders, Knights, White Gangster Disciples, 21

Porter Co. (LE):   Latin Kings, Spanish Gangster Disciples, Insane Popes, BGD's, Folks, GD's, Chicago Outlaws, Imperial Gangsters, Skinheads

Rockville (JI):   White Gangster Disciples, Hell Raisers[98], Bloods, Crips, Vice Lords, Disciples, Aryan Brotherhood, Folks, Peoples, Skinheads, Neo-nazis, Latin Kings, Black Gangsters, L.V.L., 2-1 (VL)

Tell City (W3):   Hell Raisers, BBB[99]; Black Gangster Disciples, Vice Lords; Brothers Behind Bars, Brothers of the Struggle, Crips, Disciples, Imperial Gangsters, Insane Vice Lords, Outlaws, West Side Posse

Westville (AI):   Brothers Behind Bars, Lucifer's Lot[100], Aryan Brotherhood, Vice Lords, Disciples, Folks, Peoples, Brothers of the Struggle, El Rukns, Latin Kings, Black Gangsters, Ku Klux Klan

Winslow (PC):   Vice Lords, Disciples, Aryan Brotherhood, Folks, Peoples, Skinheads, Posse, Latin Kings

IOWA:

Anamosa (AI):   Bloods, Crips, Vice Lords, Disciples, Aryan Brotherhood, Folks, Peoples, Brothers of the Struggle, Latin Kings, Black Gangsters, Bikers, Ku Klux Klan, Pagans, Sons of Silence, Mountain Church, SS Action Group

---

[96]Out of Indianapolis.

[97]Indiana University.

[98] Both are white gangs.

[99]Both white gangs.

[100] A white gang.

Anamosa (W3):   Young and Wasted (Y&W)[101]; BGD's, Vice Lords, Crips; Aryan
  Brotherhood, Aryan Nation, Bikers, BD's, BG's, Bloods, Brothers of the Struggle
  (BOS), E.M.E., Four Corner Hustlers, GD's, F.T.W., Imperial Gangsters, Insane
  Vice Lords, KKK, Latin Kings, Lynch Mob, Mexican Mafia, MSTA, Neo-nazis,
  Outlaws, Rolling 60, Satanic Cult Gangs, Shotgun, Skinheads, Sons of Silence, Vice
  Lords, White Gangster Disciples, White Pride
Black Hawk Co. (LE):   Vice Lords, BG's, Sons of Silene, BGD's, Bloods, Crips
Cedar Falls (PC):   Sons of Silence Motorcyle Gang, Black Gangsters, bikers
Cedar Falls (LE):   Sons of Silence, BGD's, Bloods, Brown Gangster Disciples, Crips,
  Outlaws, Posse Comitatus, Sharps, Skinheads
Cedar Rapids (PC):   Posse
Clinton (LE):   Vice Lords, Disciples, BGD's, BD's
Council Bluffs (JD):   Bloods, Crips, EVIL, Insane Crips, Latin Kings, Skinheads,
  Stoners
Council Bluffs (LE):   Skinheads[102], Lomas, Cholos, Latin Kings
Davenport (LE):   Vice Lords, BGD's, Latin Kings, Crips, El Rukns, Folks, Insane
  Vice Lords, Insane Crips, La Raza, Posse Comitatus, Satanic Cult Gangs
Des Moines (LE):   BGD's, Vice Lords[103], Young & Wasted[104], BD's, BG's,
  Bloods, B.O.S., Crips, Dirty White Boys, Disciples, El Rukns, Folks, Four Corner
  Hustlers, GD's, Insane Vice Lords, KKK, Latin Kings, Lynch Mob, NWA, Posse
  Comitatus, Rolling 60, Santana Block, Sharps, Skinheads, Sons of Silence, Warlocks,
  Warlords, West Side Boyz
Dubuque (PC):   Posse
Eldora (JI):   Bloods, Crips, Vice Lords, Disciples, Brothers of the Struggle, Latin
  Kings, PYRU, Black Mafia, Sons of Silence, Young & Wasted, Chop Ticks
Fort Madison (W2):   Aryan Brotherhood, BGD's, Bikers, Brothers of the Struggle
  (B.O.S.), Crips, El Rukns, Four Corner Hustlers, Gangster Disciples, Moors, MSTA,
  Rolling 60, Santana Block, Sons of Silence, Vice Lords, White Pride
Humboldt Co. (CS):   Sons of Silence
Indianola (JA):   The Young & Wasted, Black Gangsters, Vice Lords; BGD's, Crips
Iowa City (LE):   Bikers, KKK, Sons of Silence
Jessup (PC):   Bloods, Crips, Posse
Mitchellville (AI):   Crips
Montrose (JA):   Bikers, Bloods, El Rukns, Chosen Few, Grim Reapers
Oakdale (W3):   Bikers; Vice Lords, Aryan Brotherhood, Crips; Aryan Nation,
  BGD's, Bloods, Crazy White Boys, El Rukns, Skinheads
Ottumwa (LE):   Niggaz For Life (NFL), Other Peoples Property (OPP), Crips -
  Hoover 57
Rockwell City (W2):   Black Gangsters, Crips, Latin Kings, Vice Lords
Rockwell City (W3):   Crips, Aryan Brotherhood, Black Gangster Disciples
Scott Co. (CS):   Bloods, Crips, Vice Lords, Neo-nazis, Latin Kings

---

[101]An all white gang.

[102]AKA "White Rats".

[103]Black, like BGD's.

[104]White gang.

Scott Co. (LE):   Big Top Locos, Black Dragon, Bloods, Cross Suns, Latin Locos,
Village Boys
Waterloo (JD):   Black Gangsters, Bloods, Crips, Vice Lords
Woodbury Co. (LE):   Folks, El Forestero, West Side Locos, BGD's, Bloods, Crips,
Eight Balls, F-13, GD's, KKK, Latin Kings, Posse Comitatus, Vice Lords

KANSAS:
Atchison (JI):   Bloods, Crips, Disciples, Black Gangsters,
Beloit (JI):   Bloods, Crips, Disciples, Jr. Boys, Black Mafia
El Dorado (JA):   Crips, Nasty White Boys[105]
Ellsworth Co. (CS)[106]:   Bloods, Crips
Ellsworth (W3):   Aryan Brotherhood; Bloods, Crips; BGD's, Aryan Nation, Imperial
Nation, Insane Crips, KKK, Latin Locos, Skinheads, White Knights, Jr. Boys
Hutchinson (JD):   Junior Boyz, Aryan Brotherhood, BGD's, Bloods, Crips, Disciples,
Insane Vice Lords, Jr. Boys, Posse, Satanic Cult Gangs, Skinheads, Sons of Silence,
Vice Lords
Johnson Co. (LE):   Aryan Brotherhood, Aryan Nation, BGD's, Banditos, BG's,
Bloods, Bomber Boys, Crips, Imperial Gangsters, Insane Crips, Latin Counts, Posse
Comitatus, White Gangster Disciples, 9th Street Dawgs
Kansas City (PP):   Black Gangster Disciples, Bloods, Crips, Vice Lords, Brothers of
the Struggle, Latin Kings, Insane Crypts
Lansing (AI):   Bloods, Crips, Vice Lords, Disciples, Aryan Brotherhood, Skinheads,
El Rukns, Ku Klux Klan
Lansing (W2):   Aryan Brotherhood Nation, BGD's, Black Gangsters, Bloods, Crips,
El Rukns, Folks, Gangster Disciples, Insane Crips, Pyru, People, Vice Lords
Lansing (W3):   Crips, Bloods, Black Gangster Disciples; Aryan Brotherhood, BD's,
BG's, El Rukns, Folks, Four Corner Hustlers, Insane Crips, Jr. Boys, Latin Counts,
Latin Kings, Moors, Peoples, Rolling 60, Satanic Cult Gangs, Skinheads, Vice Lords
Larned (JI):   Bloods, Crips, Disciples, Skinheads, Posse, Black Gangsters, Mexican
Mafia, Jr. Boys, Insane Crypts, Banditos, Sons of Silence, Spruce Park Gangsters,
Brown Gangster Disciples, Blue Devil Gangsters
Lawrence (LE):   Bloods, BGD's, Vice Lords,Crips, Four Corner Hustlers
Norton (W2):   Outlaws, White Power[107], Aryan Brotherhood, BGD's, Black
Gangsters, Bloods, Brothers of the Struggle (B.O.S.), Crips, Disciples, Folks,
Gangster Disciples, Insane Crips, Jr. Boys, Pyru
Olathe (PP):   Bloods, Crips, Black Gangster.Disciples, Vice Lords, Latin Kings
Osawatomie (W3):   Aryan Brotherhood; Latin Kings, Bloods, Crips; BGD's, BD's,
BG's, Crazy White Boys, Dirty White Boys, Eight Balls, Folks, GD's, Insane Crips,
Skinheads, White Gangster Disciples, White Power, 18th Street Gang
Scott City (JA):   Raiders, Mexican Mafia
Sedgwick Co. (LE):   Neighborhood Crips, Junior Boys, Insane Crips, Aryan
Brotherhood, BGDs, Bloods, Black Mafia, Blue Devil Gangsters, Born To Kill
(BTK), Cholos, GDs, Hells Angels, KKK, Latin Kings, Lynch Mob, Mexican Mafia,

---

[105]A white gang.

[106]Not in immediate area, some within 120 mile radius.

[107]Both, white gangs.

Posse Comitatus, Piru, Skinheads, Sons of Silence, Spruce Park Gangsters, Stoners, Vice Lords, White Knights, 8-Balls
Shawnee Co. (LE):   Bloods, Crips, Basin Street Gang, BGD's, BD's, Black Mafia, Disciples, Folks, GD's, Insane Crips, Posse Comitatus, Warlords
Shawnee Mission (PC):   Crips, Bloods, Black Gangster Disciples, Posse, Bikers
Topeka (PC):   Posse
Topeka (JI):   Bloods, Crips, Vice Lords, Disciples, Folks, Posse, Latin Kings, Black Gangsters, Mexican Mafia, KKK, Jr. Boys, Insane Crypts
Topeka (LE):   Four Corner Hustlers, Vice Lords, Buchanan Street Bloods, Aryan Brotherhood, BGD's, BD's, Folks, Crips, Insane Vice Lords, Peoples, Rolling 60
Wallace Co. (CS):   Posse
Wichita (JD):   Aryan Brotherhood, Bloods, Crips, Insane Crips, Jr. Boys, Skinheads
Wichita (W2):   Bloods, Crips, Insane Crips, Jr. Boys
Winfield (AI):   Bloods, Crips, Aryan Brotherhood

KENTUCKY:
Ashland (LE):   Brothers of the Wheel, Pagans, Outlaws
Eddyville (AI):   Aryan Brotherhood, Ku Klux Klan
Eddyvillel (W3):   Aryan Brotherhood, BGD's, Crips, Bloods; Aryan Nation, Black Guerilla Family, Black Mafia, Folks, Vice Lords
Elizabethtown (JI):[108]   Bloods, Crips, Aryan Brotherhood, Outlaws, KKK, Cobras, The True Niggers[109], Monks[110]
Floyd Co. (CS):   Ku Klux Klan
Frankfort (AI):   Aryan Brotherhood, Skinheads, Bikers
LaGrange (AI):   Bloods, Crips, Aryan Brotherhood
LaGrange (AI):   Aryan Brotherhood, Neo-nazis, KKK
LaGrange (W2):   Aryan Brotherhood, Bikers
LaGrange (W3):   Aryan Brotherhood
La Grange (W3):   Aryan Brotherhood, Black Guerilla Family, Unjustifed Brotherhood
Lexington (AI):   Outlaws (Motorcycle gang), Bloods, Aryan Brotherhood, Bikers, Ku Klux Klan
Lexington (JI):   Bloods, Crips, Skinheads, Posse
Louisville (JI):   Bloods, Crips, Skinheads, Bikers, Outlaws, Hell's Angels, KKK, Monks
Louisville (JA):   Aryan Brotherhood, Insane Crips, KKK, West End Rockers
Middlesboro (JI):   Outlaws, Hells Angels, KKK
Newport (JI):   Sin City Boys[111], Bloods, Crips, Aryan Brotherhood, Skinheads, Neo-nazis, KKK, Hell's Angels
Pewee Valley (AI):   Aryan Brotherhood, Bikers, KKK
Pineville (AI):   Aryan Brotherhood, Bikers, KKK
West Liberty (AI):   Ku Klux Klan

---

[108]Gangs noted in area, but not a problem in the facility.

[109] Lexington, KY.

[110] Louisville, KY.

[111] White gang.

West Liberty (W2):   Aryan Brotherhood, Bikers
West Liberty (W3):   Aryan Brotherhood[112]

LOUISIANA:
Angie (W3):   5th Ward, 7th Ward[113]; Black Mafia, Satan's Disciples, Vice Lords
Baton Rouge (JI):   Bloods, Crips, KKK, 19th St. Gang
Bridge City (JI):   Bloods, Crips, Skinheads, Posse, Hoosier, Village Boys
Caddo Parrish (LE):   Bloods, Crips, Skinheads
Concordia Parish (PP):   Crips, Bloods, Posse, Bikers, KKK
Covington (LE):   Northside Posse, Lacombe Posse, Playboy Crips, Banditos, BGD's, BD's, Bloods, Folks, Latin Kings, Outlaws
DeQuincy (W2)[114]:   Bloods, Crips, KKK
Hammond (PC):   Bloods, Crips
Homer (AI):   Bloods, Crips, Aryan Brotherhood
Homer (W3):   Crips, Bloods
Lafayette (LE):   8 Ball Posse, Q-Balls, Prayer Boys, Banditos, Lynch Mob, Posse Comitatus
LaFayette (JA):   Banditos
Monroe (JD):   Lynch Mob, Crips, Posse
New Orleans (JD):   Bikers, Bloods, Crips, KKK, Posse, Blue Hat/Blue Rags, Red Hats/Red Rags, Satanic Cult Gangs, Satans Disciples
Pineville (AI):   Bloods, Disciples, Skinheads, Neo-nazis, Ku Klux Klan, Basin Street Gang, Knights
Pineville (W2):   Bloods[115], Crips[116]
Port Allen (LE):   Eight Ball Posse, Bum Rush, South 17th, Eazy Town, Aryan Nation, Banditos, BGDs, Bloods, Crips, Hells Angels, Head Bangers, KKK, Neo-nazis, Skinheads, Sons of Silence
Shreveport (JD):   Banditos, Bloods, Bomber Boys, Crips, KKK, Rolling 60
St. Charles Par. (LE):   40 Oz. Posse, St. Rose Posse, Size Aint Shit (S.A.S.)
St. Gabriel (AI):   Crips, Bloods, Bandidos, Skinheads, Bikers, Ku Klux Klan
St. Martinville (LE):   8-Ball Posse, Brother-in-laws, 4 Horsemen, Airheads, Banditos, BBMF, Chicago Outlaws, Hells Angels, Insane Crips, Korean Dragon, Outlaws, Pagans, Posse Comitatus, Rolling 60 Crips, Sons of Silence, Texas Mafia, Warlocks
W. Baton Rouge Par.(CS):   Bloods, Crips, Aryan Brotherhood, Skinheads, Miami Boys, Posse, Black Gangsters, Bikers, KKK, Head Bangers, Sons of Silence
Winnfield (W2):   Aryan Brotherhood, Bloods, Crips, KKK

---

[112]Wannabes.

[113]Both, local New Orleans cliques.

[114]Facility reports they do not allow gangs, they do not have gangs; they do have a recognized situation in that everyone from a particular city or area groups together - i.e., New Orleans, Baton Rouge, Shreveport, etc.

[115]New Orleans area.

[116]Shreveport area.

MAINE:
Lewiston (LE):   Crips, Folks
Oxford Co. (CS):   Bikers, KKK, Pagans
Richmond (PC):   Mountain Boys (motorcycle)

MARYLAND:
Baltimore (LE):   Korean Power, Korean Fuk Ching, Bikers, KKK, Pagans, Skinheads
Baltimore (JI):   Skinheads, Mad Dogs, Head Bangers, Knockers
Baltimore (PC):   Bloods, Aryan Brotherhood, Peoples, Skinheads, Neo-Nazis, Black Gangsters, Bikers, Ku Klux Klan, Pagans, Knights, Hell Raisers
Baltimore (AI):   Pagans
Baltimore (AI):   Pagans
Baltimore (W2):   KKK, MSTA, Pagans, Posse, Skinheads
Baltimore (W2):   Brothers of the Struggle (B.O.S.), Pagans, Posse, Skin   heads
Baltimore (W3):   Aryan Nation, Bikers; BGD's; Five Percenters, Fruits of Islam, Pagans
Berlin (PC):   Posse
Queen Anne's Co. (CS):   Raiders, Knights, Posse
Fruitland (PC):   Posse, Ku Klux Klan
Hagerstown (AI):   Ku Klux Klan, Pagans
Hagerstown (LE):   Aryan Brotherhood, Hell's Angels, KKK, Outlaws, Pagans
Hagerstown (W3):   Black Guerilla Family, Five Percenters, Fruits of Islam, KKK, Mexican Mafia, Pagans
Harford Co. (LE):   Skinheads, Fates Assembly (motorcycle gang), KKK
Jessup (AI):   Pagans, Bikers
Jessup (W2):   KKK[117]
Jessup (W3):   Moors; Aryan Brotherhood, KKK, Pagans, Posse, Skinheads
Upper Malboro (JA):   Aryan Circle, Aryan Nation, Insane Vice Lords, KKK
Westover (W2):   Aryan Brotherhood, Bikers, Black Mafia, Bloods, Crips, Five Percenters, Hell's Angels, KKK, Mexican Mafia, Pagans, White Knights
Westover (W3):   Pagans, Organization of African Unity
Worchester (W2):   Intervale, Humboldt, X-Men, Five Percenters, Giants, KKK, Satanic Cult Gangs, Warriors

MASSACHUSETTS:
Boston (LE):   Castlegate, Humbolt, Vamp Hill; Aryan Nation, BBMF, Born to Kill (BTK), Boston Boys, C.I.A. (Criminals in Action), Corbet, Five Percenters, Flying Dragons, Franklin Park Giants, Ghost Shadows, Highway Men, Intervale, KKK, Lynch Mob, Miami Heat, Neo-nazis, Orchard Park, Red Dragons, Skinheads, Warlords, X-Men
Boston (PP):[118]   Posse, Humboldt, Orchard Park, Castlegate, Corbet, Vamp Hill, Intervale, Franklin Park Giants
Boston (JD):   Bloods, Crips, Satanic Cult Gangs, Warlords
Brewster (JI):   Humbolt, Orchard Park, Castlegate, Franklin Park Giants
Bridgewater (AI):   Humboldt Street, Intervale Street, Franklin Park Giants, Corbet

---

[117]Facility, however, reports "no gangs at this facility".

[118] Statewide jurisdiction.

Bridgewater (AI):   Posse, Bikers, Humboldt, Orchard Park, Castlegate, Corbet, Five Percenters, Intervale

Bridgewater (W2):   Boston Bandits, Townies, Southies[119], Corbet St., Humboldt St. Raiders, Intervale/Mission Hill, Aryan Brotherhood, BGD's, Bikers, Boston Boys, Castlegate, Crips, Five Percenters, Franklin Park Giants, Latin Kings, Orchard Park

Bridgewater (W3):   Humbolt, Castlegate, Intervale, Corbet, Franklin Park Giants, KKK, Orchard Park, X-men

Brockton (JD):[120]   BBMF, Castlegate, Franklin Park Giants, Humboldt, Intervale

Carver (JI):   Crips, Cobras

Gardner (AI):   Aryan Brotherhood, Humboldt, Castlegate, Corbet, Five Percenters, Intervale, Franklin Park Giants

Grafton (JI):   Skinheads, Posse, Neo-nazis, Humbolt, Orchard Park, Castlegate, Corbet, Vamphill, NWA, Intervale, L.V.L., Franklin Park Giants

Greenfield (JI):   Skinheads, Neo-nazis, Humbolt, Orchard Park, Castlegate

Malden (LE):   Boston Boys, X-Men

Mattapan (JI):   Humbolt, Orchard Park, Castlegate, Franklin Park Giants

N. Chelmsford (JI):   Humbolt, Tiny Rascal Gang, Red Gang

Norfolk (W3):   Thunder Gang, Highland Avenue Blackhawks, Castlegate

Roslindale (JI):   Humbolt, Orchard Park, Castlegate, Corbet, Vamp Hill, Intervale, Franklin Park Giants, Pistons

Roxbury (W2):   Castlegate, Humboldt, Intervale,

Shirley (W3):   Notra Dame[121]; Humboldt, Insane Vice Lords, Latin Kings, Orchard Park

South Carver (AI):   Intervale, Castlegate, Kilos & Ounces, Corbet

South Carver (W2):   Castlegate, Corbet, Intervale

South Walpole (AI):   Corbet, Intervale, Castlegate, Aryan Brotherhood, Disciples, Posse, Bikers, Humboldt, Orchard Park, Franklin Park Giants

South Walpole (W2):   Castlegate, Corbet, Five Percenters, Franklin Park Giants, Humboldt, Intervale, Orchard Park, Vamp Hill

South Walpole (W3):   Intervale/Vamphill, Aryan Brotherhood, Almight Latin King Nation; Aryan Circle, Boston Boys, Center City Locos, Cobras, El Rukns, Freak Blasters, F.T.W., Giants, Hydros, Insane Vice Lords, Iron Coffins, Latin Locos, Los Solidos, Monks, Neta, NIC, Outlaws, TKK, Young Boys Inc

Springfield (JI):   Posse, Little Rascals, Eastern Avenue Posse

Taunton (PP):   Humbolt, Castlegate, Orchard Park, Skinheads

Westboro (JI):   Disciples, Aryan Brotherhood, Skinheads, Neo-nazis, Outlaws, Hell's Angels, KKK, Humbolt, Orchard Park, Castlegate, Jr. Boys, Corbet, Vamp Hill, Intervale, Franklin Park Giants, TG (Thunder Gang), TRG (Tiny Rascals Gang), OSB (Oriental Street Boys), the Kings, Pistons, Raiders.

Westfield (JI):   Bloods, Posse, Humbolt, E.S.P., Saints,[122] AV's[123].

---

[119]All three are indicated as white gangs.

[120]Female facility.

[121]A white gang.

[122] E.S.P. and Saints: Holyoke, Mass.

Woburn (LE):   Intelligent Young Hoodlems, Niggers With An Attitude, Spring Ct. Posse, Aryan Brotherhood, Banditos, Hell's Angels, Humboldt, Skinheads, 8-Balls
Worcester (JI):   Humbolt, Orchard Park, Castlegate, Corbet, Intervale
Worcester (JD):   Boston Boys, Castlegate, Corbet, Disciples, Dukes, Franklin Park Giants, Intervale, Miami Heat, Orchard Park, Vamp Hill
Worcester (LE):   Kilby Posse, Out of State Boys (OSB), Herbs, Born To Kill (BTK), Hartford Posse, The Kings Posse, King Cobra, Latin Kings, X-Men

MICHIGAN:
Allen Park (LE):   Latin Counts, Cobras, Sudden Impact, BBMF, Spanish Cobras, White Gangster Disciples, X-Men
Bay City (JI):   Folks
Berrien Center (JD):   BGD's, Black Gangsters, Gangster Disciples, Vice Lords
Coldwater (AI):   Aryan Brotherhood, Skinheads, El Rukns, Bikers, Young Boys Inc, Pit Bull Boys[124]
Coldwater (W3)[125]:   Aryan Brotherhood, Bikers, Pit Bull Boys, Young Boys Inc
Detroit (JI):   Skinheads, Neo-nazis, Vice Lords, Latin Counts
Detroit (LE):   Latin Counts, Cash Flow Posse, Spanish Cobras, Folks, Four Corner Hustlers, GD's, Highway Men, Dirty White Boys, BGD's, Insane Vice Lords, Latin Kings, Vice Lords, X-Men
Eastpointe (LE):   Children of the Night (C.O.N.), 187 Posse, Square Boyz, BGD's, Bloods, C.I.A. (Criminals In Action), Cobras, Folks, Latin Counts, Latin Kings, La Familia, Peoples, Rolling 60, Vice Lords, White Gangster Disciples, X-Men
Flint (LE):   Up Folks, Down Folks, Mexican Posse, Avengers, BG's, Bloods, Cobras, Crips, Eightballs, Top Cats
Grandville (PC):   Bloods, Bikers, Ku Klux Klan
Grass Lake (W2):   Young Boys, Incorporated, BKU's, Bikers, Aryan Brotherhood, BGD's, Crazy White Boys, Neo-nazis, skinheads
Inkster (LE):   Garden Boyz Down, Task Force, Compton Gang
Ionia (AI):[126]   Aryan Brotherhood, Folks, Skinheads, Posse,, Black Gangsters, Bikers, Nuestra Familia, Ku Klux Klan
Ionia (AI):   Black Jacket Gang (Bikers), Vice Lords, Aryan Brotherhood, Skinheads, El Rukns
Ionia (AI):   Aryan Brotherhood, Bikers
Ionia (AI):   Aryan Brotherhood, Folks, Brothers of the Struggle, Latin Kings, Black Gangsters, Bikers, Nuestra Familia, Avengers, Knights
Ionia (W2):   Aryan Brotherhood, Brothers of the Struggle (B.O.S.), Disciples, El Rukns, Satanic Cult Gangs

---

[123]Springfield, Mass.

[124] These gangs are not in this institution, but in the Department of Corrections or the community is what the respondent indicated.

[125]A female facility; respondent remarked "some females were involved in Detroit youth gangs but not really a significant problem here". But some of the gangs from the check-off list were marked.

[126] Multiple obervations for Ionia because of multiple institutions.

Ionia (W3):   Aryan Brotherhood; MSTA; KKK, Melanics, Young Boys Inc; Aryan
   Nation, BBMF, Bikers, BGD's, BD's, BG's, Black Guerilla Family, Black Mafia,
   Bloods, Born To Kill (BTK), Brick City Outlaws, Crips, Dirty White Boys, Down By
   the Laws, Four Corner Hustlers, Hilltop Hustlers, Hoods, Insane Vice Lords, Inca
   Boys, King Cobra, Knights, Latin Kings, La Familia, La Mafia, Macomb Street
   Gang, Satan's Disciples, Skinheads
Jackson (AI):   Aryan Brotherhood, Brothers of the Struggle, Bikers, Nuestra Familia
Kalamazoo (JI):   Vice Lords, Disciples, Posse, El Rukns, Black Gangsters, Raiders,
   G-Boys, NFL, Pink Hill Boys, Paid in Full, Dexter Boys, Goochie Boys
Kalamazoo (JD):   Disciples
Kalamazoo (LE):   Young Boys, Inc; Iron Coffins
Kincheloe (AI):   Melanics[127], Moors[128]
Lapeer (AI):   White Brotherhood, Melonics, Moors, Aryan Brotherhood, Folks,
   Skinheads, Neo-nazis, Mexican Mafia, Bikers, Ku Klux Klan
Lincoln Park (LE):   Cobra's, Latin Counts, Folks Nation
Livonia (LE):   West Side Posse
Marquette (AI):   Aryan Brotherhood, Moorish Science Temple of America, Melanic
   Palace of the Rising Sun, Bikers
Marquette (W2):   Christian Vanguard[129], Aryan Brotherhood, Avengers, Brothers
   of the Struggle (B.O.S.), KKK, Moors, MSTA, Outlaws, Melanic Islamic Palace of
   the Rising Sun, Bikers
Marquette (W3):   Aryan Nation; MSTA, Melanics, N.O.I.; Fruits of Islam
Muskegon (W2):   Aryan Brotherhood, Bikers, Moors, MSTA, Neo-nazis, Skinheads,
   Melanics
Muskegon (W3):   Mobites, Melanics, N.O.I. (Nation of Islam); Brothers of the
   Struggle (BOS), Cobras, Fruits of Islam, Latin Counts, MSTA, Young Boys Inc
Ottawa Co. (LE):   Tiny Rascal Gang (T.R.G.), Crips, Crips With Attitude (C.W.A.),
   Latin Kings, Aryan Brotherhood, BGD's, Bloods, Neo-nazis, Outlaws, Pit Bull Boys,
   Skinheads, Road Knights
Plymouth (W3):   Melanic Palace of the Rising Sun
Prudenville (JI):   El Rukns
Riverview (LE):   Latin Counts, Cobra's, Sudden Impact, BGD's, Nuestra Familia,
   Skinheads
Saginaw (PC):   Wilders, Iron Coffins, Highway Men, Bloods, Crips, Bikers
Southgate (LE):   Cobras, Latin Counts, Sudden Impact,BDGs, Crips, Folks, Latin
   Kings, Peoples, Rolling 60, Spanish Cobras, Vice Lords, X-Men
Standish (W2):   Aryan Brotherhood, Moorish Science Temple, Melanics, Nation of
   Islam (B.O.S.), BGD's, Satanic Cult Gangs
Taylor (LE):   Cobras, Latin Counts, X-Men, BKU's, Black Disciples, C.I.A.
   (Criminals in Action), Lynch Mob, Mad Dogs, South Side Tracy, Spanish Cobras,
   S.S.G.

---

[127] An inmate religious group, AKA Melanic Palace of the Rising Star; AKA
Melonics.

[128] Inmate religious group; the Moorish Science Temple of America.

[129] A white gang.

MINNESOTA:

Anoka Co. (LE):   Vice Lords, Disciples, Latin Kings, BGD's, BD's, Cobras, Crips, Disciples, El Rukns, Latin Kings, Lobos, Outlaws, Pagans

Arden Hills (PC):   Bloods, Crips, Vice Lords, Disciples, Aryan Brotherhood(W), Skinheads(W), Posse, El Rukns, Neo-Nazis(W), Latin Kings, Miami Boys, Bikers, Ku Klux Klan, Pagans, BBMF, Five Percenters, Head Bangers

Austin (LE):   Gangster Disciples, Royal Cambodian Bloods

Blaine (LE):   Vice Lords, Disciples[130], Asian gangs[131], BGD's, B.O.S., Cobras, Hells Angels, Laos Boys/Angel Boys[132], Insane Vice Lords, Rolling 60 Crips[133], Vice Lords, White Tigers

Bloomington (LE):   Bloods, Crips, Disciples, Hells Angels

Faribault,MN (W3):   White Supremacists, Skinheads; BGD's, Aryan Nation/White Power groups, Vice Lords; Aryan Brotherhood, BD's, BG's, Brothers of the Struggle (BOS), Crips, Insane Vice Lords, Latin Kings, Satanic Cult Gangs

Hennipenn Co. (LE):   Vice Lords, BGD's, Crips[134], Aryan Brotherhood, Aryan Nation, BD's, BG's, Bloods, Brothers of the Struggle (BOS), Folks, Four Corner Hustlers, GD's, Insane Vice Lords, Latin Kings, Lynch Mob, Posse Comitatus, Skinheads, Sons of Silence, White Tigers

Hennipenn Co. (JA):   Vice Lords, Disciples, Bloods, Crips, Naturals; Aryan Brotherhood, Aryan Nation, BGD's, Bikers, El Rukns, Hell's Angels, Latin Kings, Skinheads

Jackson (JA):   Bloods, Vice Lords, Crips

Lino Lakes (W3):   Prison Motorcycle Brotherhood (PMB), Vice Lords, Disciples; Aryan Brotherhood, BGD's, Bikers, BD's, BG's, Bloods, Born to Kill (BTK), Brothers of the Struggle (BOS), Crips, El Rukns, GD's, Insane Vice Lords, Latin Kings, La Raza, Rolling 60, Satanic Cult Gangs, White Gangster Disciples

Maple Grove (PC):   Vice Lords, Bloods, Crips, bikers

Maplewood (LE):   Vice Lords, White Tigers, Disciples, Bloods, Crips, Skinheads

Minneapolis (JD):   BDG's, Bloods, Crips, Disciples, Neo-nazis, Skinheads, Vice Lords, Naturals

Minneapolis (LE):   Vice Lords, Disciples, Crips, BGD's, BD's, Bloods, Folks, GD's, G-Street, Hells Angels, Insane Vice Lords, Lynch Mob, Outlaws, Rolling 60, Skinheads, White Dragon

Minneapolis (LE):   Vice Lords, Disciples, Asian Gangs, Aryan Brotherhood, BGD's, Bikers, BD's, BG's, Brothers Behind Bars (BBB), Brothers of the Struggle (BOS), El Rukns, Folks, Four Corner Hustlers, Freight Train Riders of America, Hell's Angels, Imperial Gangsters, Insane Vice Lords, Latin Kings, Mexican Mafia, Prison Motorcycle Brotherhood (PMB), Rolling 60, Skinheads, Warlords, White Tigers

---

[130]Offshoots.

[131]Hmong and Laotian.

[132]Laotian.

[133]Rumor.

[134]Various different sets: Rolling 60's, Shotgun, Compton Hoover St.

Moose Lake (W3):   Disciples, Vice Lords, Bloods; Aryan Brotherhood, Aryan Nation, BGD's, Bikers, BG's, Crips, El Rukns, Foul Play, GD's, Gypsy Jokers, Latin Counts, Prison Motorcycle Brotherhood (PMB)

Oak Park Heights (W2):   Aryan Brotherhood, BGD's, Bikers, Black Gangsters, Brothers of the Struggle (B.O.S.), Crips, Disciples, El Rukns, Folks, Gangster Disciples, Hell's Angels, Insane Vice Lords, KKK, Latin Kings, Peoples, Satanic Cult Gangs, Shotgun, Skinheads, Vice Lords, White Power, White Pride, Prison Motorcycle Brotherhood (PMB)

Olmsted Co. (LE):   Royal Cambodian Bloods, GD's, Sons of Silence

Red Wing (JI):   Bloods, Crips, Vice Lords, Disciples, Folks, Peoples

Rochester (LE):   R.C.B.s, Crips, Gangster Disciples, Bloods, B.O.S., GDs, Latin Kings, Sons of Silence, Vice Lords

Roseville (LE):   Vice Lords, White Tigers, Crypts[135], Aryan Brotherhood, Aryan Nation, Black Mafia, Bloods, Disciples, Insane Vice Lords, Latin Kings, Pagans, Posse Comitatus, Skinheads

Sauk Centre (JI):   Crips, Vice Lords, Disciples, Latin Kings, Naturals (Indian)

Sauk Centre (JD):   Black Gangsters, Bloods, Crips, Disciples, Four Corner Hustlers, Hilltop Hustlers, Latin Kings, Vice Lords

St. Cloud (W2):   Aryan Brotherhood, Banditos, BGD's, Bikers, Black Gangsters, Black Guerilla Family, Bloods, Brothers of the Struggle (B.O.S.), Cobras, Crips, Disciples, El Rukns, Five Percenters, Folks, F.T.W., Gangsters, Gangster Disciples, Hell's Angels, Insane Vice Lords, KKK, Knights, Latin Kings, Moors, Neo-nazis, Peoples, Posse Commitatus, Pyru, Rolling 60, Santana Block, Satanic Cult Gangs, Shorty Folks, Shotgun, Skinheads, Spanish Cobras, Stoners, Vice Lords, Warlords, White Power

St. Cloud (W3):   Aryan Brotherhood; Vice Lords, Disciples, Latin Kings; Airheads, BGD's, Bikers, BD's, BG's, Black Guerilla Family, Bloods, Brothers of the Struggle (BOS), Cobras, Crips, El Rukns, Folks, Four Corner Hustlers, GD's, Hell's Angels, Hilltop Hustlers, Imperial Gangsters, Insane Vice Lords, Lynch Mob, Neo-nazis, Prison Motorcycle Brotherhood (PMB), Piru, Rolling 60, Sharps, Skinheads, Spanish Cobras, White Gangster Disciples

Stearns Co. (LE):   Lost Boys, Crenshaw Mafia, Lynch Mob, Insane Crips, Insane Vice Lords, Posse Comitatus

Stearns Co. (JA):   Vice Lords, Bloods, Crips

Stillwater (AI):   Vice Lords, Disciples, PMB (Prison Motorcycle Brotherhood), Bloods, Crips, Aryan Brotherhood, El Rukns, Neo-nazis, Mexican Mafia, Bikers

Stillwater (AI):   Hells Outcasts[136], Vice Lords, Black Gangster Disciples, Crips, Bloods, Aryan Brotherhood, Skinheads, Brothers of the Struggle, El Rukns, Latin Kings, Bikers

Stillwater (W2):   Prison Motorcycle Brotherhood, Aryan Brotherhood, Disciples, El Rukns, Gangster Disciples, F.T.W., Moors, Vice Lords

Stillwater (W3):   Vice Lords, Black Gangster Disciples, White Power; Aryan Brotherhood, Aryan Circle, Aryan Nation, Bikers, BD's, BG's, Bloods, Boyz of Destruction, Brothers Behind Bars, Brothers of the Struggle (BOS), Brothers of White Supremacy (BOWS), Crips, El Rukns, Folks, GD's, Hell's Angels, Insane Crips,

---

[135]This spelling syntax is as provided in response to an open-ended question: "What are the names of the largest three gangs in your area" from the 1992 Law Enforcement survey.

[136] White motorcycle gang.

Insane Vice Lords, Latin Kings, Latin Locos, Mexican Mafia, Prison Motorcycle Brotherhood (PMB), Satan's Disciples, Skinheads, Sons of Silence, Stoners, Warlords, White Gangster Disciples, White Power
St. Louis Park (PC):   Bloods, Crips, Vice Lords, Disciples, Skinheads
St. Paul (JD):   Crips, Disciples, Skinheads
Togo (JI):   Vice Lords, Disciples, Skinheads, Latin Kings
Waite Park (PC):   Bloods, Crips, Vice Lords, Disciples
Willow River (AI):   Bloods, Crips, Vice Lords, Disciples

MISSISSIPPI:
Clarke Co. (CS):   Ku Klux Klan
Columbus (LE):   BGD's, Vice Lords
Goodman (PC):   Vice Lords, Ku Klux Klan, Cobras, Disciples, Knights
Greenville (LE):   Vice Lords, Black Gangster Disciples
Gulfport (W2):   Vice Lords, Bloods, Black Gangster Disciples, Crips
Hinds Co. (LE):   Folks, Vice Lords, Lynch Street Mob, BGD's, BD's, Crips, Gangsters, GD's, G-Boys
Jackson (PC):   Folks, Vice Lords, Disciples
Leakesville (AI):   Aryan Brotherhood, Vice Lords, Black Gangster Disciples, Crips, El Rukns
Leakesville (W2):   Aryan Brotherhood, BGD's, Bloods, Crips, Insane Vice Lords, Insane Crips, Vice Lords
Lucedale (W2):   Aryan Brotherhood, Black Gangster Disciples, Bloods, Crips, Insane Vice Lords, Insane Crips, Vice Lords
Parchman (W3):   Aryan Brotherhood; Black Gangster Disciples, Vice Lords, Bloods; Crips, Insane Vice Lords
Pascagoula (PC):   Bloods, Crips, Black Gangster Disciples, Vice Lords, Disciples, Folks, Peoples, Miami Boys, PYRU
Union Co. (CS):   Lynchmob, Ghostriders, Vice Lords, Disciples
Waveland (PC):   Bloods, Crips, Ku Klux Klan, bikers
Westpoint (PC):   Bloods, Southern Homeboys, Black Gangsters, Crips, Vice Lords, Disciples, Miami Boys, El Rukns

MISSOURI:
Andrew Co. (CS):   Bloods, Crips, Aryan Brotherhood
Boonville (AI):   Bloods, Crips, Black Gangster Disciples, Vice Lords, Skinheads, Posse, Neo-nazis, SWP, Ku Klux Klan
Boonville (W2):   Bloods, C Street, Moors, MSTA, Satanic Cult Gangs
Chillicothe (AI):   Bloods, Crips, Aryan Brotherhood, Skinheads, Posse, Ku Klux Klan, Cobras
Douglas Co. (CS):   Aryan Brotherhood, Neo-nazis, KKK
Farmington (W3):   Aryan Nations; Crips, Black Gangster Disciples Nation, Bloods; Aryan Brotherhood, Bloods, Pharoahs, Satanic Cult Gangs, South Side Boys
Fordland (W3):   Aryan Brotherhood, Bloods, Crips, Colonia Chiques, Head Bangers, Hell's Angels, Inca Boys, White Power
Fulton (JI):   Bloods, Crips, Disciples, Black Gangsters, Moors, PYRU
Harrisonville (JA):   Aryan Brotherhood, Bloods, Crips, Hell's Angels, Galloping Goose[137], El Forastero[138], KKK

---

[137] Biker gang.

Independence (LE):   Eastside Latin Counts, 9th Street Dogs, Woods Chapel Posse[139], BGD's, Sons of Samoa, The Crew

Jackson Co. (LE):   Crips, Bloods, Latin Counts, Aryan Nation, KKK, Posse Comitatus, Satanic Cult Gangs, 9th Street Dawgs

Jefferson City (AI):   Aryan Nation, Crips, Bloods, Aryan Brotherhood, Ku Klux Klan

Jefferson City (LE):   Disciples, Eight Balls, Four Corner Hustlers

Joplin (LE)[140]:   Aryan Brotherhood, Banditos,

Kansas City (JI):   Bloods, Crips, Latin Kings, KKK

Kansas City, MO(LE):   Black Gangster Disciple Nation, Vice Lords, Big Top Locos, BG's, Folks, Gangsters, GD's, Imperial Nation

Lawson (JI):   9th Street Dawgs[141], Bloods, Crips, Disciples, Posse, Black Gangsters, KKK, Insane Crypts, 39th Street Gang, Latin Counts, Black Mafia

Liberty (JA):   Aryan Nation, Bloods, Crips; Aryan Brotherhood, BGD's, Cobras, Dragons, Hell's Angels, Insane Vice Lords, Latin Counts, KKK, La Mafia, Neo-nazis, Rolling 60, Skinheads, South Side Boys, West Side Boyz, White Knights, 9th Street Dawgs

Mexico (JI):   SWAS[142], Bloods, Crips, Aryan Brotherhood, Skinheads, Neo-nazis, KKK, Pagans, Banditos, Raiders, F.T.W., 69th Street Dogs, Black Knights, Black Stone Rangers[143], Church of Jesus Christ Christian (neo-nazi), The Covenant-Sword-And Arm of the Lord (white supremicist).

Mineral Point (AI):   Bloods, Moorish Science Temple #1, Crips, Aryan Brotherhood, Vice Lords, Disciples, Posse, El Rukns, Neo-Nazis, Latin Kings, Black Gangsters, Bikers, Black Guerilla Family, G-Street, Hell Raisers

Osage Beach (JI)[144]:   Bloods, Crips, Vice Lords, Disciples, Skinheads, Posse Commitatus

Poplar Bluff (JI):   Pharoahs[145], Bloods, Crips, Vice Lords, Disciples, Folks, Skinheads, Neo-nazis, Hell's Angels, KKK, Raiders, Black Mafia, 39th Street Gang, White Gangster Disciples, NWA, 19th Street Gang

---

[138]Biker gang.

[139]AKA: "inner circle".

[140]"None" gangs known, but following checked off.

[141] White gang.

[142] White gang, short for SWAStika, neo-nazis (Jefferson City, MO).

[143] 69th Street Dogs, Black Knights, and Black Stone Rangers from Kansas City area.

[144] Data taken from youth case files or self-reported during their stay at this youth facility.

[145] White gang.

Springfield (JI):   Bloods, Crips
Springfield (LE):   Bloods, Inglewood Family Gangster Bloods, Galloping Goose
  motorcycle gang, Disciples, Crips, Hell's Angels, Hell Raisers, KKK, Posse,
  Skinheads, Vice Lords
St. Charles Co. (LE):   Crips, Bloods, BGD's[146], Raiders[147], KKK, Skinheads
St. Louis (JI):   Bloods, Crips, Vice Lords, Posse, JVL Posse, BGD's, Thundercats,
  High Rollers, Hoovers
St. Louis (W2):   Bloods, Crips, Moors, MSTA, Thundercats
St. Louis (JD):   BGD's, Bloods, Boyz of Destruction (BOD's), Crips (39th Player
  Crips, Six Dueces East Coast Crips, 44 Blue Blood Crips), Disciples, Fila Boys, Five
  Percenters, Freakie Boys, Insane Gangsters, West End MOB, Posse (JVL Posse,
  Northside Posse, 98 Posse), Pagedale Boys, Rolling 60, Peabody Boys, Switchblade
  Sisters, Smith-Wesson Boys, Thundercats, Westend Rockers
St. Louis (LE):   Boys of Destruction, Semple Mob, Organized Gangster Disciples,
  BGD's, BD's, Bloods, Crips, Disciples, GD's, JVL posse, Kitchen Crips, Peaboby
  Boys, Piru, Rolling 60, S.S.G.
St. Louis Co. (LE):   Crips, Bloods
Union (JD):   Bloods, Crips
Warsaw (JA):   Aryan Brotherhood

MONTANA:
Billings (LE):   Eight Balls, Lynch Mob, Skinheads, Wolf Pack
Helena (JI):[148]   Bloods, Crips
Kaliskill (PC):   Aryan Brotherhood, Neo-nazis
Laurel (PC):   Freight Train Riders Association (transient gang)
Swan Lake (W2):[149]   Aryan Brotherhood, Crips, Bloods
Thompson Falls (JA):   Constitutionalists, White Supremecists; Aryan Brotherhood,
  Aryan Nation, Banditos, Neo-nazis, skinheads
Warm Springs (AI):   Aryan Brotherhood, Bikers
White Fish (PC):   Aryan Brotherhood

NEBRASKA:
Atkinson (PC):   Bloods, Crips, Skinheads
Dakota Co. (LE):   Cholos, Eight Balls, Crips, Insane Crips, Satanic Cult Gangs
Geneva (JI):   Bloods, Crips, Skinheads
Lincoln (AI):   Hells Angels, Crips, Bloods, Aryan Brotherhood, Skinheads, Posse,
  neo-nazis, Mexican Mafia, Bikers, Ku Klux Klan, Gypsy Jokers, Mad Dogs
Lincoln (AI):   Crips, Bloods, Black Gangster Disciples, Vice Lords, Skinheads, Latin
  Kings, Bikers, Ku Klux Klan

---

[146]From the E. St. Louis Illinois area.

[147]Athletic groups that generally congregate at local shopping mall.

[148] Both Bloods and Crips from Billings area.

[149]Admitted gang affiliations by inmates during intake.

Lincoln (W2)[150]:   Aryan Brotherhood, Bloods, Crips, BGD's
Lincoln (LE):   BGDs, Bloods, Crips, KKK, Latin Kings, Santana Block
Lincoln (W3):   Bloods, Crips; Aryan Brotherhood, BGD's, Cholos, Vice Lords
Loup Co. (CS):   Posse
Holdrege (PC):   Posse
Lancaster (PP):   Bloods, Crips
Kearney (PC):   Bloods, Posse Commitatus
Milford (PC):   Aryan Brotherhood, skinheads, bikers, Sons of Silence
Omaha (AI):   Bloods, Crips, Bikers
Omaha (W2):   Aryan Brotherhood, BGD's, Bloods, Crips, Cholas
Omaha (LE):   Crips, Bloods, Cholos, BGDs, Bikers, Black Mafia, Cholos, Hells
Angels, Sons of Silence
Omaha (LE):   Crips, Bloods, Lomas, Aryan Brotherhood, BGD's, Cholos, Folks,
Insane Crips, KKK, Latin Counts, Latin Kings, La Raza, Lynch Mob, Piru, Rolling
60, Santana Block, skinheads, Vice Lords
Omaha (W3):   Aryan Brotherhood, Skinheads; Bloods, Crips, Vice Lords, Lomas;
Aryan Nation, Cholos, El Rukns, Hell's Angels, KKK, Insane Crips, Rolling 60,
Santana Block, White Power
Ralston (PC):   Bloods, Crips, Cholos, Vice Lords, Aryan Brotherhood, Skinheads,
Black Gangsters, Bikers
York (AI):   Crips, Bloods

NEVADA:
Battle Mountain (CS):   Sundowners (bikers)
Carson City (W2):   AW's or Aryan Circle[151], Aryan Brotherhood, Bikers, Bloods,
Crips, Mexican Mafia, Neo-nazis, Nuestra Familia, Skinheads, Kingsman
Carson City (W3):   Montellos, Crips, Bloods; Aryan Brotherhood, Aryan Circle,
Aryan Warriors, Barrio Chicano Locos, La Raza, Nuestra Familia, Skinheads, White
Power, White Pride
Carson City (W3):   Crips, Bloods, White Supremacists; Aryan Warriors
Caliente (JI):   Bloods, Crips, Neonazis, Skinheads, Raiders
Douglas Co. (PP):[152]   Bloods, Crips, Skinheads
Elko (JI):   Bloods, Crips, Skinheads, Black Gangsters, PYRU, Blue Rags, Red Rags
Ely (AI):   Aryan Circle, Crips, Bloods, Aryan Warriors, Aryan Brotherhood, Bikers,
Black Guerilla Family
Ely (W2):   Aryan Warriors, Assassins Inc, Bikers, Black Gangsters, Black Guerilla
Family, Bloods, Bomber Boys, Crips, Hell's Angels, Mexican Mafia, PYRU, Rolling
60
Ely (W2):   Aryan Brotherhood, Barrio Chicano Locos, Bikers, Bloods, Crips, F.T.W.,
Gypsy Jokers, Hell's Angels, Insane Crips, KKK, Mexican Mafia, Neo-nazis, Nuestra
Familia, Pyru, Rolling 60, Satanic Cult Gangs, Skinheads, SUR 13, SWP, Stoners,
White Peoples Party, 14th Street Gang, 18th Street Gang

---

[150]Respondent reports experiencing no significant gang activity as of yet (e.g., one inmate identifying with the Aryan Brotherhood).

[151]White gang.

[152] In general Reno, Carson area.

Ely (JA):   Aryan Brotherhood, Aryan Circle, Aryan Nation, La Familia, La Mafia, Skinheads

Henderson (PC):   Hogs, Los Hermanos, Lil Locos, Crips, PYRU

Jean (AI):   Crips, Bloods, Aryan Warriors, Aryan Brotherhood, Skinheads, El Rukns, Neo-nazis, Nuestra Familia, Cobras, PYRU

Las Vegas (CS):   Bloods, Crips, Vice Lords, Disciples, Aryan Brotherhood, Skinheads, Posse, Latin Kings, SUR, Black Gangsters, Mexican Mafia, Bikers, Black Guerilla Family, Insane Crypts, PYRU, SUR 13, 28th Street, West Coast Bloods, Rolling 60's

Las Vegas (W2):   Aryan Brotherhood, Bloods, Crips, Mexican Mafia

Las Vegas (LE):   Donna Street Crips, Gerson Park Kingsmen (Crips), San Chucos, BDs, Bloods, Insane Crips, Lil Locos, Los Hermanos, Piru, Santana Block, Sons of Somoa (S.O.S.), Skinheads, 18th Street Gang

Las Vegas (JA):   West Coast Bloods, Donna Street Crips, Gerson Park Kingsman; Aryan Brotherhood, Aryan Nation, Aryan Warriors, Bikers, Lil Locos, Pagans, Skinheads, Stoners

North Los Vegas (PC):   Bloods, Cips, Little Poco's, Aryan Brotherhood, skinheads, Mexican Mafia, bikers, PYRU

Reno (PC):   Montellos, Vatos, 118 Crips, Bloods, Disciples, Aryan Brotherhood, Skinheads, Posse, Neo-nazis, SUR, SWP, Mexican Mafia, Bikers, PYRU, SUR 13

Reno (W2):   Aryan Brotherhood, Bloods, Crips, Rolling 60, Skinheads

Reno (JD):   Bloods, Crips, Diamond Street, Disciples, Mexican Mafia, Neo-nazis, Nuestra Familia, Rolling 60, SUR 13, SWP, T.C.G. (Tongan Crip Gang), 8-Balls, 18th Street Gang

Reno (LE):   Montellos, Crips, Sunset Texans, Aryan Brotherhood, Aryan Circle, Aryan Nation, Aryan Warriors, Banditos, BGDs, Big Top Locos, Black Guerilla Family, Black Mafia, Bloods, Brothers Speed, Eight Balls, E.M.E., Fruits of Islam, F.T.W., Gypsy Jokers, Hells Angels, KKK, La Familia, Mexican Mafia, Nortenos, Nuestra Familia, Pagans, Posse Comitatus, Satanic Cult Gangs, Skinheads, Sons of Samoa, Stoners, SUR 13, Tongan Crip Gang, White Power

Reno (LE):   Montellos, Sunset Texans, Mara Villa, Aryan Brotherhood, Aryan Circle, Big Top Locos, Bikers, Bloods, Crips, Nortenos, Piru, Skinheads, Surenos, SUR 13, Tongan Crip Gang (TCG)

Sparks (PC):   Montellos, Big Top Locos, Crips 11-8, Bloods, Crips, Aryan Brotherhood, Skinheads, Posse, SUR, Mexican Mafia, Bikers, Nuestra Familia, PYRU, SUR 13, 19th Street Gang

Washoe Co. (CS):   Crips, Bloods, Montello's, Aryan Brotherhood, Skinheads, Neo-nazis, SUR, SWP, Mexican Mafia, Bikers, Nuestra Familia, Gypsy Jokers, SUR 13, Sons of Silence

Wells (PC):   The Brothers

NEW HAMPSHIRE:
Concord (JI):   Bloods, Crips
Lancaster (PC):   Skinheads
Manchester (PP):   Aryan Brotherhood, Bikers, KKK
Manchester (JA):   Aryan Brotherhood, Bikers, Bloods, Crips, KKK

NEW JERSEY:
Atlantic City (LE):   Abdullah, Salaams, BG's, Black Mafia, Eight Balls, Dragons, Gangsters, Knights, Lynch Mob, Pagans, Warlocks
Bridgeton (JI):   Posse

Camden (AI):   UJAMA/African National UJAMA, Five Percent Nation of Islam, New World of Islam, Aryan Brotherhood, Skinheads, Posse, Neo-nazis, Bikers, Black Guerilla Family, Ku Klux Klan, Pagans

Cape May Co. (LE):   Outlaws, Pagans

Delmont (W3):   Aryan Brotherhood, Salaams, Abdullah's, Five Percenters, Bikers; Black Mafia, Eight Balls, Fruits of Islam, Head Bangers, KKK, Pagans, Posse, Skinheads

Freehold (JI):   Aryan Brotherhood, Skinheads, Posse, Neo-Nazis, Pagans, G-Street, Five Percenters, Head Bangers, DBL's, DBB (Devastating Black Brothers)

Freehold (JD):   Flying Aces

Garfield (LE):   Jewell St. Posse, Monroe St. Posse, Third St. Posse, skinheads

Gloucester Co. (CS):   Bloods, Skinheads, Posse, KKK, Pagans

Hopewell (JI):   Aryan Brotherhood, Skinheads, Bikers, Outlaws, KKK, Pagans, Five Percenters

Jamesburg (JI):   Five Percenters

Jersey City (JI):   Posse

Mercer Co. (CS):   Bloods, Crips, Skinheads, Posse, Neo-nazis, Five Percenters

Monmouth Co. (PP):   F.B.I, Rat Pack, Skinheads[153], Five Percenters, Devastation Black Boys (DBB's), Unique Neptune Brothers (UNB's), Bloods, Crips, Aryan Brotherhood, Neo-nazis

New Brunswick (LE):   Uptown, Downtown, Hell's Angels, Pagans, Skinheads

Plainfield (JI):   Skinheads, Posse, Neo-nazis, Latin Kings, Five Percenters, G-Boys

Ridgewood (LE):   Broad Street Posse

Somerset (PC):   Grove, Uptown Boys, Down Town Boys, Skinheads, Posse

Trenton (W2):   Five Percenters

Trenton (JD):   Five Percenters

Watchung (LE):   Arlington Ave. Posse, Latin Kings, Third Street Posse

Wrightstown (W3):   Five Percenters; Aryan Brotherhood, Aryan Nation, Bikers, Fruits of Islam, High Rollers, KKK, Neo-nazis, Pagans, Satanic Cult Gangs, Skinheads

NEW MEXICO:

Alamogordo (PC):   Deleware Locos, BKs, Bloods,Crips, Skinheads, Bikers, Nuestra Familia

Alamogordo (JI):   Bloods, Crips, Posse, Raiders, 19th Street Gang, Delaware Locals, La Familia, Surenos

Albuquerque (JI):   Bloods, Crips, Disciples, Aryan Brotherhood, Skinheads, Neo-nazis, Latin Kings, Mexican Mafia, Bikers, KKK, Nuestra Familia, Banditos, La Raza, NWK 14, Vice Lords, Juarito's, Outlaws, Hell's Angels, Cobras, Raiders, Knights, Black Mafia, Lucifer's Lot

Albuquerque (JD):   Avondale Crack Monsters, Barrio Chicano Locos, Black Mafia, Bloods, Brothers Speed, Center City Locos, Colonia Chiques, Crips, Kuang Le, La Raza, Posse, PYRU, Shotgun, Six Pack Gang, Skinheads, White Pride, 14th Street Gang, 18th Street Gang, 19th Street Gang

Albuquerque (LE):   San Jose Locos, 18th Street, Westside Locos, Aryan Brother hood, Banditos, Black Mafia, Bloods, Crips, E.M.E., F-13, Kitchen Crips, Latin Kings, La Familia, Los Hermanos, Nuestra Familia, Piru, Rolling 60, Sharps, Skinheads, 14th Street Gang

Artesia (PC):   Pie, DBL, VNS

---

[153] All three are white gangs.

Clovis (JA):   West Side, 4th St. Locos, Crips
Dona Ana Co. (LE):   45er's Dona Ana Home Boys, Eastsiders
Farmington (JI):   Bloods, Crips, Skinheads, Posse, Cobras
Fort Stanton (W3):   Mighty Whiteys[154]; Mexican Mafia, Crips, Nuestra Familia; Aryan Brotherhood, Aryan Nation, Banditos, Bloods
Hagerman (AI):   Bloods, Crips, Mexican Mafia, Nuestra Familia, Gypsy Jokers, F.T.W.
Las Crueces (PC):   Eastside, King Cobras, No Joke Posse, Bloods, Crips, Posse, Latin Kings, Nuestra Familia, Cobras
Las Crueces (AI):   Texas Syndicate, Crips, Bloods, Aryan Brotherhood, neo-nazis, Mexica Mafia, Nuestra Familia
Las Cruces (LE):   East Siders, West Siders, Dona Ana Home Boys
Las Cruces (W3):   Supreme White Peoples Party (SWP); El Paso Tip (EPT), Los Carnales, Burgue Clique; Bloods, Crips, F.T.W., King Cobra, Neo-nazis, Nuestra Familia, Skinheads, SUR 13, 8-Balls, 18th Street Gang
Los Alamos (PC):   White Trashers, Skinheads
Los Lunas (PC):   East Side Locos, 18th Street Gang, Crips, Bloods, Posse, Mexican Mafia, Bikers, Pagans
Mesilla (PC):   Bloods, Crips, Mexican border gangs, Disciples, Aryan Brotherhood, Posse, Neo-Nazis, Latin Kings, Black Gangsters, Mexican Mafia, Bikers, Nuestra Familia, Cobras, Pagans, Avengers
Socorro (JA):   Grant Streeters, Bagley Boys; Bloods, G-Street, G-Boys, 18th Street Gang
Springer (JI):   Bloods, Crips, Quaritos, Valley Gardens, Echo Park, San Jose

NEW YORK:
Albany (JI):   Bloods, Aryan Brotherhood, Skinheads, Neo-nazis, Outlaws, Hell's Angels, Five Percenters
Brooklyn (JD):   Five Percenters
Brooktondale (JI):   DBz[155], Posse, Izod Posse, Mad Dogs, Savage Nomads, Five Percenters, F.T.W., La Raza, G-Boys, DBL's, Decepticons (NYC)
Buffalo (JI):   Skinheads, Five Percenters, 10th Street
Buffalo (LE):   LA Boys, GC Crew, Mad Dogs
Canandaigua (JD):   G-Boys, Satanic Cult Gangs
Comstock (W2):   Five Percenters, Hell's Angels, Latin Kings, Posse, Machetteros
Dix Hills (JI):   Posse, Five Percenters, B.T.K. (Born To Kill)[156], Partners in Crime[157], Sprangler Posse[158]
Elmira (JD):   Crips, Skinheads
Fishkill (AI):   Five Percenters

---

[154]Obviously: a white gang.

[155] White gang.

[156]Lower east side Manhattan Asian gang.

[157] Brooklyn gang.

[158] Jamaican gang, W. 145th St., Manhattan.

Flushing (JA):   Born To Kill (BTK), Crips, Five Percenters, Fruits of Islam, Ghost Riders, Ghost Shadows, Latin Kings, La Familia, Skinheads
Hudson (AI):   Five Percenters, Bikers
Industry (JI):   Crips, Bloods, Posse, Five Percenters
Moravia (AI):   Latin Kings, Posse, Aryan Brotherhood, Five Percenters, Blue Rags, Red Rags
Rensselaerville (JI):   Bloods, Crips, Aryan Brotherhood, Skinheads, Posse, Neo-nazis, Latin Kings, Bikers, Outlaws, Nuestra Familia, Hell's Angels, KKK, Kuang Le, Orchard Park, Knights, Red Dragons, Five Percenters, Intervale, La Raza, Down By the Law (DBL)
Riverhead (JA):   Five Percenters, Hell's Angels
Rochester (PC):   F.V., Posse, G-Boys
Schenectady (LE):   Hell's Angels[159], Little John[160], Five Percenters[161], Ghost Shadows, Satanic Cult Gangs, Sprangler Posse, KKK
Scotia (PC):   Hells Angels, The Breed, Bikers, Five Percenters
Syracuse (JI):   North Syracuse Players[162], Five Percenters, South Side Posse
Westbury (JI):   Skinheads, Neo-nazis, Five Percenters
Westchester Co. (PP):   Aryan Brotherhood, Skinheads
Yonkers (LE):   Doing the Most Damage (DMD), Lawrence Street Posse, BP Boys

NORTH CAROLINA:
Asheville (CS):   KKK, Aryan Brotherhood
Brunswick (W3):   Fayetteville Posse, Sanford Posse, Mohawks
Clinton (W3):   Fayetteville Posse
Concord (JI):   Skinheads, Posse, Neo-Nazis, KKK, Outlaws, Hell's Angels, Pagans
Davidson Co. (LE):   Outlaws, Crips, KKK, Pagans
Durham (LE):   Hell's Angels, Pimps, Few Crew, Lynch Mob, West End Mob, West Side Boyz, 8-Balls
Durham (W3)[163]:   Aryan Brotherhood, Blades, Bloods, Satanic Cult Gangs
Gastonia (JA):   Eight Balls
Goldsboro (LE):   45 Kings, Butt Naked, Jungle Boys, L.A. Kings
Greensboro (LE):   Benagers, Outlaws, Crips, KKK, Pagans
Henderson (W3):   Posse[164]; Hell's Angels; JVL Posse, K-A Posse
Kinston (PC):   Skinheads, Ku Klux Klan, Pagans

---

[159]Nomad chapter.

[160]Juvenile drug gang.

[161]Juvenile Black gang.

[162] White gang.

[163]Respondent remarked regarding white inmate gangs "more of a group than a gang - no name"; and regarding the top three gangs among inmates in the facility "no known gangs"; but checked off several gangs on the checklist.

[164]A white gang.

Lexington (W3):   Folks
McCain (AI):   Hell's Angels
Morgantown (JI):   Posse, KKK, Five Percenters
Mt. Pleasant (W3):   Hell's Angels, Outlaws
Murfressboro (PC):   Bikers, Ku Klux Klan
Raeford (PC):   Ku Klux Klan
Troy (AI):   Aryan Brotherhood, Bikers
Troy (W3):   Aryan Nation
Washington (JA):   Aryan Brotherhood, Crips
Wilmington (JA):   Hell's Angels, Hell Raisers, Highway Men
Wilson (PC):   Aces, Klu Klux Klan
Yadkinville (W3):   Outlaws, Hell's Angels, Jamaican Posse; Jokers, JVL Posse,
    Pagans
Zebulon (PC):   Crew, Nike, OP (On Probation), Skinheads, Posse, Miami Boys,
    Bikers, Ku Klux Klan

NORTH DAKOTA:
Bismarck (AI):   Aryan Brotherhood, Bikers
Bismarck (W2):   Aryan Brotherhood, Hell's Angels
Bismarck (W3)[165]:   Bikers, Posse Comitatus, Raiders, Satanic Cult Gangs
Bismarck (LE):   Raiders, Aryan Nation, Banditos, Bloods, Crips, Hells Angels,
    KKK, Outlaws, Prison Motorcycle Brotherhood (PMB), Satans Disciples, Skinheads,
    Sons of Silence
Ellendale (JA):   Posse Comitatus
Fargo (LE):   Latin Kings, Freight Train Riders Association of America, Posse
    Comitatus
Jamestown (JA):   Posse Comitatus
Mandan (JI):   Bloods, Crips
Mandan (JD):   Bloods, Crips, Raiders
Mercer Co. (CS):   Posse
Minot (PC):   Raiders, Crips
Ward Co. (CS):   Raiders

OHIO:
Akron (JD):   8-Balls, Bloods, Folks (Po Boys)
Barberton (LE):   9-Kings[166], Dew Rag Posse[167], East Side Posse,[168]
    West Side Posse[169]

---

[165]Respondent indicated "we don't have any" regarding the top three major gangs
that are represented among inmates in the facility; but checked off several gangs from
the gang checklist, as a gang that has been active in any capacity in the area.

[166]Akron - predominantly Black males.

[167]Akron, predominantly white males.

[168]Black males.

[169]White males.

Butler Co. (LE):   Skinheads, Outlaw M.C. Gang, KKK, Bloods, Crips
Canton (JD):   Satanic Cult Gangs, Satans Disciples
Canton (LE):   Wranglers, Lynch Mob, Crips
Chillicothe (W3):   Aryan Bro., Aryan Nation, Final Chapter[170], BGD's, El-Rukns; Aryan Brotherhood, Avengers, BG's, BD's, Black Mafia, Bloods, Boston Boys, Brick City Outlaws, Brothers Behind Bars (BBB), Brothers of the Struggle (BOS), Crips, Disciples, Folks, Fruits of Islam, F.T.W., GD's, Imperial Gangsters, Insane Crips, Latin Kings, Miami Boys, NWA, Outlaws, Pagans, Rolling 60, Satanic Cult Gangs, SWP, Vice Lords, Young Boys Inc
Cincinnati (JD):   Bloods, Crips, Down By the Laws (DBL's), L.A. Kings, White Gangster Disciples
Cincinnati (LE):   Iron Horsemen Motorcycle Gang, Down By Laws, Camp Washington Crips, Aryan Brotherhood, BGD's, BD's, Boot Boys, GDs, Latin Kings, Neo-nazis, Outlaws, Rolling 60, Spanish Cobras, Vice Lords, Young Boys Inc
Cleveland (PP):   Crips, Bloods, Klu Klux Klan, Folks, Knights
Cleveland (PC):   Devil Dogs, Brick City, Posse
Columbiana Co. (JA):   Pagans, Hell's Angels, Dukes; Outlaws, Posse Comitatus
Columbus (JI):   Bloods, Crips, Vice Lords, Disciples, Folks, Peoples, Skinheads, Brothers of the Struggle, Black Gangsters, White Gangster Disciples, Peoples, Folks, Neo-nazis, Latin Kings, SWP, Bikers, Outlaws, Castlegate, Intervale, G-Boys, East 79th Street Posse
Columbus (W2):   Aryan Brotherhood, Bloods, Crips, Moors
Columbus (LE):   Assassins, Inc; Flying Dragons, Hells Angels, Hoods,
Columbus (LE):   Short North Posse, Brotherhood of Black Mafia, G.I. Boys, Avengers, Big Top Locos, Bloods, B.O.S., Crips, Insane Vice Lords, Skinheads, Vice Lords
Columbus (W3):   Crips, Bloods, Aryan Brotherhood; BGD's, BD's, Brothers of White Supremacy (BOWS), Folks, La Familia
Dayton (LE):   Bloods, Crips, KKK, Outlaw M.C.
Delaware (JI):   Bloods, Crips, Disciples, Posse, Black Gangsters, Assassins Inc
Franklin Co. (PP):   Skinheads, Bloods, Crips, Posse, Ku Klux Klan
Grafton (W2):   Aryan Brotherhood, Bloods, Crips, Bikers, BGD's, Brothers of the Struggle (B.O.S.), Crazy White Boys, Eight Balls, Folks, F.T.W., Gangster Disciples, Hell's Angels, Insane Crips, Insane Vice Lords, KKK, Latin Kings, Pagans, Outlaws, Vice Lords
Grafton (W3):   Aryan Brotherhood, Folks, Crips, White Supremacists; Aryan Nation, Avengers, Banditos, BGD's, Bikers, BD's, BG's, Bloods, Brick City Outlaws, Brothers of the Struggle (BOS), Cobras, Dragons, El Rukns, EME, Four Corner Hustlers, F.T.W., Hammer Gang, Hell's Angels, Imperial Gangsters, Insane Vice Lords, Iron Coffins, KKK, Latin Kings, La Mafia, Lynch Mob, Mexican Mafia, Moors, Neo-nazis, Outlaws, Pagans, Peoples, Piru, Rolling 60, Satan's Disciples, Simon City Royals, Skinheads, South Side Boys, Spanish Cobras, Stoners, Vice Lords, West Side Posse, White Peoples Party, Young Boys Inc, Zulu
Lebanon (W2):   Aryan Brotherhood, Bloods, Five Percenters, KKK
Lebanon (W3):   Aryan Brotherhood, BGD's, Aryan Nation, Bloods, Brick City Outlaws, Brothers of the Struggle (BOS), Crips, El Rukns, Folks, F.T.W., GD's, Insane Vice Lords, Outlaws, Vice Lords, White Power, White Pride
Liberty Center (JI):   Bloods, Crips, Folks, Skinheads, Mexican Mafia

---

[170]All white gangs.

London (W2):   Aryan Brotherhood, Avengers, Bloods, Crips, F.T.W., Hell's Angels, Outlaws (MC), Skinheads, BGD's
Lorain Co. (LE):   YBI, TNO, Avengers, BLoods, Crips, Hells Angels, Iron Coffins, KKK, Latin Kings, Young Boys Inc (YBI)
Lucasville (W2):   Aryan Brotherhood, Brick City Outlaws, Hell's Angels, KKK
Mahoning Co. (LE):   Ready Rock Boys, Posse, Aryan Brotherhood, Aryan Nation, BGDs, BKUs, BDs, BGs, Crips, Dirty White Boys, Eight Balls, Dukes, Head Bangers, Hells Angels, Lynch Mob, Partners in Crime, Pagans, Six Pack Gang, Skinheads, South Side Boys
Mansfield (JD):   Four Horsemen of the Apolcalypse, Posse
Mansfield (W2):   Aryan Brotherhood, BGD's, Bloods, Crips, Folks, White Peoples Party, Brick City Outlaws
Mansfield (W3):   Aryan Brotherhood; Black Gangster Disciples, Crips, Bloods; Aryan Nation, BG's, Brick City Outlaws, Folks, KKK, Latin Kings, Posse, Vice Lords
Maple Heights (LE):   Posse Chasers, Folks, Hoods, Insane Crips, Posse
Marysville (W2):   Bloods, Crips, Hell's Angels, KKK, Satanic Cult Gangs
Massillon (JI):   Bloods, Crips, Vice Lords, Folks, Peoples, Brothers of the Struggle, Sons of Silence, Superior Posse, Black Gangsters, Skinheads, White Gangster Disciples, NWA, East Coast Gangsters
Massillon (LE):   Detroit Boys[171], Hells Angels
Northern Dist.(PP):   Hells' Angels, Bloods, Crips
Orient (W2):   Aryan Brotherhood, Bikers, Bloods, Brothers of the Struggle (B.O.S.), Crips, KKK, neo-nazis, Outlaws, Satanic Cult Gangs, Skinheads, La Mafia
Orient (W3):   Aryan Brotherhood, Folks (BGD's), Vice Lords; Aryan Nation, Black Disciples, Brick City Outlaws, Brothers of the Struggle (BOS), Five Percenters, Four Corner Hustlers, Gangster Disciples, F.T.W., Insane Vice Lords, KKK, Posse, Rolling 60, Satanic Cult Gangs, Skinheads, Vice Lords
Painesville (JD):   BGD's, Bloods, Crips, Eight Balls, Folks, Insane Vice Lords, Jokers, Neo-nazis, Satanic Cult Gangs, Skinheads
Sandusky (JD):   BGD's, Bikers, Black Mafia, Bloods, Brothers of the Struggle (B.O.S.), Brothers Speed, Crips, Eight Balls, Gangsters, Hell's Angels, Hoods, Lynch Mob, NWA, South Side Boys
Springfield (JD):   BDG's, Black Gangsters, Bloods, Crips, Disciples, Insane Crips, Latin Kings, L.A. Kings, Lobos, Posse, Satans Disciples, Skinheads, White Knights
Stark Co. (LE):   Si Fi, Rated R, Lynch Mob, Crips, KKK, Outlaws, Pagans, Posse Comitatus
Toledo (LE):   Bloods, Crips, Avondale Posse, Avengers, BGDs, Eight Balls, Folks, Iron Coffins, L.V.B., Neo-nazis, Outlaws, Skinheads
Wood Co. (LE):   Latino Posse, Bloods[172], Crips[173]
Xenia (LE):   Bloods, Crips

---

[171]Drug traffickers.

[172]Adjoining urban jurisdiction.

[173]Adjoining urban jurisdiction.

OKLAHOMA:
Boley (W3):   Aryan Brotherhood; Bloods, Crips Del City (LE): Playboy Gangster
    Crips (PBC), 24 Karat Crips (24K), Inglewood Family Gangster Bloods (IFG), Aryan
    Brotherhood, Aryan Nation, BGDs, BDs, Eight Balls, Folks, Head Bangers, Imperial
    Nation, Insane Crips, KKK, Prince Hall Villains, Rolling 60 Crips, Satanic Cult
    Gangs, Vice Lords, White Pride, Piru
Granite (W2):   Aryan Brotherhood, Bloods, Crips, Insane Crips, Kitchen Crips,
    Skinheads
Helena (W2):   Aryan Brotherhood, Banditos, Bikers, Bloods, Crips, KKK, Neo-
    nazis, Satanic Cult gangs, Skinheads, White power
Hodgen (W2):   Aryan Brotherhood, KKK, Neo-nazis, Bikers, Bloods, Crips, Posse,
    Posse Commitatus, Satanic Cult Gangs, Skinheads
Hominy (W2):   Prison Brotherhood[174], Aryan Brotherhood, Bikers, BGD's, Bloods,
    Crips, KKK, P.V.C., Pyru, Rolling 60, Santana Block, Shotgun
Idabel (PC):   Crips, Aryan Brotherhood, Neo-nazis, Ku Klux Klan
Lawton (LE):   Vice Lords, 8-Ball Bloods, 107 Hoover, Crips, 8-Balls, NWA, Prince
    Hall Villains, Rolling 60, Shotgun, Spanish Cobras
Lexington (W3):   Aryan Brotherhood, Bloods, Crips, Aryan Nation, Banditos, Barrio
    Chicano Locos, Bikers, El Rukns, KKK, Mexican Mafia, Romeo Knights, Texas
    Mafia, Rolling 60, Skinheads
McAlester (W2):   Aryan Brotherhood, Bloods, Crips
Midwest City (LE):   Inglewood Family Gangster Bloods, West Side 60 Crips, Rolling
    20 Crips, Aryan Brotherhood, Insane Crips, Prince Hall Villains
Morris (PC):   Crips, Bloods, Bikers
Oklahoma City (PP):   Aryan Brotherhood, Bloods, Crips, Skinheads, Bikers, Nuestra
    Familia
Oklahoma City (W2):   Aryan Brotherhood, Bloods, neo-nazis
Oklahoma City (W3):   Aryan Brotherhood, Aryan Nation, Banditos, Barrio Chicano
    Locos, BGD's, BD's, Black Guerilla Family, Black Mafia, Bloods, Cholos, Crips,
    Mexican Mafia, Neo-nazis, Outlaws, Prince Hall Villains
Sand Springs (JI):   Bloods, Crips, Disciples, Skinheads, PYRU, NWA, Prince Hall
    Villains, Vice Lords, KKK, Posse, G-Street, Raiders, G-Boys, Insane Crypts
Stillwater (LE):   Crips, Bloods, 8-Balls
Tecumseh (JI):   Bloods, Crips
Temple (PC):   Bloods, Crips
Tulsa (PP):   Crips, Bloods, Skinheads, KKK
Tulsa (W2):   Aryan Brotherhood, Crips, Bloods
Tulsa (LE):   107 Hoover Crips, 111 Neighborhood Crips, Red Mob Gangster Bloods,
    Aryan Brotherhood, Aryan Nation, BGDs, Boot Boys, Cholos, Banditos, Kitchen
    Crips, KKK, neo-nazis, Posse Comitatus, Piru, Rolling 60, Sharps, Shotgun, Sons of
    Silence, Stoners, White Knights, White Pride, Oriental Green Team (OGT), 747 Rip
    Boys, Red Mob Gangsters (RMG), Grape St. Crips, Monguls, Rogues, 52nd St.
    Black Mafia Crips, South Side Locos, White Aryan Resistance, Juaritos, Athens Park
    Boys
Tulsa (Co., LE):   Red Mob Ganstas, Neighborhood Crips, Hoover Crips, Aryan
    Brotherhood, Aryan Nation, Banditos, BGD's, Bikers, BD's, Black Mafia, Bloods,

---

[174]White gang - affiliated with Church Jesus Christ Christian: Aryan Nation.

Cholos, Crips, Disciples, Folks, The Fourth Reich, Insane Crips, KKK, Lynch Mob, Neo-nazis, Outlaws, Prince Hall Villains, Piru, Rolling 60, Skinheads, Vice Lords
York (W2):   Bloods, Crips[175]

OREGON:

Baker City (W3):   Crips, Bloods, White Supremacist groups; Aryan Brotherhood, Aryan Nation, Boot Boys, Brothers Speed, E.M.E., La Familia, Neo-nazis, Nuestra Familia, Skinheads

Clackamas Co. (LE):   Bloods, Crips, Skinheads, Aryan Nation, Brothers Speed, Cobras, Gypsy Jokers, Neo-nazis, Posse Comitatus, White Pride, 18th Street Gang

Clatsop Co. (CS):   Bloods, Crips, Aryan Brotherhood, Skinheads, Neo-nazis, Bikers, Gypsy Jokers, PYRU, Red Dragons, Head Bangers

Columbia Co.(PP):   Aryan Brotherhood, Bikers, Gypsy Jokers, Bloods, Crips, Skinheads,

Corvallis (LE):   Crips, Gypsy Jokers, American Federation[176], Bloods, Hells Angels, Neo-nazis

Eugene (JD):   Aryan Brotherhood, BDG's, Bikers, Bloods, Brothers of the Struggle (B.O.S.), Cobras, Crips, Five Percenters, Folks, Gypsy Jokers, Head Bangers, Hell's Angels, Insane Vice Lords, Jesters, KKK, Latin Kings, Mexican Rap Mafia (MRM), neo-Nazis, Nortenos, Peoples, PYRU, Red Cobras, Rolling 60, Skinheads, T.C.G. (Tongan Crip Gang), Vice Lords, White Corner Pride, White Power, 18th Street Gang

Grants Pass (JA):   Posse Comitatus, Aryan Brotherhood, Mexican Mafia; Bloods, Crips, Gypsy Jokers, Nuestra Familia, Stoners

Hillsboro (JA):   18th Street, Crips, Bloods; Aryan Brotherhood, Boot Boys, Cholos, Freight Train Riders of America, KKK, Mexican Mafia, Neo-nazis, Nortenos, Piru, Rolling 60, Sharps, Skinheads, SUR 13, White Pride

Lane Co. (CS):   Bloods, Raiders, Party Boys, Crips, Aryan Brotherhood, Skinheads, Neo-nazis, SWP, Mexican Mafia, Bikers, Gypsy Jokers, PYRU

Marion Co. (LE):   18th Street (Mexican), Skinheads, Asian gangs, Aryan Nation, Bikers, Black Guerilla Family, Bloods, Brothers Speed, Cobras, Crips, Gypsy Jokers, Hells Angels, Insane Vice Lords, KKK, La Familia, Mexican Mafia, Satanic Cult Gangs,

Morrow Co. (CS):   Bloods, Crips

Newport (JA):   Aryan Brotherhood, Skinheads, Nuestra Familia; Banditos, Bikers, Brothers Speed, Freesouls M.C., Ghost Riders, Gypsy Jokers, Hell's Angels, Highway Men, Sons of Silence, Skinheads

Pendleton (W2):   Bloods, Crips

Portland (PC):   Crips, Bloods, Red Cobras, Gypsy Jokers, Brothers Speed, Sharps, Skinheads, Aryan Brotherhood, Posse, Mexican Mafia, Bikers, Pagans

Portland (JA):   Aryan Brotherhood, Aryan Nation, BGD's, Brothers Speed, Gypsy Jokers, Hell's Angels, KKK, Mexican Mafia, Nuestra Familia

Salem (W2)[177]:   Aryan Brotherhood, Bikers, Bloods, Crips, Gypsy Jokers, Hell's Angels, KKK, neo-nazis, skinheads

---

[175]A women's facility.

[176]A white supremicist hate group.

[177]Women's facility.

Salem (W3):   Skinheads, White Supremacists; Bloods, Crips, 18th Streeters; Aryan Brotherhood, Aryan Nation, BGD's, Bikers, Boot Boys, Border Brothers, Brothers Speed, Cholos, Dirty White Boys, E.M.E., EVIL, Folks, F.O.B., F.T.W., Gypsy Jokers, Hell's Angels, Hilltop Hustlers, Hua Ching, Kitchen Crips, Mexican Mafia, Neo-nazis, Nortenos, NWA, Piru, Rolling 60, Santana Block, SUR 13, The Crew, Vice Lords, White Fence, White Pride, F-13, 14th Street Gang, 18th Street Gang
Sheridan (PC):   Bloods, Crips, Aryan Brotherhood, Skinheads, Gypsy Jokers
Tillamook (JI):   Bloods, Crips, Disciples, Aryan Brotherhood, Folks, Peoples, White Pride, Skinheads, Posse, Neo-nazis, Mexican Mafia, Raiders
Troutdale (PC):   East Side PYRU's, Posse 91, Skinheads, Bloods, Crips, Aryan Brotherhood, Posse, Neo-Nazis Bikers, Gypsy Jokers
Wasco Co. (CS):   Bloods, Crips, Aryan Brotherhood, Skinheads, Posse
Woodburn (JI):   Bloods, Crips, Folks, White Pride, Skinheads, Asian Gangs, Hilltop Hustlers, Red Cobras
Yamhill Co. (LE):   Aryan Brotherhood, Bloods, Crips, Hells Angels, Jokers

PENNSYLVANIA:
Allentown (LE):   Pagans, Warlocks, Black Mafia, Skinheads
Camp Hill (W3):   KKK, skinheads, Kensington[178]; F.O.I., Bloods, Crips, F.T.W., Folks, Five Percenters, Pagans, Peoples, Warlocks
Cresson (W3):   Nation of/Fruits of Islam, Crips, White Supremacists (a composite of KKKK, NSWAP, SSAG); Black Mafia, Outlaws
Danville (JI):   Skinheads, Black Mafia
Loysville (JI):   Crips, Skinheads, Bikers, Outlaws, Cobras, Pagans, Black Mafia, Green Street Posse[179], Get Money Gang
Philadelphia (AI):   Junior Black Mafia, Aryan Brotherhood, Skinheads, Posse, Neo-nazis, Black Gangsters
Pittsburgh (JD):   Bloods, Crips, Skinheads
Pottstown (LE):   Original Gangster Posse (OGP), Criminals of Society (C.O.S.), 40 Ounces[180]
Reading (LE)[181]:   4th St. Kings, Disciples, Grizzle Posse Roaring Spring (PC): Bikers
Somerset Borough (LE):   KKK
South Williamsport (LE):   Junior Black Mafia, KKK, Raiders
Weatherly (PC):   Crips, Bloods, Flying Aces, Skinheads, Bikers, Ku Klux Klan, Cobras, Pagans, Airheads
West Mifflin Bor. (LE):   Pagans

PUERTO RICO:
San Juan (W2):   Manuel A. Perez, Monacillos (Neta), G 25 E 81

---

[178]All three are white gangs.

[179] Lancaster, PA.

[180]Refers to 40 oz. bottles of Mad Dog Beer.

[181]Repondent noted "When they were active in 1990".

RHODE ISLAND:
Central Falls (PC):   Posse
Cranston (AI):   Elma Sumtre, Fox Point Posse, Hartford Posse, Skinheads
Cranston (W2):   Five Percenters, Skinheads
Cranston (W3):   Aryan Brotherhood[182]; Five Percenters
Newport (LE):   Hillside Posse, Hells Angels, F.T.W.
North Kingston (PC):   Skinheads
Warren (PC):   Aryan Brotherhood, Skinheads, Posse, Bikers, Five Percenters, F.T.W.

SOUTH CAROLINA:
Aiken Co. (CS):   Miami Boys, Bikers, KKK
Aiken Co. (LE):   Banditos, Iron Coffins, Miami Boys, Outlaws, Pagans
Allendale (JA):   The Eliminaters, Public Enemy, Posse, Assassins Inc, Death Row Posse, KKK
Anderson (PC):   Westside, Eastside, Ku Klux Klan
Anderson Co. (LE):   East Coast Gang, West Coast Gang, Black Mafia, Hells Angels, KKK, Miami Boys, Outlaws, West Side Boyz
Berkeley Co. (CS):   DBL (Down By the Law), Hell Angels (national headquarters), Sun Downers Posse, KKK, Pagans, Miami Boys
Blackville (PC):   Ri-Lo, Miami Boys
Cheraw (PC):   K-9 Posse
Charleston (AI):[183]   Aryan Brotherhood, Skinheads, Posse, Bikers, Ku Klux Klan
Chesterfield Co. (PP):   Ku Klux Klan
Clarendon Co. (CS):   Ku Klux Klan
Columbia (PP):   Bump Boys Posse, Miami Boys
Columbia (AI):   Bikers, Ku Klux Klan
Enoree (AI):   Bikers, Ku Klux Klan
Enoree (AI):   Boston Boys, Posse, Bloods, El Rukns, Miami Boys, Bikers, KKK
Fairfax (AI):   Bloods, Crips
Florence (PC):   Aryan Brotherhood, Neo-nazis, Bikers, Ku Klux Klan, Bikers, Pagans
Greenville (LE):   West Greenville Posse, Rolling 60's, Dream Team, Bloods, Cross Suns, Eight Balls, El Rukns
Lexington Co. (CS):   Ku Klux Klan, skinheads
McCormick (W3):   Five Percenters
Pelzer (AI):   Bikers, Ku Klux Klan
Pelzer (W3):   Five Percenters, Spartanburg Gang, Greenville Gang; Bikers, Dirty White Boys, El Rukns, Fruits of Islam, Hell's Angels, Satanic Cult Gangs, Satan's Disciples, White Knights
Pickens Co. (CS):   The Crew, Skinheads, KKK, Neo-nazis
Rock Hill (LE):   Grey - Boyz[184], Cobras, Spider Boyz Spartanburg (CS): Highland, The Lynch Mob, Bloods, Skinheads, KKK, Miami Boys
Spartanburg Co. (JA):   Boston Boys, Northside Gang, Skinheads; Aryan Warriors, Bikers, KKK

---

[182]"Very few members".

[183] Near city, not in the institution.

[184]G-Boys (Grey Boys).

Spartanburg (W3):   Florida boys
State Park (W3):   Five Percenters
Woodruff (PC):   Scooter Gang, Hammer Gang, KKK

SOUTH DAKOTA:
Gettysburg (PC):   Banditos[185]
North Sioux City (PC):   Crips
Plankinton (JI):   Bloods, Crips, Vice Lords, Disciples
Rapid City (LE):[186]   The Boyz, The Original Gangster Posse (OGP), The Browns, Banditos, Dirty White Boys, Hells Angels, Macomb Street Gang, Warlords, Warrior Society
Redfield (JI):   Disciples, Hell's Angels, Banditos, Posse Commitatus
Sioux Falls (AI):   Warlords, Boyz[187]
Springfield (AI):   Bloods, Crips
Springfield (W2):   Bikers, Boyz, Warlords

TENNESSEE:
Centerville (PC):   Skinheads, Bikers, Ku Klux Klan
Chattanooga (LE):   East Dale Posse, Aton Park Posse, 8th Street Posse, Aryan Brotherhood, BGDs, Bloods, Crips, Hells Angels, Neo-nazis, Outlaws
Davidson Co. (LE):   Villains In Progress (VIP), West Side Posse, East Side Posse, Village Boys, Death Row Posse, Crips, F.B.I., Mad Dogs, Skinheads
Greene Co. (JA):   Bad Boys, Young Riders, White Power (KKK); Dirty White Boys, Ghost Riders, KKK, Warlords
Jackson (LE):   Bikers, Bloods, Crips, Hell's Angels, KKK, Pagans
Johnson City (JI):   KKK
Knoxville (W2):   Aryan Brotherhood, Banditos, Bikers, Black Mafia, Crips, Eight Balls, Hell's Angels, Hoods, Outlaws, Satanic Cult Gangs, Satans Disciples, C Street
Knoxville (LE):   NFL Boys, The Possee, Outlaws, Skinheads
Knoxville (LE):   Outlaws, Skinheads
Lebanon (JI):   Bloods, Crips, Skinheads, KKK
Memphis (LE):   Vice Lords, Disciples, Banditos, Crips, Insane Vice Lords, Miami Boys, NWA, Outlaws
Murfreesboro (LE):   Black White Connection (BWC), Lynch Mob, Ruthless Posse, Crips, Skinheads
Nashville (AI):   Aryan Brotherhood, Ku Klux Klan, Bikers, neo-nazis
Nashville (AI):   Miami Boys
Nashville (JI):   Bloods, Crips, Skinheads, Outlaws, KKK, Hell's Angels
Nashville (W2):   Aryan Brotherhood, Bloods, Crips, Pagans, KKK
Norris (PC):   Ku Klux Klan
Petros (AI):   Aryan Brotherhood
Williamson Co. (CS):   Bloods, Crips, Skinheads, Ku Klux Klan

---

[185] Only during the Sturgis Motorcycle Rally in August.

[186] Covers the Pennington Co (Rapid City) Sheriff's Office and the Rapid City Police Department.

[187] Same two reported in the W2 survey.

TEXAS:
Abilene (LE):   La Opmpa, Bloods, Crips[188], Aryan Brotherhood, Banditos, EVIL,
    Kitchen Crips, Latin Kings, La Raza, Rolling 60, Satanic Cult Gangs, Satans
    Disciples, Skinheads
Abilene (JA):   Crips, Bloods, Southside Homeboys; Southern Homeboys
Arlington (LE):   Angel Boys, Rollin '30' Crips, Vigilante Lynch Mob, Aryan
    Brotherhood, Banditos, Bloods, Born To Kill (BTK), Crips, Ghost Riders, KKK,
    Latin Kings, Mexican Mafia, Skinheads, Stoners, SUR 13, White Power, White Pride
Austin (JD):   Crips, Latin Kings
Austin,TX (CO)(LE):   Latin Kings, E.G.V., "The Bro's", 10th Street Syndicate, Aryan
    Brotherhood, Aryan Nation, Banditos, Bloods, Crips, Dirty White Boys, Fruits of
    Islam, Imperial Gangsters, Insane Crips, Mexican Mafia, Nuestra Familia, Outlaws,
    Posse Comitatus, Rolling 60, Satanic Cult Gangs, Scorpians, Skinheads, Stoners,
    Texas Mafia
Baytown (LE):   UNLV, East Side Locos, Pelly Rats, Banditos, Crips, High Rollers,
    Lynch Mob, Mexican Mafia, Miami Heat, Posse Comitatus, Texas Mafia
Beaumont (JD):   Bloods, Crips, L.A. Kings, La Raza, Lobos, Posse, Raiders
Brazoria (W3):   Aryan Circle, Aryan Brotherhood, KKK; Texas Syndicate, Mexican
    Mafia, Texas Chicano Brotherhood; Aryan Nation, Banditos, Bloods, Crips, F.T.W.,
    Latin Kings, La Familia, La Raza, Los Hermanos, Nuestra Familia, Skinheads, SUR
    13, SWP, White Knights, White Peoples Party, White Pride, X-Men
Brazos Co. (JD):   East Side Posse (Blood), Bloods, Crips, Mockingbird Run Crew
    (Crips), West Side Posse (Crips), Homeboys (H-Boys), Latin Kings, Lupers/Loopers,
    Organized Crime Posse (OCP), Playboys, Ruthless Posse, Southside Posse
Brenham (JA):   Aryan Brotherhood
Brownwood (JI):   Bloods, Crips, Posse, Banditos, Raiders
Bryan (JD):   Blood-East Side Posse, Bloods, Crips, Crips-Mockingbird Run Crew,
    Homeboys, Latin Kings, Lupers/Loopers, Organized Crime Posse, Playboys, Ruthless
    Posse, Southside Posse, Mexican Mafia, Satanic Cult Gangs
Andrews Co. (CS):   Mexican Mafia, Bikers
Ballinger (PC):   Banditos
Castroville (PC):   Crips, Latin Kings
Collin Co. (LE):   Crips, La Raza, East Side Locos
Corpus Christi (JI):   Bloods, Crips, Disciples, Aryan Brotherhood, White Pride,
    Skinheads, Posse, Neo-nazies, Latin Kings, Bomber Boys, Mexican Mafia, KKK,
    Assassins Inc, Insane Crypts, Banditos, La Raza
Corpus Christi (JD):   Aryan Brotherhood, Banditos, BGD's, Bloods, Bomber Boys,
    Crips, Disciples, Eight Balls, Five Percenters, Gangsters, Head Bangers, Hell's
    Angels, Latin Kings, L.A. Kings, La Raza, Lynch Mob, Mad Dogs, Mexican Mafia,
    Neo-nazis, Nuestra Familia, NWA, Posse, Satanic Cult Gangs, Skinheads, South Side
    Boys, Stoners, Tri-City, West Side Boyz
Dallas (JI):   Bloods, Crips, Disciples, Skinheads, Posse, Latin Kings, Bomber Boys,
    Two-Sixers, Black Gangsters, Mexican Mafia, KKK, Kuang Le, Insane Crypts, G-
    Street, Raiders, Head Bangers, NWA
Del Rio (JD):   Bloods, Crips, Disciples, Warlords
El Paso (JI):   Bloods, Crips, Black Gangsters, Mexican Mafia
El Paso (LE):   Fatherless, F-Troop, N.E. Villains, Banditos, Black Mafia, Eight Balls,
    La Familia, La Mafia, La Raza, Mexican Mafia, Pagans, Texas Mafia, White Fence
Fort Worth (JI):   Crips, Bloods, Skinheads, Posse

---

[188]All three gangs "home grown".

Fort Worth (JA):   Aryan Brotherhood, Banditos, Insane Crips, Latin Kings
Galveston (LE):   4-Trey Posse, 29 Posse, Greenville 13 ACE Posse, Aryan Brother
  hood, Aryan Circle, Aryan Nation, Aryan Warriors, Banditos, Bloods, C.I.A., Eight
  Balls, Hell's Angels, Latin Kings, Mexican Mafia, Texas Mafia
Garland (LE):   Glynn Street Gangsters, East Side Locos (Dallas), A.V. Boyz, Aryan
  Brotherhood, Aryan Nation, Bloods, Born To Kill (BTK), F.B.I., G-Boys, KKK,
  Latin Locos, My Only Brothers (M.O.B.), Neo-nazis, Piru, Skinheads, 8-Balls
Grand Prairie (LE):   Players, Crips, Latin Knights, Aryan Brotherhood, Aryan
  Nation, BGD's, KKK, Lynch Mob, Latin Kings, Mexican Mafia, Neo-nazis
Groveton (JA):   Aryan Brotherhood, Posse; Aryan Nation, Bloods, Insane Crips,
  KKK
Harlingen (JI):   Skinheads, Latin Kings, Mexican Mafia, Tri-City Bombers
Harris Co. (JA):   Aryan Brotherhood, Texas Syndicate, Texas Mafia, Mexican Mafia;
  Aryan Warriors, Black Guerilla Family, Born To Kill (BTK), Brothers of White
  Supremacy (BOWS), Lynch Mob, Nuestra Familia
Henderson (JA):   Aryan Brotherhood
Hidalgo Co. (LE):   Tri-City Bombers, Spoilers, Latin Kings, El Cinco, Lords,
  Partners in Crime, Outlaws
Huntsville, TX (W3):   Texas Mafia, A.B.T.[189]; Texas Syndicate, Mexican Mafia;
  Aryan Brotherhood, Aryan Nation, Banditos, Black Guerilla Family, Crips, Dirty
  White Boys, E.M.E., KKK, La Raza, Skinheads
Huntsville (W3):   Aryan Brotherhood of Texas, Texas Mafia, Skinheads[190]; Texas
  Syndicate, Mexican Mafia, De Hermandad Pisolero Latinos; Aryan Circle, Aryan
  Nation, Banditos, Bloods, Crips, KKK, Latin Kings, Moors, Neo-nazis, Tri-City
  Bombers, White Knights, White Peoples Party
Huntsville (JA):   5th Ward Posse[191], Mexican Rap Mafia
Huntsville (W3):   A/C, KKK; TS, MM; All Brothers Together (ABT), Aryan
  Brotherhood, Aryan Circle, Aryan Nation, Mexican Mafia (MM), Texas Mafia
Itasca (LE):   Hoova Crips, Vito Crips, Tongan Crips, Bloods, Born To Kill (BTK),
  Ghost Riders, Hell Raisers, KKK, Latin Kings, Neo-nazis, Piru, Red Dragons,
  Skinheads, White Power
Jefferson (PP):   Bloods, Crips, Bikers, KKK
Kingsville (LE):   Kingsville Lynch Crew, D-Boys (Down Boys), Kingsville Latin
  Lords
Kyle (W3):   Texas Syndicate, Aryan Brotherhood, Mexican Mafia; Nuestra Familia,
  Skinheads
Laredo (PC):   Death Row Posse
Laredo (LE):   George Town Boys, The Always Violent (AV's), Latin Kings, Los
  Carnales, Bloods, Crips, Eight Balls, Head Bangers, L.A. Kings, Mexican Mafia,
  Posse, Satanic Cult Gangs
Longview (PC):   NWA, Hoods, Horsemen, Crips, Skinheads
Longview (JD):   Bloods, Crips, Four Horsemen of the Apolcalypse, NWA, Satanic
  Cult Gangs

---

[189]White gangs.

[190]White gangs.

[191]Houston, TX origin.

Lubbock (JD):   Aryan Brotherhood, Bloods, Crips, Insane Crips, Latin Kings, Rolling 60, Satanic Cult Gangs, Skinheads, Stoners

Lufkin (JD):   Bloods, Crips, Eight Balls, Ellenwood Boys, Head Bangers, Insane Crips, KKK, La Raza, NWA, Raiders, Satanic Cult Gangs, South Side Boys, Stoners

Mesquite (LE):   Always Kicking Ass (AKA), Boys of Low Profile (BLP), Junior Latin Vatos (JLV)

Midland (LE):   Varrio South Siders, Bolchers III, Mid City Locals, Banditos, Bloods, Crips, KKK, Latin Kings, Mexican Mafia, Rolling 60, Skinheads

Mumford (W3):   Aryan Brotherhood of Texas (ABT), Texas Mafia; Texas Syndicate, Mexican Mafia, ABT; Aryan Circle, Aryan Nation, E.M.E., La Familia, La Mafia, La Raza, Nuestra Familia, Skinheads

Odessa (LE)[192]:   H.D.P., G.T.S., 8 Ball Posse, Banditos[193], Hells Angels[194], La Mafia[195], Lynch Mob, L.V.L., Mexican Mafia, Texas Mafia, Warlords

Pasadena (LE):   Criminally Minded Gangsters (CMGs), Radical Assassins (RA's), South Side Chuchos (SSC's), Flying Dragons, Get Money Gang, Latin Kings, Mexican Mafia

Port Arthur (LE):   Angel Boys, Hiep Sing, Banditos, Born To Kill (BTK), Ghost Shadows, Latin Kings, Miami Boys, Skinheads

Pyote (JI):   Bloods, Crips, SKinheads, Cobras

Randall Co. (LE)[196]:   Aces, Aryan Circle, Aryan Nation, Banditos, Barrio Chicano Locos, Big Top Locos, Black Mafia, Bloods, Crips, Texas Mafia

Raymondville (JA):   Texas Syndicate, Mexican Mafia, Westside Diablos, Southern Insanity, The Hood[197]; Banditos, Bloods, Crips, Hoods, Tri-City Bombers

Richardson (LE):   Lime Street Bloods, North Side Locos, Los Compadres Trece, Bloods, Born To Kill (BTK), Crips, Eight Balls

Richmond (W3):   Texas Syndicate, E.M.E., Crips

Rosharon (W3):   Texas Aryan Brotherhood, Texas Mafia, Aryan Circle[198]; Texas Syndicate, Mexican Mafia, Barrio Azteca; Aryan Nation, Banditos, BGD's, Bloods, Crips, E.M.E., Freight Train Riders of America, KKK, Latin Kings, La Raza, MSTA, Piru, Rolling 60, Skinheads, Surenos, Tri-City Bombers, Vice Lords, White

---

[192]"These gangs are not active at this time. Gang problems has subsided subtantially in our city."

[193]"Not active at this time".

[194]"Not active..."

[195]As with all gangs reported from this respondent "not active at this time".

[196]Very few of these make any impact in our area. We just notice if we have heard of them here or one or more is here.

[197]Texas Syndicate and Mexican Mafia are statewide. Westside Diablos, Southern Insanity, and The Hood are local groups.

[198]All white gangs.

Knights Rusk (W2): Aryan Brotherhood of Texas, Hermanos Pistoleros Latinos, Crips, Latin Kings, KKK, Mexican Mafia, Nuestra Familia
San Antonio (JI):   Bloods, Crips, Skinheads, Black Gangsters, Mexican Mafia, Nuestra Familia, Center City Locos
San Antonio (JD):   Bloods, Crips, Latin Kings, L.A. Kings, Skinheads
San Antonio (LE):   Kings, Bad Boyz, KKK, Aryan Brotherhood, Banditos, Black Guerilla Family, Bloods, Crips, Disciples, El Rukns, Folks, Imperial Gangsters, Latin Kings, L.A. Kings, La Raza, Nuestra Familia, Peoples, Rolling 60, Santana Block, Sharps, Skinheads, Texas Mafia, Two-Sizers
San Patricio Co. (LE):   Mexican Mafia, Mexican Rap Mafia, Texas Mafia
Tarrant Co. (JA):   1532 Maldonado Gang, 357 Posse, Addidas Boys, All In the Family, Alpha Omegas, American Nazi Party, America's Most Wanted, Angel Boys, Aryan Brotherhood, Ayran Legion, Aryan Nations, Bandidos, Barboza, Basse De Bombarde, Baylor Boys, Beat Down Posse, Berryhill Gang, Birdow Gang, Bitches With an Attitude, Black Cobra Clan, Black Eagles, Black Guerilla Family, Black Knights, Black Villain Assassins, Bloods, Born to Kill, Bowdy Gang, Bowery Boys, Boys of the Corner, Boys of the Hood, Bozo Gang, The Bud Club, Christian Guard, Christian Order, Como Gang, Como Original Gangsters, Confederate Hammerskins, Confederate Knights of the KKK, Confederate Strike Force, Corner Boys, Counter Attacks, Creekwood Boys, Criminal Deviant Movement, Crips, Dallas Skull Boys, Dark Side Gents, Dawgs, Death Babies, Demons/Satans Warriors, LittleJohn, Los Carnales De Nuestro Chicanos, Los Chigones, Los Cochinos, Los Crazy Boys, Los Locos, Los Locos Chicanos, Los Players Locos, Mandingo Warriors, Meadowbrook Group, Mexican Mafia, Midnite Chucas, Midnite Cruisers, Mixed Mafia, The Mob, National Socialist Skinheads, Niggers with Power, Northside Cholas, Northside White Boys, Nuestra Familia, On Leong Tong, The Only Ones Too II, Outlaws, Pecan Street Players, Phu Quy, Pink Ladies, Players in Effect, Pocos Pero Locos, Polo Boys, Polo Crew, Poly Brotherhood, Poly Untouchables, Pretty Boys, Puro Vatos Locos, Puros Chicanos Locos, Purro Little Mafia, Raza 13, Ready and Willing, Red Dragons, Richardson Crime Family, Satan Midnight Locos, Satans Clan, Scorpians (Asian), Scorpians (motorcycle gang), Self Defense Family, Sheep, Skaters, SKull Inc, Southside Hoods, Southwest Centros Locos, Southwest Latin Kings, Woodhaven Boys, Young Urban Knights, Zingarros; Texas Mafia
Temple (LE):   Bloods, Crips, Latin Kings
Texarkana (LE):   Rat - Pack, X-Clan, H.B.O.'s (Home Boyz Only)
Vidor (PC):   Ku Klux Klan, Banditos (Motorcycle gang)
Waco (LE):   Latin Kings, Tray Tray Crips, Syndicate Bloods, Aryan Brotherhood, BGD's, KKK, L.A. Kings, Mexican Mafia
Washington Co. (CS):   Bandidos, Texas Mafia, Aryan Brotherhood, Mexican Mafia

UTAH:
Cedar City (JI):   Bloods, Crips
Draper (W2):   Aryan Brotherhood, Banditos, Bloods, Crips, Hell's Angels, KKK, Neo-nazis, Skinheads, Stoners
Helper (PC): . Aryan Brotherhood, Posse Comitatus, Bikers
Hurricane (PC):   Bikers, Hell Raisers
Logan (JA):   Aryan Nation, Bloods[199], Insane Vice Lords[200]

---

[199]Pass throughs.

[200]Pass throughs.

Ogden (JI):   Bloods, Crips, Vice Lords, Skinheads, SUR, PYRU, Center City Locos, T.C.G., Neo-nazis

Provo (JI):   Aryan Brotherhood, Bloods, Crips, Skinheads, Posse, Mexican Mafia, T.C.G., SOS (Sons of Samoa), T.C.G (Tongan Crip Gang), 8-Ball, CUBO

Provo (LE):   Tongan Crip Gangsters, QVO, Sons of Samoa (SOS), Aryan Nation, Bloods, Crips, La Raza, Neo-nazis, Posse Comitatus, Piru, Quo Vo, P.V.C., Skinheads, Sun Downers Posse, SUR 13

Roy (JI):   Bloods, Crips

Salt Lake City (JI):   Bloods, Crips, Aryan Brotherhood, Skinheads, Posse, KKK, Black Mafia, Center City Locos, SUR 13, T.C.G., Quo Vo, S.L. Posse, PVC, Diamond Street, V.L.T, 8 Ball Posse, S.S.G., Sons of Samoa, Crazy White Boys

Salt Lake City (W2):   Diamond Street, SUR 13, Quo Vo

Utah Co. (LE):   Tongan Crip Gang, Eight Ball Posse, Quovo (Brown Pride, Hispanic), Aryan Brotherhood, Aryan Nation, Banditos, Bloods, Crips, Diamond Street, KKK, La Raza, Mexican Mafia, Neo-nazis, Nortenos, Nuestra Familia, P.V.C., Piru, Quo Vo, Sharps, Skinheads, Surenos, White Pride, SUR 13

Wasatch Co. (CS):   Bloods, Crips, Aryan Brotherhood, Skinheads, Mexican Mafia

Woods Cross (PC):   Bloods, Crips

VERMONT:

South Burlington (W2):   The Foundation[201]

VIRGINIA:

Albemarle Co. (LE):   Fruits of Islam, Posse, Satanic Cult Gangs

Chesapeake (W2)[202]:   Richmond Gang, Norfolk Gang, The Suffolk Boys

Chesterfield Co. (CS):   Skinheads, Neo-nazis, Pagans

Fairfax Co. (LE):   Pagans, Korean Fuk Ching, Born To Kill (BTK), KKK, Skinheads

Goochland (W2)[203]:   Pagans, local Virginia and Drug gangs

Hanover (W2):   Pagans, Bikers

Hanover (W3):   D.C. Gang, Richmond Gang; Bikers, Born To Kill (BTK), Hell's Angels, Pagans

Lorton (AI):   Skinheads, Posse, Neo-nazis, Ku Klux Klan

Lorton (W3):   LeDroit Park Crew, R Street Crew, Wheeler Road Crew, 5th & O Street Crew, 8th & H Crew

Loudoun Co. (LE):   Pagans

Newport News (LE):   Posse, The Boys, The Creek Boys, Kings Posse, Lynch Mob

Norfolk (LE):   Filamafia, Mestistos, Lake Taylor Posse, All Brothers Together (A.B.T.), Aces, B.G.D.s, Bloods, Crips, Skinheads

---

[201]white gang.

[202]Few problems with nationally identified prison gangs. Level one prison gang: i.d. is tied to geographical area as an 'informal organization' (Knox, 1991 An Introductin to Gangs).

[203]Womens Facility; Gangs do not play a large role at the facility and members soon loose their gang identity shortly after their arrival; only 3 or 4 members who do not pose an active problem.

Prince William Co. P.D.(LE):   Faiths Assembly[204]
Stauton (JI):   Posse, KKK, Pagans, Five Percenters
Virginia Beach (LE):   Diego Boyz, The Family, Trigga Mafia Family, Hells Angels, Pagans, Skinheads
York Co. (LE):   Pirates

WASHINGTON:
Belfair (JI):   Bloods, Crips, Vice Lords, Disciples, Aryan Brotherhood, Skinheads, Black Gangsters
Bellingham (JA):   Aryan Brotherhood, Nuestra Familia, Posse Comitatus; Bikers, BGD's, Bloods, Crips, Gypsy Jokers, La Raza, Neo-nazis, Satanic Cult Gangs, Skinheads, White Peoples Party
Centralia (JI):   Bloods, Crips, Disciples, Skinheads, Posse, Black Gangsters, Mexican Mafia, NWK 14
Clallam Bay (W3):   Aryan Brotherhood, Aryan Nation, BGD's, Crips, Folks, Head Bangers, skinheads
Clark Co. (LE):   Red Cobras, XIV Cholo's, West Side Piru, Bloods, Brothers Speed, Cholos, Crips, Gypsy Jokers, Latin Kings, Piru, Skinheads
Douglas Co. (CS):   Aryan Brotherhood, Posse
East Wenatchee (JI: Bloods, Crips, skinheads
Ephrata (JI):   Bloods, Crips, Skinheads, Outlaws, Gypsy Jokers, Banditos
Gig Harbor (W2):   Bloods, Crips
Goldendale (PC):   Socialist Vanguard, Neo-nazis
King (PP):   Skinheads, Crips, Bloods, Black Gangster Disciples, Aryan Brotherhood, Ku Klux Klan, Gypsy Jokers
King Co. (LE):   Loco Asian Boyz (LAB), United Blood Nation (UNB)[205], Bad Side Posse (BSP)[206], Aryan Nation, Banditos, BGD's, Bloods, Cholos, Red Cobras, Crips, El Rukns, Folks, Ghost Riders, Jokers, Kitchen Crips, La Raza, Lynch Mob, O.L.B., Piru, Rolling 60, Santana Block, Skinheads, Sons of Samoa (SOS), Tiny Rascal Gang (TRG)
Klickitat Co. (CS):   Crips, Bloods, Skinheads[207], Aryan Brotherhood, Neo-nazis, Mexican Mafia, Bikers, Pagans, Gypsy Jokers, Freight Train Riders of America (Hobo Gang)
Littlerock (W2):   BGD's, Bloods, Crips,
Littlerock (W3):   Bloods, Crips, BGD's
Monroe (W2):   Aryan Brotherhood, Aryan Nation, Bikers, Bloods, Crips, BGD's
Okanogan Co. (CS):   Aryan Brotherhood, Mexican Mafia,Bikers
Pierce Co. (LE):   Crips, Bloods, Oriental Loco Boyz[208], Aryan Brotherhood, Aryan Nation, Banditos, BGD's, Bloods, Crips, Ghost Riders, Gypsy Jokers, Hell's Angels,

---

[204]Motorcycle gang.

[205]Primarily Samoan.

[206]AKA: Blood Side Pinoy, primarily S.E. Asian.

[207] Crips, Bloods, and Skinheads "travel through" the area.

[208]AKA "O.L.B.'s".

H.T.C.G., KKK, Mexican Mafia, Neo-Nazis, Posse Comitatus, Piru, Rolling 60, Skinheads, Sons of Samoa (SOS), 109 Watts

Richland (PC):   Romeo Knights, Bloods, Crips, Neo-nazis

Richland (JI):   Bloods, Crips, Skinheads, F13

Seattle (PP):   Skinheads(W), Aryan Brotherhood, Crips, Bloods, Black Gangster Disciples, Neo-nazis, Mexican Mafia, Bikers, Gypsy Jokers, PYRU

Seattle (PC):   Black Gangster Disciples, Crips, Bloods, Vice Lords, Aryan Brother hood, Folks, Skinheads, Posse, Neo-nazis, Mexican Mafia, Bikers, Gypsy Jokers

Seattle (LE):   BGD's, Crips, Bloods, Banditos, Born To Kill (BTK), Brothers of the Struggle (BOS), Folks, Freight Train Riders of America, Gypsy Jokers, H.T.C.G., Insane Crips, Kitchen Crips, La Raza, NWA, O.L.B., Rolling 60, Santana Block, Skinheads, Sons of Samoa (SOS), SUR 13, Tongan Crip Gang (TCG), Tiny Rascal Gang (TRG), Vice Lords

Shelton (W3):   Aryan Nations, KKK, etc; Crips, Bloods, BGD's; Aryan Brotherhood, Aryan Circle, Aryan Warriors, Banditos, Barrio Chicano Locos, Bikers, BD's, BG's, Brothers Behind Bars (BBB), Brothers of the Struggle (BOS), Brothers of White Supremacy (BOWS), Brothers Speed, Cholos, Davie Boys, El Rukns, Folks, Fruits of Islam, GD's, Gypsy Jokers, Hawaiian Brothers, Hell's Angels, Insane Crips, Kitchen Crips, La Familia, Lil Locos, Prison Motorcycle Brotherhood (PMB), Piru, Santana Block, Satanic Cult Gangs, Satan's Disciples, Skinheads, Sons of Samoa (SOS), Texas Mafia, Vice Lords, White Power, White Pride, White Tigers

Skagit Co. (CS):   Bloods, Crips, Aryan Brotherhood, Disciples, Skinheads, Posse, Neo-Nazis, Black Gangsters, Mexican Mafia, Bandidos (bikers), Nuestra Familia, KKK, Pagans, Gypsy Jokers, White Gangster Disciples, 39th Street Gang, Insane Crypts, PYRU, G-Street, SUR 13

Snohomish Co. (LE):   Black Gangster Disciples, Crips, Bloods, United Blood Nation, 74 Hoover Crips, Aryan Brotherhood, Aryan Nation, Banditos, Bikers, Brothers Speed, Down By the Laws (DBL's), Folks, Ghost Riders, Gypsy Jokers, Hells Angels, H.T.C.G., KKK, Neo-nazis, O.L.B., Posse Comitatus, Piru, Rolling 60, Santana Block, Tiny Rascal Gang (TRG), White Pride

Snoqualmie (JI):   Bloods, Crips, Black Gangster Disciples

Spokane (W2):   Aryan Brotherhood, Aryan Nation

Spokane (JD):   Bloods, Crips, Skinheads

Spokane (LE):   Palmer Block Compton Crips, Rolling 60, Lynch Mob, BGD's, Aryan Brotherhood, Aryan Nation, Banditos, Bloods, Down By the Laws (DBL's), Eight Balls, F-13, Folks, Freight Train Riders Association of America, Ghost Riders, Gypsy Jokers, Hells Angels, Hilltop Hustlers, H.T.C.G., Insane Crips, KKK, La Familia, La Mafia, Mexican Mafia, Neo-nazis, Pagans, Posse Comitatus, Santana Block, Satanic Cult Gangs, Sharps, Skinheads, SUR 13, Tiny Rascal Gang, Vice Lords, Regulators, Ruthless Posse, Hardtime Hustlers Posse, Lincoln Park Crips, Grape St. Crips, Lilac City Posse, Green Street Crips, Hill Top Crips, The Order, South Hill Locos, Ole's, Shotgun Crips, Holly Hood Piru Bloods, Six Duece Crips, New School Crips, Hell Raisers

Steilacoom (W3):   Crips, Bloods, BGD's; Aryan Brotherhood, Aryan Nation

Tacoma (JI):   Bloods, Crips, Vice Lords, Disciples, Aryan Brotherhood, Folks, Peoples, White Pride, Skinheads, Brothers of the Struggle, Neo-nazis, Boot Boys, Black Gangsters, Mexican Mafia, Bikers, Black Guerilla Family, KKK, Gypsy Jokers, Insane Crypts, Shorty Folks, PYRU, G-Street, White Gangster Disciples, Watergate Cribs, A-4 Swan PYRU, Santana Block, Rolling 60, Kitchen Crib, 106 Watts, Shotgun, 25th Neighborhood

Tacoma (W2):   Aryan Brotherhood, Banditos, BGD's, Bloods, Crazy White Boys, Crips, Gypsy Jokers, Satanic Cult Gangs, White Power

Walla Walla Co. (CS):   F-13, 18th Street, Bloods, Crips, Aryan Brotherhood, Mexican Mafia, Bikers, Gypsy Jokers
Woodinville (JI):   Bloods, Crips, Black Gangsters
Yakima (PP):   Bloods, Crips, Raiders, Mexican Mafia
Yakima (JI):   Bloods, Crips, Aryan Brotherhood, 14th Street, Raiders
Yakima (LE):   14th Street, Crips, BGA (from Seattle), 13th Street, BGD's, Bloods, Disciples, H.T.C.G., La Raza, O.L.B., 18th Street

WEST VIRGINIA:
Bradshaw (PC):   Ku Klux Klan
Fayette Co. (PP):   Ku Klux Klan, Avengers[209], Pagans[210]
Huntington (PP):   Avengers, Pagans, Crips, Aryan Brotherhood, Neo-Nazis
Jackson Co. (CS):   KKK, Pagans
Moundsville (W2):   Aryan Brotherhood, Avengers, Pagans
Parkersburg (JA):   Avengers[211], KKK

WISCONSIN:
Brookfield (LE):   BGDs[212], Latin Kings, Spanish Cobras, Vice Lords
Chippewa Falls, WI (JA):   Bloods, Chicago Outlaws, Crips, Hell's Angels, Posse Comitatus
Dodgeville (JA):   Aces, Aryan Brotherhood, Blue hats/blue rags, Hell's Angels, Outlaws, Red hats/red rags
Fox Lake (W2):   Aryan Brotherhood, BGD's, Brothers of the Struggle (B.O.S.), Hell's Angels, Vice Lords
Greenbay (LE):   BGD's, Latin Kings, S.E. Asian Gangs, B.O.S., Cobras, Folks, GD's, Imperial Gangsters, Peoples, Simon City Royals, Six Pack Gang, Tri-City Bombers, Vice Lords, White Dragon, White Tigers
Iowa Co. (LE):   BKU's, Black Disciples
Janesville (LE):   Black Gangster Disciples (BGDs), KKK
Johnson Creek (PC):   Posse Comitatus
Kenosha (LE):   BGD's, Latin Kings, BOS, GD's, G-Boys, Imperial Gangsters, Outlaws
Marathon Co. (CS):   Vice Lords, Disciples, Brothers of the Struggle, Posse, Cobras, White Gangster Disciples
Madison (JD):   BGD's, Vice Lords
Manitowoc (LE):   Folks, Latin Kings, Vice Lords, BGDs, BDs, Bloods, Gangsters, GDs, Insane Vice Lords, Peoples, Satans Disicples
Marathon Co. (LE):   GD's, Asian Knights/Cobras, Laotian Posse, BGD's, Brothers of the Struggle (BOS), Folks, Knights, Latin Kings, Peoples, Posse Comitatus, Simon City Royals, Vice Lords, White Tigers
Menomenee Falls (LE):   Folks, People
Merrill (JA):   Black Gangster Disciples, Brothers of the Struggle, White Tigers

---

[209] A white gang.

[210] Like the Avengers, also a motorcycle gang.

[211]Bikers.

[212]"No gangs in this city", but are traveling there.

Milwaukee (PP)[213]:   Black Gangster Disciples, Latin Kings, Vice Lords, Skinheads, Brothers of the Struggle, Ku Klux Klan, Cobras

Milwaukee (W2):   Aryan Brotherhood, Banditos, Basin Street Gang, BGD's, Black Gangsters, Bloods, Boot Boys, Brothers of the Struggle (B.O.S.), Crips, El Rukns, Folks, Gangster Disciples, Gangsters, Insane Vice Lords, KKK, Latin Kings, Outlaws, Posse Commitatus, Spanish Cobras, Vice Lords, Maniac Latin Disciples

Milwaukee (LE):   Black Disciples, Latin Kings, East Side Mafioso, Aryan Brother hood, BGD's, BG's, B.O.S., Crips, Folks, GD's, Insane Crips, Latin Kings, Shorty Folks, Spanish Cobras

Milwaukee (DHHS):   BGD's, GD's, Vice Lords, Latin Kings, Eastside Mafiosa, Spanish Cobras, Double C.P.L., 2-4's[214]

Mosinee (PC):   Bikers

New Berlin (LE):   Latin Kings

Oneida (W2):   Prison Motorcycle Brotherhood (PMB), Simon City Royals[215], Aryan Brotherhood, BGD's, Black Gangsters, Brothers of the Struggle (B.O.S.), Cobras, Disciples, Dukes, El Rukns, Folks, Gangsters, Gangster Disciples, Insane Vice Lords, Latin Kings, Peoples, Satans Disciples, Spanish Cobras, Vice Lords

Oregon (W2):   Aryan Brotherhood, Banditos, BGD's, Black Guerilla Family, Brothers of the Struggle (B.O.S.), Spanish Cobras, Disciples, Empire Villans (EV's), Folks, Gangster Disciples, Insane Vice Lords, Latin Kings, Moors, Outlaws, Satanic Cult Gangs, Shorty Folks, Simon City Royals, S.S.G., Vice Lords

Oshkosh (W2):   Aryan Brotherhood, BGD's, Black Gangsters, Brothers of the Struggle, El Rukns, Folks, Four Corner Hustlers, F.T.W., Gangsters, Gangster Disciples, Insane Vice Lords, KKK, Latin Kings, Peoples, Posse Commitatus, Simon City Royals, Shorty Folks, Skinheads, Spanish Cobras, Aryan Nation, Vice Lords

Oshkosh (W2):   Aryan Brotherhood, BDG's, Black Gangsters, Bloods, Brothers of the Struggle (B.O.S.), Crips, El Rukns, Latin Kings, Skinheads, Spanish Cobras, Vice Lords

Racine (LE):   Vice Lords, Latin Kings, Gangster Disciples, BGDs, B.O.S., GDs, Imperial Gangsters, Insane Vice Lords, SWA's

Sturgeon Bay (JA):   Latin Kings

Sturtevant (W2):   Aryan Brotherhood, BGD's, Bikers, Black Gangsters, Brothers of the Struggle (B.O.S.), Cobras, Crips, Disciples, El Rukns, Folks, Gangster Disciples, Latin Kings, neo-nazis, Satanic Cult Gangs, Shorty Folks, Vice Lords

Wales (JI):   White Gangsters[216], Vice Lords, Disciples, Folks, Peoples, Skinheads, Brothers of the Struggle, Posse, Latin Kings, Black Gangsters, Mexican Mafia, Outlaws, Cobras, Shorty Folks

Washington Co. (LE):   Bad Boy Gang, 74 Gangster Disciples, BGD's, Bikers, BG's, Brothers of the Struggle (B.O.S.), Latin Locos, Outlaws, Skinheads, Spanish Cobras, Vice Lords

---

[213] Statewide.

[214]DHHS = Federal funding (DHHS) program report.

[215]Both, white gangs.

[216] A white gang.

Waukesha (LE):   Vice Lords, Latin Kings, Gangster Disciples, Aryan Nation, BGDs, B.O.S., Folks, Four Corner Hustlers, Imperial Gangsters, Mexican Mafia, Peoples, Spanish Cobras, White Knights, 34th Street Players
Wausau (LE):   Asian Knights, BGDs, B.O.S.
Waushara Co. (JA):   Latin Kings, Ghost Riders
Westbend (JD):   Folks, Gangster Disciples, Latin Kings, Skinheads
Winnebago (W2):   Aryan Brotherhood, Banditos, Bikers, Black Gangsters, Black Guerilla Family, Bloods, Brothers of the Struggle, Cobras, Crips, Disciples, El Rukns, Folks, Four Corner Hustlers, Gangster Disciples, F.T.W., Hell's Angels, Insane Crips, Insane Vice Lords, KKK, Latin Kings, La Raza, Mexican Mafia, Moors, Neo-nazis, Outlaws, Pagans, Peoples, Posse, Posse Commitatus, PYRU/PIRU, Rolling 60, Satanic Cult Gangs, Shorty Folks, Scooter Gang, Simon City Royals, Skinheads, South Side Boys, Spanish Cobras, Stoners, Vice Lords, White Gangster Disciples, White Knights, White Peoples Party, White Power, White Pride

WYOMING:
Basin (PC):   Wolf Pack, Aryan Brotherhood, Posse
Casper (JA):   Aryan Brotherhood, Aryan Nation, Banditos, Bloods, Crips, Hell's Angels, Satanic Cult Gangs, Skinheads
Cheyenne (LE):   Quest, Chey Town Posse (CTP), 8-Balls
Green River (PC):   Mexican Mafia, Sons of Silence
Laramie Co. (CS):   Chey-town Posse, Eight Balls, Rolling Nines[217], Bloods, Crips, Aryan Brotherhood, Skinheads, Posse, Neo-nazis, Bikers, Ku Klux Klan, Sons of Silence
Torrington (JA):   Aryan Brotherhood, Bloods, Crips, Neo-nazis, Posse Comitatus, Satanic Cult Gangs

GANGS IN JUVENILE CORRECTIONAL INSTITUTIONS BY REGION FROM THE 1990 SURVEY[218]

Region 1 (Maine, New Hampshire, Vermont, Massachussettes, Rhode Island, Connecticut):

(JI)[219]:   Giants, Castlegate, Corbet, Vamp Hill
(JI):   BBMF
(JI):   Corbet, Castlegate, Humboldt
(JI):   Intervale, Castlegate, Humboldt
(JI):   Castlegate, Humboldt, Franklin Park Giants
(JI):   Red Dragons (Cambodian gang)

---

[217] The three have ties to the CRIPS.

[218] This data is from the 1990 Juvenile Corrections survey and due to a data agreement the author is not permitted to identify these institutions by their specific states. Lumping them into regions is the only summary permitted under the 1990 survey.

[219] Each listing "(JI)" refers to a separate juvenile correctional institution responding to the survey.

Region 2 (New York, Pennsylvania, New Jersey, Maryland, Delaware):

(JI):   Izod Posse
(JI):   Mad Dogs, Knights, Madados
(JI):   Heavy metal, Head Banger, Occult Types
(JI):   Five Percenters, Abductors
(JI):   Five Percenters
(JI):   Skinheads

Region 3 (West Virginia, Washington DC, Virginia, North Carolina, South Carolina, Kentucky, Tennessee):
No gangs reported

Region 4 (Georgia, Florida, Alabama, Mississippi, Arkansas, Louisiana):

(JI):   Miami Boys, Chateau Boys, Ellenwood Boys, Skinheads
(JI):   G-Street, Airheads
(JI):   Macomb Street Gang, Basin Street Gang, Joe Louis Project
(JI):   Pennsylvania Posse, Top Cats, 13th Street Boys
(JI):   Six Pack Gang, WOPS, PSL Boys, The Posse
(JI):   Vice Lords, Black Gangster Disciples
(JI):   Folks, Bloods, Crips
(JI):   Shorty Folks, Hoover Folks, Crips
(JI):   Crips, Bloods, 19th Street Gang

Region 5 (Minnesota, Wisconsin, Michigan, Iowa, Illinois, Indiana, Ohio):

(JI):   Disciples, Vice Lords, Latin Kings
(JI):   Vice Lords, Crips, Disciples
(JI):   Brothers of the Struggle, Black Gangster Disciples, Vice Lords, Honky Love
(JI):   Black Gangster Disciples, Latin Kings, Vice Lords, White Gangster Disciples, Neo-nazis
(JI):   Bloods, Crips, Vice Lords
(JI):   Black Gangster Disciples, Vice Lords
(JI):   Vice Lords, Disciples, Latin Kings
(JI):   Vice Lords, Black Disciples, Hell Raisers
(JI):   Vice Lords, Disciples, Latin Kings, White Knights
(JI):   Vice Lords, Black Gangster Disciples
(JI):   Disciples, Vice Lords, Latin Kings, Skinheads
(JI):   Bloods, Crips, Folks
(JI):   Bloods, Crips
(JI):   Bloods, Crips, Folkz(W), Kings

Region 6 (Montana, Wyoming, North Dakota, South Dakota, Nebraska, Kansas, Missouri):

(JI):   Bloods, Crips
(JI):   Bloods, Crips
(JI):   Crips, Bloods, Disciples
(JI):   Bloods, Black Gangster Disciples
(JI):   Disciples, Vice Lords, Spanish Cobras, Simon City Royals
(JI):   Crips, Bloods, Thundercats, JVL
(JI):   Bloods, Crips, Jr. Boys

(JI):   Bloods, Crips, Black Gangster Disciples
(JI):   Jr. Boys, Insane Crypts

Region 7 (Oklahoma, Texas, Colorado, New Mexico, Alaska, Hawaii):

(JI):   Bloods, Crips
(JI):   Bloods, Crips
(JI):   Bloods, Crips, Skinheads
(JI):   Bloods, Crips, Los Casados

Region 8 (Washington, Oregon, Idaho, California, Nevada, Utah, Arizona):

(JI):   Bloods, Crips
(JI):   Crips, Bloods, Black Gangster Disciples, Bootboys
(JI):   Crips, Bloods, BGD's
(JI):   Crips, Bloods, Skinheads
(JI):   Crips, Bloods, 39th Street Gang
(JI):   Crips, Bloods, SUR, White Corner Pride
(JI):   Crips, Bloods, North vs. South Hispanic
(JI):   Crips, Bloods, SUR 13, White Power, SWP
(JI):   Crips, Bloods
(JI):   Crips, Bloods, Norte, SUR
(JI):   Crips, PYRU
(JI):   Crips, Bloods
(JI):   Crips, Bloods, Center City Locos
(JI):   L.V.L., T.C.G.
(JI):   Crips, Bloods, South Side Posse, Skinheads, White Power
(JI):   Crips, Bloods, SWP, FTW
(JI):   Crips, Bloods
         ZIPCODE LISTINGS FROM 1992-93 Law Enforcement Survey:
         And 1993 Jail Survey and 1994 L.E. Survey
PROJECT: Look up these zip codes in an Official Zip Code Directory

(1) First look up City for the zip code number.
(2) If "(County)" appears by the zip code, which
    has the marker "(CO)" then the second step is
    to look up County for the zip code.
(3) Report the correct spelling for City, County.
    Do this neatly. Do not combine two separate
    Words "Park Forest" into "Parkforest", and do
    not split one word into two "Elmhurst" into
    "Elm Hurts". Any error here means nothing
    else can be trusted and the work will not
    be used.
(4) One error will eliminate any credit, so be
    careful. Your work is going to be completely   double checked.

PROVE IT:

53709 (JA):   Vice Lords, BGD's; BG's, BD's
53709 = City County Bldg, Wisc???

55882 (County)(LE):   Posse Comitatus, Raiders, Outlaws, BGD's, Banditos, Crips, El Rukns, Freight Train Riders of America, Hell's Angels, Pagans, Skinheads, Sons of Silence, Vice Lords

65102 (W3)[220]:   Aryan Brotherhood, Aryan Nation, MSTA

****

(L4 Project zipcode listing):
SNATCH THESE

60020 (L4):	Vice Lords, Black Gangster Disciples
60047 (L4):	Gangster Disciples, Latin Disciples, Gaylords, Latin Lovers
60090 (L4):	Folks, Spanish Gangster Disciples, Spanish Cobras
60093 (L4):	Latin Kings, Vice Lords, Simon City Royals
60146 (L4):	Disciples, Latin Counts, Vice Lords
60176 (L4):	Latin Kings, Imperial Gangsters
60409 (L4):	Gangster Disciples, Black P. Stones, Latin Kings
60417 (L4):	Latin Counts, Gangster Disciples, Folks, Two-Two Boys
60429 (L4):	Gangster Disciples, Black P. Stone Nation, Vice Lords
60431 (L4):	Gangster Disciples, Vice Lords, Latin Kings
60450 (L4):	Two-Sixers, Latin Kings, Gangster Disciples
60466 (L4):	Gangster Disciples, Vice Lords, Black Stones
60466 (L4):	Gangster Disciples, ViceLords, Latin Counts
60540 (L4):	Latin Kings, Black Gangster Disciples, Two Sixers

60542 (L4):   Gangster Disciples, Latin Kings, Vice Lords, Ambrose, Black Disciples, Four Corner Hustlers, Insane Deuces, Insane Vice Lords, Satan's Disciples

60561 (L4):   Gangster Disciples, Vice Lords, Satan's Disciples, Four Corner Hustlers, Latin Kings, Two-Sixers, Two-Two Boys

60627 (L4):	Vice Lords, Black Gangster Disciples, B.P.S.N.
60633 (L4):	Vice Lords, Black Gangster Disciples, Black Stones
61021 (L4):	Black Gangster Disciples
61064 (L4):	Krazy Get-Down Boyz (K.G.B), Gangster Disciples, Latin Kings
61072 (L4):	Vice Lords, Disciples
61074 (L4):	Latin Kings, Gangster Disciples
61088 (L4):	Black Gangster Disciples, Latin Kings

61350 (L4):   Black Gangster Disciples, Latin Kings, Vice Lords, B.P.S.N., Maniac Latin Disciples, Northsiders, Simon City Royals, Conservative Vice Lords

(STAMPED: Ottawa)

61520 (L4):	Latin Kings, Gangster Disciples
61554-1399 (L4):	Gangster Disciples, Latin Kings
61761 (L4):	Gangster Disciples, Latin Kings, Vice Lords
61764 (L4):	Latin Kings, Gangster Disciples, Satan's Disciples

61820 (L4):   Gangster Disciples, Vice Lords, Black P. Stones, B.O.S., El Rukns, Four Corner Hustlers, Insane Unknowns, Insane Vice Lords, Ku Klux Klan, Neonazis, Peopls, Skinheads

---

[220]Respondent remarked, regarding the top three major gangs that are represented among inmates in the facility "we have none, because we will give them status by recognition".

61944 (L4):   Gangster Disciples, Vice Lords
62075 (L4):   Skinheads
62206 (L4):   Disciples, Metros, Vice Lords, Gangster Disciples, Park Avenue
Players, White Gangster Disciples
62207 (L4):   Gangster Disciples, Vice Lords, 38 Specials, Bloods, Crips, Metros,
Park Avenue Players
62326 (L4):   Gangster Disciples, Latin Kings
62656 (L4):   Gangster Disciples, Vice Lords, Latin Kings
62701 (L4):   Black Gangsters, Simon City Royals, Latin Kings
62812 (Co.)(L4): KKK, Aryan Brotherhood, Vice Lords
62932 (L4):   Storm Riders, Knights, Christian Patriots

USE THIS FORM TO RECORD INFO IN THE SAME ZIP CODE SEQUENCE

ZIP CODE	CITY	State	COUNTY
*********	*********************	**************	**********
_____	_____	_____	_____
_____	_____	_____	_____
_____	_____	_____	_____
_____	_____	_____	_____
_____	_____	_____	_____
_____	_____	_____	_____
_____	_____	_____	_____
_____	_____	_____	_____
_____	_____	_____	_____
_____	_____	_____	_____
_____	_____	_____	_____
_____	_____	_____	_____
_____	_____	_____	_____
_____	_____	_____	_____
_____	_____	_____	_____
_____	_____	_____	_____
_____	_____	_____	_____
_____	_____	_____	_____

APPENDIX A

ACT 147. STREETGANG TERRORISM OMNIBUS PREVENTION ACT

Section
147/1.   Short title.
147/5.   Legislative findings.
147/10.   Definitions.
147/15.   Creation of civil cause of action.
147/20   Commencement of action.
147/25.   Venue.
147/30.   Service of process.
147/35.   Injunctive relief, damages, costs, and fees.

147/1. Short title

§ 1. Short title. This Article may be cited as the Illinois Streetgang Terrorism Omnibus Prevention Act. P.A. 87-932, Art. II, § 1, eff. Jan. 1, 1993.

Formerly Ill.Rev.Stat., ch. 38, 1751.

Title of Act:

An Act to create the Statewide Organized Gang Database Act and the Illinois Streetgang Terrorism Omnibus Prevention Act. P.A. 87-932, Art. II, approved Aug. 27, 1992, eff. Jan. 1, 1993.

147/5. Legislative findings.

§ 5. Legislative findings.

(a) The General Assembly hereby finds and declares that it is the right of every person, regardless of race, color, creed, religion, national origin, sex, age, or disability, to be secure and protected from fear, intimidation, and physical harm caused by the activities of violent groups and individuals. It is not the intent of this Act to interfere with the exercise of the constitutionally protected rights of freedom of expression and association. The General Assembly hereby recognizes the constitutional right of every citizen to harbor and express beliefs on any lawful subject whatsoever, to lawfully associate with others who share similar beliefs, to petition lawfully constituted authority for a redress of perceived grievances, and to participate in the electoral process.

(b) The General Assembly finds, however, that urban, suburban, and rural communities, neighborhoods and schools throughout the State are being terrorized and plundered by streetgangs. The General Assembly dins that there are now several hundred streetgangs operating in Illinois, and that while their terrorism is most widespread in urban areas, streetgangs are spreading into suburban and rural areas of Illinois.

(c) The General Assembly further finds that streetgangs are often controlled by criminally sophisticated adults who take advantage of our youth by intimidating and coercing them into membership by employing them as drug couriers and runners, and by using them to commit brutal crimes against persons and property to further the financial benefit to and dominance of the streetgang.

(d) These streetgangs' activities present a clear and present danger to public order and safety and are not constitutionally protected. No society is or should be required to endure such activities without redress. Accordingly, it is the intent of the General Assembly in enacting this Act to create a civil remedy against streetgangs and their members that focuses upon patterns of criminal gang activity and upon the organized nature of streetgangs, which together have been the chief source of their success.

P.A. 87-932, Art. II, § 5, eff. Jan. 1, 1993.

Formerly Ill.Rev.Stat., ch. 38, 1755.

147/10. Definitions

§ 10. Definitions.

"Course or pattern of criminal activity" means 2 or more gang-related criminal offenses committed in whole or in part within this State when:

(1) at least one such offense was committed after the effective date of this Act;

(2) both offenses were committed within 5 years of each other; and

(3) at least one offense involved the solicitation to commit, conspiracy to commit, attempt to commit, or commission of any offense defined as a felony or forcible felony under the Criminal Code of 1961.1

"Designee of State's Attorney" or "designee" means any attorney for a public authority who has received written permission from the State's Attorney to file or join in a civil action authorized by this Act.

"Public authority" means any unit of local government or school district created or established under the Constitution or laws of this State.

"State's Attorney" means the State's Attorney of any county where an offense constituting a part of a course or pattern of gang-related criminal activity has occurred or has been committed.

"Streetgang' or "gang" means any combination, confederation, alliance, network, conspiracy, understanding, or other similar conjoining, in law or in fact, or 3 or more persons:

(1)(I) that, through its membership or through the agency of any member and at the direction, order, solicitation, or request of any conspirator who is a leader, officer, director, organizer, or other governing or policy making person or authority in the conspiracy, or by any agent, representative, or deputy of any such person or authority engages in a course or pattern of criminal activity; or (ii) that, through its membership or through the agency of any member engages in a course or pattern of criminal activity.

(2) For purposes of this Act, it shall not be necessary to show that a particular conspiracy, combination, or conjoining of persons possesses, acknowledges, or is known by any common name, insignias, flag, means of recognition, secret signal or code, creed, belief, structure, leadership or command structure, method of operation, or criminal enterprise, concentration or specialty, membership, age, or other qualifications, initiation rites, geographical or territorial situs or boundary or location, or other unifying mark, manner, protocol or method of expressing or indicating membership when the conspiracy's existence, in law or in fact, can be demonstrated by a preponderance of other competent evidence. However, any evidence reasonably tending to show or demonstrate, in law or in fact, the existence of or membership in any conspiracy, confederation, or other association described herein, or probative of the existence of or membership in any such association, shall be ad-

missible in any action or proceeding brought under this Act.

"Streetgang member" or "gang member" means any person who actually and in fact belongs to a gang, and any person who knowingly acts in the capacity of an agent for or accessory to, or is legally accountable for, or voluntarily associates himself with a course or pattern o f gang-related criminal activity, whether in a preparatory, executory, or cover-up phase of any activity, or who knowingly performs, aids, or abets any such activity.

"Streetgang related" or "gang-related" means any criminal activity, enterprise, pursuit, or undertaking directed by, ordered by, authorized by, consented to, agreed to, requested by, acquiesced in, or ratified by any gang leader, officer, or governing or policy-making person or authority, or by any agent, representative, or deputy of any such officer, person, or authority:

(1) with the intent to increase the gang's size, membership, prestige, dominance, or control in any geographical area; or

(2) with the intent to provide the gang with any advantage in, or any control or dominance over any criminal market sector, including but not limited to, the manufacture, delivery, or sale of controlled substances or cannabis; arson or arson-for-hire; traffic in stolen property or stolen credit cards; traffic in prostitution, obscenity, or pornography; or that involves robbery, burglary, or theft; or

(3) with the intent to exact revenge or retribution for the gang or any member of the gang; or

(4) with the intent to obstruct justice, or intimidate or eliminate any witness against the gang or any member of the gang; or

(5) with the intent to otherwise directly or indirectly cause any benefit, aggrandizement, gain, profit or other advantage whatsoever to or for the gang, its reputation, influence, or membership.
P.A. 87-932, Art. II § 10, eff. Jan. 1, 1993.
Formerly Ill.Rev.Stat., ch. 38, 1760.
1 720 ILCS 5/1-1 et seq.

147/15. Creation of civil cause of action

§ 15. Creation of civil cause of action.

(a) A civil cause of action is hereby created in favor of any public authority expending money, allocating or reallocating police, firefighting, emergency or other personnel or resources, or otherwise incurring any loss, deprivation, or injury, or sustaining any damage, impairment, or harm whatsoever, proximately caused by any course or pattern of criminal activity.

(b) The cause of action created by this Act shall lie against:

(1) any streetgang in whose name, for whose benefit, on whose behalf, or under whose direction the act was committed; and

(2) any gang officer or director who causes, orders, suggests, authorizes, consents to, agrees to, requests, acquiesces in, or ratifies any such act; and

(3) any gang member who, in the furtherance of or in connection with, any gang-related activity, commits any such act; and

(4) any gang officer, director, leader, or member.

(c) The cause of action authorized by this Act shall be brought by the State's Attorney or attorneys, or by his or their designees. This cause of action shall be in addition to any other civil or criminal proceeding authorized by the laws of this State or by federal law, and shall not be construed as requiring the State's Attorney or his designee to elect a civil, rather than criminal remedy, or as its officers, directors, leaders, and members shall be joint and severable subject only to the apportionment and allocation of punitive damage authorized under Section 35 of this Act.1

P.A. 87-932, Art. II, § 15, eff. Jan. 1, 1993.

Formerly Ill.Rev.Stat., ch. 38, §1765.

1 740 ILCS 147/35.

147/20. Commencement of action.

§ 20. Commencement of action.

(a) An action may be commenced under this Act by the filing of a verified complaint as in civil cases.

(b) A complaint filed under this Act, and all other ancillary or collateral matters arising therefrom, including matter relating to discovery, motions, trial, and the perfection or execution of judgments shall be subject to the Code of Civil Procedure,1 except as may be otherwise provided in this Act,

or except as the court may otherwise order upon motion of the State's Attorney or his designee in matters relating to immunity or the physical safety of witnesses.

(c) The complaint shall name each complaining State's Attorney or his designee, and the public authority represented by him or by them.

(d) The complaint shall also name as defendants the gang, all known gang officers, and any gang members specifically identified or alleged in the complaint as having participated in a course or pattern of gang-related criminal activity. The complaint may also name, as a class of defendants, all unknown gang members.

(e) When, at any point prior to trial, other specific gang officers or members become known, the complaint may be amended to include any such person as a named defendant.

P.A. 87-932, Art. II, § 20, eff. Jan. 1, 1993.

Formerly Ill.Rev.Stat., ch. 38, 1770

1 735 ILCS 5/1-101 et seq.

147/25. Venue

§ 25. Venue.

(a) In an action brought under this Act, venue shall lie in any county where an act charged in the complaint as part of a course or pattern of gang-related criminal activity was committed.

(b) It shall not be necessary for all offenses necessary to establishing a course or pattern of criminal activity to have occurred in any one county where the State's Attorneys of several counties, or their designees, each complaining of any offense, elected to join in a complaint. In such instance, it shall be sufficient that the complaint, taken as a whole, alleges a course or pattern of gang-related criminal activity, and each count of any such joint complaint shall be considered as cumulative to other counts for purposes of alleging or demonstrating such a course or pattern of activity.

(c) Where a course or pattern of activity is alleged to have been committed or to have occurred in more than one county, the State's Attorney of each such county, or their designees, may join their several causes of action in a single complaint, which may be filed in any such county agreed to by or among them, but no such joinder shall be had without the consent of the State's Attorney having jurisdiction over each offense alleged as part of the course or pattern of activity.
P.A. 87-932, Art. II, § 25, eff. Jan. 1, 1993.
Formerly Ill.Rev.Stat., ch. 38, 1775.

147/30. Service of process

§ 30. service of process.

(a) All streetgangs and streetgang members engaged in a course or pattern of gang-related criminal activity within this State impliedly consent to service of process upon them as set forth in this Section, or as may be otherwise authorized by the Code of Civil Procedure.1

(b) Service of process upon a streetgang may be had by leaving a copy of the complaint and summons directed to any officer of such gang, commanding the gang to appear and answer the complaint or otherwise plead at a time and place certain:

(1) with any gang officer; or

(2) with any individual member of the gang simultaneously named therein; or

(3) in the manner provided for service upon a voluntary unincorporated association in a civil action; or

(4) in the manner provided for service by publication in a civil action; or

(5) with any parent, legal guardian, or legal custodian of any persons charged with a gang-related offense when any person sued civilly under this Act is under 18 years of age and is also charged criminally or as a delinquent minor; or

(6) with the director of any agency or department of this State who is the legal guardian, guardianship administrator, or custodian of any person sued under this Act; or

(7) with the probation or parole officer of any person sued under this Act; or

(8) with such other person or agent as the court may, upon petition of the State's Attorney or his designee authorize as appropriate and reasonable under all of the circumstances.

(c) If after being summoned a streetgang does not appear, the court shall enter an answer for the streetgang neither affirming nor denying the allegations of the complaint but demanding strict proof thereof, and proceed to trial and judgment without further process.

(d) When any person is named as a defendant streetgang member in any complaint, or subsequently becomes known and is added or joined as a named defendant, service of process may be had as authorized or provided for in the Code of Civil Procedure for service of process in a civil case.

(e) Unknown gang members may be sued as a class and designated as such in the caption of any complaint filed under this Act. Service of process upon unknown members may be made in the manner prescribed for provision of notice to members of a class in a class action, or as the court may direct for providing the best service and notice practicable under the circumstances which shall include individual, personal, or other service upon all members who can be identified and located through reasonable effort.

P.A. 87-932, Art. II, § 30, eff. Jan. 1, 1993.

Formerly Ill.Rev.Stat., ch. 38, 1780.

1 735 ILCS 5/1-101 et seq.

147/35. Injunctive relief, damages, costs, and fees

§ 35. Injunctive relief, damages, costs, and fees.

(a) In any action brought under this Act, and upon the verified application of the State's Attorney or his designee, the circuit court may at any time enter such restraining orders, injunctions, or other prohibitions, or order such other relief as it deems proper, including but not limited to ordering any person to divest himself of any involvement or interest, direct or indirect, in any illegal streetgang activity and imposing other reasonable restrictions on the future illegal activities of any defendant.

(b) A final judgement in favor of a public authority under this Act shall entitle it to recover compensatory damages for all damages, losses, impairments, or other harm proximately caused, together with the costs of the suit and reasonable attorney's fees. Punitive damages may be assessed against any streetgang, against any streetgang officer or member found guilty of actual participation in or to be legally accountable for a course or pattern of criminal activity under this Act.

P.A. 87-932, Art. II, §35, eff. Jan. 1, 1993.

Formerly Ill.Rev.Stat., ch. 38, 1785.

ABOUT THE AUTHOR

George W. Knox teaches in the Department of Corrections and Criminal Justice, Chicago State University (Ph.D., University of Chicago, M.A., University of Texas at Arlington, B.A., University of Minnesota). He is certified beyond the Ph.D. in "Law and Social Control" by the American Sociological Association and is a Certified Consultant by the American Correctional Association. Dr. Knox is Director of the National Gang Crime Research Center at Chicago State University and is Editor-in-Chief of the *Journal of Gang Crime Research*.